❧ The ❧
MILLIONAIRE
AND THE
BARD

*Henry Folger's Obsessive Hunt for
Shakespeare's First Folio*

Andrea E. Mays

SIMON & SCHUSTER PAPERBACKS

New York London Toronto Sydney New Delhi

Simon & Schuster Paperbacks
An Imprint of Simon & Schuster, Inc.
1230 Avenue of the Americas
New York, NY 10020

First Simon & Schuster trade paperback edition April 2016

SIMON & SCHUSTER PAPERBACKS and colophon are registered trademarks of Simon & Schuster, Inc.

For information about special discounts for bulk purchases, please contact Simon & Schuster Special Sales at 1-866-506-1949 or business@simonandschuster.com.

The Simon & Schuster Speakers Bureau can bring authors to your live event. For more information or to book an event, contact the Simon & Schuster Speakers Bureau at 1-866-248-3049 or visit our website at www.simonspeakers.com.

Interior design by Ellen Sasahara
Jacket design by Christopher Lin
Jacket photograph: Shakespeare (engraving), Droeshout, Martin, the elder (c.1560–c.1642) / Private Collection / © Look and Learn / Bridgeman Images

Manufactured in the United States of America

1   3   5   7   9   10   8   6   4   2

Library of Congress Cataloging-in-Publication Data

Mays, Andrea E.
The millionaire and the bard : Henry Folger's obsessive hunt for Shakespeare's first folio / by Andrea E. Mays.
    pages cm
Includes bibliographical references and index.
1. Folger, Henry Clay, 1857–1930.   2. Shakespeare, William, 1564–1616—Bibliography—Folios. 1623.   3. Book collectors— New York (State)—New York—Biography.   4. Millionaires— New York (State)—New York—Biography.   5. New York (N.Y.)—Commerce—History.   6. New York (N.Y.)—Intellectual life.   7. Shakespeare, William, 1564–1616.   8. Shakespeare, William, 1564–1616—Friends and associates.   9. Publishers and publishing—England—London—History—17th century.   10. London (England)—Intellectual life— 17th century.   I. Title.
        Z989.F66M28   2015
822.3'3—dc23   2015001458

ISBN 978-1-4391-1823-8
ISBN 978-1-4391-1825-2 (pbk)
ISBN 978-1-4391-4124-3 (ebook)

*To my first teacher, my mother, Rosemarie Greb.
And in memory of my father, Lewis Mays, who,
as a lad of seventeen during the Second World War,
left the countryside for the sea and, aboard HMS Nelson,
defended Shakespeare's England.*

Thou in our wonder and astonishment,
Hast built thyself a live-long monument.

—*John Milton, "An Epitaph on the Admirable Dramatic Poet, W. Shakespeare"*

And now I will unclasp a secret book,
And to your quick-conceiving discontents
I'll read you matter deep and dangerous.

—*Henry IV, Part 1*

Contents

Note to the Reader

THROUGHOUT THE text, in order to make it easy for the reader to keep track of which copy of the First Folio is being described, I have used a numbering system proposed by Anthony James West in *The Shakespeare First Folio: The History of the Book*, Volume 1. Numbers in parentheses refer to the West assigned numbers, preceded by a *W*, and Folger Library assigned numbers, preceded by an *F*.

Prologue

꽃Y꽃

"He was Not of an Age, but for All Time!"

—BEN JONSON

*I*T STARTED, as many great obsessions do, with an unremarkable incident, an encounter between a man and a book. It happened during the Gilded Age, in New York City. Henry Clay Folger was a recent graduate of Columbia Law School living in rented rooms, working as a clerk at a local oil refinery, and trying to make his way in the world.

He walked into Bang's auction gallery in Manhattan with, as he later admitted, "fear and trepidation."[1] The books to be sold that day overflowed from the shelves. As an undergraduate at Amherst College he had studied literature, including Shakespeare, whose plays he "read . . . far into the night."[2] He had continued reading for pleasure ever since. He saved every book he ever read. He had always been a collector. At college, he made scrapbooks for his most trivial ephemera, including theater and lecture tickets. But his hoarder's impulse was still in search of a grand obsession.

Henry had never bought a rare book. The closest he had ever come was when he purchased a gift for his young wife. She shared his literary enthusiasm, so he had bought her an inexpensive facsimile of the First Folio of the collected plays of William Shakespeare. He had never seen a real one. The old book that caught his eye at Bang's was not, however, a coveted First Folio published in 1623, but to his amateur's eye it seemed close. It was an authentic Fourth Folio, printed in 1685; it was a less valuable edition than a First. Its antiquity excited his fancy. He bid on the book until the auctioneer hammered it down to him for $107.50. He asked if he could pay in installments. When he took it home, he and his wife gazed at the familiar engraving of Shakespeare on the title page. They turned the thick, durable rag paper pages, and savored the familiar words of the plays they both loved, and which they had read many times before in cheap, modern editions. Holding that old book in his hands changed Henry Folger's life, just as the publication of its first edition more than two hundred fifty years earlier had come to define its author's.

Soon, Folger found himself in the thrall of obsession. The young man who could barely afford a hundred-dollar book would spend a year's salary for another one, and devote the rest of his life, and millions of dollars, to chasing the rare books he coveted. The apprentice clerk would rise in the world of Gilded Age titans—John D. Rockefeller, J. P. Morgan, Henry Huntington—and join them in a frenzied competition for some of the rarest books in the world. Soon, he would own more volumes than he knew what to do with. They would overwhelm his shelves, his rented rooms, and then his home, and fill secret warehouses and storage lockers to their ceilings. Before long, Henry Folger's books would dominate his life. But in this ocean of books he prized one above all the others.

Today, it is the most valuable book in the world. And, after the King James Bible, the most important. In October 2001, one of the First Folios sold at Christie's for more than six million dollars. No more than 750 copies were printed, and two-thirds of them have perished over the last 391 years. Around 244 of them survive, and most of those are incomplete. Shakespeare's First Folio—Folger wanted to own them all.

As Victor Hugo wrote, "England has two books, one of which she has made, the other which has made her—Shakespeare and the Bible." Published in London in 1623, *Mr. William Shakespeares Comedies, Histories, & Tragedies* revolutionized the language, psychology, and culture of Western civilization. Without the First Folio, published seven years after the playwright's death, eighteen iconic works, including *Macbeth*, *Measure for Measure*, *Julius Caesar*, *Antony and Cleopatra*, *Twelfth Night*, *The Winter's Tale*, and *The Tempest* would have been lost.

Recognizing that every folio was superficially the same book but that each surviving handmade copy was in fact unique with its own idiosyncratic typographical fingerprint, binding, and provenance, Folger decided that the only way to rediscover Shakespeare's original intentions and language—what he called "The True Text"—was to buy every copy he could find and subject it to meticulous comparative analysis.

Believing that the mysteries of the folios could be fully understood only in the context of their time, he amassed an equally stupendous collection of artwork, books, letters, manuscripts, and antiquities from sixteenth- and seventeenth-century England. He wanted to own Shakespeare. And he did. He came to own more copies of the First Folio than anyone else in the world, more than even the British Library, the ultra-repository in Shakespeare's homeland. Folger collected more than twice the number of copies known to exist in all of England. How this happened is more than the tale of one passionate bibliophile. It is a story of the Old World giving way to the New, of the power of modern economics and transatlantic trade, and of the irresistible democratization of taste.

Everyone knows William Shakespeare. He was born in 1564, and died in April 1616. He wrote approximately thirty-nine plays[3] and composed five long poems and 154 sonnets. He failed to publish his collected works—during his lifetime plays were considered ephemeral amusements, not serious literature. By the time of his death he was retired, was considered past his prime, and by the 1620s many of his plays were no longer regularly performed in theaters. No one—not even Shakespeare himself—believed that his writings would last, that he was a genius, or that future generations would celebrate him as the greatest and most influential writer in the history of the English language.

Harold Bloom has argued that Shakespeare transformed the nature of man and created modern consciousness. If that is so, then the

First Folio—not the works of Darwin, Marx, or Freud—is the urtext of modernism. If the Bible is the book of God, then Shakespeare is the book of man on earth. We use the words he invented, we speak in his cadences, and we think in his imagery. The epitaph that fellow poet Ben Jonson penned for William Shakespeare proved to be prophetic: "He was not of an age, but for all time!" Without the First Folio, the evolution from poet to secular saint would have never happened, and the story of that book is an incredible tale of faith, friendship, loyalty, and chance. Today, few people realize how close the world came, in the aftermath of Shakespeare's death, to losing half of his plays.

Henry Clay Folger, however, remains one of the least-known industrial titans of his time. Folger, from the twilight years of the Gilded Age through the comet's arc of the Roaring Twenties, built the greatest Shakespeare library in the world, transporting it across the Atlantic piece by piece and hoarding it in thousands of unopened shipping crates, locked away in secret New York warehouses. And yet his life remains curiously unexamined. He is a forgotten man.

This is a story of resurrection, of a magical book and two men, an American millionaire and an English playwright—the man who coveted the First Folio, and the man who composed it.

Chapter 1

❦❦❦

"The Good [That Men Do] Is Oft Interred with Their Bones"

—WILLIAM SHAKESPEARE, *Julius Caesar*

ILLIAM SHAKESPEARE died in April 1616, on or around his fifty-second birthday. He was mourned by a small group of devoted family members, friends, and theatrical colleagues. His most productive years and major creative accomplishments were long behind him. Several years earlier, in 1610 or 1611, he had retired to his hometown of Stratford, in Warwickshire. Had he lived longer, it is doubtful that he would have picked up his pen again and written significant new plays or poems. He had abandoned the stage to assume new roles: real estate investor, landowner, and businessman. Indeed, his death entry in the parish registry lists him not as "Poet" or "Playwright" but as "Gentleman."

The circumstances of Shakespeare's death and burial were modest, unlike the dramatic, violent, and fantastic deaths experienced by many public figures in Elizabethan and Jacobean England; death by burning at the stake, beheading, imprisonment and torture, or, as in the case of Shakespeare's literary peer Christopher Marlowe, being stabbed above the eye in a rowdy tavern brawl (possibly a bizarre assassination plot) was not uncommon. Without violence or political intrigue,

William Shakespeare died at home in his bed from an unknown illness. As recently as January 1616, he had been in good health, and when he expired three months later no cause of death was recorded. About a half century later, the Reverend John Ward, vicar of Stratford, made an unreliable and probably apocryphal entry in his diary on what killed Shakespeare: "Shakespear, Drayton, and Ben Jonson, had a merry meeting, and itt seems drank too hard, for Shakespear died of a feavour there contracted." Given that the diary entry was made so much later, it was probably based on town gossip rather than personal knowledge.

Whatever ended Shakespeare's life, he died within one hundred yards of the place where he was born. The chapel bell, familiar music from his boyhood as it summoned children to school, pealed for him once again to mark his passing. The bell tolled to honor not a great artist but a prosperous local parishioner. The theater was a suspect trade in Stratford, and none of his plays had ever been performed there. The Puritans condemned acting as a vice and had kept the trade and touring companies of actors out of town. Indeed, the borough chamberlain of this small countryside place had once paid Shakespeare's own acting company, the King's Men, *not* to perform in the town hall. Thus Shakespeare, because he was a dramatist, was not Stratford's favorite son.

If his family followed the funerary customs of Renaissance England they would have had his body wrapped in a winding sheet on the evening of his death, either the sheet he died on or a finer linen sheet in the household accompanied by flowers and fragrant herbs. Rosemary, symbolic of remembrance, was favored for its pungent yet pleasing odor. "There's rosemary, that's for remembrance, pray you, love remember," says Ophelia in *Hamlet*.[1] A female servant or midwife would have cleaned and dressed him for burial, then wrapped him in the sheet. If the servant was an old woman long in the family's employ she might have had the privilege of wrapping the deceased at both ends of his life. Then his friends and neighbors would have viewed the body at his home.[2]

The body would then have been "watched" by a member of the

household—as a sign of respect but also to be sure he was fully dead and would not awaken in the grave—until it was moved to nearby Holy Trinity Church, and buried indoors, beneath the floor in the chancel, along the north wall.

The inscription that was cut into the big, flat gray stone that sealed Shakespeare's body in its tomb evidenced his fear of being disinterred:

> Good friend for Jesus sake forbeare,
> To dig the dust enclosed here.
> Blessed be the man that spares these stones,
> And cursed be he that moves my bones.

The verse refers to a common and ghoulish practice of the time. Whenever burial grounds became overcrowded, gravediggers emptied the old graves of their occupants' bones, dumping them in the charnel houses to make way for fresh corpses.

In *Hamlet*, Shakespeare wrote of such a dead man evicted from his grave to make room for the drowned and still-wet Ophelia. The gravedigger clown picks up a skull that has lain in the earth for "three and twenty years." Curious, Hamlet asks, "Whose was it?" The clown answers, "This same skull . . . was . . . Yorick's skull, the King Jester." Hamlet takes the disinterred skull in hand. "Alas, poor Yorick! I knew him, Horatio, a fellow of infinite jest, of most excellent fancy. He hath bore me on his back a thousand times . . . Here hung those lips that I have kissed I know not how oft. Where be your jibes now?" When Hamlet throws down the skull, and the gravedigger tosses Yorrick's inconvenient bones into an undignified pile, they are consigned to the trash heap of memory. Did Shakespeare have these very scenes in mind when he composed the warning that would admonish visitors to his own tomb?

News of his death could travel no faster than a man on horseback. Within a few days, it reached London. When it did, that great city— scene of his many triumphs as actor and author—did not pause to weep. His fellow writers and performers mourned that one of their brightest stars had been extinguished, but his loss did not reverberate in wider London as a national tragedy.[3] His theater friends and admirers there did not march in a procession to his Stratford graveside or to London's famous Poets' Corner at Westminster Abbey, where the immortal poets Geoffrey Chaucer and Edmund Spenser were memorialized. Shakespeare's April twenty-fifth burial away from London made such honors impossible, even if anyone had been inclined to render them. Nor did his friends write poems of eulogy. In no way did the people of England respond to his death with a gesture that suggested they believed a great man had died.

The circumstances of Shakespeare's birth were no more illustrious than those of his death. He was born in the town of Stratford-upon-Avon around April 23, 1564. Stratford's Holy Trinity Church recorded his baptism on April twenty-sixth. It is assumed but not certain, based on Elizabethan custom, that he was born three days earlier, on a national holiday, St. George's Day, celebrating the patron saint of England. Stratford was a thriving market town, connected to London trade via a stone bridge across the river Avon, though it had been recently ravaged by the plague.

Almost all the information about Shakespeare's childhood and early life has been lost. We know that he was the son of John Shakespeare, a man who made and sold gloves, was the town ale-taster, and later became Chamberlain of the borough of Stratford. We know he had seven brothers and sisters. Beyond that, we know little more than what can be recovered about the early life experiences of any typical sixteenth-century English child born into his class and region. In 1582, when he was eighteen, he married Anne Hathaway, a woman eight years his senior. They had three children: a daughter, Susanna, born within six months of the marriage, and then twins baptized in 1585 (a son named Hamnet who died very young, and a daughter named Judith). That year, when he was twenty-one, the historical Shakespeare disappeared from view for the next several years.

Probably by the end of the 1580s, when he was twenty-five, but no later than 1592, when he was twenty-eight, Shakespeare left Stratford for cosmopolitan London. When he arrived it was still a walled city, medieval in its look and layout, crowded, dirty, noisy, dangerous, exciting, and prosperous. Exactly why, how, or when he went to London no one knows. But he arrived there at an unprecedented moment in English arts and letters. Elizabeth I was in the fourth decade of her reign, and in her capital city there flourished a thriving theater scene.

Christopher Marlowe and the University Wits were writing the greatest dramas of the era. The Wits were educated poets and included Cambridge graduates Marlowe, Robert Greene, and Thomas Nashe, as well as Oxford men George Peele, Thomas Lodge, and Thomas Lyly. Thomas Kyd, although not university trained, was also part of the group, writing plays, including the hugely successful *Spanish Tragedy*, full of ghosts, blood, and revenge. Equally popular was Marlowe's *Tamburlaine*, a violent tale of a man devoured by his military ambition and passions. In the late sixteenth century these playwrights and poets transformed English drama from monotonous, hidebound verse, delivered in a stilted, unnatural style, to the rich, action-filled poetry of early seventeenth-century blank verse. They knew one another, lived near one another, dined and drank together, sometimes whored together, and, occasionally, coauthored plays together.

Elizabethan London was mad for the theater, and its popularity was well entrenched prior to Shakespeare's arrival. In 1576, James Burbage had built the city's first public playhouse, which he called simply the Theatre. He located it in Shoreditch, outside the City of London's walls, primarily to avoid regulation by the fussy and capricious Puritan London civil authorities, the Corporation of London. It was a turning point in the history of the English stage. Before Burbage, plays were performed on improvised stages at Inn-Yards, the rectangular, open courtyards of inns ringed by two or three covered balconies, or in small, exclusive private theaters. But the Inn-Yards layout was unfortunate from both an actor's and a businessman's perspective. There was no tiring room where actors could switch costumes between characters or scenes. For most patrons there was little protection from the elements, and none at all for those standing in the "pit" in the yard, closest to the actors. These venues could not accommodate large crowds. In contrast, the Theatre could hold three thousand people, thus making playgoing more accessible to the masses.

Burbage modeled the Theatre on the Roman circus and the bear-and bull-baiting arenas in London. It was octagonal, with benches and seating constructed like bleachers, but with plenty of empty space in front of the stage where the groundlings could pay a penny and stand, shoulder-to-shoulder, to watch the play from directly in front of the stage. Although the people standing in the pit were still exposed to the elements, anyone willing to pay two pennies enjoyed a seat and some shelter from the weather. Tiers of galleries formed the circumference of the theater. There was no proscenium separating the stage from the audience, no movable scenery, and scarcely any props. Language created the geography and the atmosphere. Burbage earned extra cash by selling food and drink to his captive audience.

By 1587 Philip Henslowe, entrepreneur, diarist, and proprietor of the Rose theater, another prominent London playhouse, was running, besides his brothel, a thriving theater business on the south bank of the Thames River. Henslowe's stepson-in-law, Edward Alleyn, a contemporary of Shakespeare's, was the foremost actor of his time—equaled perhaps only by Richard Burbage, James's son.

Plays were so popular that theatergoing distracted people from work and other entertainments. Shop owners complained that their apprentices abandoned their jobs during the day to attend performances. Proprietors of bull- and bear-baiting establishments—in which blinded and chained bears were tormented and attacked by savage, hungry dogs for the amusement of the public—complained to the Crown that the theater had become too popular and that no one was attending their establishments. They lobbied against their competitors and demanded a law to close the theaters on Thursdays, to protect the interests of the animal combat industry.

Later, other theaters opened in London, including the one more closely associated with Shakespeare's name than any other—the Globe. On performance days, its grounds were transformed into a temporary bazaar, with merchants peddling food, wine, and ale occupying the streets and plazas surrounding the theater. Like the Theatre, the Globe could hold about three thousand patrons, many of whom milled around in the vicinity before the show began. A trumpet sounded to announce the imminent start of the performance, and as patrons entered, they dropped a penny in the box held by a "gatherer." That penny entitled them to unsheltered standing room on the ground in front of the stage and earned them the moniker "penny public." If they desired a seat and could afford one, they could pay an additional penny, dropping it in another box as they climbed a small set of stairs. A seat in the second gallery cost them yet another penny, dropped in the box of the gatherer standing at the base of the second flight of stairs. After the patrons had taken their seats, and actors had taken their places, the boxes of pennies were taken to a room backstage—the original "box office"—for counting. The proceeds of the performance were split among the "householders," those men, including actors, who had made the transition from hired man to profit participant.

In the last decade of the sixteenth century, Shakespeare's arrival in London coincided with a historical phenomenon that contributed to his success; the audience for theatrical performances was larger than it had ever been in England's history. That audience had an almost insatiable appetite for new plays, and access to large theaters where they could see them performed.

The undistinguished and unknown young Shakespeare landed in London without prospects. He did not carry in his satchel a stack of manuscripts of finished plays ready for the stage. Given the average life span of a man at the time, half of Shakespeare's life was over before he even began his theatrical career. But Shakespeare immersed himself in an intoxicating milieu of actors and poets. How exactly an outsider without proper university credentials or an established literary reputation was able to penetrate the tight-knit circle of wits, poets, and actors who orbited the London theaters remains unknown. But somehow he did. He began by performing in plays written by others. He must have displayed a natural talent for it, for he became a regular figure on the stage. But he was not content to remain an actor. Not long after he arrived in London, Shakespeare picked up a quill and wrote his first play. It was *Titus Andronicus*, a bloody revenge story set in ancient Rome. It was not his best work, but it was an astonishing debut.

By 1592, Shakespeare had become prominent enough to provoke a jealous literary attack from a fellow author. It was the first mention of Shakespeare's name in print. Robert Greene, a talented but dissipated poet embittered by his failed youthful promise, reached out from his deathbed to condemn Shakespeare. In a biting little pamphlet called *Greene's Groatsworth of Wit*, he warned three other playwrights, including Christopher Marlowe, that there was a preening "upstart crow" in their midst.

This interloper, warned Greene, reminded him of the crow from Aesop's fables who struts around in borrowed feathers. This particular crow was an actor, one of "those puppets . . . that spake from our mouths" and who, onstage, "perform those antics garnished in our colors." Greene complained about one such actor who did not know his place. "Yes, trust them not; for there is an upstart crow, beautified with our feathers, that with his *Tiger's heart wrapped in a player's hide* supposes he is as well able to bombast out a blank verse as the best of you: and being an absolute *Johannes fac totum* [jack of all trades], is in his own conceit the only Shake-scene in a country." In a clever turn, Greene twisted the words from one of Shakespeare's own plays to mock the upstart. In *Henry VI Part 3*, the Duke of York is crowned with an imitation paper crown before his enemies kill him. Before his death, York rails against Queen Margaret of France, "O tiger's heart wrapp'd in a woman's hide!" Greene rewrote the line to suggest that Shakespeare was an actor masquerading as a poet.

Greene did not live long enough to enjoy seeing his insults in print. In August 1592, while dining with fellow author Thomas Nashe and others, he gorged himself on Rhenish wine and pickled herring. Taken ill, he died on September 3, 1592. Before the month was out, the publisher Henry Chettle posthumously printed *Greene's Groatsworth of Witte, bought with a million of Repentance. Describing the follie of youth, the falshoode of makshifte flatterers, the miserie of the negligent, and mis-chiefes of deceiuing Courtezans.* It must have created discordant ripples in the theater world, for it provoked strong statements from Chettle and Nashe. Chettle apologized to Shakespeare, regretting that he had published the pamphlet in the first place: "With neither of them that take offense was I acquainted, and with one of them [Marlowe] I care not if I ever be. The other [Shakespeare], whom at that time I did not so much spare, as since I wish I had . . . I am as sorry, as if the original fault had been my fault, because myself have seen his demeanor no less civil than he [is] excellent in the quality he professes. Besides, divers of worship have reported his uprightness of dealing, which argues for his honesty, and his facetious grace in writing that approves his art."

But Chettle was just the publisher. Playwright Thomas Nashe found himself in a more uncomfortable position—accused of ghostwriting *Greene's Groatsworth.* A bit of tantalizing evidence supported the charge. A few years earlier, in 1589, Nashe had written the introduction to another work by Greene. In it Nashe complained about inferior authors "who (mounted on the stage of arrogance) think to outbrave better pens with the swelling bombast of a bragging blank verse." It is only three words—"bombast," "blank," and "verse"—but the parallel is there. Alternatively, Greene might simply have appropriated the words from Nashe. In any event, Nashe issued a vehement denial that he was the secret author of Greene's mockery of Shakespeare. "Other news I am advertised of, that a scald, trivial, lying pamphlet, called *Greene's Groatsworth of Wit,* is given out as being my doing. God never have any care of my soul, but utterly renounce me, if the least word or syllable in it proceeded from my pen, or if I were in any way privy to the writing or printing of it."

This long-forgotten incident is more than a tempest in a teapot over bruised egos and sullied reputations. The *Groatsworth* controversy offers fundamental revelations about who William Shakespeare was at a particular moment in time, and captures him during his metamorphosis from player to playwright. Greene froze the moment in time when Shakespeare's reputation as a playwright eclipsed his celebrity as an actor.

The episode also suggests that by 1592, William Shakespeare was already a man to be reckoned with. What else but his rising status can account for the fulsome retraction from printer Henry Chettle or the fervid denial from poet Thomas Nashe?

Greene was right about one thing. At the beginning of Shakespeare's literary career, he was not a singular talent or the only remarkable writer working. It was a golden age in the history of the English language.

It had been Christopher Marlowe (1564–1593), not Shakespeare, who had changed theater forever, adapting blank verse used in poetry for dialogue. Blank verse is poetry that has meter—a particular rhythm—but no rhyme. Lines of Elizabethan verse customarily used groups of five iambs: each iamb a pair of syllables, in delivery the first unstressed, the second stressed. Rather than delivering speeches in a declamatory and unnatural style, actors could deliver blank verse in a more natural speaking cadence.[4]

In London, Shakespeare joined a coterie of established star writers. His singular position in English literary history was ensured by his effective use of blank verse. Not content to excel at a single type of poetic form, he also took Petrarch's Italian sonnet (introduced to England by Sir Philip Sidney) and perfected it, too. A sonnet, Italian for "little song," is a fourteen-line lyric poem with a very rigid set of rules for meter and rhyme, written in iambic pentameter. "Shall I compare thee to a summer's day?" "My mistress' eyes are nothing like the sun."

He excelled at both sonnets and long poems. In the theater, he mastered histories, tragedies, and comedies. His competitors might each excel in one or two of these arts, but no one else mastered them all.

But as Shakespeare's early acting and playwriting careers gained momentum, they were interrupted by disease. When the plague of 1592 to 1594 struck London, Edmund Tilney, the Master of the Revels—the royal official who approved all plays for public performance—shut down the theaters and other public places, save church, for health reasons.[5]

The actors fled to the country and reorganized themselves into temporary, ad hoc touring companies performing plays in the towns and provinces. During this time, Shakespeare wrote two long poems. The first, *Venus and Adonis*, was an elaborate, ornate, and extremely erotic narrative work of six-line stanzas almost 1,200 lines long; "backward she push'd him, as she would be thrust" gives a fair idea of the steamy content. On April 18, 1593, the poem was registered with the Stationers' Company, which kept a list of works to be published by its members. When *Venus and Adonis* was printed later that year, Shakespeare included his name on the title page. It was a sign of pride of authorship. Poems were considered more highbrow than plays. Authors boasted of their poetical works and never published their plays. The following year, on May 9, 1594, Shakespeare's second long poem, *The Rape of Lucrece*, almost two thousand lines long, was registered. Seeking to attract a sponsor, Shakespeare dedicated it to Henry Wriothesley, Third Earl of Southampton, with the obsequious language of a poet hoping to engage a patron: "The love I dedicate to your lordship is without end . . ."

While Shakespeare was writing and publishing poems, friends and fellow actors John Heminges and Henry Condell were performing in his plays in London. Heminges and Condell, living in the same neighborhood and worshippers in the parish of St. Mary the Virgin, Aldermanbury, were members of the Earl of Derby's Men, in which company they had performed in *Titus Andronicus*.[6] When their patron Derby died in April 1594 they joined with Shakespeare and fellow actor Richard Burbage as investors and performers in the Lord Chamberlain's Men, one of two rival theater companies in London. Shakespeare, aside from sharing in the receipts, was also the company's writer-in-residence. He and his colleagues built it into the most accomplished theatrical company in the English-speaking world.

In 1594, for the first time, one of Shakespeare's plays appeared in print. It was his first play, *The Lamentable Tragedy of Titus Andronicus*, published in quarto format, the equivalent of a cheap, modern paperback selling for five pence. It was printed by pirates without permission or attribution—Shakespeare's name does not even appear on the title page. *Quarto* is a printing term referring to the format in which a book appears. In a quarto, each sheet was folded twice, at right angles, producing four leaves, or eight pages. The pages were stitched together, and the book was sold unbound. This would not be the last time that an unauthorized, pirated edition of a Shakespeare play would appear in print.

By late 1594 or early 1595, Shakespeare had written a formidable portfolio of plays, but it is difficult to determine exactly when he wrote them, or in what order. Often it is impossible to even date a play to a certain year. His credits by this time seem to have included the comedies *Love's Labour's Lost*, *The Two Gentlemen of Verona*, and *The Comedy of Errors*; the histories in the *Henry VI* series; and, of course, *Titus Andronicus*. Some scholars also believe that by the end of 1594 he may have also written *King John*, *The Taming of the Shrew*, and also three of his finest plays: *A Midsummer Night's Dream*, *Romeo and Juliet*, and *Richard III*.

Had Shakespeare died in 1595, he had already made a sufficient mark to qualify as one of the major literary voices of the Elizabethan era. An early death in his thirties would not have been unusual—several of his peers had died young. If twenty-nine-year-old Marlowe had not been murdered at the dawn of a brilliant career, and if he had enjoyed another decade or two of productivity, we might remember him, and not the poet of Stratford, as the star playwright of his age. If Shakespeare had written only *A Midsummer Night's Dream*, *Romeo and Juliet*, and *Richard III*, and then had vanished from the stage, we would still remember him as long as those three texts survived. But what he accomplished over the next fifteen years, between 1595 and 1610, immortalized him.

By late 1594, Shakespeare had, in little more than five years in London, transformed himself from an undistinguished man from the hinterlands into a talented and celebrated actor and writer in the greatest city in the English-speaking world. In the next stage of his career, he leveraged his considerable talent and achievements into greater success. Already a prominent figure in the Lord Chamberlain's Men, Shakespeare connected his name with another illustrious institution when he became a shareholder in the now-renowned Globe Theatre. The Globe was run as a joint-stock company, with Shakespeare, Heminges, Condell, and Burbage as some of the principal stockholders. Shakespeare continued to serve as in-house playwright, taking a percentage of the gate as a householder, and a percentage of the profits as a shareholder. In other words, he was an author, actor, producer, co-owner of the acting company, and co-owner of the theater that sold the tickets. Thus Shakespeare prefigured the economic vertical integration that characterizes much of the modern entertainment industry.

Two events signaled his rising social status and financial prosperity. In 1596 the Shakespeare family was granted a coat of arms in William's father's name, enabling the playwright to sign his name, "William Shakespeare, Gentleman." And in 1597 Shakespeare glanced homeward to Stratford, where he purchased New Place, one of the two best properties in town. It was a source of pride to a glover's son.

The plays kept coming: *Othello*, *Measure for Measure*, *The Merchant of Venice*, *Julius Caesar*, *Antony and Cleopatra*, *King Lear*, *Henry V*, and more. Neither Shakespeare's burgeoning fame as a playwright nor his financial success as a theatrical entrepreneur diminished his love of acting. We find him on the stage in 1598, appearing on the list of "principal comedians" who acted in Ben Jonson's *Every Man in His Humour*.[7] He performed a number of times before the most important theatergoer in England, Queen Elizabeth I. Although she enjoyed watching plays, she did not, contrary to modern cinematic portrayals in films such as *Shakespeare in Love*, attend public theaters. Instead, she summoned the Lord Chamberlain's Men to come to her and perform at Richmond, Greenwich, or Whitehall, wherever she happened to be in residence—particularly around Christmas and Twelfth Night.[8]

The popularity of Shakespeare's plays inspired pirates to publish unauthorized quartos of several of them, and in 1599 a brazen London printer and bookseller, William Jaggard, gathered and published what he claimed was a collected group of Shakespeare's poetry. The bold fraud, titled *The Passionate Pilgrim*, was a collection of various poems, some actually written by Shakespeare, followed by another set of works that Jaggard labeled "sonnets" (none of them fourteen lines long and thus not true sonnets at all) which he attributed to William Shakespeare. Today, scholars accept only five of the twenty pieces as authentic Shakespeare compositions. Jaggard had lifted three lyrics from the play *Love's Labour's Lost* and had somehow purloined the other two from Shakespeare's own private, unpublished collection of sonnets. Hedging, Jaggard also included in the volume *another* fifteen poems that he implied were written by Shakespeare, but were not. Shakespeare was not amused. One of his contemporaries wrote, "The author I know [is] much offended by M. Jaggard . . . that (altogether unknown to him) presumed to make so bold with his name."[9]

The queen died in 1603, but fortunately for the Lord Chamberlain's Men, England's new ruler, King James I, also loved plays. He granted a royal patent—similar to a franchise—to Shakespeare's troupe and changed its name to the King's Men, sealing the company's premier place at court. It performed there about twelve times a year. Shakespeare continued to act. In 1603 he appeared on the cast list of "principal tragedians" in Ben Jonson's *Sejanus*. Although it was his last documented stage performance, as late as 1608 Cuthbert Burbage, Richard's brother, listed Shakespeare among the "men players" who arranged to begin using the Blackfriars Theatre. That word, *players*, suggests that perhaps he acted longer than we know.[10] With or without Shakespeare onstage, the new king savored his plays. In the winter of 1604–5, James I watched performances of *Love's Labour's Lost*, *The Merry Wives of Windsor*, *Othello*, *Measure for Measure*, *Henry V*, and *The Merchant of Venice*, the last of which he insisted on seeing twice.

By 1608, when Shakespeare was forty-four years old, the catalogue of his plays included *Twelfth Night*, *Troilus and Cressida*, *Hamlet*, *Macbeth*, *Coriolanus*, and *Antony and Cleopatra*. It had been a miraculous fourteen-year run, unmatched in the history of the English theater. As other Jacobean dramatists—talented rivals like Thomas Middleton, John Fletcher, and Francis Beaumont—came into vogue, Shakespeare responded with his late plays, *Pericles*, *Cymbeline*, *The Tempest*, and *The Winter's Tale*.

On May 20, 1609, another rogue printer, Thomas Thorpe, listed "a Booke called Shakespeares sonnettes" in the Stationers' Register and published it in quarto, as Jaggard had done in 1599, without Shakespeare's authorization or supervision. It was sold by William Aspley, whose bookshop, the Parrot, was in the churchyard of St. Paul's Cathedral. Contemporary accounts provide little information about the printing history of these "sonnettes," aside from the name of the publisher and the price of the book. But this time, at least, the poems were authentic. The handwritten sonnets had been circulated by Shakespeare privately in manuscript form only among his friends. It remains a mystery how they ever got into a printer's hands. The poems also served as private homage to royals who, he hoped, would become financial patrons. Francis Meres, a churchman, scholar, and theater enthusiast of the time, wrote in a commonplace book about how "the sweet, witty soul of Ovid lives in mellifluous and honey-tongued Shakespeare: witness his *Venus and Adonis*, his *Lucrece*, his sugared Sonnets among his private friends."[11]

And then, by 1610 or 1611, it was over. One of the last plays Shakespeare wrote, *The Winter's Tale*, a melancholy conjuring trick of loss, memory, and regret over the passage of time, which ends with a magical resolution where past becomes present, stands as a coda to Shakespeare's career. It had been a grand one, spanning almost twenty years. Unlike so many of his peers, he had survived the vicissitudes of life and death in seventeenth-century England, and his talent had endured. He had proven that he was more than a brilliant flash in the pan. He had written five long poems, 154 sonnets, and thirty-seven plays.[12] He had not become famous in his lifetime because of his "readers"—his popularity resulted solely from the public performance of his plays and his reputation as an excellent comic and tragic actor. Then he just walked away, and retired to Stratford, to New Place, at the corner of Chapel Lane and Chapel Street, to enjoy his impressive home and its surrounding grounds.

But he could not resist the lure of keeping his hand in the game. Shakespeare continued to dabble with playwriting. In 1613 he collaborated with his protégé John Fletcher, who had followed in his footsteps as in-house writer to the King's Men, on *Henry VIII*, *The Two Noble Kinsmen*, and *Cardenio*. But his greatest days were behind him.

On June 29, 1613, a theatrical disaster symbolized the end of his run, and destroyed the company's most valuable assets with it: its costumes and the prompt copies of its plays. The theater had long used cannons for special effects during performances. Situated beneath the thatched roof in the attic in the "heavens"—an area above the stage—cannon fire was used to punctuate dramatic entrances. Loaded with gunpowder and wadding, the cannon was fired during Act I, Scene iv, to announce the arrival of the character Henry VIII during a performance of one of Shakespeare's own plays, *All Is True*, an early version of the play we now know as *Henry VIII*.[13]

An eyewitness account written in a letter by Sir Henry Wotton a few days after the fire, on July 2, 1613, recalled the events:

> The King's players had a new play called All is True, representing some principal pieces of the reign of Henry the Eighth, which set forth with many extraordinary circumstances of pomp and majesty even to the matting of the stage. . . . Now King Henry making a Masque at the Cardinal Wolsey's house, and certain cannons being shot off at his entry, some of the paper or other stuff, wherewith one of them was stopped, did light on the thatch, where being thought at first but idle smoak, and their eyes more attentive to the show, it kindled inwardly, and ran round like a train, consuming within less than an hour the whole house to the very ground.

No human casualties were recorded, except for "only one man [who] had his breeches set on fire, that would perhaps have broiled him, if he had not by the benefit of a provident wit, put it out with a bottle of ale."

Three years later, 1616, was another bad year for London's theater community. Impresario Philip Henslowe and playwright Francis

Beaumont died. Beaumont, at least, had reached the social stature necessary for burial in Poets' Corner in Westminster Abbey, where he took his place near legendary poet Edmund Spenser, who had died in 1599.[14] On April 23, Shakespeare died. Half of his plays existed only in pirated, corrupted, and bastardized printings far removed from his original language, which would, without action, soon become extinct.

Even worse, the other half of his plays—eighteen works, including some of his greatest—had never been published in any form and were about to vanish into "airy nothing."[15] So, on that sad day in April 1616, William Shakespeare's grave claimed his body, and was prepared to do the same with his words. Unless, that is, someone found and saved them.

Chapter 2

❦❦❦

"Adieu . . . Remember Me"

—WILLIAM SHAKESPEARE, *Hamlet*

S HAKESPEARE'S WILL directed the distribution of his worldly goods. To his daughter Susanna Hall he left the home at New Place, presumably subject to the life tenancy of his widow, Anne, along with all his other real estate interests. To his daughter Judith he left a sum of cash and "my broad silver gilt bowle"; to his granddaughter Elizabeth Hall he left his "silver and plate." To Thomas Combe he left his sword. To his Stratford friend Hamnet Sadler and to William Raynoldes, "gentleman," he left money for memorial rings. And to three of his theatrical comrades, "my fellowes John Hemynges, Richard Burbage, and Henry Cundell," he set aside twenty-six shillings and eight denarius each to "buy them ringes" to wear in remembrance of him.[1]

Shakespeare's sword, gilt bowl, silver, and plate would be prized relics today, but they are long lost, either destroyed or divorced from their historical provenance and unrecognizable today as his property. The same is true of the rings Shakespeare left his friends. Surviving examples from the period suggest that these were not ordinary, decorative pieces of jewelry. Fashioned from gold, such rings bore sober signs of death: skulls, bones, or other symbols of mourning.

Who were these three "fellowes," to merit such gifts? Richard Burbage was the son of the great theater owner and entrepreneur James Burbage. Richard, a member of the Lord Chamberlain's Men and the King's Men, was the most famous actor in England, playing—indeed, creating—the lead roles in *Hamlet*, *Richard III*, *Othello*, and *King Lear*. He also excelled in plays by Ben Jonson and other dramatists. Like Shakespeare he was more than just an actor. He was a businessman, too—a shareholder along with Shakespeare in the King's Men and also, with his brother Cuthbert, an owner of half of the Globe Theatre.

John Heminges and Henry Condell, fellow shareholders with Burbage and Shakespeare in the King's Men, had been actors in various companies since the 1590s, ending up as members of the Lord Chamberlain's Men around 1597 or 1598.[2] These memory keepers were privileged members of the small band of stage brothers who actually saw with their own eyes Shakespeare's fugitive handwritten manuscripts, and who acted in the plays under the author's eye, receiving from him coaching as well as stage direction.

Heminges's acting career began before he met Shakespeare, and there is evidence that he performed in a number of Ben Jonson's plays—*Every Man in His Humour*, *Every Man out of His Humour*, *Sejanus*, *Volpone*, *The Alchemist*, and *Catiline*. Though he was a competent actor he was limited by a stutter, but he appears to have had a talent for numbers and logistics, becoming, around 1611, an administrator for the troupe.[3]

Condell, the younger of the two, played Benvolio in *Romeo and Juliet*, Don Pedro in *Much Ado about Nothing*, Oliver in *As You Like It*, and Horatio in *Hamlet*. Although his name appears in the top ten of the King's Men's list of actors, he never matched the success of Richard Burbage. Heminges and Condell raised their families—Heminges had fourteen children, Condell nine—in the area around St. Mary Aldermanbury.

After the Globe Theatre burned down in 1613, a poem commemorated the tragedy. This piece, *A Sonnet upon the pitiful burning of the Globe Playhouse in London*, incorporated the names of Burbage,

Heminges, and Condell into the verse, thus suggesting the trio's prominence. Had Shakespeare not already retired, no doubt the text would have mentioned him, too.

> This fearful fire began above
> A wonder strange and true,
> And to the stage-house did remove,
> As round as tailor's clew;
> And burned down both beam and snag,
> And did not spare the silken flag,
>   O sorrow, pitiful sorrow, and yet all this is true.
> Out run the knights, out run the lords,
> And there was great ado;
> Some lost their hats and some their swords;
> Then out run Burbage too;
> The reprobates, though drunk on Monday,
> Prayed for the Fool and Henry Condye,
>   O sorrow, pitiful sorrow, and yet all this is true.
> The periwigs and drum heads fry
> Like to a butter firkin;
> A woeful burning did betide
> To many a good buff jerkin.
> Then with swoll'n eyes, like drunken Flemings,
> Distressed stood old stuttering Heminges.
>   O sorrow, pitiful sorrow, and yet all this is true.[4]

Burbage, Heminges, and Condell did not need to behold their golden rings to recall their fond memories of William Shakespeare. Everywhere they turned, they were reminded of him: pursuing the theatrical life, performing for king and queen, living it up in London with dinners and drinks at the local tavern.

Three years after Shakespeare's death, the fellows of the King's Men suffered another loss. In March 1619, Richard Burbage died. He was only fifty-one, one year younger than Shakespeare had been when he died.

EXIT BURBAGE, read his simple tombstone. More eloquent was the anonymous *Funerall Elegye on the Death of the famous Actor Richard Burbage*:

> He's gone and with him what a world are dead.
> Which he review'd, to be revived so,
> No more young Hamlet, Old Hieronimo
> Kind Lear, the Grieved Moor, and more beside,
> That lived in him have now forever died.[5]

The melancholy verse mourned not just the loss of a great actor; it foreshadowed the day when *all* the King's Men would join Burbage—and
Shakespeare—in the grave. When that happened, then Shakespeare's
world would truly be gone.

A few years after Shakespeare's death, and probably no later than
1620, the year after Burbage died, Heminges and Condell conceived
of a way (more permanent than rings) to remember William Shakespeare. It would make them the two most unsung heroes in the history of English literature. They decided to do what Shakespeare had
never done for himself—they would publish a complete record of his
dramatic works. Their motives did not include money or fame. They
did not expect the book to become a bestseller, or to make them rich.
They did it for love. Later, in a prefatory letter to the First Folio, "To
the Great Variety of Readers," they wrote that their objective was to
compile Shakespeare's work "without ambition either of self-profit or
fame, only to keep the memory of so worthy a friend and fellow alive
as was our Shakespeare." Through this book, which they would call
Mr. William Shakespeares Comedies, Histories, & Tragedies, Heminges
and Condell hoped to create a memorial more permanent than the
golden rings on their fingers. In their prefatory letter they mourned
that the author was not alive to publish his own plays. By publishing
them for him, Heminges and Condell did more than honor a departed
friend; they resurrected him from the grave. In time, it would have
repercussions beyond their wildest imaginings.

But Heminges and Condell were not the first men to conceive of collecting Shakespeare's plays between the covers of a book. In 1619, three years after Shakespeare's death, there had been an aborted and unauthorized attempt to collect at least some of them. William Jaggard, earlier the perpetrator of the *Passionate Pilgrim* fraud of 1599, was hired to print an incomplete collection. This volume, not authorized by the King's Men, who owned some of the plays, failed to live up to its intended purpose and ran afoul of the actors in the process.

This first attempt at collecting Shakespeare's plays came to be known as the False Folio or the "Pavier Quarto," named for its publisher. The name is confusing because the book was not in folio format at all. It contained only ten works, two of them—*Sir John Oldcastle* and *A Yorkshire Tragedy*—not written by Shakespeare at all. The others were *Henry V*; *King Lear*; *The Merchant of Venice*; *The Merry Wives of Windsor*; *A Midsummer Night's Dream*; *Pericles, Prince of Tyre*; and a combined version of *Henry VI Part 2* and *Henry VI Part 3*.

The printed book—slightly larger than a conventional quarto size—was sold at Thomas Pavier's shop at the sign of the Cat and Parrots in Cornhill, a ward of London, in loose sheets or bound, with each play bound separately, or all of them together, per the customer's choice. The endeavor quickly failed. Once the King's Men, who held rights to some of the plays, became aware of the project, they, along with Heminges and Condell, shareholders who were possibly already planning their own publication, sought the assistance of a higher power to stop the project. The Lord Chamberlain intervened on behalf of the players, instructing the Stationers' Company—a printer's guild of which Jaggard was a member—"That no playes that his maiesties players do play shalbe printed without the consent of somme of them."[6] This order against unfair competition would ensure that any hitherto unpublished Shakespeare plays would not appear in print while the First Folio was being produced. But William Jaggard and Pavier, in an act of brazen deception, fraudulently backdated the title pages, making it appear the plays had been published years earlier, in 1608 instead of 1619.[7]

Perhaps the Pavier episode inspired Heminges and Condell to publish a legitimate volume. Or they might have had their own project in mind prior to the incident. Regardless, it would not be easy. Heminges and Condell confronted several obstacles. The fact that Shakespeare failed to publish his plays himself made the project immeasurably more difficult. The two actors had to locate a source—sometimes multiple and conflicting sources—for every play, half of which had never appeared in print before. Could reliable texts for all the plays even be found?

Shakespeare had never authorized the publication of any of his plays for two reasons. First, it simply was not the custom. Dramas were meant to be seen, not read. Shakespeare and his fellow playwrights thought of themselves as entertainers, not literary paragons. They did not write for all time, but for their own. In 1604, playwright John Marston published a comedy in which he conveyed the typical Elizabethan attitude toward publication: "Only one thing afflicts me, to think that scenes, invented merely to be spoken, should be enforcively published to read." During Shakespeare's lifetime common people went to the theater and saw his plays performed: they did not desire to go home and read them. And for a population that was largely illiterate, it was not possible for them to do so. Plays were public entertainment for the royals and for the masses, not serious literature.

The second reason is that playwrights, Shakespeare included, did not own the rights to their plays. The idea of intellectual property was in its infancy in early modern England. For a fee of two to five pounds, a play's author sold all commercial rights to the theater company that would produce it. Writers did not license performance rights, nor did they retain for themselves separate publication or other rights. The idea of splitting intellectual property into a bundle of various rights to be sold or licensed off one by one, which is commonplace today, would have been incomprehensible to Elizabethan authors or theatrical companies. Had Shakespeare attempted to publish a collection of his own plays, the rights holders to whom he had sold them would have treated him no differently from any other infringer, and enlisted the help of the Company of Stationers to prevent the publication of "their" work. Shakespeare owned only a *partial* interest in whatever plays he had sold to the Lord Chamberlain's Men or the King's Men, not because he wrote them, but because he was a shareholder in the theater companies.

The acting companies, as owners of the plays, did not publish them to sell printed copies for profit. On the contrary, they kept the plays secret so much as it was possible. In the competitive world of Elizabethan theater, rival groups pirated one another's plays with virtual impunity. Competing companies sent spies to listen to the plays being performed, memorize them, and write down the words as best they could recall. A troupe of actors could thus plagiarize a script, take it for its own, and perform the play in the countryside far from London, paying neither the theater nor the playwright royalties. An acting company's best protection against piracy was to keep its plays out of print and, thus, out of the hands of the competition.

The fugitive nature of the First Folio source material has bedeviled scholars for more than a century. Today there exist *no* first-generation sources for the plays. Nothing survives from Shakespeare's original, handwritten manuscripts—not one play, not an act, not a scene, not a single page of dialogue, not even a sentence. Heminges and Condell must have had more sources available to them four centuries ago. But they left no account of what sources they used, making it impossible to retrace their steps and reconstruct exactly how they derived the final text of each play. They left us no bibliography, no files, no memoirs, no notes. All that survives is the incandescent climax of their work, the First Folio itself.

Still, we can imagine the universe of possible sources from which they worked. There are only six possibilities: Shakespeare's original, handwritten manuscripts; complete handwritten copies of those original scripts written out by scribe Ralph Crane for use by the acting troupe; manuscript "sides" used by the actors, which were stand-alone fragments containing only the lines in the play to be spoken by the actor for whom each individual, unique side was prepared; printed quartos that published unauthorized and sometimes multiple, confusing versions of some of the plays; after-the-fact memorial reconstructions of dialogue furnished orally by the few dozen actors who had performed in the plays; and, finally, the personal memories of Heminges and Condell themselves.

Without doubt, the single best source for the First Folio text would have been Shakespeare's original manuscripts. Those pages, recording in his own handwriting the dialogue, strikeouts, emendations, substitutions, rearrangements, and other edits as they flowed from his mind to his pen, from first to final draft, could have offered nonpareil documentation of his artistic process. Not only did Shakespeare fail to make an effort to publish his complete works, but he apparently also made no attempt to preserve the originals. He failed to keep copies. In his will, he left behind no manuscripts, prompt books, or hand-corrected printed quarto editions. Once he turned his manuscripts over to a scribe like Ralph Crane for copying, he abandoned the originals. He was, it turned out, one of his own legacy's worst enemies.

Shakespeare wrote in an age before scholars and collectors fetishized an author's original manuscripts. It is hard for a modern reader to fathom that in Shakespeare's time these manuscripts possessed no intrinsic value. In our own age, they are prized. A single page written in Shakespeare's hand might now fetch several million dollars. His complete manuscript for one of the great plays—*Hamlet, Romeo and Juliet, Richard III*—might bring twenty million, or possibly more, at auction. In Shakespeare's time, an original manuscript was worth little more than the paper it was written on.

Indeed, the high cost of paper in early modern England might explain the disappearance of at least some of Shakespeare's manuscripts. Paper was too valuable to use only once. In an otherwise excellent depiction of an Elizabethan playwright's working life, the film *Shakespeare in Love* fails on this point, depicting Will crumpling up sheets of paper as he writes drafts of poems, and tossing wads of paper on the floor. Paper was purchased in small amounts, handwriting was small to squeeze as many words as possible onto a sheet, and paper was reused whenever possible. Centuries ago, the pages of a disbound copy of the First Folio were once used in Spain to wrap fish. A fragment of the oldest-known surviving manuscript written in England, an obscure religious tract from the seventh century,[8] survived for nine hundred years until 1578, when it was dismissed as printers' waste, and recycled as a stiffener inside the binding of an old medical text. The manuscript fragment remained hidden inside that book for another four hundred years, until it was unearthed during the dissection and conservation of the volume. It is possible that someday, during rebinding of an old book from Shakespeare's time, one of his manuscript pages might accidentally be discovered under the spine, or glued as reinforcement under one of the binder's boards.[9]

Although the Elizabethan (1558–1603) and Jacobean (1603–1625) periods of English history were prolific times for poets and playwrights, very few manuscripts from that era survive, and more than half the manuscripts that we know once existed can no longer be found. As with another art form three centuries later, when a large percentage of all the silent films ever produced would be lost forever, the manuscripts of Renaissance England suffered a high attrition rate. The Dead Sea Scrolls enjoyed better preservation than the manuscripts of Shakespeare and many of his peers. Thus, the disappearance of all Shakespeare's manuscripts was not a unique—or even rare—occurrence. Even before Shakespeare's death, it is likely that some of his papers had perished. Today, no authenticated writing of Shakespeare's exists save three examples of his signature on documents, plus the words "by me" on his will.

This dearth of documentary evidence has been seized upon by a cult of naysayers who suggest that William Shakespeare never wrote the plays that we credit to him. His manuscripts failed to survive not, they claim, because they were lost, but because they never existed in the first place. These Anti-Stratfordians, as they have come to be known, advance two principal arguments against Shakespeare's authorship: first, no physical evidence survives to prove he wrote the plays, and second, he did not possess the intellectual or social qualifications necessary to write them. Although this is decidedly the minority view, a cottage industry has grown around the thesis that Shakespeare was not Shakespeare.

The idea that Shakespeare was a man of mystery about whom we know nothing has been exaggerated by those who say that our incomplete knowledge of his life is inherently suspicious, giving credence to the accusation that he did not write the plays. We may know little about him, but we know more about him than any of his contemporaries, save playwright Ben Jonson. The Elizabethan English were efficient record keepers, resulting in a trail of thirty-six government and church references to Shakespeare in contemporary documents— his baptism, marriage, lawsuits he was party to, real estate transactions, mortgages, a deed to Blackfriars real estate, and also citations to him not only as a person who actually existed but also specifically as a playwright and shareholder of the Globe Theatre. Yes, the surviving documents are inadequate to flesh out the life story of such an important writer. This absence of evidence of his everyday life plus his humble origins and un-illustrious social status have caused some contrarians to insist that the man named "William Shakespeare" is not the same man who wrote the plays.

Those who question Shakespeare's authorship rely heavily upon the lack of manuscript evidence. It is also frustrating that, although he enjoyed the patronage of earls and monarchs, not a single letter of his has been unearthed. But although Shakespeare was a professional author, writing letters was more a pastime of the leisure class of his age. Moreover, in this regard, Shakespeare is not an outlier. The inference drawn—that as an artist he did not exist—would be more persuasive if the manuscripts of Shakespeare's contemporaries showed up in significant quantity, which they do not. Not a single manuscript of a Marlowe play survives, not one by Robert Greene, and only one by John Fletcher. Does this mean they, too, are not the authors of their plays?

Lurking below the surface is the elitist prejudice that such an ordinary man could not possibly have created such magnificent literature. Surely, these incredulous critics argue, only a man of breeding and education could have written such timeless works. Shakespeare was from the wrong class. It was impossible. This reasoning is based on the wishful thinking that genius can only be earned through education and hard work. It denies the time-proven truth that genius can strike like a random bolt of lightning, at any time in any place, even in a humble glover's home in a small town in Elizabethan England.

During Shakespeare's lifetime the plays were attributed to him and to no one else. In fact, several of his peers praised him as a poet and playwright. Dramatist John Webster praised Shakespeare's "copious industry" in his preface to *The White Devil*. None questioned his authorship. Another of his contemporaries, Robert Greene, mocked Shakespeare's talent. If the dyspeptic Greene had suspected that Shakespeare was fronting for a secret author operating behind the scenes, Greene would not have hesitated to expose Shakespeare as a fraud—a mere actor *truly* masquerading as a playwright. Furthermore, allusions to Shakespeare as an author occurred in the plays, poems, and literary criticism of several of his peers. The records of the Master of the Revels name him as a playwright. Other records, including personal diaries, scrapbooks, and letters, reveal the existence or performance of Shakespeare's works.

After Shakespeare's death his fellow actors, shareholders, and colleagues all continued to acknowledge him as the author of the plays that they had attributed to him in life. It would have required a conspiracy of dozens of men, including fellow actors Burbage, Heminges, and Condell, to keep the secret that Shakespeare was not the author of the plays the public had come to know as his. And for the next one hundred fifty years, no one challenged his authorship until after Shakespeare had become an icon. Weighing all the evidence, two things are certain: William Shakespeare did exist, and he is the man who wrote the plays. One might say it does not matter. We have the plays, whoever wrote them. But vexatious conspiracy theorists notwithstanding, the plays' author *is* William Shakespeare.

In the absence of Shakespeare's original manuscripts, the next best source for Heminges and Condell to establish the First Folio text would have been the theatrical "prompt" books based upon those manuscripts. An author's draft—with its cramped handwriting disfigured by marginalia, corrections, amendments, and stage directions—could be a messy thing to behold. This draft, the so-called foul papers of the play, was too disorganized for the director and actors to work from. Plays sold by a playwright to the theater troupe were hand-copied from the author's draft by a scribe into a neater, more legible manuscript called the fair copy. Thus, Shakespeare hired Ralph Crane to transform his manuscripts from "foul" to "fair." *Macbeth* contains an allusion to this literary process in the scene where the three witches mix a brew and cast a spell so that "fair is foul, and foul is fair."

The director annotated this fair copy with stage directions, scene divisions, actors' names, and any changes he wished to incorporate. During a performance a theater factotum, an employee standing at the foot of the stage, used it to "feed" a line to an actor who had forgotten his text. It was from such a prompt book that *Titus Andronicus* was set up when the plays for the First Folio were gathered.

The prompt book was, in turn, the source for the actors' sides—small sheets of paper with an individual character's lines written on them that were copied by the guardian of the prompt book, the "bookkeeper," and then distributed to the players. The actors were not given a complete script, so they could not sell it to publishers or rival companies, as they possessed or had memorized only fragments of it. By gathering together all the sides, one could, hypothetically, reassemble the dialogue of an entire play. As with the original manuscripts, the prompt books and the sides have all since been lost.

But what is lost to us today was not lost to Heminges and Condell almost four centuries ago. They may well have had all these sources available to them. As members of the King's Men, they would have had access to any unpublished and annotated prompt books, and possibly, tantalizingly, some of Shakespeare's own manuscripts, both his foul papers and fair copies, and collated them into the most reliable texts, as close as possible to Shakespeare's original language.

Heminges and Condell hired Crane to transcribe some of the plays from the foul papers and other sources. Now, after Shakespeare's death, he put quill to paper again, this time not for performance but for publication.

Heminges and Condell were fortunate to locate *any* manuscript sources. Although we know that the fire that burned the Globe Theatre to the ground on June 29, 1613, destroyed the principal physical asset of the King's Men—their theater—we do not know to what extent the fire damaged their other precious asset, their intellectual property. The loss of the prompt books would have been devastating to the company and its shareholders. Second in value only to the costumes as assets of the theater, they were stored under lock and key by the book-keeper to prevent theft by rival companies. Perhaps some manuscripts burned. Or perhaps the trunk that secured them was spirited out of the Globe in time. Whatever happened, the fire, however catastrophic, could not have destroyed *all* the documents and sources for Shakespeare's plays. For without them—if the flames had consumed them all—then the First Folio would not exist.

Beyond the potential manuscript sources, the compilers could also have turned to printed sources: the quartos. The subject of the Shakespeare quartos is a field unto itself, vast and controversial. Prior to the publication of the First Folio, eighteen of the plays were published as quartos, and some, such as *King Lear* and *Hamlet*, in multiple and conflicting editions. By tradition, scholars have divided Shakespeare's quartos into three categories intended to describe the integrity of the text: "good," "bad," or "doubtful." A good quarto, such as the second quarto edition of *Hamlet* published in 1604, was used as a source by Heminges and Condell because it derived from a trusted manuscript. Rival troupes or publishers paid scribes or "reporters" to sit in the audience and write down the words of the play. The results were abridged, sometimes "bad," incoherent, low-quality reconstructions of the play containing text that corrupted the original. A bad quarto, like the 1597 printing of *Romeo and Juliet*, might be based on no more than the recollections of one player with a minor part, who had performed in the production and who could be bribed to sell his recollections to a pirate publisher. Actors with major parts, who memorized large parts of the play, were sometimes also sharers—that is, they kept a portion of the take at the door—and did not want to undercut their own livelihoods by enabling other companies to perform the plays in which they appeared. They had a financial interest in keeping the plays out of the hands of rival acting companies, and would have been unlikely to have cooperated with pirates.

Heminges and Condell could have consulted a variety of published quartos, some of which contain widely—and occasionally, absurdly—different texts of the same play. They warned readers in the prefatory material of the First Folio against "stol'n and surreptitious copies, maimed and deformed by frauds and stealths of injurious impostors." It would fall to them to be "the office of their care, and paine, to have collected & publish'd them."

The 1603 "bad" quarto of *Hamlet* is replete with errors and distortions—a butchery of what would later become the version of the play in the First Folio:

> To be, or not to be, Ay, there's the point,
> To Die, to sleepe, is that all? Ay, all:
> No, to sleep to dreame, I mary there it goes.
> For in that dreame of death, when wee awake,
> And borne before an everlasting Judge,
> From whence no passenger euer retur'nd
> The undiscovered country, at whole sight
> The happy smile and the accursed damn'd.[10]

The more familiar version of the speech is from the First Folio:

> To be, or not to be—that is the question:
> Whether 'tis nobler in the mind to suffer
> The slings and arrows of outrageous fortune
> Or to take arms against a sea of troubles
> And by opposing end them. To die, to sleep—
> No more—
>   *Hamlet*, Act III, scene i, lines 56–61, First Folio

Here is another example from the "bad" quarto of Hamlet:

> Why what a dunghill idiote slave am I?
> Why these Players here draw water from eyes:
> For Hecuba, why what is Hecuba to him, or he to Hecuba?
> What would he do and if he had my losse?

In the First Folio edition these lines become the more familiar:

> O, what a rogue and peasant slave am I!
> Is it not monstrous that this player here,
> But in a fiction, in a dream of passion,
> Could force his soul so to his own conceit
> That from her working all his visage wan'd;
> Tears in his eyes, distraction in's aspect,
> A broken voice, and his whole function suiting
> With forms to his conceit? And all for nothing!
> For Hecuba?
> What's Hecuba to him, or he to Hecuba,
> that he should weep for her?

❧ While recent scholarship has reexamined and conferred new status upon some of the quartos, textual analysis of all their known editions, copies, and variants proves that Heminges and Condell derived the First Folio text for the eighteen previously published plays from much more than the quartos alone. For the eighteen hitherto unpublished plays, quartos played no role in their recovery.

Once they had exhausted all the physical sources, they and their fellow King's Men had a monopoly on a unique source that could never be stolen, pirated, or taken away from them: their memories of what they had seen and heard. But memory and life itself were ephemeral. Their recollections would die with them. One by one, the old King's Men were dying off: Heminges, Condell, and Burbage were the last three of the original troupe. Soon, no one would be left alive who had performed onstage with William Shakespeare. For eighteen years following a September 1642 act of the Puritan-controlled Parliament, theaters were banned from performing plays. By the time of the Restoration of 1660, when theaters began to stage performances again, almost every actor who had known Shakespeare would be dead. Eventually, all collective public memory of Shakespeare would expire when, in time, every last soul who had seen William Shakespeare walk the stage, or had watched one of his plays performed during his lifetime, would, like him, be dead. Soon all the living witnesses would be gone. But that time had not yet come.

For now, Heminges and Condell and their memories of Will had not exited the scene. They had seen him as a "poor player" who "struts and frets his hour upon the stage." They had watched with their own eyes the first time Hamlet encountered his father's ghost; they had heard the first time that Will the actor, playing the slain King Hamlet, spoke these haunting lines to his son: "The glowworm shows the matin to be near, / And 'gins to pale his uneffectual fire. / Adieu, adieu, adieu! Remember me."[11] Later, as they labored on the First Folio, did Heminges and Condell hear Shakespeare's voice echoing that entreaty across the years?

Thus, when complete and accurate source material did not exist, Heminges's and Condell's recollections proved invaluable. They knew their fellow's idiosyncratic language and allusions. They had seen him standing in the wings, directing or watching a rehearsal. They knew how he had instructed them to deliver a line, how or when to enter, running or staggering, when to kiss the maiden, how to menace a Roman nobleman with a dagger, fight with a sword, or when to exit, pursued by a bear.

They were present at the creation. In their daily routine they had lived the privileged life that modern Shakespearian scholars might sell their souls to experience: Shakespeare onstage playing two simultaneous roles—artwork and artist, performer and author—speaking the lines he had written. They had seen wonders that a legion of scholars burrowing in one hundred libraries can never recover. How long did it take Shakespeare to write a play? What did his manuscripts look like? Which were his favorites? How did he intend his lines to be read? Was it, in *Macbeth*, for instance, an urgent "tomorrow, and tomorrow, and tomorrow" or the more languid "to morrow, to morrow, and to morrow"? (Act V, scene v, lines 19–20). On the page, such variants might read as a minor difference of no consequence; on the stage, spoken aloud for the ear, such differences might alter the whole mood of a line or scene.

Of course the First Folio, especially its eighteen hitherto unpublished plays, could never have been conjured up by Heminges and Condell from memory alone. But their recollections must have, in ways that we will never fully know, been indispensable in the making of the book.

By the fall of 1622, they had assembled sufficient source materials to allow them to go forward with the publication. If they had waited any longer, it might never have been printed. Within a generation, a Puritan dark age of antitheatrical mania, an attempt to "appease and avert the wrath of God," would create an eighteen-year gap in theater history. There would be no stage performances to keep the plays alive, no passing of Shakespeare's torch from one generation of actors to the next. By 1660, and the renaissance of English theater under the patronage of Charles II, it would have been too late; the age of Shakespeare's King's Men would have long passed, and with it all hope of recovering what, a generation earlier, Heminges and Condell had saved.

Chapter 3

✿❦✿

"Whatever You Do, Buy"

—John Heminges, Henry Condell
"To the Great Variety of Readers"

*I*f heminges and Condell wanted to publish a book in London, there seemed only one place to go: the plaza surrounding St. Paul's Cathedral. It was to seventeenth-century English publishing what Broadway in New York City and the West End in London are to the theater today: the symbol of an entire industry. All aspects of publishing, from printing to binding to bookselling, were crowded into Paul's Cross Churchyard. The Crown regulated the printing industry to control the dissemination of ideas. It limited the number of presses, as well as their locations, to facilitate censorship of dangerous ideas, particularly to protect the Crown from sedition and heresy, and to protect the economic interests of the guild members.

Booksellers also occupied Paternoster Row, the street just north of St. Paul's. Other printers established themselves just beyond the city walls, at the corner of the Barbican and Aldersgate. Here was the shop of printer William Jaggard, at the sign of the Half Eagle and Key. Heminges and Condell needed no introduction to *this* printer. Indeed, given the *Passionate Pilgrim* and Pavier Quarto or "false folio" episodes, there were a number of reasons for Shakespeare's friends to shun Jaggard's shop. And yet Heminges and Condell chose him to print their collection of Shakespeare's plays. Several business and professional reasons justified their otherwise inexplicable choice. For better or worse, the players already knew him, and he enjoyed the Queen's and then the King's grant of a monopoly for printing theater playbills. Jaggard had been appointed Printer to the City of London, a privilege that gave him, for a fee, the right to print proclamations, "Acts of Coen Counsell and other matters for the service of this Cittie."[1] He had undertaken other large book publishing projects, so Heminges and Condell knew his two-press shop could handle the enormity of the task. And they knew he could negotiate with his business associate—the same Thomas Pavier of the "false folio" episode—for rights Pavier had acquired to four of Shakespeare's plays that they wished to include in their project. It was not the first time a printer had been awarded a job based on the rights he controlled. And so, Heminges and Condell went into business with the blind printer William Jaggard and his son, Isaac.

Heminges and Condell obtained permission from members of the Stationers' Company who had earlier registered and printed some of the plays in quarto form and therefore controlled the right to print them. They paid the King's Men for the rights to publish the plays the company owned. William Aspley and John Smethwick traded the right to publish plays they controlled in exchange for a share of the project's profits. Heminges and Condell's inability to acquire the rights to *Troilus and Cressida* and *Pericles* led to their exclusion from the collection. The former eventually received a reprieve and was printed in the First Folio, while the inability to agree on rights to the latter made it the sole Shakespeare play excluded from the collection.

The plays were not the only material that the editors included in the First Folio. They solicited authors—from minor poet Leonard Digges to Shakespeare's illustrious friend, playwright Ben Jonson—to compose memorial poems. These works varied widely in quality and ranged in tone from elegiac to hagiographic. Heminges and Condell themselves made four contributions to the front matter: a catalogue of the plays, a roster of the principal actors who had performed in them, a dedication, and a memorial essay which was a personal tribute to their friend. Hoping they might attract financial support from two earls, they dedicated the book to them. This collection of material, earmarked for the front of the Folio, became known as the "preliminaries."

Their choice of folio format was part solution to a practical problem, part artistic statement. In a folio-size book, a single sheet of paper measuring thirteen by eighteen inches is printed on both sides with text from a play, and folded once in half to yield four printed pages in the final book. Publishing Shakespeare's plays in folio size would result in a nine-hundred-plus-page volume measuring approximately nine by thirteen inches. This was a massive tome for its time, but it could still be bound into a single volume that a reader could hold in his hands, open, and turn the pages without cracking the spine. The First Folio could not have been printed in a smaller format and still be contained in one volume. Heminges and Condell could have elected to print the plays in smaller, quarto size, resulting in a book measuring approximately six by nine inches. But in quarto the thirteen-by-eighteen sheet is folded twice at right angles, resulting in eight pages per sheet. Thus, a nine-hundred-page folio-size work, when reduced to quarto, would be eighteen hundred pages and twice as thick, making it impossible to bind into a single volume.

Although folio was the only practical way to print a book of so many plays in a single volume in manageable size, the folio format was likely to provoke some controversy. By tradition, publishing in folio signified that the content was of serious historical or intellectual importance— reference works, religious and political works, or the collected writings of important and serious authors. It was almost unheard of for plays to enjoy such a prestigious format.

In 1616, Poet Laureate and popular playwright Ben Jonson supervised the publication of a folio collection of his writings, *Workes*. The volume was prefaced with dedicatory verses, including three by Francis Beaumont, and it contained plays, poems, masques, epigrams, and entertainments. It had the distinction of being the first folio-sized book that included plays. A Puritan antitheatricalist, William Prynne, lamented the publication of mere entertainments in that format, complaining that "some Play-books . . . are growne from Quarto into

Folio."[2] Jonson's critics accused him of claiming a higher, more exalted status for his plays than they deserved. He was ridiculed for mistaking the difference between "workes" and "playes." One cheeky fellow wrote:

> *To Mr. Ben Jonson, demanding the reason*
> *Why he call'd his playes works.*
> Pray tell me Ben, where doth the mystery lurke,
> What others call a play you call a worke,
> *Thus answer'd by a friend in Mr.*
> *Jonson's defense.*
> The authors friend thus for the author sayes,
> *Bens* plays are works, when others works are plaies.[3]

Heminges and Condell's choice of supersize format risked inciting similar mockery. Perhaps it was Jonson's *Workes* that inspired them to print Shakespeare's plays in one complete, impressive, and expensive volume. After they chose the format, they had to decide how many copies to print. Once Jaggard started to manufacture the book, its print run would, for technical limitations, be unalterable. The publisher and editors did not have the luxury of knowing in advance whether the First Folio would sell out quickly, unlike a famous text published twelve years earlier, which was destined to be a bestseller. During the reign of Queen Elizabeth I, Puritans in Parliament proposed a new translation of the Bible. In 1604, the year after King James ascended to the throne, forty-seven writer-scholars began the work. Published in 1611, it sold out quickly. It would become the most important nonsecular work in the English language.

Expectations for the First Folio were more modest. If Jaggard printed too few copies—just a couple of hundred—the cost per book would be high, and the booksellers could not charge enough per copy to earn a profit. If they printed too many—more than one thousand—it might take years to sell enough copies just to cover the costs. They had to estimate how many copies they believed they could sell and assume the risk of the cost of time, paper, ink, and labor. Heminges and Condell wished to reach as wide an audience as possible, educated or barely literate, "From the most able, to him that can but spell."[4] Based on these economic considerations, scholars have estimated the size of the print run to be around 750 copies.[5] It was both a leap of faith and a vote of confidence in the marketability of their friend's plays—not just for performance, but also for reading. And this in a country where the literacy rate for males was below thirty percent.

Printing the First Folio required a lot of paper. A print run of 750 copies contained 225 sheets per book, totaling 168,750 sheets. Jaggard did not store that much at his shop, nor would he have tied up funds in such a large stock over the many months it would take to complete the print job. It would have to be imported and it would be expensive; good-quality rag paper was not manufactured in England, so it would have to come from Normandy. Most books printed during the seventeenth century in England were printed on handmade Normandy rag paper. It began its life as discarded rags and clothing, and then, after cleaning, bleaching, soaking, and boiling in quicklime, it became the liquid "stuff" that the papermakers scooped into trays, drained, then dried on felt.

The paper used to print the First Folio was of medium quality, one hundred percent rag, with a supple but substantial feel, and a crown watermark. A watermark is a distinct decorative shape or pattern visible when the paper is held up to the light, with some areas allowing more light to pass through than others because of the different thickness of "stuff" scooped into a mold where a wire ornament has been placed. The wire ornament embosses the fibers of the paper, making them thinner in some areas than others. Prior to printing, the paper was creased down the middle of the long side, to make it easier to drape while drying. In comparison to the Normandy paper, the modern paper used in books today feels tissue-thin. The Puritan William Prynne, so bothered by the status that folio size conferred on the First Folio, was also disturbed that it was printed on such fine-quality paper, complaining "with grief" that "Shackspeers Plaies" are "printed on farre better paper than most Octavo or Quarto Bibles."[6]

Jaggard's shop, equipped with two presses and staffed by more than a half dozen employees, had a variety of typefaces from which to choose.

The Shakespeare folio would be typeset in well-worn type, in two columns per page, with running titles at the top of each page of text. Skilled workmen called compositors sorted each individual letter of metal type into its standard assigned place in a "case." The "case" was an array of small wooden boxes, placed on a table on a slant within easy reach of the compositor. Each letter had its own compartment; more frequently used letters required more copies of the type. Standing before the case, the compositor, holding a composing stick in his left hand, placed the type into the rectangular trench in the composing stick, placing each letter next to the previous, forming words, then lines. When a line of text was complete, the compositor would fill any leftover space at the end of the line with spacers. This process is called justifying. The line of type was lifted from the stick, placed on a wooden board, and the next line of text composed, and then placed on the board below the previous line. To make the printed text read correctly from left to right, the letters and words were composed backward. Once two pages were set, they were placed on a flat surface within an iron frame, the chase. The pages thus arranged, and the frame tightened with screws or wooden wedges called quoins, the whole apparatus, called a forme, was moved to the press, where a proof was pulled to check for errors and make corrections.

A proof was a single sheet held in a tray called a galley. By removing the sheet through an open side of the galley, the printer or one of his employees could mark corrections on the proof sheet while the printing of pages continued. Each uncorrected sheet that came off the press was hung to dry. A worker marked the proof sheet with proofreaders' marks: carats for insertions, strikeouts through text for deletions, marks to insert or delete a space, or to change a letter or word. Next, compositors corrected the galleys, removing, rotating, or adding type as necessary. The high price of paper meant that proof sheets containing mistakes were not discarded, but included in the finished book. The end result was that a particular page of a play exists in one of three possible states: the uncorrected page, a single proof sheet with corrections marked by hand, and corrected pages with errors fixed by having reset the type. These three states were intermingled, stacked, and collected into quires—four or six sheets of paper folded once and gathered together. Jaggard's employees sewed together the gathered pages. The process of making corrections while the printing was under way explains the numerous printed errors that appear in the book.[7]

Once the compositor had reset the type with corrections, the final, corrected state of the sheet could be printed. Between printing the front and back—the recto and verso—of a sheet, they were dried, hung on strings stretched across the print shop or from rounded battens extending from the walls of the shop. The employees used a long-handled wooden paddle to hang the wet sheets as though draping a bedsheet over a clothesline.

Jaggard did not print the pages of the First Folio in sequential order, from beginning to end. Instead, he and his workers typeset the text from the middle, backward and forward to the first and last pages of each quire. In other words, each quire of the First Folio was printed from the middle out. The pages of a quire of six would be printed in the order 1, 2, 11, 12, 3, 4, 9, 10, 5, 6, 7, 8. A compositor estimated how much text would fit on each page, and in a process called casting off he would typeset the pages, starting with the two middle pages of the quire. The process was more prone to error if the source was in manuscript or, if printed, had a number of insertions and emendations. If the compositor incorrectly estimated the amount of text that would fit on a page of a quire, he compensated for his error. If he had too much text to fit on a page, he had to cram the text into the allotted space by deleting line breaks, omitting or altering printer's decorations, converting poetry to prose, or otherwise modifying—even excising—text to fit into its allotted space. If he had too little text to fill a page, he added blank lines, divided complete lines in two, or inserted ornaments until the page was filled. The printer set "catchwords" to help him correctly sequence the pages as they were printed, and later, after they were dried, when they were gathered: the same word appeared at the bottom of a page, below and separate from the last line of text, and as the first word printed in the text of the next page.

Two men worked each press. One pressman smeared ink onto one of two big, soft inking balls made of stuffed animal skin and, by a series of gymnastic manipulations, spread the viscous substance evenly over the surface of both balls. Next, he "beat" the forme by daubing ink onto the type in uniform thickness, neither missing spots nor leaving excess ink on any portion of the type. The ink, made of boiled oil and lampblack, had to be sufficiently gooey that it did not drip off the surface of the type. It took some skill to ink a forme properly: if a pressman applied too much ink, indentations within letters filled in, resulting in letters called monks. Application of too little ink resulted in weak or invisible letters, called friars. The other pressman, careful not to touch the ink, placed the clean sheet of paper on the press and maneuvered the forme beneath the plate of the press. When the pressman pulled a bar attached to the screw, the plate was pressed against the paper, and the ink that coated the type was transferred onto the paper, creating an image and making a three-dimensional printed impression.[8]

When all 750 copies of the two pages of a forme were printed, the men cleaned the type with lye soap, rinsed it with water, dried it, unlocked it from the forme, and redistributed it to the case for use in composition of the next page. Some parts of the assembled type, such as the running titles printed above the text, head ornaments, and tailpieces, were used on multiple pages. Jaggard's men tied these—called furniture—with string and set them aside for reuse. Once the compositors redistributed the type into the case, it was too late to go back and increase the print run. The composition began anew for the next forme, a process that the pressmen would have to repeat several hundred times before the First Folio printing job was complete. It would take centuries for scholars to discover the process and the order in which the First Folio was printed.

This printing process, already prone to error, required flexibility, and circumstances often led to improvisation. Pages of one play, *Troilus and Cressida*, were printed prematurely; Henry Walley, who had printed the play in quarto, had not given his permission to include it in the First Folio. Rather than discard the sheets containing one page of *Troilus*, the printers drew a big X across the superfluous page and continued printing the next play in the catalogue. The disfigured page was kept in the quire, and so some copies of the First Folio contain the canceled page. *Troilus and Cressida* was printed later and appears in some copies of the First Folio, but the title of the play is excluded from the Catalogue page in the preliminaries. Either Jaggard finally secured permission from Walley, or he decided to print it anyway.

Beginning in the fall of 1622, Jaggard and his men methodically typeset, printed, and assembled thousands of sheets of paper. It was a quiet process, mechanical, powered only by hand, slow, methodical, and rhythmic. It was still part art, part industry. The printing process would remain essentially the same, powered by the muscle of the pressmen, for hundreds of years. Machinery did not drown out the voices in the shop, or the sounds from London's streets—the everyday cacophony of rolling carts, horses, and pedestrians.

The pressmen did not know that they were printing what would become the most important secular book in the English language. Although we do not know the names of all the men who set the type for the First Folio, we can identify their work. In the seventeenth century, spelling was not standardized: people often spelled the same word differently. For example, Shakespeare's name was variously spelled as Shakspere, Shaxpere, Shaxberd, or other variants. Even in an era without standard spelling, each compositor tended to spell (or misspell) a given word consistently. For example, Compositor A would usually spell the same word the same way on each page he composed. But Compositor B might use a different spelling for the same word. From the records of Jaggard's shop and the Stationers' Company, scholars have identified at least two compositors and one apprentice. They have been given the code names of Compositors A, B, C, and so forth, plus the so-called Teenage Apprentice, whose identity scholars can only guess. Whatever his name, he was a youth exceedingly prone to error. Meticulous detective work has allowed scholars to infer which sets of hands composed which pages of the Folio. The image of these anonymous tradesmen slowly printing, gathering, and piling in stacks the pages of what would become, unbeknownst to them, one of the most important books in the world is a magical scene worthy of Shakespeare himself.

———

Other work on the First Folio proceeded elsewhere while Jaggard's shop printed the pages. Heminges and Condell wanted to present Shakespeare's image as well as his plays. For the first time in the history of English literature, an author's portrait would become the central feature on a title page. True, other books had included author portraits, but not in such a prominent position. Heminges and Condell could have commissioned a cheap, crude woodcut portrait. But they went to extra effort to have their friend's image engraved on a copper plate, to achieve a more detailed and accurate portrait. Why did they go to this trouble and additional expense? It was as though they were saying, "You cannot just have the words. You must behold the man."

Just as they did not want Shakespeare's words to vanish, they did not want his physical appearance to vanish, as Prospero said in *The Tempest*, "into thin air." Thanks to them, we have the only authentic portrait of William Shakespeare. This illustration, the only one in the book, was executed by the twenty-two-year-old Flemish émigré engraver Martin Droeshout. The most recognizable extant image of Shakespeare, it was made neither from life nor by someone who had known or even seen Shakespeare. Engravers did not "sketch" or do "rough drafts" on metal. So Heminges and Condell must have supplied the engraver with more than a verbal description of their friend. Droeshout must have based his work upon some preexisting source, perhaps a drawing or even an oil painting, now long lost. Engravers were copyists, not police sketch artists.

The process for creating and printing an engraving differed substantially from the method for printing text, and Jaggard lacked the expertise and equipment necessary to execute the portrait. Another shop printed the engraving at the center of a blank page, then turned the sheets over to Jaggard, and he added the title and text that surrounded the portrait. The engraving left crisp images on the early impressions, but the soft copper surface of the plate wore down over time and had to be retouched or reengraved. To the untrained eye, one specimen of the portrait looks no different from another, but three "states" of the engraving exist. The three, laid side by side, vary slightly: the earliest state can be recognized by the *absence* of a shadow cast by Shakespeare's hair on his ruffled collar. The second state has a shadow cross-hatched in, but lacks the little white lines at the centers of the pupils of Shakespeare's eyes that identify the third state.

The composition is amateurish and has invited centuries of mockery. Shakespeare's head seems to float above his body like a roast on a platter, and it appears that his tunic sprouts two left sleeves. Despite these shortcomings, Droeshout displayed his talent in the rendering of his subject's face, creating what became one of the most recognizable and ubiquitous images in Western art.

The portrait has also inspired conspiracy theories. In Ben Jonson's short introductory poem to the First Folio, his play on words regarding the engraving has been seized upon by Shakespeare deniers as some sort of secret code "proving" that Shakespeare did not write the plays:

To the Reader

This Figure, that thou here seest put,
It was for gentle Shakespeare cut,
Wherein the Graver had a strife
With Nature, to out-doo the life:
O, could he but have drawne his wit
As well in brasse, as he hath hit
His face, the Print would then surpasse
All, that was ever writ in brasse.
But, since he cannot, Reader, looke
Not on his Picture, but his Booke.

Conspiracy theorists translate Jonson as saying: if you wish to find the man who wrote the words, look in the book, and not on his face, because the man whose face you see is not the author. What Jonson really meant was that no static likeness could ever convey the zest and wit of the living Shakespeare that he and the King's Men knew and heard. Rather, to know the true man, Jonson says, read his words, and perform them. And yet Heminges and Condell thought it important for the reader to gaze upon that face.[9]

After the printed text, title page, and preliminaries were printed and dried, Jaggard's men gathered and stitched them together. While pages within the quire were sequenced with the help of catchwords, gatherings were put in correct order using a unique signature in the lower margin of the first leaf of the quire. It might seem logical to use the page numbers as a guide to collating the pages, but pagination was notoriously flawed in books of such length—and the First Folio is no exception—because the casting-off process was imperfect. Thus, the First Folio pagination is incomplete, containing unnumbered pages and repeated numbers.

To Heminges and Condell, the preliminaries were as important as the main text. They intended these pages not only to speak to an audience of the 1620s, but also to reach across time to all of Shakespeare's future readers. They wanted us to know their friend, not just his words. The first page of the preliminaries contains Jonson's "To the Reader."

The title page, which faces Jonson's verse, displays the complete title *Mr. William Shakespeares Comedies, Histories, & Tragedies, published according to the True Originall copies*, cites the place of publication as London, and announces that the book was printed in 1623 "by Isaac Jaggard and Ed. Blount"—a slight misstatement as the Jaggard shop did all the printing. Isaac's name had replaced his father's as William had died a short time before publication.

The third preliminary, the dedication epistle, was written by Heminges and Condell "To the Most Noble & Incomparable Paire of Brethren" William Earl of Pembroke, who served as "Lord Chamberlaine to the King's Most Excellent Majesty," and Philip Earl of Pembroke and Montgomery, from whom the editors sought patronage: "We have but collected them, and done an office to the dead, to procure his Orphanes, Guardians; without ambition either of selfe-profit, or fame: onely to keepe the memory of so worthy a Friend, & Fellow alive, as was our S H A K E S P E A R E . . . therefore, we most humbly consecrate to [you] these remaines of your servant Shakespeare." They ask that the two nobles "shew their gratitude both to the living, and the dead."

Next, Heminges and Condell appealed to the public—"The great Variety of Readers," from educated men to those who could barely read, "From the most able, to him that can but spell"—to "read, and censure . . . but buy it first." They beseech the public to read, and even criticize the plays, pleading, "But, whatever you do, Buy."

The editors expressed regret that "the author himselfe" did not live to oversee the publication of his plays. And so they published them on his behalf, not from "diverse stolne, and surreptitious copies, maimed, and deformed by the frauds and stealthes of injurious impostors" but "cur'd, and perfect of their limbes, and all the rest, absolute in their numbers as he conceived them." Heminges and Condell evoked the apparent ease and speed with which Shakespeare composed his texts: "His mind and hand went together: And what he thought, he uttered with that easinesse, that wee have scarse received from him a blot in his papers." In other words, his hand moved so quickly across the page that his quill did not rest long enough to leave a blot of ink behind. But it is not up to us, say Heminges and Condell, to praise Shakespeare. It is up to you to find in the text "enough, both to draw, and hold you: for his wit can no more lie hid, than it could be lost. Reade him, therefore; and againe, and againe."

The next preliminary, "To the Memory of My Beloved, Mr. William Shakespeare and what he hath left us," is a most romantic and complimentary eulogy. Here Jonson, as famous as Shakespeare was during their lifetimes, pays a stunning homage. First, he elevates him to the pantheon of English literature, comparing him to the gods Chaucer, Spenser, and Beaumont. Then Jonson ranks Shakespeare above all his contemporaries, including John Lyly, Thomas Kyd, and Christopher Marlowe, singling him out as the "Soule of the Age!"

While I confesse thy writings to be such,
As neither Man, nor Muse, can praise too much.
. . . Soule of the Age!
The applause! delight! the wonder of our Stage!

My Shakespeare, rise; I will not lodge thee by
Chaucer, or Spenser, or bid Beaumont lye
A little further, to make thee a roome:
Thou art a Moniment, without a tombe,
And art alive still, while thy Booke doth live . . .
And tell, how farre thou dist our Lily out-shine,

Or sporting Kid or Marlowes mighty line.
And though thou hadst small Latine, and lesse Greeke, . . .
He was not of an age, but for all time!

Not all contributors to the preliminaries possessed Jonson's eloquence. Hugh Holland's elegiac sonnet, "Upon the Lines and Life of the famous Scenicke Poet, Master William Shakespeare," was not very good, but contains a few couplets worth remembering.

Those hands, which you so clapt, go now, and wring
You Britaines brave; for done are Shakespeares dayes:
His dayes are done, that made the dainty Playes, . . .
For though his line of life went soone about,
The life yet of his lines shall never out.

Next in order came "A CATALOGVE of the Seuerall Comedies, Historie, and Tragedies in this Volume"—what modern readers would call the table of contents—listing the plays. The classifications mimicked the practice at the Globe Theatre of using a colored flag on the roof to communicate what genre of play was being performed that day: red flag for history, white for comedy, and black for tragedy.

The next preliminary, Leonard Digges's "To the Memorie of the deceased Authour Maister W. Shake-speare," was, like Hugh Holland's verse, no masterpiece. Still, it contained a heartfelt sentiment.

This Booke,
When Brasse and Marble fade, shall make thee looke
Fresh to all Ages: . . .

Be sure, our Shake-speare, thou canst never dye,
But crown'd with Lawrell, live eternally.

Printed on the same page as the Digges verse is James Mabbe's forgettable "To the Memorie of M.W. Shake-speare," which imagines the playwright in the dressing room of the great Globe Theatre in the sky. "Wee thought thee dead," Mabbe laments, but Shakespeare lives on in the First Folio, "this thy printed worth."

WEE wondred, Shake-speare, that thou went'st so soone
From the Worlds-Stage, to the Graves-Tyring-roome.

Last, Heminges and Condell listed "The Names of the Principall Actors in all these Playes." They wanted to record for all time the names of the men who had first breathed life into Shakespeare's characters. The twenty-six actors included William Shakespeare, John Heminges, Henry Condell, Richard Burbage, Will Kemp, Samuel Gilburne, and the rest, many of whom would have been lost to history but for this list.

❧ The First Folio was not the most important project on which Jaggard's men labored from February 1622 to December 1623; and they were in no particular hurry to finish it. A book by Jaggard's friend Augustine Vincent was rushed into print ahead of both Shakespeare's First Folio and André Favyn's *Theatre of Honour and Knight-Hood*.[10] Jaggard periodically stopped printing books whenever he could make money on other, smaller jobs—proclamations, broadsides, copies of the Ten Commandments, and playbills. He had no idea that he was delaying a historic undertaking. But then, neither did anyone else.

The Vincent book was also folio size and shared with Shakespeare's volume a variety of printers' ornaments, the decorative woodcuts easily recognizable in previous and subsequent works printed by Jaggard and his son. Publication of Vincent's *Discoverie of Errours in the First Edition of the Catalogue of Nobility, Published by Raphe Brooke, Yorke Herald, 1619* was accelerated ahead of the First Folio to beat to publication a book that would contain accusations concerning Jaggard's professional competence. The author of that book, Raphe Brooke, blamed Jaggard for the large number of errors that had appeared in a book that Jaggard had printed for him. Augustine Vincent defended Jaggard in *Discoverie of Errours*, and time was of the essence in getting that volume to market.

The Shakespeare folio was announced to the trade in advance of its publication. The Frankfurt Book Fair was the publishing industry's largest event of the year, and in 1622, John Bill, printer to the King of England, issued an English translation of the Frankfurt catalogue as well as a list of books printed in English. It contained this modest announcement: "Playes, written by M. William Shakespeare, all in one volume, printed by Isaack Iaggard, in fol." Also listed for publication that year was Augustine Vincent's *Discoverie of Errours*.

From the summer of 1622 through the fall of 1623, the printing continued; the same set of motions, repeated hundreds of times in setting the type, and tens of thousands of times inking the type, laying down the sheet, and pulling the lever. Month by month, the stacks of printed pages grew taller. No single book could be stitched and bound until all the pages had been printed.

When at last the printing was finished, the First Folio was a physically impressive object sitting in Blount's bookshop, at the sign of the Black Bear in St. Paul's Churchyard. At more than nine hundred pages, it was a solid book with size and heft. The tallest copies, right off the press, untrimmed by the binder's plow, measured 13½ by 8¾ inches. The project was finished. It had taken two years to print the massive First Folio. At last it could be made available for sale. Publishing it had been an unprecedented, ambitious, complicated, and risky project. The public was not lining up outside Blount's shop to buy copies.

The book was sold as is, in unbound leaves "in sheets," or in one of three bindings available from Jaggard. Forel, the least expensive, was a limp, creamy white parchment. Untanned calf or goatskin, with one side smooth and the other rough, was more expensive. Tanned calfskin, at one pound, was the most costly standard binding, and was light brown to mahogany in color. Some buyers purchased the text in sheets and paid their favorite bookbinders to clothe the First Folio in exquisite calfskin with elaborate decoration. Sometimes, the owner had the edges of the paper trimmed to eliminate the rough, deckled edge. He might have the resulting smooth edges gilt with a thin layer of gold using an adhesive of egg white and water. Such a treatment was expensive, but would serve a greater purpose than the owner's vanity; gilt edges would also provide a barrier against dust and moisture, protecting the book from the elements and preserving it. If the buyer could not afford to gild every edge, he might treat only the top one, where the most dust would settle. Further adornment could be achieved by gauffering the edges of a gilt or silvered book, pressing heated decorative tools into the edges.

Some bibliophiles have romanticized the First Folio as a magnificent example of the printer's art. To Heminges and Condell, its physical appearance was never of much importance. What was vital to them was the content: its significance was, is, in saving the oeuvre of Shakespeare, rather than in its aesthetic merits. Imagine an accurate catalogue description that could have been printed at the time:

> Each copy unique, some copies missing one play, pages misnumbered, different copies containing the portrait of the author in varying states, some copies with one page of crossed-out text, table of contents not necessarily accurate. May include uncorrected proof pages within the text. Prose occasionally printed as verse, and vice versa. Stage directions missing in some parts. Spelling and punctuation haphazard, though less in some copies than in others, printers' ornaments worn and broken, inconsistent page numbering. Prologue to *Romeo and Juliet* missing in some copies. Sold in a variety of bindings or in sheets, ready to take to your favorite binder to indulge your preferences at your expense.

On November 8, 1623, the publishers entered in the Register at the Stationers' Company "Master William Shakespears Comedyes, Histories, and Tragedies so many of the said Copies as are not formerly entered to other men."[11] By the mid-sixteenth century, members of any theatrical company had to present to the warden any proposed publication not protected by royal grant. This list, the "register of Copies," in which Jaggard and Blount entered the First Folio, was the official record of their exclusive right to print the complete works of William Shakespeare. The entry in the Register was intended to protect not the author, but the printer—only a member of the Worshipful Company of Stationers of London could enter a book. Jaggard and Blount now "owned" the publishing rights, and they could exploit them, neither compensating the author nor requiring his permission. No work previously registered by a member of the Company could be printed by another member, and disputes as to ownership were settled through the Company. Printers who were not also booksellers usually had to arrange with one or more booksellers to market their books; William Aspley, member of the syndicate that published the First Folio, owned the Parrot, a few feet west of Blount's shop at the sign of the Black Bear.

Flawed though the First Folio was as an example of the printer's art, without it we would not possess definitive texts closest to Shakespeare's original intentions for the plays that would, absent the First Folio, have come down to us only in some lesser form via various quartos. And without the First Folio, we would have lost the text of half the plays that were never printed during Shakespeare's life, and perhaps even the knowledge that some of those plays had ever existed: *The Tempest*, *The Two Gentlemen of Verona*, *Measure for Measure*, *The Comedy of Errors*, *As You Like It*, *All's Well That Ends Well*, *Twelfth Night*, *King John*, *Henry VI Part 1*, *Henry VIII*, *Coriolanus*, *Timon of Athens*, *Julius Caesar*, *Macbeth*, *Antony and Cleopatra*, *Cymbeline*, *The Taming of the Shrew*, and *The Winter's Tale*.

Were Heminges and Condell's choices perfect? No. Does the First Folio reflect the text of each play exactly as written by Shakespeare? Almost certainly not. But it is the best we have. And scholars have spilled much ink disagreeing on what the "true" text is. The casual reader might be astonished to know that there isn't one true text. If Shakespeare could return to us and read the First Folio from cover to cover, and we asked him, "Is it word for word exactly as you wrote it?" he might well answer, "No, but close enough."

Postmodern scholars (dubious of the sole-author-as-genius creative model) dispute whether the texts of Shakespeare's plays were ever truly fixed. On the contrary, they argue, the texts were always changing, even during Shakespeare's lifetime, in constant flux due to alterations by the author, the players, and even the publishers of the quartos. Thus Shakespeare was not the "sole" author and the play texts were never permanent but constantly evolving.

Others think the canon of Shakespeare was always settled, but that is not so. What we accept as the canon today is a result of choices made by Heminges and Condell as well as the vicissitudes of chance, according to the sources available to them. The First Folio did not include all the plays: some, like *Pericles*, were known but not included. Some, like *Love's Labour's Wonne*, were known but already "lost" or surviving under another name. Heminges and Condell were unable to secure the rights to publish *Pericles*. *Love's Labour's Wonne*, attributed to Shakespeare, appeared in a bookseller's record in 1603, but no copy has ever been found. It is possible that the title was changed to *Love's Labour's Lost*. Scholars have speculated that Heminges and Condell excluded plays that were not entirely Shakespeare's own work, like *The Two Noble Kinsmen*, but such a strict standard would also have resulted in the exclusion of *Henry VIII*, on which Shakespeare had also collaborated with Fletcher, which *is* included in the First Folio.[12]

Little is known about the first buyers, though the first recorded retail sale appears as an entry on December 5, 1623, in the account book of Sir Edward Dering. It shows that he attended a play, which cost one shilling, six denarii, and he purchased "two volumes of Shakespear's playes" for two pounds. He also purchased "Jhonson's playes" for nine shillings. We also know what happened to two more of the earliest copies to leave the shop. Jaggard sent one free copy, unbound in sheets, to the Bodleian Library at Oxford, as required by an agreement between the library and the Stationers' Company. The other was the first presentation copy of the Shakespeare First Folio, whose story begins with Raphe Brooke.

Raphe Brooke, a member of the College of Arms (or Herald's College), objected to the coat of arms given to the Shakespeares. Three centuries later, Henry Folger would describe him thus: "Brooke, a man without a past, had forced his way into the sacred precincts. His very name and lineage were assumed." When the esteemed heraldic scholar William Camden supported the legitimacy of the Shakespeare grant, Brooke published in 1596 a defamatory book that attacked Camden's book *Britannia*, a distinguished genealogical volume. Then, in 1619, Brooke published, through the printer William Jaggard, his own book on peerage, riddled with errors and containing further defamations against Camden. Outraged, the Windsor Herald of Arms, the state official charged with control over issuance of arms and maintenance of heraldic records, Augustine Vincent, rose in defense of Camden and exposed Brooke's ridiculous mistakes.[13] Brooke responded by issuing a second edition of his book, blaming whatever errors it contained on his "rascally printer" by whom many "divers faults and many mistakings were committed." Now Brooke had defamed not only Camden but also William Jaggard, future printer of the First Folio.

In 1622, Augustine Vincent escalated the feud by publishing a rejoinder, *A Discoverie of Errours in the Catalogue of Nobility, Published by Raphe Brooke*.[14] Vincent chose as his publisher none other than Jaggard, who was eager to repay Brooke's offense. Jaggard included in Vincent's book several pages of his own accusing Brooke of "falsifications, suborning of incestuous matches, bastard issues, and changing children in the cradle, and such scumms of his ranke eloquence." *A Discoverie of Errours* pronounced Brooke guilty of all manner of offenses, including "Your owne intolerable arrogance and pride of conceite, your vilifying and contempt of others, as if you had stoode on the toppe of Powles, and saw all men under you no bigger than Jacke-dawes; your familiar vaine of detracting from the best and Worthiest men; your tongue gliding over no man's name, but that it left a slime behind it." Brooke, finally, was finished.

In 1623, Jaggard printed the First Folio and, in gratitude for the punishment Vincent had meted out to Brooke, presented him, the Windsor Herald, with one of the earliest copies to be bound. The impression of the engraved portrait of Shakespeare on the title page of this copy is so fresh and brilliant that it must have been one of the first copies struck from the copper plate. The volume was bound in calfskin, and the front cover was embossed with Vincent's coat of arms—"a bear, holding in his left paw a banner, and in his right a squire's helmet, surrounded with a crest of a bear's head, standing on a scroll with the motto 'Vincenti Augusta' (Laurels for a conqueror)." The motto was meant to be a pun on Vincent's own name. William Jaggard could not inscribe the book to his friend, because the blind printer had died before the First Folio job was completed. So Augustine Vincent inscribed the title page in his own hand: "Ex donno Willi Jaggard. Typographi a 1623," identifying the book as a gift from the printer. Then the book vanished for the next 278 years.

The publication of the First Folio, despite Ben Jonson's stirring proclamation that its author was the "Soule of the Age!" who merited eternal fame because he was "Not of an age, but for all time," did not set the world aflame. It took nine years to sell out the first printing. But it made possible what was to come, a story that would take another century and a half to unfold.

The First Folio saved all of Shakespeare's plays from textual corruption, and half of them from oblivion, but it also left a great mystery that remains unsolved to this day. What did Heminges and Condell do with all the source materials they collected, which they distilled into the final text of the First Folio? It is not likely that they turned everything they found over to their printer. Jaggard played no role in editing these sources down to a final draft. He needed no more than a legible copy of each play for his compositors to set the type. Once Heminges and Condell generated those fair copies, what happened to the sources that they gathered to create them? Did they destroy them, or preserve them in some safe place? And what did Jaggard do with the pages his compositors used to set the type? Did he return them to Heminges and Condell, or did he destroy them seriatim as each printed quire transferred text from manuscript to type? Or did he sell the paper for scrap? Was it consigned to the fire? And what of the preliminaries— the manuscript tributes by Jonson and the others, and the message to the reader from Heminges and Condell? All gone. Not one page from the archives of Shakespeare's editors has survived.

Of course it is possible that somewhere in England, in a private library at a remote country house, set high upon a dusty shelf, there lies an old, forgotten leather portfolio, stuffed with hundreds of manuscript pages and quartos, hand-marked with heavy strikeouts and emendations—the long-lost Heminges and Condell hoard. Or perhaps in the attic of that house, there rests a small, locked trunk that once belonged to the loyal friends who wore Shakespeare's rings. There is precedent for such astonishing discoveries; that is how the famous sixteenth-century Waldseemüller map was discovered. It was the first map that ever printed the name "America." Long known to scholars, no copy had ever been found. Its huge size and fragile nature argued against its survival. Then, several years ago, the only known copy in the world turned up in a private German library and was sold to the Library of Congress for ten million dollars. The discovery of the archives of Heminges and Condell would answer one of the most puzzling literary mysteries of all time: How did they create the First Folio?

Chapter 4

❧✿❧

"My Shakespeare, Rise"

—Ben Jonson

THE PUBLICATION in 1623 of the First Folio did not immediately lead to Shakespeare's apotheosis. The folio was a necessary precondition for Shakespeare's rebirth, but it took another 140 years, and three distinct stages of evolution, for the playwright, and his book, to achieve immortality. Over the next century and a half, a colorful cast of proclaimers, editors, bowdlerizers, biographers, literary critics, actors, and collectors—curators of his reputation—elevated him to the pantheon of the greatest writers in the English language.

During the first phase, between 1623 and 1709, a consensus formed in England that Shakespeare was one of the preeminent writers of the Elizabethan and Jacobean ages. His plays were no longer considered second-class stepchildren to his high art, poetry. But sales of the First Folio suggest that this recognition took time. A book printed in such a limited quantity could never enjoy widespread distribution in a nation of several million people.

By 1632, Jaggard and Blount had exhausted their stocks of First Folios. A second edition of the book was published that year. Heminges and Condell were no longer alive to supervise the reprinting, which was executed not by Jaggard but by the firm of Smethwick and Aspley, et al. This edition, called the Second Folio, corrected some errors in the First but it introduced others. Essentially a reprint of the First Folio, it is most famous for its inclusion of John Milton's verse, "An Epitaph of the admirable Dramaticke Poet, W. Shakespeare," the first time a poem of Milton's appeared in print.

Shakespeare's collected plays would not be printed again for another thirty-one years. The cause of the delay was not literary but historical. The London plague of 1636 paralyzed the theatrical world for a time. More ominously, the English Civil War of 1642–1651 enforced radical changes in popular culture, including the banning of performances of plays. The beheading of King Charles I (who had kept a copy of the Second Folio close during his captivity) on January 30, 1649, signaled dark days for the English theater during the era of Puritan dominance. Only the death of Oliver Cromwell in 1658 and the restoration of the monarchy, which brought Charles II to the throne in May 1660 and saw him crowned on Shakespeare's birthday, April 23, 1661, revived the theater. The contemporary diary of Samuel Pepys offers wonderful evidence of how plays, including ribald versions of old favorites, flourished under the new king, a man sympathetic to the arts as a cultural force.

The good news for Shakespeare's reputation was that in Restoration England, almost fifty years after his death, some of his plays were being staged again. The bad news was that some of them were barely recognizable as the plays he wrote and that we know today. Characters were subtracted (the fool vanished from Lear) and tragic endings were lightened up (*Romeo and Juliet* ended with a happy marriage). One theater treated audiences to alternating tragic and romantic endings every other night. In 1667 William Davenant (D'Avenant), Poet Laureate of England, collaborated with John Dryden to adapt *The Tempest*.[1]

A Third Folio of the plays appeared in 1663, forty years after publication of the First. Shakespeare was still popular enough to justify a new printing of his works. The big selling point of the third edition was that it contained seven new plays hitherto unattributed to him: *The London Prodigal*; *The Life and Death of Thomas, Lord Cromwell*; *The History of Sir John Oldcastle, the Good Lord Cobham*; *The Puritan, or the Widow of Watling Street*; *A Yorkshire Tragedy*; *The Tragedy of Locrine*; and *Pericles*. Unfortunately, of the seven additional plays, six were spurious.

Scholars believe that only one of them, *Pericles*, was actually, at least partially, written by Shakespeare at all.

Because the Third Folio purported to include additional material, it superseded the importance of the First in the mind of the public, and thus supplanted it in many libraries. It is impossible to know how many owners of the First Folio disposed of their old copies once they obtained the new Third Folio, but in one instance that became notorious centuries later, the Bodleian Library sold the First Folio as surplus and shelved the Third Folio in its place. The library's records suggest that it went to Richard Davis, an Oxford bookseller, for twenty-four pounds. It was a trivial, improvident act that would set in motion unanticipated reverberations 250 years later. No one realized at the time that the text of the First Folio was superior to that of the Second or Third, or that the number of perfect copies of the First Folio was dwindling year by year.[2]

The Third Folio, although not the most desirable or most valuable of the seventeenth-century Shakespeare Folios, is the rarest, not because of sustained losses over the vicissitudes of time but due to a mass disaster—many copies were destroyed during the 1666 Great Fire of London. Because this folio had been published just three years prior, a large unsold stock was still on hand at the booksellers around St. Paul's. No doubt the Great Fire also counted among its victims a number of First Folios. But these were not lost en masse; the stockpile of First Folios had sold out decades earlier, and the 750 copies had been dispersed—safely, it turned out—throughout London, England, and even Europe. As it had been during Shakespeare's lifetime, London in 1666 was still medieval in its street plan, an overcrowded warren of half a million inhabitants, living in narrow, winding, cobbled alleys, slippery with dung and urine, both animal and human. The houses were primarily wooden, many with thatched straw roofs and wood chimneys. The more expensive and more fireproof stone houses were located in the center of town. Spark-belching workshops, including blacksmiths, bakers, and glaziers, had cropped up within the crowded city despite having long been forbidden, as a precaution against fire, from doing so. One such bakery, Farriner's on Pudding Lane, would soon become notorious. Many buildings were top-heavy, constructed with their upper floors larger than their ground floors, so that protruding "jetties" almost touched neighboring structures. Like tree limbs, these timber-framed Tudor structures grew and curved above the narrow streets below until the upper stories of these homes and shops practically touched, "like old crones whispering secrets to each other."[3] The result? London was one giant firetrap.

On the evening of Sunday, September 2, 1666, fire broke out in Farriner's and spread quickly. Many people, before fleeing the city, buried their valuables to protect them from flames and looters. Some Londoners believed that St. Paul's, with its mighty stone walls, ingenious lead-covered roof, and wide plaza surrounding the church, offered obvious sanctuary from the firestorm. And royal decrees had long required that churches keep firefighting supplies available—leather buckets, ladders, barrels of water. But in the years since London's previous great fire, much of that equipment had disappeared, been stolen, or been left in disrepair. A recent drought had all but dried up the water stored in the cisterns, and there was insufficient manpower or equipment to fight the blaze by hand.

Printers and booksellers from adjoining Paternoster Row rushed to St. Paul's with carts crammed full of their goods—printed unbound sheets, books sewn and ready for binding, and bound books—and carried them into the underground, airtight crypt of St. Faith's Chapel in St. Paul's. Fire requires three factors in order to combust: a source of fuel, a source of ignition, and oxygen. The combustible goods stowed in the airtight crypt were, it was presumed, protected from the onrushing fire by the lack of oxygen in the underground chamber and the stone construction of the building. But although the huge, six-acre wooden roof had been protected with a fire-resistant sheet of lead, the edges of the roof had not been so covered. The flames took hold at these narrow but vulnerable wooden edges. The vaulting underneath was all timber—dried out from weeks of scorching sun without rain—an ideal fuel to feed the fire. As flames consumed the underlying roof, the superheated lead began to melt. The roof collapsed, and tons of timber and stonework crashed down to the slate floor below.

The roar of the falling roof could be heard all over London, above the cacophony of the fire, the screams of fleeing inhabitants, and even the gunpowder explosions announcing the intentional demolition of houses to deny fuel to the fire. The stone of the outer skin of St. Paul's heated and exploded

> like Granados . . . the melting lead running down the streets in a stream and the very pavements glowing with fiery redness, so as no horse, nor man, was able to tread on them, and the demolition had stopped all the passages, so that no help could be applied. The eastern wind still more impetuously driving the flames forward. Nothing but the Almighty power of God was able to stop them for vain was the help of man.[4]

Inside St. Paul's, the collapsing roof broke the slate floor and cracked the ceiling of the crypt. Oxygen seeped into the chamber and molten lead dripped onto the contents. The books and papers were destroyed. Samuel Pepys described the loss: "The cathedral was quickly a ruin," but books and paper stored in the crypt burned for two weeks. "I hear the great loss of books in St. Paul's Church-yarde, and at their Hall also, which they value about £150,000; some booksellers being wholly undone . . . they trusting St. Fayth's and the roof of the church falling, broke the arch down into the lower church and so all the goods burned. A Very great loss."[5]

The Fourth Folio was published in 1685. It included the seven new plays—six of them apocryphal—introduced by the Third Folio, and perpetuated errors from both the Second and Third Folios. But the era of Shakespeare folios was coming to an end, in more ways than one. There would be no Fifth Folio. No later printings of the plays would resemble the physical appearance of the first or the three that followed. To an untrained eye, a later folio might look very much like a First—they shared the same large-size format, were printed in double columns, and included the engraved portrait by Droeshout, although the once-fine details captured by its copper printing plate were now worn away from decades of use. So, too, did the language preserved by the First Folio degrade over time. The subsequent folios had strayed from the urtext blessed by Heminges and Condell.

No one had yet realized the unique literary value of the First Folio. By the end of the seventeenth century, book dealers began to list in their sales catalogues used, out-of-print copies of the 1623 edition, but without any indication that the volume was held in high esteem.[6] Still, Shakespeare's reputation was slowly on the rise. As early as 1668, in *An Essay of Dramatic Poesy*, John Dryden gushed, "I admire [Ben Jonson], but I love Shakespeare."[7] But what Heminges and Condell hoped to achieve by their careful editing and arranging of the plays was being undermined by the success of the later folios. By 1685, it was by no means certain that Shakespeare's original language would survive as they had preserved it. This was a double cruelty. First, Heminges and Condell had died too soon for them to know the importance of what they had accomplished. And now, what they had accomplished was in jeopardy. By 1700, seventy-seven years after they completed the First Folio, there was no guarantee that the new century would belong to "their" Shakespeare.

In 1709, the age of Heminges and Condell and the four folios had passed. Now began the second stage in the evolution of Shakespeare's reputation and the preservation of his texts, the era of "the editors" and literary criticism. In that year Nicholas Rowe published his edition of the plays in an entirely new format, a multivolume octavo size, based on the Fourth Folio text. Rowe became the first "real" editor of Shakespeare since Heminges and Condell. In his quest to retrieve the true text, Rowe relied on a 1685 Fourth Folio. He was the first to add a list of dramatis personae, to insert act and scene divisions, and to insert stage directions for actors' entrances and exits. In his dedication he claimed:

I have taken some Care to redeem [Shakespeare] from the In-juries of former Impressions. I must not pretend to have restor'd this Work to the Exactness of the Author's Original Manuscripts: These are lost, or, at least, are gone beyond any Inquiry I could make so that there was nothing left, but to compare the several Editions, and give the true Readings as well as I could from thence.

Notwithstanding Rowe's boast to protect Shakespeare from "injuries," the editor included in his new edition the apocryphal plays from the Third and Fourth Folios.

Rowe also wrote a biography of Shakespeare, the first one attempted in the more than ninety years since the playwright's death. But it was too late. By then, everyone who had known the poet was dead. Anne Hathaway had died in August 1623. Shakespeare's last surviving child, Judith, had died in 1662. No one alive could provide the raw facts of his life or vivid recollections of events. If only Heminges and Condell had thought to include in the First Folio a short biography, even one of just thirty or forty pages, their anecdotes might have answered many of the questions that have gnawed at generations of Shakespeare scholars.

Rowe inspired other editors to try their hand at taming and packaging Shakespeare. The appearance over a short period of multiple, posthumous editions of the same work is a sign that an author's reputation is on the rise.

In 1725, Alexander Pope issued his six-volume quarto edition based largely on Rowe's work. Pope also claimed to have used as sources the First and Second Folios, as well as twenty-seven quartos of various dates. He inserted into the plays passages that he believed should have been present from the beginning, but that were "missing" from the folios. In 1733, Lewis Theobald, a critic of Pope's edition who is credited by some as "the first Shakespearean scholar," collated the quarto printings of the plays, investigated Shakespeare's literary sources, and published his edition in octavo.[8] Other editions followed, from Thomas Hanmer in 1744 and from William Warburton in 1747.

In another measure of Shakespeare's growing importance, his Holy Trinity Church monument was restored in 1748–49, the historic preservation funded with the first known performance of a Shakespeare play in Stratford. Town records do not indicate which play it was. In the progression of Shakespeare's apotheosis, the first academic lectures on his work at an English university occurred at Oxford in 1751.[9] In

1765, the great lexicographer Samuel Johnson published his *Plays of William Shakespeare*, in eight octavo volumes, with a magnificent preface praising Shakespeare's drama as the "mirrour of life." And in 1768, Edward Capell published in ten volumes his thirty years' worth of quarto collation and other research into Shakespeare's sources.

By the 1750s, more than 125 years after its publication, English editors and bibliophiles had finally recognized the First Folio for what it had always been: a rare and desirable book of the utmost literary and historical importance. It also attained status as a cultural icon. In eighteenth-century England, the conspicuous display of antiquarian objects or texts indicated a fashionable reverence for the past. Prior to the mid-eighteenth century, the later editions—the Second, Third, and Fourth Folios—superseded the First in the minds of readers, who failed to realize that, rather than containing improvements, each subsequent edition strayed further and further from Shakespeare's original language. Then, when the new Rowe edition of 1709 was published, it supplanted all of the preceding folios. By then, many copies of the First Folio had already been lost, sold off as superfluous, discarded, or broken up. Only later did scholars realize that it was irreplaceable, and superior to all subsequent editions. But by then, two-thirds of them had vanished, and over the next century and a half, many more were cannibalized to repair incomplete copies.

By the 1750s, Shakespeare's reputation as a great author was secure in the British literary world. In 1769, a peculiar event made him a national icon in British popular culture. In that pivotal year, the famed actor David Garrick staged the world's first Shakespeare festival. Garrick, a close friend of Shakespeare biographer Samuel Johnson, made his first appearance on a London stage in 1741, and later that year he played the character for which he became renowned: Richard III. Garrick owned that role for the next two generations, and he also gave beloved performances of other tragic and comic characters. His associations with royalty raised the status of actors in general. Like Shakespeare, Garrick was actor, playwright, and businessman. Garrick, the Richard Burbage of his age, was England's first modern stage star.

Born in 1717, Garrick was credited with rescuing Shakespeare's plays "from the rust of antiquity by his excellence of acting."[10] Slight of build and short of stature, he created and then popularized a more natural style of delivering Shakespeare's lines, shunning the declamatory speech and bombastic style popular at the time. Alexander Pope, an enthusiastic Garrick fan, insisted, "He will never have a rival." By 1769, after enjoying more than a quarter century of fame, David Garrick honored the man whose plays had catapulted him to stardom and whom he praised as "the God of our Idolatry." He concocted what he hoped would be an incomparable festival, a grand Shakespeare Jubilee, and he planned to stage it not in cosmopolitan London but in Stratford-upon-Avon, the playwright's sleepy hometown.

Garrick overwhelmed the bewildered Stratfordians with his proposal. In exchange for his pledge to fund a renovation of the town hall, city officials gave him free rein to organize a three-day Shakespeare festival in September. Stratford was not a destination for literary tourists on a quest for the wellspring of Shakespeare's greatness. So Garrick decided to build a shrine to Shakespeare there, a replica of the elaborate, classical rotunda he had already built at his own home. It was a sublime example of English folly architecture.

Garrick, a master at public relations, lover of his own fame, and loudly proclaimed lover of Shakespeare, had ambitious plans. The Jubilee's main attraction would be an unprecedented literary pageant, a parade through the town by actors costumed as the most memorable characters from Shakespeare's plays. The three-day-long party would be filled with feasting, pageantry, processions, fireworks, and balls. The Jubilee was concocted to appeal to the masses, not scholars and intellectuals. Strangely, at the world's first Shakespeare publicity event, not a single play was to be performed, and not one poem written by Shakespeare was to be recited.

Some scholars made fun of the whole enterprise, satirizing it in print before it even happened. Others, including Garrick's friend Samuel Johnson, declined to attend. Still, Garrick had created massive advance publicity for the Jubilee and all signs pointed to its success. Garrick appointed his literary agent as the head of merchandising. In a surprising twist, the merchandise being sold was only tangentially related to Shakespeare. It was mostly Garrickiana—Garrick plays, songbooks, broadsides, engravings, and more. Indeed, from the catalogue of goods and paraphernalia sold there, one might wonder whom this festival was *really* intended to celebrate.

It was a fiasco. Rains swelled the nearby river Avon and flooded the shrine under half a foot of water. The fireworks display—the promised exciting finale—was rained out. Mud paralyzed traffic on Stratford's unpaved streets, and on the third day Garrick canceled the remaining festivities, including a pageant of characters from Shakespeare's plays. The high point of the Jubilee was Garrick's performance of what came to be known later as "the Ode"—an *Ode upon Dedicating a Building, and Erecting a Statue, to Shakespeare, at Stratford upon Avon.* Garrick spoke the piece—more like an opera recitative than delivery of a poem—over musical accompaniment.[11] The Shakespeare Jubilee was a financial failure. Garrick had to reimburse the town of Stratford for two thousand pounds in expenses. Despite the mocking news reports that followed, the actor was able to salvage something from his considerable efforts. He moved the pageant and the *Ode* to Drury Lane in London. There he presented it as a standalone entertainment called *The Jubilee*, which ran for ninety-one nights in 1769 and 1770. The scheme worked, despite biting criticism in the press and the simultaneous London theater production of a satire making fun of Garrick's colossal ego and the festival's failure. The *Ode* became an old chestnut in Garrick's repertoire, and he performed it again in 1776.

With the Jubilee of 1769, David Garrick had created a Shakespeare industry and buttressed the author's transformation from mortal man to English god. Although George Bernard Shaw did not coin the term *bardolatry* until the very early twentieth century, it offers a perfect description of Garrick's enterprise, as it was the first ultra-manifestation of the cult of Shakespeare. Garrick, master image-maker, impresario, and publicity hound, had single-handedly created an entire industry around the worship, commemoration, performance, and marketing of all things Shakespeare. Indeed, Garrick's intuitive grasp of the importance of marketing and merchandising in the entertainment business was prophetic.

Stratford took notice. After the participants in the failed Jubilee departed and the deluged town dried out, local boosters hit upon a brilliant idea. The Jubilee had been planned as a onetime event. Recognizing a good opportunity when they saw it, the corporation of Stratford capitalized on Garrick's idea by honoring their most famous son not once but yearly ever after. Over time, Stratford's annual Shakespeare's birthday festivities evolved into a year-round celebration luring tourists to his birthplace. The Bard's former homes became shrines, and wooden souvenirs—goblets, boxes, and small chests—carved from a mulberry tree allegedly planted by Shakespeare, like fragments of Christ's true cross coveted by religious pilgrims, fetched handsome sums.

Bardolatry spread to continental Europe. In October 1772, Johann Wolfgang von Goethe delivered a speech in Frankfurt in honor of the first German "Shakespeare Day." The author of the incomparable *Faust* and *The Sorrows of Young Werther* described his personal awakening to literature as coincident with his discovery of Shakespeare.[12]

In 1789, in another extravagant sign of apotheosis, an English Shakespeare fanatic named John Boydell opened an art gallery devoted exclusively to displaying a collection of specially commissioned oil paintings depicting famous characters and scenes from the plays. Such a scheme might sound static and dull to a modern reader in the age of photography, motion pictures, animation, and the Internet, when a variety of images can be summoned up anywhere in the world with the tap of a finger, but in the eighteenth century, painting was the only art, aside from a live performance itself, that could offer a full-color visual depiction of scenes from the plays.

An engraver, successful entrepreneur, and onetime Lord Mayor of the City of London, Boydell had been searching for an artistic business project that could "wipe away the stigma that all foreign critics threw" on British art, particularly French skeptics who defamed English historical painting as inferior.[13] Boydell sought a suitable subject for the soon-to-be-commissioned English paintings, settling on the one "National" subject that he believed everyone could agree on: Shakespeare.

Boydell's business plan was to commission paintings, and from them have the leading engravers of the time make copies in various sizes and prices, affordable to less affluent Londoners. The prints were also to be included as artworks in a new literary endeavor—an eight-volume, quarto-sized, illustrated collected works of Shakespeare, edited by George Stevens, a noted eighteenth-century Shakespeare scholar. The prints could also be purchased separately as a folio of engravings. The original paintings would hang in the Boydell Shakespeare Gallery as a celebration of British nationalism and greatness. At least that was the plan.

Boydell commissioned some of the biggest names in British art, including Joshua Reynolds, George Romney, and Swiss émigré Henry Fuseli (né Johann Heinrich Füssli), to create the first visual images of scenes from Shakespeare's plays. On May 4, 1789, the Shakespeare Gallery opened at Fifty-Two Pall Mall, London, to positive reviews. It was a year in which British pride needed some bolstering: in April, George Washington had been inaugurated as the first president of the Empire's lost jewel, the former American colonies. On opening day, the gallery exhibited thirty-four paintings by eighteen artists. Boydell's hope to sell large quantities of prints foundered from production delays, impatient customers, disputes with temperamental engravers, and other problems, but he pressed forward with the paintings. By the end of its run sixteen years later, the gallery's inventory had climbed to around 170 paintings, and Boydell had done much to fix Shakespearian visual imagery in the popular mind.

In 1790, Irish-born lawyer and friend of Samuel Johnson Edmond Malone, considered the best of the eighteenth-century Shakespeare editors, published his ten-volume octavo edition of the plays. The number and variety of editions that appeared between Rowe's in 1709 and Malone's eighty-one years later indicates the increasing amount of scholarly and commercial interest in Shakespeare's works, and the reverence in which he was then held.

As Shakespeare rose in esteem, so did prices for the First Folio. In the mid-eighteenth century, a copy of the First Folio was still affordable. Samuel Johnson, close to abject poverty, owned one, as did many of the editors of Shakespeare. As late as 1777, a First Folio could still be purchased for five pounds. Prices rose during the Revolutionary War. Soon, booksellers began to give the volume more prominent notice in their catalogues, rather than a brief listing under the "miscellaneous" section. In 1781, Thomas Payne featured a First Folio on the cover of his catalogue.[14]

Within a few years of the war's end, prices had risen sevenfold. At a famous sale in 1790, the Duke of Roxburghe paid a record price of £35 14s for a copy of the First Folio. Thomas Frognall Dibdin described the dramatic purchase in his book *Bibliomania*:

> A friend was bidding for him in the sale-room: his Grace had retired to a distance to view the issue of the contest. Twenty guineas and more were offered from various quarters for the book: a slip of paper was handed to the Duke, in which he was requested to inform his friend whether he was "to go on bidding." His Grace took his pencil and wrote underneath, by way of reply,
> "Lay on, Macduff;
> "And damned be he who first cries, 'Hold, enough!'"
> Such a spirit was irresistible, and bore down all opposition. His Grace retired triumphant, with the book under his arm.

By the end of the eighteenth century, discriminating collectors demanded perfect copies of the First Folio complete with no missing pages, and with all preliminaries present. To satisfy collector demand, a cottage industry grew around the work of making defective copies perfect. Bookbinders, sellers, and artisans replaced missing pages, trimming them to size to match the folios into which they would be inserted; stained pages were washed so as not to stand out; engraved Shakespeare portraits from later folios were disbound from their original volumes and inserted into First Folios; and artists even drew by freehand ingenious and near-perfect pen-and-ink copies of missing pages, or even of the Shakespeare portrait. Some of these alterations would defy detection for more than two centuries.

The price of the First Folio tripled over the next thirty years. In 1818, at the Saunders Library sale, the Grenville copy brought £121 16s. Individual copies of the First Folios already had proper names, usually from their illustrious previous owners. Some skeptical observers considered it the high-water mark for First Folio prices and predicted that never again would a copy fetch so much money. Collector and bibliographer Thomas Frognall Dibdin wrote that it was "the highest price ever given, or likely to be given, for the volume." His pronouncement proved to be one of the most colossal errors in the history of book collecting.

The study of Shakespeare became further professionalized when in 1840 four eminent editors and scholars—John Payne Collier (who in 1831 had published in three volumes his influential *The History of English Dramatic Poetry to the Time of Shakespeare; And Annals of the Stage to the Restoration*), the Reverend Alexander Dyce, Charles Knight, and scholar-collector James Orchard Halliwell-Phillipps—established the first Shakespeare Society. Knight's and Collier's editions of Shakespeare represented material changes from the predominant Edmond Malone 1790 text. Charles Dickens and English Shakespearian actor William Charles Macready served on the council of the organization. The purpose of the Shakespeare Society was "the elucidation of the productions of our great Dramatist." The Society's papers, published between 1844 and 1849, are really the first example of a Shakespeare journal. The volumes of papers included essays on English theater history, the study of Elizabethan culture, the sources of Shakespeare's plays and music, editorial suggestions, and more. Not the least of the Society's accomplishments was to introduce the commonly accepted modern spelling of Shakespeare's name.

The club was to be short-lived, however. Collier's reputation was so elevated by the Society that he was asked to issue a new edition of Shakespeare's works, which he published in eight volumes between 1841 and 1843. A few years later, he announced a stunning discovery. He had found, so he claimed, a copy of the Second Folio filled with marginal notations and emendations in a contemporary hand. The notes were not merely corrections, but contained stage directions and even new additions to Shakespeare's text. When Collier was exposed as a hoaxer who had forged the notes, his career as a scholar ended. The Shakespeare Society folded.

In the 1850s, another sign of Shakespeare's apotheosis appeared—the emergence of specialty dealers who made it their business to know all there was to know about all things Shakespeare. Halliwell-Phillipps was the first great dealer in Shakespeariana, and thus he had a huge influence over the sale and pricing of First Folios. According to one expert, "The interest in collecting the early editions of Shakespeare had never entirely disappeared, but its real revival was due to the unflagging industry of the laborious Shakespearean scholar J.O. Halliwell."[15] In 1852, Phillipps issued a catalogue of "Shakespeare reliques," books, manuscripts, and other material that he sold to the collector Lord Warwick.[16]

By the 1850s, more than 225 years after the publication of the First Folio, Shakespeare's literary reputation was secure. But something else was in the air in early Victorian England, and he was undergoing an additional transformation. Scottish writer Thomas Carlyle expressed the feeling as well as anyone when he declared: "This King Shakespeare, does he not shine, in crowned sovereignty, over us all as the noblest, gentlest, yet strongest of rallying-signs; indestructible; really more valuable in that point of view than any other means?"

Carlyle predicted that Shakespeare would live forever as an eternal touchstone to the English-speaking world: "We can fancy him as radiant aloft over all Nations of Englishmen, a thousand years hence. From Paramatta, from New York, wheresoever, under what sort of Parish-Constable soever, English men and women are, they will say to one another, 'Yes, this Shakespeare is ours; we produced him, we speak and think by him; we are of one blood and kind with him.'"[17]

Carlyle captured the moment when Shakespeare became celebrated as more than a great author. He was much more than the most important playwright and poet in British history. Now he transcended literature. His name became synonymous with empire, civilization, and the Anglosphere. His apotheosis, now complete, spanned a trajectory of more than 225 years. And now, by the middle of the nineteenth century, Shakespeare was no longer just the greatest author in the history of the English language. William Shakespeare *was* England.

Across the Atlantic, Shakespeare's American apotheosis began much later. From the publication of the First Folio in 1623, it had taken about 150 years for Shakespeare to morph into a secular English god. From the establishment of the first permanent, English-speaking North American settlements in Jamestown and Plymouth, Shakespeare's rise in the New World would take more than two centuries.

While Shakespeare was all the rage on the stages of cosmopolitan London, North America was still a wilderness. When Englishmen landed at Jamestown, Virginia, in 1607 and founded the first permanent American settlement, they brought no plays or actors. The same was true a few years later, when in 1620 the English landed at Plymouth, Massachusetts. Indeed, actors were unwelcome in the early colonies. What vital role could such idle, frivolous characters play in the life-and-death struggle for survival in the New World?

American Puritans were no more tolerant of the theater than their counterparts back in England. In 1687, in Massachusetts, Increase Mather complained, "Persons who have been corrupted by Stage-Plays are seldom, and with much difficulty, Reclaimed," and in 1714, plays were banned in Boston.[18]

Shakespeare's plays did not reach America until more than fifty years after the publication of the First Folio. William Byrd II of Virginia possessed a copy of the Fourth Folio of 1685, and a separately printed quarto copy of *Macbeth* had reached America by 1700. Harvard and Yale had acquired copies of the collected works by the 1720s. In 1730, the first known performance of a Shakespeare play in the colonies—*Romeo and Juliet*—took place in New York City, more than 130 years after Shakespeare's works were first performed in England.

The Revolutionary War generation embraced Shakespeare in print. In 1746, Benjamin Franklin had the Library Company of Philadelphia purchase a six-volume set of the collected works; *Richard III* was performed in New York City in 1750; John Adams wrote about the "great Shakespeare"; and in 1771, Thomas Jefferson recommended

Shakespeare as essential for a gentleman's library. George Washington owned a copy of Shakespeare's collected works in his private library at Mount Vernon.

Still, by the time of the Revolutionary War in 1775, not a single copy of the First Folio, published more than 150 years earlier, had crossed the Atlantic. Instead, the colonists collected later English editions, or one of several American editions published by the late 1700s. The earliest known First Folio to arrive in America was autographed by its owner, William Parker Jr., in 1791. Within a half century, six copies were sold in the United States, then nine more in the following decade. In the 1830s, as young French observer Alexis de Tocqueville traveled through the country, he found Shakespeare present in "the recesses of the forests of the New World." He recalled "reading the feudal drama of Henry V for the first time in a log cabin."

In 1847, the Shakespeare Birthplace Trust in Stratford-upon-Avon raised money to buy the house where Shakespeare was said to have been born. The campaign was successful, perhaps in part due to the rumor that American impresario and exhibiter of oddities P. T. Barnum wished to buy the house, dismantle it, and ship it to America.[19] Oddly, Barnum also prefigured the historic preservation movement in America, which began in Deerfield, Massachusetts, and Mount Vernon, Virginia. The impudent American's tactic to preserve something was to buy it. Barnum prefigured the Gilded Age moguls and their European buying sprees, and European resentment.

Two prominent Shakespearian actors, American Edwin Forrest and Englishman William Charles Macready, knew each other and crossed each other's paths as they toured Britain and the United States performing the plays. Forrest, First Folio owner and the first true American theater "star," was a muscular, physical, flamboyant, energetic actor known for his powerful voice. Macready possessed none of those traits. More a scholarly, introverted performer, he possessed a more elite, aristocratic following than did Forrest, who was immensely popular with the working classes.[20]

By 1845, they had seen each other perform for decades, had socialized amiably with each other's family, and recorded their encounters in their respective diaries. Forrest was the younger of the two by thirteen years, the American challenger to Macready's position in English theater as "the Eminent Tragedian." Both enjoyed theatrical success.

But Forrest, a man "whose enormous ego matched his physical proportions," was not well received in England during his 1845 tour. He seized upon the reason for his surprising failure: Macready must have poisoned the British press against him. In retaliation, during a performance of *Hamlet* in Edinburgh, Scotland, Forrest hissed at Macready, who was outraged; the friendly veneer was off, as was the friendship.

From 1845 through 1849, the two men separately toured the United States, each performing Shakespeare's plays in all the big theater towns: New Orleans, Boston, Philadelphia, and New York.

It had been only sixty-nine years since the colonies declared their independence. And the new nation was in a boundary dispute with Britain once more. President James Polk's rallying cry in setting the boundaries of the Oregon Territory was "Fifty-four Forty or Fight!" American nationalist anti-English feeling was stirred up further by Charles Dickens's writings, which expressed his outrage that the United States still permitted slavery and over the uncouth behavior he observed as he traveled through the country. On May 10, 1849, Forrest and Macready were each scheduled to play *Macbeth* in separate theaters in New York City. A passionate dispute erupted among their fans over who was the better Shakespearian actor. Anti-English sentiment ran hot, augmented by class warfare between the working and upper classes, and the argument led to madness and violence. On May 10, Forrest was performing at the Broadway Theatre for the coarse and boisterous blue-collar men and women. Macready was performing for people of refinement, concerned with their outward appearance and dress, at the white-glove Astor Opera House uptown. Broadsides, posted by Forrest supporters at Tammany Hall, incited fans to express their nationalistic displeasure with the English by meeting at the "ENGLISH ARISTOCRATIC! OPERA HOUSE!" asking "WORKING MEN SHALL AMERICANS OR ENGLISH! RULE IN THIS CITY?"

Instigators supplied Forrest's fans with free tickets to crash Macready's performance. Many of them were turned away at the door of the Astor Opera House that night, and thousands of them surrounded the building. They attacked the Astor, threw stones, and rioted. Macready fled for his life through the back door, never to perform on an American stage again. To quell this "Shakespeare Riot," the mayor of New York called out the state militia, which fired on the wild mob, killing at least 22 and leaving 120 injured on the streets of Manhattan.

Notwithstanding the violence in New York, prominent American authors began to celebrate Shakespeare not only as a great writer but also as something more—as a vessel that transmitted the core values of Western civilization from England to America. His works accounted for a quarter of the plays performed in America during the nineteenth century, with his popularity reaching beyond the cities into the countryside and out to the frontier. Shakespeare's reputation was evolving from literary icon into Anglo-American cultural hero, and his earliest printed works—especially the First Folio—became coveted relics that connected a modern audience to "King Shakespeare." As had happened in England, Shakespeare was now more than mere entertainment. He had become a symbol of civilization, of the superiority of the Anglosphere.

By the 1850s, Shakespeare was an Anglo-American hero. Although his reputation had conquered America, few original sixteenth- and seventeenth-century Shakespeare source materials—folios, quartos, and the like—had crossed the Atlantic. Indeed, as late as 1857, ninety-five percent of all known copies of the First Folio remained in England. A proud Britannia hoarded her literary treasures to which she had given birth. But in that year, unbeknownst to her, in Brooklyn, New York, a boy was born who would one day do everything in his power to turn that state of affairs topsy-turvy. By the turn of the century, he would declare Shakespeare his cause, proclaim his obsession with all things Shakespearian, and seek to convey the material culture of Shakespeare to America. He would not be content to worship Shakespeare; he wanted to own him.

Chapter 5

☙❦☙

"Had I the Money, You Would Come . . ."

—HENRY CLAY FOLGER

IN 1635, twelve years after the publication of the First Folio, an undistinguished man named Peter Folger emigrated from Norwich, England, to Watertown, Massachusetts. He later lived on Martha's Vineyard before settling on Nantucket in 1663, off the coast of the Massachusetts Bay Colony. He married in America and had many children, one of whom, Abiah, became Benjamin Franklin's mother. The family was involved in the whaling industry, which provided oil for the lamps that illuminated preindustrial America. In the early 1800s, two hundred years after the first Folgers came to Nantucket, Samuel Folger, a direct descendant of Peter, married and had several children, including three sons, Henry, Edward, and James. In 1849, these three brothers left Nantucket for San Francisco, en route to the California gold country to make their fortunes in mining. Fourteen-year-old James stayed in San Francisco, where he became a carpenter and worked in a mill that he later purchased.[1] In that era, San Francisco coffee drinkers bought, roasted, and ground their own beans. Young James Folger, possessed by an entrepreneurial spirit, saw an opportunity. He roasted and ground the beans, then delivered the product in bulk to groceries to save consumers from the inconvenience of grinding their own beans. Later, he packaged and sold ground, roasted coffee to miners.

His innovation lay not in inventing a new product—coffee had been around for many years—but in offering customers that product in a new, convenient, ready-to-brew form. From this small enterprise, based at 101 Howard Street in San Francisco, grew the Folger Coffee Company. Later, his brother Edward returned to San Francisco and opened a whale oil business next to James's coffee mill.

Henry Folger eventually left California and moved to Brooklyn, where he married grade-school teacher Eliza Jane Clark, opened a millinery supply business, and had eight children. His first son, Henry Clay Folger Jr., was born in Manhattan on June 18, 1857. Two things— one a cultural phenomenon already in place on the day he was born, the other a monumental discovery made when he was two years old— would shape Henry Junior's destiny. By 1857, William Shakespeare had conquered American popular culture. The great actors Edwin Forrest, Junius Brutus Booth Sr., James H. Hackett (soon to become a favorite of Abraham Lincoln's), and Charlotte Cushman toured the country and became some of the nation's first "stars" by performing Shakespeare. Soon Junius Booth's sons and fellow actors, Edwin, Junius Jr., and John Wilkes, joined them onstage as American celebrities, worshipped by devoted "fans." The love of Shakespearian drama was part of the spirit of the age into which young Henry Folger was born.

Then, in 1859, when Folger was two years old, oil was discovered in Titusville, in northwestern Pennsylvania. Long before strikes in Kansas, Oklahoma, Texas, and California, Pennsylvania served for decades as the main source of oil production in the United States. The crude oil revolution would define this child's life and make it possible for him to live his dreams.

Henry Folger attended public school in Brooklyn, earning commendations as well as a scholarship to Adelphi Academy. Founded in 1863 by businessman Charles Pratt and abolitionists Reverend Henry Ward Beecher and Horace Greeley, the academy offered Pratt's son and Folger an excellent education. It was at Adelphi that Henry met and became friends with young Charles Millard Pratt. Henry ranked in the top five of his graduating class, delivering an oration at commencement. The speech, "Every Man Is the Architect of His own Fortune," contained the prophetic remarks that it was up to each of them "to decide . . . whether, at death, we shall leave them [our characters] lasting monuments of imperishable marble, or the mouldering remains of abandoned ruins."[2] One of their science teachers, William Clark Peckham, encouraged the boys to attend college at his alma mater, Amherst, and so, upon graduation, Folger and Pratt set off for western Massachusetts. In time, Folger's friendship with Pratt and his family would affect his personal and professional lives in ways that he could not have imagined.

Nothing about Henry Folger's early years hinted that he would become a passionate Shakespearian or an obsessive collector. He did not descend from a line of educated antiquarians or wealthy arts patrons. Nor was he the son, nephew, or protégé of a great bibliophile. Unlike, say, J. P. Morgan, the financier and bibliophile, Folger was not born into the habits of the wealthy or privileged. His mother taught him a love of reading and a facility with numbers, and his father may have provided hard-bitten lessons on how to deal with financial difficulties.

Henry's letters home to his mother during his freshman year at college reveal a young man enjoying his education but challenged by Amherst's academic rigor, and continually worried about—one might say obsessed with—his finances.[3] He wrote home every Sunday, sometimes more frequently. He complained in his letters to his siblings that they sent him fewer letters than he alone was writing to them. In that era, Amherst was still primarily a preparatory school for men who planned to go into the ministry. Henry described his daily routine: awaken early, breakfast by 7:15 AM at his lodgings, chapel, calisthenics, and first recitation. He asked his mother to send him some "cheap writing paper" so he could keep up his family correspondence.[4] Unlike his wealthy friend Charles Pratt, who enjoyed more luxurious lodgings, Henry counted every penny he spent, well aware that others did not have to scrimp and save as he did.

Henry described his plight in an almost Dickensian style, laced with humor. In one letter, he joked to his mother that "when [my roommate] and I get rich we propose to have curtains."[5] Even the basic conveniences were a financial stretch for him. Pratt occupied a room in a society (fraternity) house that, Folger observed, contained such miraculous luxuries as a clock, marble-topped table, armchair, and writing desk: "He must have spent considerable in fitting up his room."[6] Concerned with husbanding not just every dollar but every cent, Folger mailed one letter home, enclosing it in a monogrammed envelope, about which he said, "We like it very much, but each envelope costs a cent and a half, so we don't use them often." One letter to his mother, written on borrowed stationery instead of his own plain writing paper, showed Folger's frequent humor: "I am writing in Pratt's room, on his paper. Rather fancy to send to an old lady, don't you think so?"[7]

In October 1875, during his first semester, Henry changed lodgings because of the "toughness of the meat" served at meals, as well as the "odors arising from the Deacon's books"—an amusing complaint suggesting that Henry had not yet fallen under the spell of bibliomania. Henry wrote his mother often about his fastidious housekeeping habits, reassuring her almost weekly how he cleaned and swept his room, including the dusty carpet, and washed the windows. It was an early first hint of an obsessive nature.

Later that year, as a further economy, Folger decided to "take in his own washing" instead of sending it out to the laundresses who served the college men. He detailed to his mother how he washed his laundry in his room—fetching a pail of water, heating it on the stove in his shared quarters, soaping the clothing and linens, then rinsing and hanging them up to dry. For two pairs of stockings, three towels, and a handkerchief, Henry boasted, "in all twenty-five cents worth of washing saved."[8] But his scheme proved flawed. He confessed that he left the clothes to dry above the stove, and had then gone ice-skating. By the time he returned, the unattended items had been reduced to cinders, prompting him to ask the rhetorical question, "How long can one do without a towel?"[9] A few days later, he wrote to his mother, telling her not to send replacement towels; he would buy them locally in Amherst. But could she please "write how much towels should cost so that I may have the satisfaction of knowing whether I have been cheated."[10] When his roommate also scorched a towel, Henry reconsidered their strategy, writing: "I have begun to debate whether or not it is a real saving to wash our own cloths [*sic*]."[11]

Henry spent most of his time studying, attending lectures, and attending church. However, he and his friends took time to enjoy simple New England pleasures: not only ice-skating but also sledding, long walks, and gathering apples, pears, or chestnuts. Years later, when Henry worked in Manhattan, he would continue to enjoy eating the hot chestnuts sold in wintertime by street vendors.

One college ritual involved the sharing of food treats sent from home. The boys would pool their bounty and put on a "spread." One Thanksgiving feast featured a big turkey that a student received in a shipping box that "looked like a coffin," Henry recalled. Pratt apparently had the best gustatory treats to share; Folger wrote, "We are compelled to yield the palm of supremacy in spreads to him."[12]

At home from college for Christmas in 1875, eighteen-year-old Henry received from his seven-year-old brother Stephen a gift of an edition of the *Complete Works* of William Shakespeare. Henry began reading the plays, for his college courses as well as for his own enjoyment. He acquired a commonplace book, a kind of intellectual journal in which its owner lists books read, records observations made, gathers curious miscellanea, and inscribes favorite quotations. Henry started to copy down comments about Shakespeare uttered by various luminaries such as Thomas Carlyle, Abraham Lincoln, and the transcendentalist Ralph Waldo Emerson. Folger would keep this book for the rest of his life.

Henry had arrived at Amherst College around the same time that Shakespeare was becoming part of the curriculum at American colleges. His coursework included Greek, history, Latin, math, orthography, declamation, and literature. He and Charles Pratt joined the Alpha Delta Phi fraternity, to which Henry Ward Beecher had also belonged. He participated in the Alpha Delta Phi Shakespeare discussion group.

Henry matured into a short man of slight build. He possessed a fine, loud, and deep bass-baritone voice and sang in the glee club as well as in an Amherst production of Gilbert and Sullivan's operetta *H.M.S. Pinafore*, playing the part of Dick Deadeye. It was from this character that his future wife, Emily, chose one of her nicknames for Henry, whom she sometimes referred to as "Dick." Friends and classmates described him as a studious, gentle, and shy but friendly young man.

In his junior year, a family disaster threatened to destroy Henry's world. His father's current business, a water meter company, failed during the financial panic of 1873, and his family could no longer afford to pay his Amherst tuition and expenses. Henry wrote to his father beseeching him to pay room and board of $68.50, "a fearful large amount, but I find that I have got through this term on about half the money I had the first one, and can't see a place where I could have been more 'economous.'"[13] Henry moved back home to Brooklyn and enrolled in the tuition-free City College of New York. But two of his Amherst classmates, Charles M. Pratt and William M. Ladd, were unwilling to see their promising friend leave school over finances.[14] They arranged a personal loan for Henry from Pratt's father, with his assurance that he would pay them back. Thanks to their friendship and assistance, Henry would graduate on time, and from Amherst.

Despite the loan he received, which allowed him to stay at Amherst, his finances were far from secure. In spring of his senior year, he wrote his mother about the sacrifices he made in his own personal comfort, relating that "our coal has given out—cheering prospect. I have to forage around the cellar picking up a hand-full here and there when the fellows are not looking. It is ruining my spiritual worthiness, but we can't freeze."[15]

On March 19, 1879, in his senior year, he paid twenty-five cents for a ticket to hear the seventy-five-year-old literary statesman Ralph Waldo Emerson speak in College Hall at Amherst on the topic "The Superlative, or Mental Temperance."[16] The lecture, which admonished the audience to write plainly and simply, was not an Emersonian classic. Folger saved his ticket to that talk, and preserved it with his growing collection of personal memorabilia as a reminder of what turned out to be a life-altering event, not because of the content of the lecture but because of where Emerson's other writings would lead him.[17] Listening to this literary star inspired Henry to read another of his lectures, "Remarks at the Celebration of the Three Hundredth Anniversary of the Birth of Shakespeare," which Emerson had delivered in 1864 at the Revere House in Boston.[18] There Emerson had waxed: "Wherever there are men, and in the degree in which they are civil, have power of mind, sensibility to beauty, music, the secrets of passion, and the liquid expression of thought [Shakespeare] has risen to his place as the first poet of the world."

Owing money weighed heavily on Henry. His desire to erase his indebtedness extended to sacrificing his mother's attendance at his commencement: "Had I the money, you would come. . . . If, however, you had the money my circumstances are such that I would rather use it to pay my indebtedness than your expenses."[19] He would have been proud to have his mother attend his commencement: "There are just two fellows in the class who have two orations," wrote Henry in the third person, "and Folger is one of them."[20] Indeed, Henry had won several cash prizes at Amherst for oratory, including, at commencement, the prestigious Hyde Prize.[21]

Henry Folger graduated Phi Beta Kappa, ranking fifth in the class of 1879. He had gained a fine liberal arts education. But he also learned a harder, sometimes bitter life lesson at college. The penny-pinching habits of those early lean years molded him. Some of his economizing schemes sound almost comical, but the painful experience of being in financial difficulty, and the humiliation of being forced to withdraw from Amherst, even temporarily, must have seared the value of money into him. Money meant more than the things it could buy. Money meant opportunity and freedom from his past. Soon he would learn that the same frugal habits of an impecunious college boy trying to save a few pennies on laundry soap would, when applied on a grand, massive scale, become the very catalyst of his success. For the rest of his life, Henry Folger would scrutinize the smallest expenditure with the same attention that he paid to the largest sums, in both his business and personal lives.

He had a choice to make: he could remain at Amherst, where he had been invited to stay on as a tutor; teach public speaking in Minnesota; or return home to Brooklyn, where he had been offered a position at the company owned by the father of his best college friend, Charles

Pratt. Folger chose business over academia. He moved back to Brooklyn and a week after graduation started as a clerk at Charles Pratt's Astral Oil Works.

Prior to the American Civil War, Charles Pratt worked for a company selling paint and whale oil products. After the war, he moved to New York and opened a kerosene refinery in Brooklyn—Astral Oil Works—that produced not only kerosene but other petroleum products including naphtha, engine oils, greases, paints, waxes, lubricants, and even a waste product called gasoline, which was not yet used to fuel engines but was marketed as "Pratt's Spirit." Pratt's kerosene advertising campaign made the ludicrous but charming assertion that "the holy lamps of Tibet are primed with Astral Oil." Pratt was not the only man who saw that whale oil's reign was in decline and that kerosene was the lighting fuel of the future. As it became cheaper, it would permit the common man to extend the day beyond nightfall.

Another man, John D. Rockefeller, founder and president of Standard Oil Company, led the kerosene revolution and undertook plans to consolidate and dominate the industry. Rockefeller, possessed by a conservative, religious, and unquenchable work ethic, recognized talent when he saw it, boasting he could buy it on the open market the same way he bought coffee.[22] He approached Pratt and his partner, H. H. Rogers, offering them cooperation or consolidation with Standard, on whatever terms Pratt dictated, as long as he kept the alliance secret. While Henry and classmate Charles M. Pratt progressed in their studies, Pratt's father agreed to a business deal that would change his, his son's, and Henry Folger's lives forever. In October 1874, Standard Oil joined with Pratt's large refinery works in Brooklyn, New York, continuing Standard's eastward expansion. When their companies merged, Pratt and Rogers gained positions of power and influence, with Rockefeller first among equals. Pratt and Rogers received Standard Oil stock and became part of the organization. Like many of Standard's mergers at the time, this one was done quietly and kept secret for many years, giving the public and smaller oil producers the illusion that they were doing business with the independent Pratt, rather than with the detested Standard Oil.[23]

On August 27, 1859, Edwin Drake drilled a well 69.5 feet deep and struck oil on Watson's Flats near Titusville, Pennsylvania, inaugurating the petroleum era. It was a moment that exemplified a transition in America, away from agriculture and small business toward giant enterprises. Expansion and improvement in transportation networks meant companies could efficiently produce and transport product over longer distances, across the country and across the world, at scales hitherto unimagined. The whaling industry had already been in decline, reflected in both higher prices and the desire of consumers for a less pungent source of home lighting. Drake's well produced a meager twenty-five barrels per day. Two hundred miles west of the strike in Titusville, Cleveland, Ohio, emerged as one of the competitors to Pennsylvania oil refining. The key product refined from crude oil was kerosene, the inexpensive but volatile source of illumination that supplanted increasingly scarce and expensive whale oil.

In 1865, John Davison Rockefeller, age twenty-six, and his partners Maurice Clark and Samuel Andrews bet on the future of the oil business. Rather than investing in the risky boom-and-bust oil exploration and extraction aspects of the business, they invested in a refinery in Cleveland. Oil prices could fluctuate widely, and independent wells could and did run dry at any moment, but all crude producers needed refineries. It was not a sure thing, but Rockefeller and his partners believed that by investing in a modern, safe, large refinery, they could profit by producing kerosene for a mass market. By 1865, Cleveland had thirty refineries. By 1869, the expanding firm of Rockefeller, Andrews & Flagler operated not only in Cleveland but also in Oil City, Pennsylvania, and New York City.

Two elements accounted for Rockefeller's success as a businessman: his personal talents as a manager and his ability to realize small cost savings for each gallon of kerosene his company refined. He achieved cost savings through vertical integration—essentially cutting out the middleman—and enormous economies of scale. Rockefeller and one of his partners, railroad titan Henry Flagler, secured quantity discounts from the railroads by guaranteeing shipment of large volumes of oil from wells to refineries, and from refineries to customers. No other oil producer or refiner could guarantee similar volumes or receive such discounts, and it infuriated them. With transportation a significant portion—more than a third—of the total cost of refined kerosene, this amounted to an insurmountable cost advantage for Standard, and a boon to its customers, who profited handsomely from the cost reductions the company was able to achieve.

Not all of Rockefeller's dealings with the railroads benefited consumers.[24] The arrangement between Standard and the railroads was of the "you scratch my back, I'll scratch yours" variety. In later years, Rockefeller "evened" traffic across the railroads, spreading his business around in proportions agreed upon by the railroads. They gave him preferential rates over his competitors, deterring refiners from entering the business, and he would serve to enforce the railroad cartel arrangement. The end result was a decrease in Standard Oil's costs relative to its competitors'—good for Standard's customers, bad for its competitors.

Rockefeller continued to lower his firm's average cost by vertically integrating his firm, including more stages of production in the company. Rather than contracting with other firms, he used company employees to minimize his costs. The purchase of barrels accounted for a significant expense in shipping crude. Rockefeller soon realized that barrel makers were unreliable and charged prices that he could beat if he hired his own coopers and made the barrels in-house. He reduced the cost per barrel to his company by two-thirds, and ensured a steady supply. Not satisfied that he had squeezed every penny out of his barrel costs, he purchased timberland, so that his barrel makers could use staves cut from the company's own lumber, cutting out the lumber supplier. Frustrated that the wooden barrels leaked during transport, and aware of the high labor costs of loading and unloading barrels, Rockefeller produced the first primitive railroad tanker cars. Just as the automobile would finish off the buggy-whip industry, Rockefeller's cost cutting resulted in the collapse of the barrel-making industry. By 1872, he had vertically integrated his operations into almost every aspect of refining—including storage, loading, marketing, barrel making, and wagon production.[25]

Rockefeller was an exceptional manager and leader. While his enterprise grew to an enormous size, covering dozens of locations in several states, he managed to create an esprit de corps among the men who worked with and for him. He surrounded himself with talented men with various skills, inviting them to join the company as he encountered them. Some, such as H. H. Rogers, had begun as vociferous opponents, but later became officers or employees of the company. A man who exercised great self-control, Rockefeller, a devout Baptist, treated his coworkers, from officers to clerks, with respect; he listened without interrupting; if he felt the need to disagree with his partners, he did so in private, without embarrassing them in public. In a note to an office of Ohio Standard in 1885, Rockefeller suggested that a decision on a contentious issue be delayed for a while: "There has been so much discussion on this, and some warmth."[26] Rockefeller was the conciliator when forceful men's strong opinions differed. No public acrimony marred the organization; decisions were conveyed from the executive committee not as orders but rather as suggestions and requests. Not dictatorial, Rockefeller was *primus inter pares*. Men who disagreed with the direction the company was taking were free to leave; Rockefeller or other shareholders would buy back the stock at any time. Although no large organization—run by committees or otherwise—can operate completely without acrimony, the men running Standard worked hard at minimizing it. The executive committee received information and recommendations from the other committees, including frequent statistical updates from the committee clerk, then laid down general policies for the committees to implement. In 1878, the price of kerosene continued to fall, the transition from whale oil to kerosene for home lighting continued, and Standard controlled ninety percent of the nation's refining capacity.[27] Nevertheless, the firm's long-term position and profits were hardly guaranteed: in 1879, just one year later, Thomas Alva Edison invented the first commercially viable carbon filament incandescent lightbulb. Rockefeller foresaw that the future would involve fierce competition among kerosene, natural gas, and electric light. He prepared the company for the coming changes. By the time Folger graduated from Amherst, Standard was already a huge and profitable enterprise. Soon Henry's future would be inextricably linked to the fortunes of Standard Oil and its founder.

While Henry Folger worked during the day to pay off his college loan from Pratt, he enrolled in night classes at Columbia Law School. Despite this double workload, he pursued his literary interests by reading the works of many of the writers influenced by Shakespeare— Jean-Jacques Rousseau, John Ruskin, Johann Wolfgang von Goethe, Friedrich Schiller, Samuel Taylor Coleridge, William Hazlitt, James Russell Lowell, Victor Hugo, and Thomas Carlyle. In December 1879, he bought a copy of Carlyle's *On Heroes, Hero-worship, and the Heroic in History*, which exceeded even Emerson's wild enthusiasm for Shakespeare.

Henry also purchased an inexpensive copy of Shakespeare's collected works, a thirteen-piece set called the Handy Volume Edition. He never liked going anywhere without bringing along a book to fill idle time, and he often kept a volume from this set within reach, reading from it whenever he could steal a free moment. By then, Shakespeare had become a minor but recurring theme in Henry's life. He read and analyzed Shakespeare's plays for education and pleasure. It would be another ten years before the obsession took hold.

In 1880, kerosene sold for nine cents per gallon. Falling product prices are not usually an indication of an all-powerful giant flexing its muscles. Rather than *raising* market prices, the usual fear of politicians and lawmakers, prices *fell* while Standard grew. Falling prices delighted customers. However, not everyone was grateful. The prices Rockefeller charged were profitable for him but not for his competitors. The evolution of the economy from agriculture and small business to large corporations caused social upheavals and hard feelings. Many firms went under, and small-business owners blamed their failures not on their own inability to compete but on what they believed were predatory and unfair business practices by their larger rivals.

Eighteen eighty-one was an important year for Henry Folger. Henry repaid the loan, including seven percent interest, from Charles Pratt and earned his law degree cum laude from Columbia. That year, Standard Oil operations were run by a series of committees made up of Rockefeller's men plus former officers or owners of the firms with which Standard had merged. The most important committee at Standard Oil of New Jersey, the manufacturing committee, was chaired by H. H. Rogers. Its first statistical clerk was Henry Clay Folger Jr., protégé of domestic trade committee member Charles Pratt. On May 1, 1881, Folger, just twenty-three years old, issued the now legendary *Manufacturing Book A,* a precise, careful compilation and illustration of data on all phases of Standard's processing of crude oil, "with emphasis on comparative costs and yields of various refineries in the combination."[28] The result of this publication and his myriad reports on the products Standard made was that in 1886, he was promoted to secretary of the manufacturing committee. During the 1890s, he was part of management of the Standard refinery on the East River and within five years became chairman of the manufacturing committee.

The manufacturing committee, along with several other specialized committees, advised the company on how it might benefit from coordination and standardization, as well as integration. Centralized purchasing of supplies, for example, with a single Standard buyer, leveraged the company's cost-cutting power.

By 1881, Henry Folger was distilling numbers for each phase of the business, charting and explaining cost and yield statistics of all refining operations in monthly, quarterly, semiannual, and annual reports, sending them to H. H. Rogers, with a copy dutifully forwarded to Rockefeller. Folger possessed a talent for and took personal delight in presenting complex facts in a useful and comprehendible way. His exceptional mathematical ability combined with his detailed knowledge of the industry, from crude to kerosene and beyond, made him a pioneer in industrial efficiency. He continued to learn, at a prodigious rate, becoming an expert in the history and technical aspects of the refining business.

———

By 1882, Lily Richardson Pratt, sister of Henry's friend Charles M. Pratt, had played matchmaker. At a gathering of the Irving Literary Society, she introduced her Vassar classmate, Emily Clara Jordan, to Henry. Emily had grown up in Washington, D.C., the daughter of Edward Jordan, the Solicitor for the Treasury Department under Lincoln and Johnson. She had met President Lincoln when she was four years old. Her older sister, who taught at Smith College, had financed her education at Vassar. Emily had been class president, presiding over a cohort of thirty-six women. After graduating Phi Beta Kappa in 1879, she taught school and wrote. Like Henry Folger, she had an intense interest in literature, debate, and theater. The match took: Emily and Henry were married on October 6, 1885, in Elizabeth, New Jersey. The Pratts had already secured Henry's college education, then his employment. Now they had found him a compatible wife.

Henry and Emily began their life together living with his parents in Brooklyn. Soon they rented Brooklyn homes of their own, first at 212 Lefferts Place, then at nearby Twenty-Four Brevoort Place. In their first year of marriage, Henry bought a special gift for his new wife. It was a copy of a recently published facsimile of the First Folio, one of a wave of such editions published at the end of the nineteenth century, as Shakespeare's popularity flourished. Henry paid $1.25 for the reduced-size facsimile, published with an introduction by English bibliophile and scholar James Orchard Halliwell-Phillipps.[29] In a note to Emily presenting the volume, Henry wrote, "Here you may see Shakespeare's plays as they were actually given to the world." It was the first time that Henry and Emily saw what a First Folio looked like. Yes, it was just a cheap copy. And it was the wrong size—significantly smaller than the original. But it gave them a taste of the real thing. If they read the scholarly introduction, they learned that there was a wonderful history behind the making and printing of the First Folio. Now they peeked below the surface of the plays, to the lore of their creation.

Henry's position required him to distribute periodic charts and explanatory memoranda to the members of the manufacturing committee. He sent copies of these reports to Rockefeller. In 1885, Rockefeller responded to one of Folger's reports, writing in appreciation of his contributions. "Let the good work go on. We must ever remember we are refining oil for the poor man and he must have it cheap and good."[30]

Four years later, in 1889, the words that Henry used when he gave Emily the facsimile of the First Folio—"Shakespeare's plays as they were actually given to the world"—might still have been lingering in his mind. For some time, he had been adding books to his home library. Nothing fancy—just some good volumes of important literature. But he felt his holdings were good enough to report, in a letter to the historian of his Amherst class, that he had, in the decade since graduation, assembled a "modest library."[31] He was still a reader, not a collector.

That changed the day in 1889 when Henry walked into Bang's auction house in Manhattan. He examined the books to be sold that day. The one that caught his attention was not the most beautiful book of the lot. Many fine leather bindings adorned with decorative gold leaf were prettier than the volume that caught his eye, an unremarkable copy of Shakespeare's Fourth Folio. Henry Folger did the bidding himself and the auctioneer hammered it down to $107.50 for him. He had spent more than he could afford to pay at that moment, but the auction house agreed to extend him credit for thirty days.

What lured Henry Folger into the auction that day remains a mystery. He left no written account of the event. He was thirty-two years old on the day he tiptoed into the world of rare books and bought that copy of the Fourth Folio. He and Emily had been married four years. They lived in a rented brownstone in the Bedford-Stuyvesant area of Brooklyn, with rented furniture.[32] His destiny as a captain of business and millionaire still lay ahead of him. Standard Oil was already an industrial giant, but no one could have imagined how large, profitable, and infamous a company it would become with Henry Folger's help. It was good that his fortunes were linked inextricably to the rise of Standard Oil. Unless he became rich, he could never pursue the dream that was about to possess him.

Chapter 6

❧✿❧

"Had I the Means, I Would Not Hesitate . . . to Buy . . ."

—Henry Clay Folger

ENRY FOLGER'S purchase of the Fourth Folio did not transform him into an obsessive collector overnight. Between 1889 and 1891, he bought no important rare books. Indeed, he devoted much of the next decade to advancing himself in the oil business. The 1890s were key years for Henry and Standard Oil. As the company prospered, so did Henry's fortunes. His intelligence, facility with numbers, and work ethic, plus his personal qualities of amiability and lack of pretention, attracted the keen interest of his superiors, including Rockefeller himself. The titan developed an affection for this young man who shared a similar, humble background and commitment to religion, and who also possessed many of his own characteristics. But as Henry rose in business, he took a series of steps—tentative at first and bolder as the decade unfolded—toward becoming a real collector.

In 1890, in response to increasing public sentiment against the power—real or imagined—of big business, Congress passed and President Benjamin Harrison signed into law the Sherman Antitrust Act. It forbade any contract, scheme, or conspiracy "in restraint of trade." The goal of the law was to protect competition in the marketplace, which benefited consumers through lower prices, better product quality, and greater variety of choices. The text of the act was vague and short—just over one hundred words long—and while it prohibited restraints of trade, it failed to define them. Congress abdicated to the courts the burden of interpreting the Sherman Act and wrestling with which business practices "restrained trade," and which did not. The Sherman Act was a ticking bomb planted beneath the edifice of Standard Oil, and when it exploded years later it changed the lives of John D. Rockefeller and Henry Folger.[1] That time had not yet, however, arrived. There was still time to go on with business as usual.

In 1891, Henry and Emily went on vacation, taking the steamer *Minnehaha* across the Atlantic on their first trip to England. They did not book expensive tickets aboard a fast luxury liner that could make the trip quickly. Instead, they sailed on the proverbial slow boat, a "cattle boat," on which their improvised cabin was a former officers' mess.[2] This unpretentious ship became their favorite vessel, and in the years to come they made every future crossing on it until their favorite seaman, Captain John Robinson, a fellow lover of Shakespeare, retired. Long after Folger attained the wealth and status of other men who would not dream of crossing the Atlantic without first-class tickets aboard anything but a White Star or Cunard luxury liner, he still preferred the modest pleasures of the *Minnehaha*. Henry and Emily enjoyed the unhurried voyage, the sea air, and their conversations with Captain Robinson. Between voyages Henry kept up an active correspondence with the captain.

More than two and a half centuries after Peter Folger's emigration to America, Henry returned to the land of his ancestors, and of Shakespeare. The Folgers' itinerary from this trip is long lost, but they probably made the rounds of the London bookshops. There, at any one of the better establishments, they might have had their initial encounter with a copy of the First Folio.

Sometime between 1891 and 1893, he bought one (W 113, F 55).[3] More than a century later, it remains his most mysterious acquisition. Its price and source are unknown. Some scholars suggest that he bought it in 1893, but that date is no more than an educated guess. The Folgers might have purchased it as early as 1891 during their trip to England, or perhaps they saw one there and ordered it by mail after their return to America. In any case, it was not an auspicious purchase. Henry and Emily's *first* First Folio was a second-rate specimen, suffering from various flaws. This copy was missing two of the nine preliminaries, and of the ones that remained most were mutilated badly enough to affect the text. One play, *The Merry Wives of Windsor*, was made up completely from pages taken from another First Folio. In an uncharacteristic lapse, Henry failed to record for posterity the price he paid. Given its condition, and the state of the rare book market at the time, it is doubtful that they paid more than one thousand dollars for it.

In the early 1890s, Folger was a member of the management team of the Standard Oil Works on the East River of New York. In 1895, he argued that Standard Oil benefited consumers through cost cutting, innovative management, and superior refining techniques. His article, "Petroleum: Its Production and Products," appeared as a chapter in the massive, two-volume book *One Hundred Years of American Commerce, 1795–1895*, and provided a reasoned exposition of the history, economics, and evolving technology of the industry. He wrote with admiration about the "capital and energy required to establish an industry of such magnitude." He called attention to the size of the growing retail market: "Wherever commerce has made its way it has found a welcome. It is carried wherever a wheel can roll or a camel's foot be planted. The caravans on the Desert of Sahara go laden with Astral oil, and elephants in India carry cases of Standard White."

In 1895, Folger had the opportunity to purchase through a London book dealer a large collection of many volumes of Shakespeariana. The prospect of a bulk purchase excited him. He coveted the material, but its cost was beyond his means. Although he could not buy it himself, he could not bear to let the collection go. Better, he reasoned, to control where it went, so he could enjoy future access to it. In a bold move, he tried to persuade Rockefeller, not known as a bibliophile, to buy the collection. Believing it was reasonably priced, and a good investment, Folger encouraged Rockefeller to purchase the entire grouping as the nucleus for a world-class library at the new University of Chicago, which the titan had endowed in 1892. Perhaps hoping to tweak Rockefeller's pride, he mentioned that "the Astor, Lenox, Harvard, and Boston libraries have valuable Shakespearian collections to which they are adding at every opportunity." Henry described some choice items: "early portraits, artistic illustrations, original contemporaneous documents" relating to Shakespeare and the Hathaways, "deeds, etc." related to the properties Shakespeare owned in Blackfriars and at New Place.[4] Henry proposed that Rockefeller purchase the collection, and then recover some of the cost by publishing and selling reproductions of the most important items. "[H]ad I the means," Henry vowed, "I would not hesitate as a businessman to buy the collection with the expectation that the profit on . . . reproductions and the money for the originals if sold at auction would net a handsome margin on the investment."[5] And Henry, of course, would volunteer his expertise to help examine the library and select the best items to publish.

For a man of Folger's customary caution and risk aversion, it bordered on a hare-brained scheme. The idea that one of the richest men in the country would divert his attention from an empire of crude oil and kerosene to publish and peddle small-print-run facsimiles of obscure Shakespeare texts seems absurd. Perhaps the newfound zeal of the novice collector's passion clouded Folger's judgment. The fact that Henry even dared to make this unusual request suggests that by 1895 he had cemented a close relationship with Rockefeller. But Rockefeller declined to make the purchase. The collection was sold to Marsden Perry, a Providence, Rhode Island, banker, industrialist, and Shakespeare collector who would soon become one of Folger's chief rivals.[6]

In 1896, Folger visited Los Angeles to prepare an analysis of California crude oil, concluding in a discouraging report that the yields and quality of the kerosene were not up to Standard's requirements.[7] That year, Rockefeller, not yet sixty, retired from running the day-to-day operations of the company, though he retained his title of president, and continued to take an interest in the business. Standard Oil would not go in any direction that he did not steer it. Key executives, including Folger, still treated him as the mastermind behind the operation.

Henry licked his wounds from losing out on the first collection of Shakespeare books he had tried to purchase. The next time he had the chance to buy a major collection, he would be ready. In the meantime, he assuaged his disappointment by buying, in 1896, a second copy of the First Folio (W 72, F 14). It had been three years since he had bought the first. This time he paid more and did better. For $4,500, he purchased a fine example. Called the Pope-Hoe copy after two of its former New York owners, it contained all original leaves, though some had been patched, repaired, and touched up with hand-drawn facsimiles.[8] It was the most expensive thing he had ever bought in his life.[9] In today's dollars, he had spent the equivalent of more than $40,000 for a single book.

It was a turning point. Folger decided that if he was about to get serious about Shakespeare, he must have an advisor. Henry was fast becoming an expert on the First Folio and other rare Shakespeariana, and soon he would become one of the most knowledgeable men in the world on those subjects, but he never pretended to be a great literary scholar. He began to correspond with Horace Howard Furness, a famous Shakespeare scholar in Pennsylvania and editor of the variorum editions of some of the plays. A variorum edition shows, alongside the main text of a play, all the various editorial decisions made by the major editors over time. Not only was Furness an expert who possessed an enormous research library, he was also the son of a great scholar. It was obvious to Furness that Folger was no dilettante, and he encouraged Henry and Emily in their study of Shakespeare and his plays. The correspondence blossomed into friendship, and Furness became a kind of mentor to the couple. Indeed, he outlined a course of study for Emily, eventually advising her on her master's thesis. Emily was an intelligent, devoted Shakespearian in her own right. Furness advised her on the best method to study Shakespeare: total immersion. "Take . . . the First Folio," Furness wrote, "and read a play every day consecutively. At the end of the thirty seven days you will be in a Shakespearean atmosphere that will astonish you."[10] In an era when it was unusual for a woman to earn a graduate degree or pursue literary scholarship, she became a student of how Shakespeare's plays were published and edited over time.

She examined the various editions, beginning with the texts of the quartos published during his lifetime, then the 1623 First Folio, and then the versions published by the various eighteenth- and nineteenth-century editors and adapters. In 1896, she received her master's degree from Vassar. Her thesis, "The True Text of Shakespeare," explored the question of how to determine the most accurate texts of the plays, as Shakespeare actually wrote them. Now Emily was a formally trained part of a team. According to a rare book dealer who knew the Folgers well, her "knowledge was always at the beck and call of her husband. She would hunt up bibliographical details and investigate difficult allusions, and frequently she would advise him to purchase a book or manuscript when he was wavering and undecided."[11]

Furness was pleased that the Folgers pursued their interest in Shakespeare together, as he and his wife had done. In 1897, Henry received a letter from Furness encouraging him to keep collecting at a fevered pace: "the sight of husband and wife, both eager in the same pursuit, always touches me deeply." The academic, who could never afford a First Folio of his own, took vicarious pleasure and pride in the acquisitions of his protégés, whom he nicknamed "the kids." Every year, on Good Friday, the Folgers visited the Furnesses to discuss and read Shakespeare, and to reveal their recent Shakespeariana acquisitions.

In that same year, Folger had a chance to act on Furness's advice. This time he did not wait to receive an auction catalogue in the mail, or a private offering from a dealer, to prompt him to pounce. This time Henry decided to try to buy something that wasn't even for sale. A New York book dealer, hoping to secure a commission, tipped Folger off that a large and important English collection—whose owner he declined to name—might be sold. The dealer hinted that the hoard included four First Folios and twenty-two quartos. This was the kind of opportunity about which rapacious collectors dream—the death of an envied, fellow bibliophile who, during his lifetime, would never have parted with his books. Henry bypassed the American and engaged Alexander B. Railton from the London book dealer Sotheran's. Find the collection, Folger instructed and, if it was worth having, secure it by private treaty before it went to auction. Railton did not disappoint. He discovered that the Fifth Earl of Warwick had inherited a magnificent library with the estates of his father, the Fourth Earl, George Guy Greville, who had died in 1893. The Fifth Earl was less interested in owning a pile of old books than he was in his sporting pursuits.[12] There was more good news. The Earl had not yet committed to an auction sale. Folger pressed Railton to pursue the collection, holding out the promise of future business he would bring to Sotheran's: "I will not write to any of the other London bookhouses until I hear from you."

Upon examination, the Warwick trove proved to consist largely of items that the Fourth Earl had bought from collector and bibliophile James Orchard Halliwell-Phillipps's 1854 catalogue of "Shakespeare Reliques." Before purchasing the collection, Folger studied the catalogue, which he found "as fascinating as a novel, for the clever collector told how each item earned its place with the other gems and how he had tracked down his quarry with patience and skill."[13] It contained many treasures: seven copies of the Second, Third, or Fourth Folios; hundreds of other rare books, artworks, and manuscripts; and two priceless quartos, the 1599 *Romeo and Juliet* and the 1600 first quarto of *The Merchant of Venice*. Such quarto editions are more fragile and therefore more rare—imagine the fragility of a paperback or a comic book versus the durability of a hardcover book—and thus the scarcest quartos come to market less frequently than even First Folios. Ownership of this library would transform Folger overnight into an important collector, and the breadth of its holdings appealed to his growing appetite not just for First Folios, but for all Shakespeare rarities.

Folger's confidence in Sotheran's was justified when, on April 3, 1897, the firm secured the Warwick collection for him at the lot price of £10,000, or about $50,000.[14] While that success might seem the end of the matter, it was not. Time was of the essence. Folger wasn't just eager to view his prizes; he was racing against an expensive ticking clock. On March 15, the U.S. Congress had begun to consider raising—nearly doubling—tariffs to 46.5 percent. If Folger could get his books into America before the increase, he would save in the neighborhood of $12,500 in import tax. Within three days of its purchase, the entire collection was packed in six crates, rushed aboard the SS *Teutonic*, and steaming its way to New York City. To Folger's relief, his cargo arrived in plenty of time to avoid the tax. But he need not have worried; the tariff would not be increased until July, and furthermore, books more than twenty years old were exempt from the tariff altogether, a carve-out that would, over time, save him hundreds of thousands of dollars.

By 1897, Folger's personal finances had improved over a couple of years earlier, when he had lost a collection he could neither afford to buy nor persuade Rockefeller to acquire. That failure had stung. His circumstances were different now. Now he could afford to purchase an entire collection, *en bloc*. In one transaction, with Sotheran's assistance, Folger landed the Warwick Castle hoard. Its crown jewel was one of the half dozen or so known copies of the First Folio called "perfect" because it contained a complete, undamaged, and original title page with the Droeshout portrait, the facing leaf of dedicatory verses, the table of contents, and the last page in the book. It contained one hundred percent original leaves, including the preliminaries, though some of those were "supplied" from another genuine, but shorter, copy of the First Folio, and thus do not match the other pages in size (W 64, F 6). It is impossible to say what this volume had cost Folger. Because he had paid one lot price for the entire collection, his records did not attribute individual prices to each book. Given the high quality of this folio, Sotheran's and Folger probably valued it at somewhere between $2,500 and $4,000. It was Henry's third and finest copy. Now he owned more First Folios than anyone else in America. Most collectors would have been content to stop there, but Henry was just getting started. Amazingly, he managed to keep his purchase of the Warwick Castle collection secret from the public for the next twenty years, illustrative of a penchant for secrecy that would become one of his trademarks.

By now the Folgers owned too many books, documents, and other objects to keep track of in their heads. They began to catalogue their collection. On hundreds, and then thousands, of five-by-eight-inch cards, Emily wrote, in her flowery hand, extensive bibliographic information: title, author, which dealer handled the transaction, and the date of purchase of each of the items acquired. Over time, her handwriting disappeared, replaced by more efficient typewritten cards. As the cards increased in volume, the Folgers stored them in tall dressers called chiffoniers.

By 1897, their collection had gotten too big to store at home. Once they had filled their bookshelves, and also their living quarters and basement, Henry and Emily rented a room at Eagle Warehouse & Storage, 28 to 44 Fulton Street, Brooklyn, at four dollars per month. They had their books and objets d'art hauled by the crate load to Eagle's premises. Folger had the sturdy, wooden crates—originally meant to hold oilcans—made in a Standard Oil workshop. Every piece in the collection was handled directly by them. They examined, inventoried, and then packed away every book, manuscript, painting, and playbill for future use.

In April 1898, Henry returned to Bang's where, thirteen years earlier, he had bought that unremarkable Fourth Folio. Now he was back to bid on a First Folio. How different he now was from the unsophisticated, young clerk who could barely afford to pay one hundred dollars for a book. Now he was a successful executive at the most valuable business on earth, a knowledgeable bibliophile, and a passionate collector on the verge of unleashing the most unquenchable appetite for all things Shakespeare that the world had ever seen. The auctioneer hammered down the First Folio to Henry's agent, the New York dealer George D. Smith, for $561. It was Folger's fourth (W 102, F 44). It was a pedestrian example, with several defects. Multiple pages had been supplied from other copies. It was missing several preliminaries; others were touched up or replaced in full by hand-drawn facsimiles by John Harris, the most accomplished facsimilist of the nineteenth century. Harris had an unsurpassed talent for perfect pen-and-ink facsimiles, which he employed at the request of collectors unhappy with flaws in their old books and manuscripts. One assistant in the department of printed books at the British Museum noted that "some of the leaves that [Harris] has supplied are so perfectly done that, after a few years, he has himself [been] puzzled to distinguish his own work from the original, so perfect has the facsimile been, both in paper and typography."[15] But Henry had not been fooled. He was expert enough to recognize all of the volume's faults, and wealthy enough to do better. It was the kind of cheap, second-rate copy that a new collector without the expertise or means to buy the best would acquire. He did not care. It was part of his plan.

Henry and Emily continued to educate themselves about the worlds of bookselling and antiquarian books, becoming familiar with the phrases and euphemisms used in a bookseller's or auctioneer's catalogue. The specialized verbiage, like the language of any all-encompassing pursuit, was a private tongue, peppered with its own jargon, incomprehensible to an outsider. The Folgers became familiar with a multitude of languages, not of other nations, but of printers, binders, publishers, bibliographers, and cataloguers. In some cases, many words retained their common usage: *new, clean, faded, frayed, stained, browned, broken, worn, polished, refurbished, rust-hole, alignment.*

In other cases, words that had a positive meaning in everyday life—like *washed*—were negative when applied to a book. *Unwashed* might be undesirable in a spouse, but it was a prized trait in a rare book. In a once popular process used to "improve" a book and make it more salable by removing unsightly page stains, and to make centuries-old paper look cleaner and brighter, dealers, auctioneers, or collectors would have a book disbound, the pages removed and separated and then washed by immersion in a solution of water and bleach. Then the pages were pressed flat, sewn back together, and rebound. The process may have brightened the paper, but when done too aggressively, washing could turn warm, age-toned pages unnaturally white. Washing also ruined the original, crisp feel of the Normandy rag paper, making it feel limp to the hand, soft and soggy. Pressing the pages flattened the original, three-dimensional impression of the type into the paper created by the letterpress. Henry and Emily learned how to detect washed pages with the touch of a hand, rolling the paper between the thumb and the index and middle fingers. They discovered the trick to identifying a pressed page: open the book, eyeball the page almost sideways in raking light, and look for the absence of tiny surface indentations of individual letters stamped into the paper by the pressure of the printing press. Washing reduced the desirability and value of a First Folio.

The Folgers learned to prize most highly the copies with unwashed leaves that still possessed a slight golden tinge and the pristine, crisp texture they had when they left Jaggard's shop almost three hundred years before. The presence of washed leaves was not, however, fatal. The treatment was not sufficient to deter advanced collectors, including the Folgers, from acquiring such copies, especially ones that were fine in other ways and complete.

The Folgers also learned that the word *unsophisticated* had an entirely different meaning in the world of bibliophiles. To describe a book as an "unsophisticated" copy was high praise. It meant that the book was as close to its original state as possible: unmarred by the meddling of later binders who stripped books of their simple, original, and early seventeenth-century bindings in favor of later fancy, overelaborate, and inappropriate bindings; leaves unspoiled by washing; pages still the original size, with margins untrimmed by misguided collectors; minor tears and damage left undisturbed by restorers; and no pages missing. Henry and Emily learned that the majority of First Folios were missing at least a few pages. After almost three hundred years of reading, neglect, and abuse, two-thirds of the print run of 750 copies had perished, and most of the surviving copies had suffered some form of damage. Thus, when acquiring a First Folio, they had to leaf through each copy's nine-hundred-plus pages to confirm that every single page was present, or which ones were missing. They also learned a shortcut for discovering whether the volume was complete. If a First Folio was "lacking" pages, to use the bibliographer's term, the odds were that at least one of what collectors called the three "grand leaves" was missing.

The most vulnerable—and thus most valuable—pages of any First Folio are the title page bearing Martin Droeshout's engraved portrait of Shakespeare, the table of contents or catalogue from the preliminaries at the front of the book, and the last leaf of the play *Cymbeline*, which is the final leaf in the volume. Of the nine hundred pages in the book, those three were the ones most likely to be missing or badly damaged. Of the three, the most coveted was the title page with the portrait. The Folgers learned that it was not sufficient to confirm that these and all other pages were present—they had to be the *right* pages. To confirm this, the Folgers had to ask a series of questions about any First Folio that came their way: Are all the pages original to this particular volume, being the ones folded into quires at Jaggard's shop in 1623, assembled there and sewn together, and then bound into the book? If not, have any missing pages been replaced by ones taken from another, authentic First Folio? If not, have any missing pages been substituted with pages removed from the Second or later Folios? A careful study of the paper and its different watermarks might reveal from how many different editions the monster had been created. And finally, are any replaced pages hand-drawn facsimiles? One artist became renowned for his brilliant, near-perfect, hand-lettered imitations of printed pages that often passed without detection. It was not easy to vet the authenticity of each page of a First Folio, and at their zenith, Henry and Emily were as skilled as the best dealers in the world in flyspecking and analyzing a copy of the book. Henry's manuscript notes reveal that he was well aware of all the possibilities for chicanery and deception on the subject of replaced pages.

A whole cottage industry grew up to supply missing pages to imperfect First Folios. Some dealers squirreled away hundreds of loose leaves, and used them to complete defective copies in their own stock, or to sell under the table to other dealers or collectors. Missing the first leaf from *Henry V*? Buy the sheet from a London book dealer's basement stock of surplus First Folio leaves and replace it. When one American dealer advertised "First Folio leaves" for sale, Folger annotated the advertisement—"ask about Shakespeares." Maybe he could buy them all? In time, as printing technologies improved, mass-produced, machine-made facsimile pages replaced unique, hand-drawn copies. The coveted title page was especially subject to substitution as very few First Folios possessed their original Shakespeare portrait. One bookseller advertised facsimile printed pages for sale, with the pages most in demand actually listed in his catalogues. Book dealers touted badly damaged or seriously incomplete First Folios in their stock as ideal for harvesting pages to complete other, superior copies. A copy of the First Folio might even be entirely made up, a Frankenstein's monster of parts assembled from the corpses of several other genuine but defective copies of the same book. A group of folios ruined beyond redemption could be dismembered and the best leaves salvaged and combined to make up one complete copy.

The Folgers complemented each other. Beginning in the mid-1890s, Emily read thousands of booksellers' catalogues, marking them with dog-eared corners and making pencil squiggles in the margins next to the items she recommended that Henry consider buying. Henry worked "zealously" late into the night going over catalogues and sorting through her notes. One famous bookseller observed, "The physical work alone was enormous as Mr. Folger had correspondents everywhere. He was known to every bookseller and collector throughout the world, all of them rendering enthusiastic assistance."[16] As a result, he developed a list of items he wished to acquire, and calculated bids for what he hoped to buy at auction. He took meticulous notes on condition, completeness, binding, provenance, and prices paid (and by whom), saving thousands of catalogues over the nearly four decades to come so that he might refer to them whenever a similar item came up at auction or private sale again. Emily wrote the catalogue cards that documented their acquisitions, keeping meticulous track of what they owned. She cross-referenced the cards with items offered for sale in the catalogues, either to prevent the accidental purchase of duplicate copies, or, after comparing the condition of a volume in their collection with one new to the market, to upgrade their copy with a superior one. Of course, the hoarder in Henry could usually not bear to part with the supplanted copy. To him, two copies were always better than one. And no two copies were ever exactly the same. Each copy was different, possessing its own unique physical characteristics and personality. Henry kept up active correspondence with dealers and others who wrote to him about Shakespeare rarities, and he negotiated through the various dealer-agents he engaged to bid at the London auctions or to pursue private sales in England or Europe.

The Folgers collected for themselves, for their private pleasure. They became regular vacationers at the Homestead Resort in Hot Springs,

Virginia, spending several weeks there each spring between 1914 and 1929. He played golf while Emily took what a friend referred to as "the nasty waters," but neither took a holiday from collecting.[17] They traveled with their massive chests holding the handwritten cards on which Emily had catalogued the collection. These chiffoniers containing the precious cards were shipped to the Homestead during their stays. The Folgers' personal files are filled with notes scribbled on scraps of paper bearing the Homestead letterhead: lists of books, catalogue prices, and records of auction bids. Even on vacation, they would scrutinize catalogues and review communications from dealers, because an opportunity might arise that was too good to pass up and might require prompt action. They might need instant access to information about what they already owned if they were to act quickly to obtain an item.

For two reasons, Henry chose not to attend the major auctions. The first was strategic. He sought to maintain his anonymity. He reasoned that if he could keep his name out of the papers, and swear the book dealers to secrecy, he would be able to buy books much more cheaply. He knew if word got out that a wealthy American was buying multiple copies of the First Folio, plus other choice Shakespeariana, opportunistic sellers would distort the market by raising prices across the board. Of course, several of the top rare book dealers discovered his identity as soon as he made an initial private purchase from each of them, but that could work to his advantage—some booksellers began offering him first choice before their catalogues went to print. And so, for the rest of his career, secrecy became one of his signature traits. Second, he failed to attend the most important auctions of rare books because, in that era, most of them took place in London, and his increasingly important job at Standard Oil did not permit him the luxury of taking several days to sail across the ocean just to spend a few hours at an auction. Furthermore, any money he did not spend on travel he could spend on more books. Folger deputized trusted agents to represent him at the auctions, and he stayed in close touch with them by letter and by cable. Henry often paid for his purchases through his Standard Oil account, so his personal checkbooks are poor guides for how much was spent. He paid each seller in British pounds, with currency conversions resulting in a memorandum of exchange as part of the paper trail. Customs duties changed over time, but often the items were exempted from charges because they were antiques. When books or artworks were shipped from abroad, they entered America duty-free because, in a colossal understatement, they were "over twenty years old." If an old painting arrived in a new frame, only the frame was dutiable. The New York customs house was only a block away from Folger's office at Twenty-Six Broadway, which made it easy for him to take possession of his treasures quickly.

It was a fortuitous time for Henry Folger to begin collecting First Folios. An alignment of historical, cultural, and economic forces had brought about a sea change in the transatlantic trade of art treasures and rare books. By the end of the nineteenth century, just as great waves of European immigrants landed on America's shores, another great western migration, not of people, but of objects, flooded America. That tide swept across the sea paintings, furniture, tapestries, sculptures, arms and armor, jewelry, silver, religious art, and rare books and autographs from the Middle Ages to the Edwardian era. Centuries earlier, European explorers had sailed to the New World to carry away her riches—gold, furs, tobacco, cotton, and more—to their homelands. Now, in a reversal of fortune, the former colonies plundered the Continent. American money was flushing First Folios from their hiding places. In 1899, one of the premier London booksellers, Bernard Quaritch, a frequent dealer in First Folios, wrote to the bibliophile Sidney Lee saying, "perfect copies are usually sold by us dealers to American collectors."[18] The British did not put up much of a fight. If English millionaires don't "bestir themselves," Lee predicted, "there is a likelihood that all the . . . privately held copies of the volume still in [Great Britain] will make tracks across the Atlantic."[19] But, as the world's expert on the provenance and history of the First Folio Anthony West later observed, "there was no bestirring."[20]

Henry Folger's good fortune in business coincided perfectly with these developments. No one knew it then, but the years 1895 to 1930 would be looked back upon with nostalgia as the golden age for collecting British literary treasures. Never before and never again would so many great English books, volumes of rare Shakespeariana, and First Folios come to market. And there was Henry Folger, present from the dawn to the dusk of that age.

Of the twenty-three First Folios known to have been sold in the 1890s, he had purchased four, one-sixth of the copies that came to market during the entire decade, and that was before he had matured into a serious collector. He had also purchased an entire library. In 1899, on the twentieth anniversary of his graduation from college, he reported to the historian of the Amherst Class of 1879 a summary of his achievements. Playing to type, he did not boast about his role at Standard Oil, or of his wealth, nor did he advertise his growing collection of Shakespeare treasures. He downplayed everything that he had accomplished in the previous twenty years as a businessman and collector:

> My annals record little that is of even passing interest. A business position with the Standard Oil Co. has called for my best efforts to meet added responsibilities; while for diversion, the gathering of a modest library—for the most part as yet unread— had helped to keep me interested in matters literary.

As the nineteenth century came to a close, many historic changes were around the corner. The new era would become the century of the automobile. Henry was poised to rise with the coming of that new technology. Cars meant a new industry and an unprecedented demand for rubber and steel. And a new source of fuel: gasoline. Once a worthless by-product of the refinement of crude oil, gasoline was a godsend to the fortunes of Standard Oil. The product fueled not only cars, but also a modernization, mobility, and a new state of mind that changed the country and led to an era of prosperity and confidence that historians would call "the American Century."

By New Year's Eve 1899, Henry and Emily Folger had settled upon the habits and practices that they would use in the new century to develop their collection. They would avoid publicity; become experts in their own right and not rely exclusively upon dealers and auctioneers for information; document their purchases with meticulous catalogue cards; review sales and auction catalogues together and promptly; travel abroad to experience the milieu of Shakespeare's England and meet the top dealers; inventory, crate, and store thousands of books, manuscripts, and artworks in warehouses so that their home would not become a bizarre warren for crazed packrats; and not limit themselves to the best First Folios—they would consider any copy if the price was right. They would buy all rare Shakespeariana and not limit themselves to First Folios; they would not attend the British auctions and bid in person, but they would engage trusted London dealers to represent them; when efficacious, they would make bulk purchases and acquire entire libraries; they would leverage their buying ability by using Henry's Standard Oil resources; they would work together as a team (Emily has never received proper credit for her role, perhaps because Henry wrote the checks and handled the correspondence, but their acquisitions were the result of their collective judgment); they would not wait for coveted books to come up for sale, but they would track down their owners and entice them to sell; Henry and Emily would keep track of what was for sale, what had been sold, to whom, and at what prices, information that was gathered through correspondence with book dealers and auction houses as well as through subscriptions to multiple domestic and international clipping services, which sent articles gleaned from thousands of newspapers and periodicals; and, finally, the pair would live frugally—except when spending thousands on a single book. Perhaps the Folgers' most important secret was that they were "hands-on," refusing to delegate or outsource their passion, knowledge, or decision-making.

By the close of the nineteenth century, they possessed the will, expertise, and growing financial resources to dominate the world of Shakespeare in ways that no one had ever even imagined. The new century would bring Henry Folger word of a stupendous discovery that would transform his enthusiastic pursuit into all-out obsession.

Chapter 7

❧Y❧

"The Most Precious Book in the World"

—Henry Clay Folger

Henry welcomed the twentieth century with the acquisition, in 1900, of his fifth First Folio, paying $9,000 for an especially attractive copy (W 66, F 8). It was the highest sum he had paid for a book, double what he had paid for his second copy in 1896. It contained one hundred percent genuine First Folio leaves, though some were supplied from other copies. Although the preliminaries were included, some pages were "cropped, mounted and ruled in red."[1] Then, in April 1901, he paid $892.50 for his sixth copy (W 94, F 36). Like any inexpensive example, it was flawed. The book, bound in goatskin, had all of its preliminaries present, but the text leaves were taken from at least five other copies. By now, Henry had solidified one of his signature traits as a collector: he knew every First Folio was unique, each having slight differences from any other, so he was willing to buy inferior or incomplete copies for research and comparison purposes—if the price was right. By 1900, he had paid between $561 and $9,000 each for his copies, plus the $50,000 he had paid for the Warwick Castle library. It is quite clear that he had chosen to become a scholar-collector. No matter how damaged or incomplete the volume, each surviving page was precious to him.

From the outset, Folger possessed two distinguishing characteristics that gave him a comparative advantage over other collectors. First, he began early. Many American millionaires waited until their fortunes had reached extraordinary size, until late middle age or retirement, to pursue their passions. Folger started young, before he became wealthy or even knew that he would prosper.

Second, he was not a passive collector, reacting to fixed-price sale catalogues, private correspondence offering items, or public auction catalogues, as was the custom for a number of other famous book collectors. In the beginning, in particular, there were other collectors far wealthier than he, and dealers were more likely to offer them first choice. They could also outbid him at public auctions. And some of them lived in England. He had to find a way to get ahead of the other, more prestigious, more established, and more moneyed collectors in the queue. As Folger had done in the business world, he decided to go out and get what he wanted, including from owners who weren't immediately willing to sell. The skills he honed during his early years at Standard Oil served him well. He could distill numbers into a nugget of a concept. He could gather information; detect a trend; find a way to do something more efficiently. Why, for example, wait for copies of the First Folio to come up for sale at auction when he could chase their owners down? This was also useful in cutting out the middlemen—often the auction houses and sometimes the dealers—to buy direct. In 1902, the publication of a remarkable book enhanced his opportunities to do just that.

When Henry Folger began collecting First Folios, no one had ever compiled a census of extant copies. In 1824, the celebrated bibliophile Reverend Thomas Frognall Dibdin had tried to locate and describe all of the known copies, but his pioneering effort yielded incomplete results, locating forty-five examples.[2] Collectors operated in the dark, without knowing how many copies existed, and they were ignorant of the true rarity of fine, complete volumes.

At the turn of the twentieth century, another man, the English Shakespeare scholar Sir Sidney Lee, set out to collect all available information about the surviving copies. He sent typed, personalized letters to all known owners of First Folios, to suspected owners, and to book dealers and auction houses that might know the identities of owners, requesting that they complete the survey he enclosed with his letter.[3] This ill-designed questionnaire asked each owner to reveal facts and opinions about his or her copy of the First Folio: its provenance, or ownership history; the size and binding; the presence or absence of the front matter or preliminaries; the number of pages, if any, missing from the text; its present location; and last, in a cheeky question that must have offended the privacy of a number of its recipients, the price that the owner had paid for the volume.

Lee located 156 First Folios.[4] He divided them into three subjective, arbitrary categories based on the condition and completeness of the books. He classified the best copies as Class IA, those less perfect as IB, and the most defective as IC. Lee inspected few of the folios personally, leaving him at the mercy of their owners to describe accurately the condition of the books. Many, of course, overlooked significant flaws, while others embellished their treasures to inflate their value.[5]

The *Lee Census*, as it became known, was published in 1902 as a separate volume to accompany the Oxford facsimile, collotype edition of Shakespeare's complete works, which carried the awkward title *Shakespeares Comedies, Histories, and Tragedies, being a Reproduction in Facsimile of the First Folio Edition 1623 from the Chatsworth copy in the possession of the Duke of Devonshire, K.G. with an Introduction and Census of Copies by Sidney Lee*. It was the first complete attempt ever made to locate every single copy of a book. Even a century later, only four other books have been the subject of such a complete census: Charles Darwin's *On the Origin of Species*; James Audubon's *The Birds of America*, a massive 26.5-by-39-inch volume of 435 color plates known as the Double-Elephant Folio; the Gutenberg Bible of 1455; and Copernicus's 1543 *De revolutionibus orbium coelestium* (*On the Revolutions of the Heavenly Spheres*), describing the heliocentric model of the universe.

When a copy of Lee's *Census* landed on Henry Folger's desk and he flipped through its pages for the first time, he must have been elated. Lee listed only one copy as belonging to Folger, when he already owned six.[6] His secret remained safe. From the *Census* alone, no one could guess that he was accumulating First Folios. But now, thanks to Lee, Folger had an idea of the universe he was trolling and for the first time he possessed answers to important questions. How many copies of the First Folio had survived, and in what condition? How many were held by institutions (and presumably out of Folger's reach), and how many were still in the hands of individuals, and ripe for the plucking? Though Lee's motive was scholarly, he had inadvertently created a wish list for Folger.

Henry annotated his copy of the *Census* like a shopping list. First he checked off the copies he owned but which Lee had attributed to other collectors. Folger also wrote marginalia about other copies in his own tiny, neat hand. This was no amateur. Not only familiar with Shakespeare's text itself, but also he had mastered the skills and language of bibliography, and he assessed the provenance, completeness, and condition of each copy inventoried in the *Census*. These notes, Henry hoped, would prove useful in the future whenever a copy listed in Lee came up for sale. Folger had to buy many books, including folios, sight unseen from English dealers and auction houses. Without a personal inspection, or accurate and expensive photography, he was at the mercy of descriptions written by book dealers and auctioneers—hardly disinterested parties. Sellers often concocted subjective and self-serving catalogue descriptions of rarity that wove together over-the-top phrases like "highly desirable," "very rare," and "exceptionally choice," with optimistic and even delusional condition reports like "very minor restoration," "only a few leaves supplied," "very tall copy," "original binding," and "one of the finest extant." Folger planned to use the descriptions in the *Census* to checkmate such hyperbole whenever copies included in it came up for sale. He would keep Lee's checklist within reach for the rest of his life.

Sidney Lee's *Census* was not without flaws. He had located just 156 First Folios, and, perhaps because he relied upon the owners' subjective and often inexpert answers to his survey questions, Lee's published descriptions of the condition of the First Folios included many errors. Lee had failed to collate each copy, check it for missing or replacement leaves, note damage, measure the height and width of the pages, examine the binding, inspect for washing, or confirm the originality of the engraved portrait. Many owners, through ignorance or dishonesty, failed to report significant flaws. But soon Lee would try again, and he would not overlook Henry Folger.

Although the *Lee Census* had revealed a number of mouthwatering specimens, for Henry Folger the years 1900 to 1903 were marked, on the surface, by little collecting activity. If Folger was quiet, others were active. On December 13, 1902, the *New York Times* published a major article about a remarkable sale of Shakespeare quartos at top prices, including a 1611 *Titus Andronicus* with uncut leaves that sold to an American buyer for £620, a world-record price for any quarto edition of the plays. It was not even the first *Titus* quarto from 1596, a legendary rarity of which no copy has ever been found. The buyer was not Henry Folger.[7] There were reasons for his temporary retreat from the market. First, he was still digesting the Warwick Castle library. Second, he was busy assuring his rise at Standard Oil. By the turn of the century, his responsibilities and income dwarfed what he had been doing and earning a decade earlier. He enjoyed more than a good salary. Now he had the ear and unquestioned trust of John D. Rockefeller. He was accumulating one of the most valuable commodities in the world: shares of Standard Oil stock. It was the value of that stock, more than anything else, that would fuel Henry's future acquisitions.

In 1902 and 1903, Folger's assets—and the value of the entire Standard Oil Company—faced a dangerous attack. While the *New York Times* was covering rare books, *McClure's* magazine rocked the very foundation of Standard Oil. Ida Minerva Tarbell, a pioneering, muckraking journalist obsessed with exposing corruption, created the narrative of "the Trust" with a series of articles that *McClure's* published between November 1902 and October 1904. In her detailed nineteen-part exposé, she revealed what she claimed were abuses by Standard Oil. Driven by an obsession to destroy Rockefeller, Tarbell ignored the consumer welfare that Standard had created by cutting its costs and reducing prices to consumers and demonized Rockefeller as a ruthless, pitiless mogul who crushed his rivals. She caricatured Henry Folger's regular golfing partner as "the oldest man in the world—a living mummy"; "money mad"; "a hypocrite"; and "ungentlemanly." She concluded that "our national life is on every side distinctly poorer, uglier, meaner, for the kind of influence he exercises." In Tarbell's anticompetitive religion, Rockefeller's original sin was that he "had never played fair."

Tarbell, the daughter of a failed barrel maker and independent oilman, and sister to another, began a one-woman crusade to influence public opinion about the activities of the Standard Oil Company. She blamed the trust for putting her father out of the oil business years earlier in Pennsylvania, and for robbing her of her comfortable life. She conceded her bias in an interview in *The Bookman*: "My childhood was spent in the oil regions, and if I have any natural sympathy, it is with the independent operators." Horrified by the devastation and poverty left behind in some Pennsylvania towns in the aftermath of the "bust" of the oil expansion, and depressed by scenes of vacant landscapes and dried-up wells, she sought an explanation; someone had to be blamed. The press had already demonized and lampooned Standard Oil as a greedy corporation with its tentacles wrapped around the U.S. Capitol. It was common knowledge that Standard had participated in the two failed attempts at forming a refiners' cartel.

Tarbell was not the only one complaining. Accusations also came from Standard's competitors: independent crude oil producers, barrel makers, refiners, and marketers, many of them cut out of the production chain by Rockefeller's earlier campaign of vertical integration. The *McClure's* articles convinced many that Standard had used unfair means to eliminate its competitors and control the market. More than any other writer, Tarbell created the persistent but largely mythical narrative of the bad behavior of the Standard Oil Company. In her zeal to influence public policy, she was not afraid to bend the truth. The preferential railroad rates, along with rebates and drawbacks, were the "abuses" Tarbell found most offensive. The rebates and preferential treatment were real, but her interpretation of the events was skewed in favor of the small, inefficient competitor, rather than in favor of consumers, who benefited from Rockefeller's vigorous cost cutting.

Standard Oil did not tolerate her accusations without comment.

After a long period of silence during which Rockefeller refused to speak to the press, his lawyer S. C. T. Dodd, principal attorney advising Standard on antitrust issues, published and distributed to libraries free of charge four hundred pages of testimony that company officers had provided to the government in an attempt to explain its practices. Not only did they refute many of the accusations made against the company, but Dodd and Rockefeller also explained how Standard, far from harming the consumer, created advantages for the public. They distinguished between combinations of firms whose goal was to limit production—to restrict output, raise prices, and harm consumers—and those that took advantage of the economies of scale, mass production, and advanced technologies, which lowered costs and benefited consumers. After all, wasn't the intention of the Sherman Antitrust Act to encourage competition and promote consumer well-being, rather than to protect inefficient producers? If Standard was guilty of anything, wasn't it too much competition rather than too little?

Tarbell's literary indictment foreshadowed a legal one, and it disturbed Henry Folger. He knew Standard's business strategies and practices inside out. Indeed, for the past quarter century, he had helped Rockefeller build the largest industrial organization in the world. As a lawyer, he was familiar with the new antitrust law. As far as Folger was concerned, Standard Oil was an ethical and law-abiding company. And Ida Tarbell was nothing but a vexatious intermeddler who had defamed not only John D. Rockefeller but him too.

Tarbell's journalistic siege may have annoyed and distracted Rockefeller, Folger, and the rest of the Standard Oil leadership, but that alone could not deter Henry from pursuing Shakespeare. Ida Tarbell was not the cause of the lull in his acquisitions. There is another explanation for the absence of major purchases—aside from the $9,000 First Folio of 1900—between 1900 and 1903. Folger was keeping his powder dry. In private, behind the scenes, he was in the grip of a furious but secret pursuit of what he believed was the single most valuable and desirable copy of the First Folio in the world.

That hunt, which climaxed in 1903, had begun in March 1899, on the day Henry Folger received a letter from the London bookseller

Sotheran & Co., the firm that had acquired the Warwick Castle library for him. Sotheran, explained the letter's author, Alexander B. Railton, had discovered a most extraordinary and hitherto unknown specimen of the First Folio. Its condition, history, provenance, ownership, and contemporary handwritten inscription revealed multiple cross-connections to Shakespeare's contemporaries, and to the origins of the First Folio. It might have been the very first copy sewn and bound. From the moment Henry Folger learned of its existence, he was seized by an irresistible compulsion to own it. His pursuit of this book also signaled a turning point in his development as a collector, and in the intensity of his intellectual and financial commitment to his Shakespeare obsession. He was far from the world's richest man. He had been promoted from secretary to chairman of the manufacturing committee that year, but he had not yet climbed anywhere near the top of Standard's ladder. This chase would determine whether he was willing to pay the world's richest price for a book.

A. B. Railton's letter of March 4, 1899, tempted Folger with a copy not present in the Lee catalogue, observing that "at present my own belief is that it is without exception the most interesting copy extant."[8] The story, continued Railton, began in 1891, when he was summoned to an English country house to evaluate the library kept there. In a flashback, Railton recounted what happened:

In April 1891 I was engaged on behalf of my firm Messr. H. Sotheran & Co. in weeding out worthless books and arranging, preparatory to a catalogue being made of the Library of Mr. Coningsby Sibthorp of Canwick Hall, Lincoln.

Having finished work in the library which was also used as a Billiard Room, I was taken to the Coach-House in which was a very large case of books; on the top of the case outside were stacked a great number of old folios covered with dust, these were being thrown down to me by an assistant who lived on the estate. On throwing down a folio volume which lacked one of the covers, had many leaves in tatters, and was tightly wound with a rough piece of cord, he remarked to me "that is no good. Sir, it is only old poetry."[9] I unloosened the string, opened the book, and at a glance saw what a treasure was found. Having shown it in due course to Mr. Sibthorp, I took it to London, supplied several missing leaves from another copy in the possession of Messrs. H. Sotheran & Co.

So far Railton's story was exciting to Henry Folger—the discovery of a lost copy of the First Folio was always that—but not amazing. At that moment Railton could not have understood the magnitude of the discovery. All he knew was that he had found a hitherto unrecorded copy of the First Folio.

But Railton continued: "[I] had it finally restored by Mr. Pratt as nearly as possible to the state in which it was originally presented by Jaggard the printer to his friend Augustine Vincent."

"Presented by Jaggard"? Now Railton had Folger's full attention. In nearly three centuries, no presentation copy of the First Folio had ever been discovered. That fact alone made this copy special. But presented by Jaggard, the printer of the book? It seemed almost too incredible to be true. Railton laid out the evidence. The volume contained a handwritten inscription written in ink and dated 1623. But who had written it? And the front cover of the binding, which appeared to be original and seemed to date to the 1620s, was decorated with a coat of arms. But whose coat of arms did it proclaim? It had, Railton revealed, taken eight years to find out. In an effort worthy of a team of cryptographers, only the combined talents and patience of paleographers, the bibliographer Sidney Lee, and three librarians from the British Museum—Principal Librarian Sir Edward Maunde Thompson, Mr. Warner of the manuscript department, and Alfred W. Pollard of the books department—could decode the triple mysteries of the book. The presentation inscription was in the hand of Augustine Vincent, the Windsor Herald; the book was the very copy given to him 276 years earlier by Isaac Jaggard, printer of the First Folio; and the decoration stamped on the front cover was Vincent's coat of arms.

The condition of the book was not perfect, Railton reported. Sotheran had restored the volume, replacing two missing pages with pages from other copies of the First Folio, and had also replaced two leaves in facsimile. When the treasure was discovered, its binding was held on with a piece of string; Sotheran's had the book rebound, incorporating much of the original calf binding—including the coat of arms—into the new cover.

Despite the volume's flaws, it was exceptional in that the pages had never been trimmed—reduced in size by previous binders. The stunning provenance of the Sibthorp volume, combined with its status as the tallest known copy, and the likelihood that it was one of the first copies assembled by the printer, made it the most important and coveted copy of the First Folio in the world.

To Henry Folger, this was all good news. It would make a perfect addition to his collection. Even better for Henry, Sotheran, an important dealer with whom, through the Warwick Castle purchase, he had established a satisfactory, prior business relationship, had discovered the volume. If Sotheran offered him first choice now, it would just be a matter of settling upon the price. Folger was ready to cable funds to London at once to complete the purchase.

But there was more, advised Railton. And this news was not good. Sotheran had failed to gain control of the volume, and it was not for sale. After Sotheran & Co. had researched, identified, and repaired the book, Coningsby Sibthorp went to London to reclaim his property. Railton tried to purchase the First Folio that day:

When the volume was ready, Mr. & Mrs. Sibthorp called together for it, I held it out and said "Which is it to be, the book or a Cheque?" Naming a large sum; Mrs. Sibthorp replied "Ah, Mr. Railton, if we take the Cheque we may spend the money, but in taking the book we shall always have a treasure to look at."

To Henry that report, though unwelcome, was not disastrous. At least Sibthorp had not sold the book to a rival collector, an institution, or a dealer not loyal to Folger. He calculated that he would still have a chance to buy the Sibthorp Folio. He could direct Sotheran to stay in touch with the owner, and pounce when the time was right. Then Railton dropped a bombshell that must have dismayed Folger. Sidney

Lee had just written an article about the remarkable Sibthorp Folio, and had published it in the April 1899 issue of the *Cornhill Magazine*. Railton included a copy of the article in a letter to Folger.[10] Now the whole world was in on the secret. Soon, Folger worried, every important collector in Great Britain and America would covet the book. Railton confirmed those fears: "As I expected Mr. Lee's article has put hounds upon the track and now Mr. Sibthorp is being sorely tested." Railton assured Folger that if Sibthorp sold the book at all, he had agreed to sell it through Sotheran: "He as good as promised if he fails he will do so into our hands—naturally nothing is certain in this life. Now do you wish the volume and if so we will act for you but the price must be high, 1,000 pounds will not do it—a long way above that in my opinion."

On May 3, 1899, Sotheran & Co. sent Folger a cryptic telegram: "Approached about folio do you wish it (signed) Bookmen" (Sotheran's telex address). Henry confirmed his interest two days later: "To Bookmen London. Any progress Sibthorp. Folger." Railton cabled Henry the next day. Sibthorp was now willing to sell his folio, but at a record high price of almost $25,000: "May 6, 1899. Bookmen to Folger: Owner replies five thousand pounds which I take to be prohibitive." It was almost three times what Folger had paid for his best copy, and at least two and a half times the record price for any First Folio. Railton assumed that Folger would never pay it. After cabling Folger, he also wrote him a letter, describing his failed attempt to visit Sibthorp and negotiate in person. Sibthorp had declined to meet, telling Railton he should write him a letter, which he did. Railton quoted Sibthorp's reply to Folger: "I am not wishing to sell my 1st Folio Edition of Shakespeare. I have been twice asked to answer a price and have replied 5,000 pounds—which I take to be prohibitive." Railton ended his letter on a discouraging note: "As I anticipated Mr. Lee's article has advertised the volume. . . . I may go further and say that Shakespearian students look upon it as a 'National Treasure' and desire its retention here."

Henry Folger hesitated. From the moment that Henry learned of the Sibthorp Folio, he had longed to possess it. Sotheran had come to him first, and in turn he had asked Railton to act as his agent and convince Sibthorp to sell. Railton had brought the eccentric Sibthorp to the table—but at an astonishing price that the owner secretly hoped that Sotheran's client would not meet. Uncharacteristically, Folger's negotiating skills failed him during this first, disastrous attempt to acquire the book. He made several amateurish mistakes. He wanted this Folio so badly that he restrained himself, fearing that his passion might overcome his judgment, causing him to pay an obscenely high price. His Shakespeare obsession had become so widely known among sellers that they used it against him to drive up the prices of the best books. Just as he had feared, the more famous he became, the more money sellers tried to charge him. Had Sibthorp guessed his identity? Is that why he had named such a preposterous price for the book? Folger overcompensated, and treated this unique transaction too casually, as though he were bargaining over any unremarkable commodity. But this was not a shipment of crude oil, of which there was a vast supply. This was the only known copy in the world of a presentation First Folio. If Henry failed to obtain it, he would regret it for the rest of his life.

He did not cable orders to Sotheran to act at once and grab the book. Instead, he tarried seven weeks before replying to Railton's telegram. Then he bargained. On June 25, Folger cabled Railton: "To Bookmen London. Offer Sibthorp up to Four thousand pounds, half cash half January first. Commission 250. Folger." On July 6, Sibthorp, perhaps believing that bargaining over money was ungentlemanly, said no. "I beg you to decline offer on my behalf," he cabled Sotheran. Folger's bargaining had alarmed his agents. They had known Coningsby Sibthorp for several years, and were in the best position to judge his quixotic nature. If he said £5,000, the price was £5,000. It was not an invitation to negotiate. Railton knew this and warned Folger by telegram the same day: "We urge cash offer full price hopeless otherwise."

Henry, still eager to bargain and save at least £500, did not grasp the nuance coded within Railton's advice and cabled another offer on July 6: "Think 4000 cash enough but see Sibthorp do your best 4500 half cash half January first. If 5000 [then] 2000 cash 3000 January first purchase kept secret." In other words, Folger made two separate offers: $4,500 with $2,250 payable now and $2,250 due six months later, or

$5,000 with $2,000 payable now and $3,000 paid six months later. Unwisely, Folger asked Railton to offer £4,500, conceding that he would go to £5,000 if absolutely necessary, but only if he could pay in two installments. Railton ignored Folger's bargaining over a measly £500, knowing that it would infuriate Sibthorp.

Frustrated with Folger's dithering, and acting in what he believed was Henry's best interest, Railton chose not to inform Sibthorp of the lower, £4,500 offer. Instead, on July 8, he simply wired Sibthorp, "five thousand now offered [by] our client." Then Railton wrote to Folger to confess what he had done. He told Henry that he had stayed late at the office "in anticipation of cabling you Mr. Sibthorp's reply. . . . I shall cable you . . . feeling assured that you, like myself, are a little anxious as to the result." On July 10, in a follow-up letter to Sibthorp, Railton breached Folger's confidence by revealing to Sibthorp Henry's private instructions to Sotheran: "His suggestion that we should offer an intermediate price we decided not to carry out, as we quite understood from the first that your price of 5000 pounds was final . . . [Y]ou will also note that our customer makes a proposition as to payment by two installments, this also we did not telegraph . . . but we shall say to him . . . that we do not anticipate you will wish to part with the folio before the completion of the payment . . . [W]e shall of course respect our customer's request that the transaction be kept strictly secret." Railton had done this not to harm Folger but to flatter Sibthorp's sense of propriety and enhance the likelihood that he would close the deal.

On July 13, Sibthorp cabled Railton with his answer: "Accept your offer 5000 clear." Railton wrote to Henry with the good news: "The precious treasure is now secured for you and Mr. Sotheran joins me in congratulating you heartily upon its acquisition. I scarcely ventured to think that the volume would leave the old country."

Sibthorp even agreed to Folger's terms of split payments, and also agreed to deposit the book with Sotheran pending payment in full by January 1, 1900. Sibthorp understood Folger's penchant for privacy—he wanted to keep the transaction secret, too: "One point I am anxious about is that the sale (& price) should not appear in the public papers. Some of my friends & acquaintances will be extremely mortified to hear that the Book (as I suppose is the case) is likely to go out of England. I beg you to use your influence and oblige me in this particular."

Folger had done it. After uncharacteristic and dangerous delay, he agreed to pay Coningsby Sibthorp's price. It was a record sum, but he had purchased the most desirable First Folio in the world. He sent a £2,000 deposit to Sotheran on July 21, 1899, believing that with it he had secured the Folio. So did everyone else involved in the transaction. The book dealer, always alert for an opportunity for the up sell, proposed that Folger take advantage of its binding services: "Would it not be well to have a nice morocco case made to hold the volume? Our idea in suggesting such is to prevent the old calf binding . . . from being rubbed." Lloyd's insurance issued a letter on July 28 confirming that it would insure the book for up to £5,250 during its journey across the Atlantic. Sibthorp agreed to deposit the book with Sotheran, requesting a receipt to relieve him of liability. Folger, worried about the risk of fire or damage, asked that the book be locked in a safe-deposit box.

Then, just a few months later, in the fall of 1899, Henry Folger, through rash, reckless, and self-destructive behavior, set in motion a reversal of fortune that undid his triumph. He had received by mail from Railton a copy of A. W. Pollard's report describing the Sibthorp Folio. That report, Henry stated in a letter to Railton of November 24, 1899, "has surprised and shocked me greatly." "It states," complained Henry, "that the leaf of verses [in the preliminaries] and the last leaf . . . are in facsimile." Henry told Railton that he had bought the book based on Sidney Lee's *Cornhill* article, and on the various representations made by the Sotheran firm that the folio was complete. Indeed, Folger reminded Railton, he had once written to the collector that Sotheran had mended and replaced some leaves. "I presume," added Folger, "it will be conceded that I had the right to expect a complete copy." Claiming that it would cost up to £1,000 to replace the missing leaves, Folger wrote, "It seems to me I am entitled to either have the missing leaves supplied (which I would much prefer) or be given a money allowance in the purchase sum on account of them." Folger also revealed that a rival bookseller from England had visited him in New York and had disparaged the condition of the folio. Railton, perhaps miffed by Folger's accusatory tone after all he had done to persuade Sibthorp to sell the book, did not reply. Instead, Mr. Sotheran himself wrote back saying that he would propose the financial accommodation to Sibthorp. Word came back quickly—Sibthorp was not interested in further negotiations. Folger could take the book or leave it. Sotheran warned Folger: "Owner declines reducing price will return deposit if not paid this year."

Folger drafted two letters, one filled with a list of complaints about mended pages, remargined leaves, pages supplied in facsimile, and more. This version he did not send. Instead, he sent a letter containing the additional £3,000, but now requesting the right to examine the book on approval before agreeing to the final sale. This was too much for Sibthorp, and on January 3, 1900, Sotheran sent Folger an alarming cable: "Owner declines and has returned deposit implying sale is off shall we renew offer without conditions." Henry cabled back the same day to "buy without condition" but then *added* a contradictory condition—"but try to secure privilege of returning at 4800 pounds after inspection." Henry wanted the book shipped across the Atlantic "on approval," a booksellers' trade practice that meant he could return it for a refund if he did not like it. If Henry decided to cancel the transaction, he offered to toss Sibthorp a bone of £200 as compensation for his trouble. Sibthorp was a proud man who did not need the money, and Sotheran refused to insult him with these new terms and cabled back on January 4 about the urgency of the situation. Railton warned him that this tactic would offend Sibthorp and certainly kill the sale. "Trying fatal know owner too well firm offer only chance cable immediately." Finally, Henry followed his dealer's advice. "Buy using judgment," Folger answered.

But it was too late. Under the terms of the original agreement, Henry was required to pay £5,000 for the folio by the end of 1899— £2,000 in July, and the balance of £3,000 before January 1, 1900. It was now several days into the new year. Sibthorp had had enough. He told Railton to return Folger's money. He had changed his mind. He no longer wanted to sell the Augustine Vincent First Folio. On January 3,

1900, Coningsby Sibthorp wrote to Sotheran: "Will you be so good as to present my compliments to Mr. Folger and say that I have decided to keep the Shakespeare in my possession. Should he visit England and wish to see the Book I will try & oblige him." Sotheran cabled Folger the bad news: "Made firm offer owner finally declined."

Henry cabled to Sotheran a curt message saying that he expected the firm to send him the folio, which was still in its possession, and that the law was on his side: "I fulfilled my side of contract in sending money before January 1st Look to you to secure Folio." As a matter of law, Folger was wrong. His attempt to modify the terms of the original agreement was a counteroffer, which canceled that agreement. Sibthorp was no longer bound by it. And even if the agreement was still in effect, Henry had breached it by failing to pay the seller in full by January 1, 1900. He had given Sibthorp an out, and the piqued and canny Englishman took advantage of Folger's twin blunders to slip out of the deal. Henry realized that he had negotiated badly and had mishandled Sibthorp. He tried again, this time without haggling or impertinent conditions. On the contrary, he raised his offer to £6,000: "Railton see Sibthorp please explain I intended if Sibthorp unwilling to accede my request you should make payment completing purchase before January first. Pay now if necessary six thousand. Will keep purchase secret." Folger even added that Sibthorp could retain possession of the book for five years. Perhaps Henry intended this as an olive branch to appease his antagonist, or perhaps it was a stalling tactic to delay making final payment.

By now Folger was desperate to have the folio. He broke his self-imposed rule of privacy and authorized Sotheran to reveal his identity to Sibthorp, and even suggested that the owner should feel at liberty to make direct contact with him. It is doubtful that Folger meant this as a boastful "don't you know who I am?" gesture. He probably wanted to impress upon Sibthorp that he was a serious Shakespearian worthy of owning this great folio.

Sotheran tried to smooth things over but Sibthorp would not budge. In a letter to the firm dated January 9, 1900, he scolded Folger for his conduct:

As regards my Shakespeare it was Mr. Folger who was anxious to buy rather than I to sell.

If the book were not as perfect as he had been led to suppose from the perusal of Mr. Sidney Lee's article I should in no way have resented his declining to complete the bargain made between us—but he made a mistake, in my opinion, in suggesting that I should reduce the price and in asking me to allow the Book be sent to New York for inspection.

Furthermore, Sibthorp crowed, the book would be Folger's property now if only he had paid by the deadline: "I should have felt bound to have sold the Book to Mr. Folger had he paid me the £5000. Before the end of last year as we had agreed—now I feel at liberty to keep it and for the present intend to do so."

Sotheran was as eager as Folger to consummate the deal. There was much more at stake than the modest five percent agent's commission of £250 that the firm stood to earn upon the sale. At risk was not just this transaction, but also the future of Sotheran's lucrative relationship with a millionaire American collector who showed every sign of becoming the most important Shakespeare buyer in the world. Sotheran refused to take no for an answer and escalated its effort to capture the folio. The firm sent a long letter to Sibthorp on January 10 to persuade him that it had all been a misunderstanding, and that a malicious book dealer had unduly alarmed Folger with a false and slanderous attack on the folio's condition:

We beg to thank you for your letter of yesterday and must admit that you have some ground for feeling as you do. But we much regret it, for we believe that had not Mr. Folger been strongly disquieted as to the condition of the book he would never have raised any questions whatever before bringing the purchase to completion.

We therefore think it right to put before you a letter from him of November 8th last, in which he refers to the visit to him of a representative of a somewhat well-known firm in Pall Mall, who described the book in such remarkable terms as naturally to cause him great anxiety, so that even Mr. Pollard's eulogistic report failed to convey its true impression to him. We have no doubt ourselves that this visit was the sole cause of all Mr. Folger's later action.

Had you been able to see Mr. Railton he would have put before you the last message we have received from Mr. Folger in accordance with which we asked for the interview. We feel that we should now communicate it to you and do so as follows verbatim.

"New York, Jany. 7th 1900. Railton see Sibthorp please explain I intended if Sibthorp unwilling to accede my request you should make payment completing purchase before January first. Pay if now necessary six thousand will keep purchase secret."

We cannot but hope that these facts may put Mr. Folger's action in a much more favorable light.

In a nutshell, Sotheran's message was "it wasn't Folger's fault." And, after all, the letter implied, only a few days had passed since January 1. What harm would it cause Sibthorp to accept payment a few days late? Folger had offered an additional £1,000 in exchange for that courtesy, and to make amends. What Sotheran did not tell Sibthorp was that Folger had cabled the firm, asking it to refuse to return the folio to Sibthorp—"request not surrender . . . purchase." Sibthorp was unmoved by Sotheran's letter of January 10. He replied the next day:

I am obliged to you for sending me the enclosure for my perusal which I return—

I have been more surprised than pleased to read the very unfavorable opinion of Mr. Wheeler (of whom I know nothing) as regards my Shakespeare—I admit it was "disquieting"—Still there was ample time to communicate and receive your unbiased opinion as to the merits of the book before the date fixed for completing the purchase had expired.

I did not regret that the sale had not taken place but felt some resentment as regards the way I had been treated.

Sotheran's had, as proof of its tenacity, been copying Folger on all its correspondence with Sibthorp. Folger saw that the dispute had become about more than money. He had, however unintentionally, offended Sibthorp. Folger decided to try personal diplomacy. Perhaps if he wrote a letter he could assuage the Englishman's hard feelings. Henry explained his agitation upon learning of the two facsimile leaves, and said that his harsh complaints to Sotheran were never meant for Sibthorp's eyes. But then Henry went on to list for Sibthorp every nitpicky complaint he had made about the folio's condition.

Folger could not resist reminding Sibthorp that he had offered him "the largest sum ever paid for a single book," implying that Sibthorp should be grateful for this largesse. It is possible that Henry never sent the letter. The undated draft in his personal papers is unfinished, and ends abruptly. But it preserves Folger's state of mind.

In the meantime, Sotheran advised Henry by cable on January 13 that they "have done everything possible without avail" and will write to him shortly. In a letter mailed the same day, Railton informed him that Sibthorp "will not yield at present but I am not altogether without hope that sometime in the future we may be successful." The book dealer promised Folger "we shall not lose sight of your interests" but warned Henry "on no account must pressure be used. Mr. Sibthorp is not the gentleman to give way under it." Folger ignored the advice and applied the pressure. By reflex he resorted to a proven tactic of American business: if someone won't do what you want, then offer him more money until he does. He cabled Sotheran: "Use discretion about conditions including Sibthorp retaining possession for period paying up to eight thousand if necessary." It was the first in a flurry of telegrams they exchanged that day. Sotheran cabled back, telling Folger to calm down—"most strongly urge waiting till personal interview occurs." Impatient, Folger could not restrain his emotions. He wanted that folio, and he wanted it immediately. Not only had he raised his offer to £8,000, now he even offered to drop everything and sail across the Atlantic at once to close the deal in person. "Would my coming to London help," he cabled. Railton warned him that he had irked Sibthorp so much that the best policy was to watch and wait several months before daring to broach the subject again. "Effect of your visit quite problematical doubt whether would influence sale."

On January 16, Folger and Sotheran exchanged another series of cables. These telegrams read more like the stuff of Sherlock Holmes than William Shakespeare. "Strongly urge delay premature action fatal," cautioned Bookmen. Heeding the warning, Folger answered, "Bookmen. Gladly leave everything to you 8000 limit." Then he cabled a postscript: "Remember if necessary Sibthorp may retain book five years." Sotheran suggested that Sibthorp was an English *gentleman*; they knew better than Folger how to deal with such a man. In a letter dated January 17, the firm advised the impetuous American—for the third time—to be patient:

> Our advice strongly urging delay arose not only from the tenor of Mr. Sibthorp's letters, copies of which we sent you, but of our more intimate knowledge of the gentleman himself. Any further attempt on our part, just at present, would we feel certain prove fatal to your prospects of securing the volume; meanwhile the volume is still in Chancery Lane safe deposit and we propose awaiting Mr. Sibthorp's visit when he will probably take a different view (at least we hope so) after hearing our explanation as to the origin of the misunderstanding.

It was too late. Sometime between January 10 and 15, Henry Folger must have sent a letter to Coningsby Sibthorp, if not containing the exact language of his unfinished draft, then something similar. It prompted a reply from Sibthorp on January 20:

> I beg to acknowledge with thanks, the receipt of your letter. In reply I offer my sincere regrets that you would have been disappointed of your expectations.
> I do not think that any blame is to be attached to Messr. Sotheran. As far as I can judge they have acted—as I have always found them to do—straightforwardly in the matter. . . .

The gentleman (unknown to me, though he appears to have seen my Book) who spoke so depreciatingly to you about the Shakespeare & unwittingly induced you to delay completing the purchase within the limit of the date I had fixed.

I have just heard that Mr. Sidney Lee has been invited to Lincoln to give a lecture on Shakespeare. I cannot say I regret being in the position to grant the request which: I have reason to believe will be made me—to view my 1st Folio edition for inspection on the occasion.

With sentiments of my highest esteem,
    Coningsby Sibthorp

Sidney Lee! The name struck Folger like a dagger from *Julius Caesar*. It was Lee's article that had announced the discovery of the Augustine Vincent First Folio to the world, and that revelation, in Folger's opinion, had complicated his attempt to purchase it. No doubt Lee planned to also publicize the copy in his forthcoming *Census*, thus making it even more desirable to Folger's rivals. Two days later, before Folger could have received Sibthorp's letter by boat, he wrote *another* letter to him. Meandering, self-pitying, and long-winded, the missive exposed how Henry could no longer suppress his impatience or control his obsession:

It is not my purpose to burden you with continued correspondence about our Shakespeare. But should it never be my good fortune to come to an understanding by which I may purchase the book, I trust I may still make clear that I have aimed to deal in regard to it as one gentleman should with another.

Folger blamed his inadvertent insult on the actions of an "untrustworthy" book dealer who was eager to ingratiate himself to him. In the process the dealer, claiming firsthand knowledge, disparaged the condition of the Vincent copy by calling it a "beast of a book." Folger also explained that the recent death of his father-in-law and illness of his brother-in-law had distracted him from the Vincent deal and led him to write a letter to Railton that was less precise than Henry would have liked.

Henry had never invested so much of himself in the pursuit of anything. This was no longer a business transaction but a courtship, with Henry playing the role of the spurned suitor. Or it was a contest between gentlemen, fought not with dueling pistols on a field, but with letters. Henry, insisting that he had behaved honorably, pledged that he had not intended to insult or offend Sibthorp. He agreed that he should suffer for the misunderstanding, and hoped that the extra £1,000 would make amends. Sibthorp insisted that he had behaved honorably, too, and that he would have lived up to the contract if Henry had not tried to alter its terms or failed to pay by the deadline. Appeasing Sibthorp's resentment demanded a delicate touch. Sotheran admonished Folger that it required nuance and timing, and not the crude bludgeon of more money. For that reason Sotheran chose not to inform Sibthorp of the latest offer of £8,000. Indeed, giving the impression that Henry believed he could influence Sibthorp with money would only make him more intransigent. Henry must go along with the ruse that this was not about money, and that Sibthorp was above mere commerce. In miniature, the battle between them reenacted the larger cultural conflict between two worlds. Below the surface of the transatlantic trade in rare books and art treasures, there lay a more elemental struggle between American triumphalism and British decline.

Henry's personal appeal fell flat. Indeed, Sibthorp's reply of February 15, 1900, seemed designed to tweak and then torture Folger. The Englishman could not help but notice Henry's sleight-of-hand reference to the First Folio as "*our* Shakespeare" (italics added). Sibthorp would have none of it. The irritating American had forfeited all rights to the book. It was not "*our* Shakespeare" but "*my* Shakespeare":

Indisposition for this house has been suffering from a visitation of the Influenza which has been raging around us is my apology for the delay in acknowledging the receipt of your letter in which you explained fully to me the circumstances of your postponing to complete the purchase of my Shakespeare according to our agreement by the end of last year. Having once consented to accept your offer of £5000 (if paid within the specified time) I was prepared to keep my word, tho I was by no means anxious to part with my Folio.

That paragraph was designed to make Folger regret his actions. If only he had paid Sibthorp by the end of 1899, and had not demanded a last-minute return privilege, Augustine Vincent's folio would now be his. Then Sibthorp rubbed salt in Folger's wounds. He taunted the collector that the folio was even more valuable than anyone had imagined:

That you were misled in your opinion as to its true value is certain. In spite of Mr. Wheeler's opinion (Mr. W is unknown to me) I have now the best authority for believing my Folio is the most valuable from its size & interesting as a Presentation Copy, of any Folio known. Under these circumstances you will not be surprised that, with many thanks, I beg to decline £6000. The sum you now generously offer me for it.

Stung by the response, Folger failed to reply. Instead, he wrote to A. W. Railton on March 2 complaining that Sibthorp had rejected his generous offer of £6,000. Folger suggested that the folio was worth nowhere near that, or even the original price of £5,000. After all, no one else had offered to pay so much:

Of course we all recognize that the price named by Mr. Sibthorp did not represent the commercial value of the book, he did not so claim or intend. And we were ready to pay the price knowing that we could never sell except at a large loss. Mr. Sibthorp had named the price to others and we conclude received no response. The additional £1000 we now offer is the penalty we are ready to pay for showing any hesitation.

The American businessman could not comprehend the English gentleman's stubbornness. Why did he refuse to sell, when Folger had offered to pay much more than the book was worth, and far more than anyone else in the world was willing to pay for it? Folger was as baffled as if a driller had refused to sell him a barrel of crude oil at double the market price. It wasn't rational.

What Folger did not know was that Sibthorp was now troubled by concerns more profound than the sale of a book. Just days after his most recent letter to Henry, Coningsby Sibthorp's wife died of illness on February 19. It was she who had influenced her husband at the outset, telling Railton, "If we take the Cheque we may spend the money, but in taking the book we shall always have a treasure to look at."

Sotheran advised Folger to give up. Sibthorp had visited the firm, and both Railton and Mr. Sotheran had worked him over, but the widower still refused to sell. The dealers left Folger with forlorn hope. Sibthorp promised that if he ever changed his mind and decided to sell the book, he would offer it to Sotheran. With that, on March 20, 1900, Sotheran drew a check on Lloyds Bank of London for $23,783 and refunded Folger's money.

❧ Henry Folger's quest for Augustine Vincent's First Folio ended in bitter failure, but taught him several important lessons, and transformed him as a collector. He learned that there was a crucial difference between business and collecting. As an executive at Standard Oil, he had mastered the art of striking the best financial deal for the firm. If a particular transaction was not profitable, Rockefeller's vast wealth and resources made it easy to walk away from the negotiating table. There was always more oil to pump from the earth; there were always multiple suppliers; and there was always more kerosene to be refined. Standard never needed to buy one particular barrel of oil pumped from a particular well on a particular day. The supply seemed infinite. Whatever Standard wanted, it could buy in the open market. Henry Folger's experience with Coningsby Sibthorp taught him that the business principles that had served him well in the oil business could lead to disaster if applied to his pursuit of Shakespeare. Folger's misguided attempt to get the best *deal* from Sibthorp distracted him from his true objective: buying the best *book*. It had been a mistake to bargain over a unique treasure for which there was no substitute. Henry had lost sight of that and had allowed the most desirable First Folio in the world to slip through his fingers. He also learned that money did not always win the day. In business, no one said no to Standard Oil. There was nothing and no one that John D. Rockefeller could not buy, if the price was right. Sibthorp defied Folger's rational economic universe of supply, demand, and price. Folger had encountered a book, and a man, that money could *not* buy. The Sibthorp family had occupied Canwick Hall since the eighteenth century, and its current owner, Coningsby Charles Sibthorp, had been a magistrate and High Sheriff of Lincolnshire. His ancient lineage stretched back to Norman times and the Domesday Book. Folger learned how psychology, personality, and pride factored into the buying and selling of rare books. He also learned something about himself as a collector: no price was too high for something he treasured. He was willing to break all precedents and price records in his quest. Most important, from his failure he learned to never hesitate again when he had an opportunity to buy a great book.

The Sibthorp debacle intensified Folger's appetite for other fine First Folios. On April 6, 1900, just over two weeks after Sotheran refunded his £5,000, Henry wrote to the dealer, asking Railton to try to buy one of the finest folios in England, then in the collection of the banking heiress Baroness Burdett-Coutts:

> Some months ago, one of our New York book dealers said to me that he had been told that the Burdett-Coutts copy of the First Folio could be purchased. I paid little attention at the time as I had the Sibthorp copy in mind, and also because I felt that if there was any truth in the rumor you would know about it and would not fail to advise me. Have you heard anything, and if not can you make some judicious inquiries? Should you learn anything favorable, please get [first] refusal and advise me of the price. You know there are two copies in the Burdett-Coutts library. I will

be glad to secure both if the price is not prohibitive. This is not to displace any effort to get the Sibthorp copy. I am ready to buy all, at any figures not ridiculously high.

The phrase "I am ready to buy all" shows how far Folger had advanced as a Shakespearian. His quest for the Sibthorp copy had been a trial by fire from which he emerged a more aggressive and decisive collector. Now he was willing to digest three copies simultaneously: Sibthorp's at £8,000 and the two Burdett-Coutts copies at probably £5,000 each on average. His April 6 letter was one of several communications in 1900 between him and Railton about teasing folios and other important books in English private collections onto the market. Having lost the Augustine Vincent First Folio, Folger targeted the Baroness and began another long quest for her copies. On April 21, Railton posted a prompt reply and promised to chase down news of her folios.

Folger now asked Railton to pursue other folios and rare books all over England, whether or not they were for sale. If Sibthorp's hitherto unknown copy had turned up in a dusty coach house, who knew what other neglected treasures awaited discovery in the town and country houses of Edwardian Britain? The Vincent copy stirred up something inside Folger. Now he wanted to go after all the best copies, and the best libraries. The Vincent pursuit emboldened him—and its failure made him insatiable. Folger was also racing against a ticking clock. He feared that Lee's forthcoming *Census* would make it more difficult and more expensive to buy First Folios.

On December 29, 1900, Railton wrote Folger a long letter to bring him up-to-date on the results of his multiple inquiries. He reported that, as a general matter, Folger could no longer hope to operate in secret with Sotheran acting as his front man. "I cannot well advertise your wants in the trade here," Railton wrote, "as you are now well known to the majority [of dealers] as a collector and they naturally prefer to sell direct to you" and cut out Sotheran as the middleman. Folger's passion was affecting the entire market for First Folios and other choice books. "The leading auctioneers as well as their catalogues are in full sympathy with us and spirit me early advice of any good Shakespeariana," Railton reported, but "on account of the high prices obtained under the hammer they naturally do not care to sell privately."

Railton then advised Folger on the status of the best copies in private hands, beginning with the one owned by the dreaded master of Canwick Hall: "1st Mr. Sibthorp—you may quite rely upon his keeping his word to the effect that if he sells we shall have the offer. We are on the best terms possible with him and no opportunity will be lost should an opening occur of reminding him—unfortunately he does not require money."

Railton ran down the list:

2nd Baroness Burdett-Coutts copy since my interview with her secretary I consider the matter hopeless.

3rd The Ellesmere Collection: I am assured by the agent will not be sold during the life of the present owner; if any chance I should be in the market we shall hear early.

4th the Duke of Devonshire is too well off & his library is too well known to admit the possibility of its sale.

5th I know of several folios in private hands but there is only one where I have the slightest hope of tempting, should he consent I shall get a full description of each volume and advise you. . . . You are probably aware that a facsimile reproduction of the first folio is in progress and when issued will contain a preface by Mr. Lee.

And speaking of Sidney Lee, continued Railton, the bibliographer threatened to become a vexatious intermeddler in the market for First Folios. "Meantime he has appealed to owners of copies of the first folio to send him particulars for registration so that as far as possible the sale of copies for America or elsewhere may be stopped; of course we have no sympathy with this scheme at some time it will have a deterrent effect on owners selling who have registered, unless in the case of death or hard pressure for money." It was naïve of Lee—and Railton—to suppose that national pride and fear of shame would stop the owner of a First Folio listed in the *Census* from selling the book abroad.

For the next year and a half, from December 1900 until the summer of 1902, Henry Folger made no progress in his pursuit of the Augustine Vincent First Folio. By midsummer, Mr. Sotheran reminded Coningsby Sibthorp that Folger still wanted the book. On July 16, Sibthorp wrote Sotheran that now was not the time, but gave him permission to ask him about it once a year:

> In reply to your letter of July 14 I write first to assure you that you are always at liberty to communicate with me about any of my Books. At the present time there would be an outcry in my own family (& outside it) if I parted with the particular book you allude to, that I cannot entertain Mr. Folger's renewed offer.
>
> If it would be any satisfaction to him you are welcome to write to me once a year on the subject (say at Xmas time) to ascertain if there be any change in my views.

Despite Sibthorp's protestations, Folger's failure to close the deal in the fall of 1899 when he had the chance had left an opening for others to pursue the Vincent Folio. He was not the only collector who knew about the treasure, and it was only a matter of time before some other supplicant journeyed to Canwick Hall and knocked on Sibthorp's door. With each passing year, the value of the Vincent Folio climbed ever higher in Sibthorp's mind. In the meantime, English prejudice against American collectors ripened. On August 16, 1902, the *New York Times* published an article—"England's Shakespearean Losses"—encapsulating the resentment over the "well-known fact that Great Britain is practically drained of purchasable examples of the early editions of Shakespeare's plays" and of "the manner in which England is losing the most valuable memorials of her literature." The author of the article, Robert F. Roden, quoted an article by Sidney Lee, "The Shakespeare First Folio," which had circulated in England in early 1899:

Public sentiment ought to demand that whenever any specially valuable Shakespearean treasure, which should be regarded as a national treasure comes into the market, the Director of such a national institution as the British Museum should have funds placed by the Government at his disposal to enable him to enter into competition on something like level ground with American amateurs.

Roden, sympathetic to Britannia's plight, editorialized, "that was three years ago, and our bibliographical invasion of England has not ceased. Her losses during that time, particularly in the Shakespearean department, were never greater. Mr. Lee and the London *Times* may well ask themselves, 'What is the end to be?'"

Would that sentiment influence Coningsby Sibthorp? In the fall of 1902, Sibthorp, despite the numerous assurances he had given Sotheran and Folger, tested the market for his First Folio without telling them. Instead, he went to America's nemesis, Sidney Lee. By now Sibthorp possessed a copy of Lee's *Census*, which allowed him to compare the tantalizing qualities of his folio with all the other known copies. Its dual status as the tallest and only surviving presentation copy intoxicated him with delusions of monetary grandeur.

On October 25, before Lee sailed for America to examine rare books and meet important collectors, he wrote to Sibthorp, asking if his folio was for sale. Sibthorp wrote back on November 1:

I am much obliged for your letter of the 25th. I have received several offers to purchase my 1st Folio Edition of Shakespeare. An American gentleman (but not your friend Mr. Perry of Providence) offered me £6000 for it and I declined it. I do not wish to sell the Book. But if Mr. Perry (or anyone else) were to offer me £10000 I might be tempted to part with it.

Sibthorp had betrayed Folger's and Sotheran's trust. He had told Lee enough to expose Henry's identity—in 1902 only two other Americans, J. P. Morgan and Henry Folger, could possibly have been in the market for such an expensive book. Not only had Sibthorp hinted at Folger's identity, but he had disclosed the amount of Folger's confidential offer of £6,000, and he had all but offered to sell it to one of his chief competitors, Marsden Perry of Rhode Island. Perry, a collector driven with fervor and means that matched Folger's, must have thought the price mad—more than three times the highest sum ever paid for a First Folio—and declined to pursue the book.

Three weeks after Christmas 1902, on January 17, 1903, Railton mailed to Sibthorp what the dealer assumed was no more than the first of the dutiful, annual letters that Sibthorp had invited him to write concerning the First Folio. Railton had no reason to hope that the resentful eccentric had changed his mind. Sibthorp dispatched a reply that must have shocked and annoyed Railton. Without telling Folger or the Sotheran firm, he had put his Vincent Folio in play:

> During last year another American gentleman (not your Mr. Folger) inquired if I were disposed to sell the 1st Folio in the Canwick Library. I replied that I had been offered and declined £6,000 that I did not wish to sell it, but that if he would offer me £10,000 I would "consider the matter."

Had Sibthorp broken his gentleman's promise to sell the book through Sotheran? Railton wondered. Folger would never forgive the firm if the folio were lost. The next sentence broke the tension: "As I have heard nothing further from the said gentleman, he considers no doubt the price to be prohibitive. So do I." Sibthorp tried to reassure Railton: "I may add that I would not have accepted £10,000 without giving you the first refusal. You are welcome to continue to write once a year to inquire if I am still of the same mind." But how could Railton be sure? Why had Sibthorp all but offered to sell the book months ago to a third party for £10,000, but failed to offer Sotheran the same courtesy? What if one of Folger's rivals decided to actually pay this exorbitant, even absurd, price? Could Sibthorp be trusted anymore to not sell Sotheran out?

Railton was not going to wait another year to send an annual

Christmas supplication letter to Sibthorp. The distressing news demanded instant action. On January 22, Sotheran sent a coded cable to Folger. In the course of their dealings, Folger and Sotheran often used code words in their cables to keep the details of their business—names or dollar amounts—secret. Folger received the following message: "Bookmen to Folger. Isoscele might buy folio shall we offer." At this critical moment, Henry had forgotten the secret meaning of the word "Isoscele." On January 23 he sent an urgent cable to London: "Folger to Bookmen. Cable translation cipher word." Back came the cable: "Ten thousand pounds." This time Henry did not delay: "Folger to Bookmen. Buy without fail even at ten thousand cash." Then Henry made the mistake of adding one of his maddening conditions of the sort that had cost him the book in 1899. "But arrange time payments if you can." He could not resist the impulse to bargain, one last time, as a businessman. The next day Sotheran wrote to Sibthorp, explaining that after reading his letter of January 22,

> We felt it our duty both to yourself and to Mr. Folger to cable him about it at once. His answer as you see is as follows:—"buy without fail even at ten thousand cash but arrange time payments if you can, Folger." In spite of the last clause we now as his agents and what we believe to be his interest make you the offer of ten thousand pounds sterling (£10,000) cash on delivery of book to us.

Henry Folger had just authorized his agents to offer the highest price in the world ever paid for a book, twice the price the book had originally been offered at. As he waited in New York City for news, Henry must have played back in his mind the torturous low points of this quest. Would Sibthorp finally agree to sell him the folio? Folger could not tarry in Manhattan to await the answer—he had to leave town on business. On January 27, 1903, the cable from Sotheran arrived: "Bought for ten thousand payable within ten days please acknowledge. Bookmen." But Henry was not there to receive the joyous news. His wife, Emily, was. She knew what to do, and acted immediately. After the fact, she penciled a quick note to her husband in Buffalo, New York, telling him what she had done: "Henry C. Folger c/o UoCo Bflo. Cablegram reads 'bought for 10000 payable within ten days. Pls acknowledge.'—[I] have answered cable gram rec'd terms accepted. Emily C. J. Folger."

Coningsby Sibthorp had surrendered in a brief, anticlimactic letter to Sotheran dated January 26:

> The reply to your letter making me the offer of £10,000 on behalf of Mr. Folger for the 1st Folio Edition of Shakespeare in the library at Canwick I write today. I will accept it—On condition that the money is paid me within a week of my placing the Book in your hands. I purpose going to town the middle of next week. I will bring the Shakespeare with me. I request that the matter may be kept secret.

Given Sibthorp's prickly nature, Folger was prompt in cabling the £10,000 to Sotheran. He did not want to lose the book a second time. At the conversion rate of $4.873 per British pound sterling, the price, according to a memorandum to Folger from Brown Brothers & Co., 59 and 61 Wall Street, came to $48,732.50. Now only one question remained: would Sibthorp hand over the book, or would he find some excuse to change his mind again? Folger was eager to receive confirmation from Sotheran. The firm cabled that Sibthorp proposed to deliver the book on Wednesday, February 4. Then the dealers cabled Folger to say that Sibthorp had postponed delivery—for a day. Had he reneged? Folger must have wondered. Only a cable from Sotheran relieved Folger's anxiety: "Safely stored." Sotheran followed up with a letter:

> In Mr. Railton's absence for two or three days on business I have the pleasure to inform you as I already have done by cable that I today received from Mr. Sibthorp his copy of the First Folio of Shakespeare paying him at the same time the price of £10000, for which I enclose you his receipt. After you had cabled the money

he wrote saying that he would let £5000 remain until April if we would retain the book for him, but we felt that you would prefer to have it at your disposal at once.

The volume proved as good condition as when we last saw it and I at once took it to the Chancery Lane Safe Deposit, where we have hired a safe to hold it. . . .

For my own part I would add my congratulations on your securing the most interesting copy of the First Folio which as far as appears now is ever likely to occur for sale.

Henry had done it. After four years of torturous and delicate negotiations with a quixotic, temperamental, and indecisive seller, after infinite patience and indefatigable persistence, and after, of course, spending a great deal of money, the folio was his. As the most expensive book in the world, it was more costly than even the finest copy of the much rarer Gutenberg Bible, of which only fifty copies had been printed on vellum. Henry and Emily decided to make a triumphant trip to England to carry the Vincent copy home.

His purchase of the Vincent copy signaled his breakthrough as a great collector. He had learned the price of hesitation and quibbling. He had overcome the psychological hurdle that all beginning collectors confront: spending big money. Some collectors do not obtain their finest pieces until the summit of their careers. Folger achieved many of his greatest triumphs at the dawn of his quest. This was his seventh First Folio (W 59, F 1). Some collectors lose great objects because they take too long to hit their stride. They lack the confidence to recognize opportunities or the will to act decisively, even when they could afford the piece. They possess the financial resources but not the will to deploy them. Great opportunities come too early in their careers, and they do not act. They fail to realize that falling stars are rare, that planets rarely align. Henry learned these lessons early in the game. The Vincent acquisition reaffirmed Henry's faith in the free market and his belief in an inexorable economic truth. Despite unyielding pride, elaborate manners, a feigned indifference to wealth, and a pose of cultural superiority, an English gentleman could, in the end, once tempted with enough money, usually be induced to part with his treasures.

Henry Folger was about to "suddenly and secretly" transport his captive prize to America. Railton advised him that the American Express Company, incapable of "sending a parcel out of the ordinary way," was not up to the job. A special messenger would be too costly. Perhaps, suggested Railton, Henry could persuade an officer on an ocean liner—the purser or the doctor—to deliver the priceless package to America. Oh, no, replied Folger. After what he had endured to acquire this First Folio, and given its great value, he would not assume the risk of trusting his precious, hard-won volume to the hands of a shipboard official. There was only one safe way to transport the folio across the sea—he would sail to England and retrieve it himself. He informed Railton of this in a letter dated May 1, 1903: "I am now planning to come over to London for a few days early in June, for the purpose of bringing back the Folio."

There remained one piece of unfinished business between Folger and Sotheran: settling upon the firm's fee for the supreme effort it spent in capturing Coningsby Sibthorp's First Folio. When Folger or other collectors engaged dealers to represent them at auctions, the custom was to pay the successful agent a fee of five percent of the purchase price. Bidding did not consume an inordinate amount of a dealer's time, and participating in an auction did not involve long and protracted negotiations. But this transaction was different. Sotheran had invested a huge effort in Folger's cause—holding numerous meetings and conversations with Sibthorp, writing dozens of cables and letters to Sibthorp and Folger, and holding Henry's hand through four years of emotional negotiations.

In 1899, when Folger thought that he had bought the folio for £5,000, he offered Sotheran the typical commission of five percent. But that was for a deal that promised to be short and simple. Now, in 1903, Folger's triumph came after a marathon that had exhausted him and the Sotheran firm, especially his point man there, Railton. In a gallant gesture, Railton wrote Henry that the firm would allow him to set its fee. Folger sent a gracious reply:

I appreciate fully your kindness in writing that you and Mr.
Sotheran were disposed to leave to me the determination of a fair
commission for the purchase of the Sibthorp Folio. . . . If I do not
write more fully next week, we will decide the question when I see
you [in June].

In view of the superb quality of professional service that Sotheran
had provided, and given the spectacular result the firm achieved, it was
not unreasonable for Messrs. Railton and Sotheran to expect Folger to
express his gratitude and reward them with some largesse. They had
just seen him open his wallet and spend more money on a book than
anyone in history. Now they were about to see another side of Folger.
In Henry's files there survives a copy of the check from him to Sotheran, issued through Brown Brothers on June 11, 1903, "in commission for the Sibthorp Folio." The check was drawn for $2,438.75—or
£500. For all their work, Henry Folger had paid them only five percent
commission.

When the Folgers sailed to England to pick up the folio, they made
their first visit to Shakespeare's birthplace in Stratford, returning to
New York carrying the book in Emily's suitcase. Years later, when it
came time to assign individual catalogue numbers to all the First Folios
he had acquired, he designated this one as "Folger #1." He would look
back on this folio as his most difficult acquisition, but also his favorite.
By tradition, the finest copies of the First Folio often bear the names
of one or more of their noteworthy owners. Sidney Lee's *Census* had
called this folio the "Sibthorp Copy." Folger renamed it, but not after
himself—he was too modest for that. Instead, he declared that henceforth it would be known as the "Vincent copy," in honor of its first
owner. That homage offered the added benefit that never again would
Henry Folger have to speak the name Coningsby Sibthorp.

The Vincent Folio aroused Folger's most profound passions and
transported him through time to the moment of its creation. "We are
carried back at once," waxed Henry, "nearly three hundred years to the
splendors and struggles of the reign of Elizabeth and James, when
poets sang a glorious note, full-throated, when felonies were punished

by branding the hand that stole, and ears were shorn to discourage eavesdropping where royalty conferred. Such is the curious history of the Vincent First Folio."[11]

Henry's pride of ownership caused him to violate his own code of secrecy. An intensely private man, he rarely wrote for publication. But a few years later, in November 1907, he could not resist writing an article, "A Unique First Folio," for *The Outlook* magazine about the amazing history and rediscovery of Augustine Vincent's First Folio, which he heralded as "the most precious book in the world." Henry mailed the piece to Sotheran, which took the bookseller by complete surprise:

> I have within the last hour received . . . the two copies of your most interesting article on the Vincent First Folio. I was startled to see you disclose your ownership as we—and I, since Mr. Railton's death—have most scrupulously kept the secret; but you have certainly had a strong temptation to do so, as it is indeed as you say the most valuable book in the world. I see however that you still do not mention the price and that will still remain a secret as far as I am concerned.

The article, which revealed that the firm had discovered the book, startled Sotheran into believing that Folger had also identified himself as its owner. But a careful reading of the text shows that Henry never disclosed his ownership. On the other hand, why would an important collector write about the discovery of a book that he did not own?

Folger's purchase of the Vincent copy unleashed a flurry of First Folio buying. In May 1903, he bought three. The first, for which he paid $2,250 (W 75, F 17), was made up from at least two other copies, the title page fashioned of pieces of a Second Folio title page, with the portrait in the third state. That month he also purchased via Sotheran for $1,750 (W 114, F 56) a patchwork of leaves from multiple copies of the First Folio, almost every page remargined to a uniform size to create the illusion that all the pages had come from a single copy. Folger's last folio purchase for the month of May 1903, also from Sotheran for $1,250, is missing its preliminaries, but contains one rare and coveted page: the proof sheet for a page of *Othello*, with the proofreader's corrections (W 105, F 47). The mistakes include the deletion at the top of a page of the phrase "and hell gnaw his bones" from Rodrigo's speech, and a misprint ("neither lip") in Emilia's (Iago's wife) line, "I know a lady in Venice would have walk'd / Barefoot to Palestine for a taste of his nether lip" in the uncorrected proof.[12]

In June he purchased another two, for $825 (W 91, F 33) and $400 (W 106, F 48). The first contains its original title page, but someone cut out the portrait. Another engraving, removed from a Second Folio, has been inlaid in its place. This copy, acquired at auction through Sotheran, had sentimental meaning to Henry and Emily. This was the very volume used to make the Chatto & Windus facsimile—also known as the Halliwell-Phillipps facsimile—that Henry had bought for Emily early in their marriage.[13] The second was a ragged copy, described as "much tattered," lacking all preliminaries, and missing the plays *The Tempest*, *The Two Gentlemen of Verona*, *The Merry Wives of Windsor*, and *Measure for Measure*. In addition, pages were missing from *Antony and Cleopatra* and *Richard III*. This volume contained one prize: a proof page of *King Lear* marked with corrections.

Sometime in 1903, Folger bought another First Folio for $850 (W 103, F 45). It was another medley of genuine leaves taken from various copies of the First and Second Folios. The original Second Folio page numbers, which were not the same as the page numbers in the First Folio, were eliminated. And in December, he bought the cheapest folio he would ever acquire, paying just $220 (W 122, F 64) for an inferior, incomplete copy missing hundreds of pages. The preliminaries are absent, as are *The Tempest*, *The Two Gentlemen of Verona*, *The Merry Wives of Windsor*, and parts of *Measure for Measure*, *The Winter's Tale*, and *Titus Andronicus*. Perhaps it would be shorter to list which plays *are* complete. The pages that remain are cropped. Only a man in Shakespeare's thrall could have cherished this shabby relic. It had been a remarkable year in which he had bought his best copy, and several of his worst.

Chapter 8

❧❦❧

"A Shakespeare Discovery"

—*The New York Times*

IN OCTOBER 1904, *McLure's* published the last installment of Ida Tarbell's marathon, nineteen-part attack on the Trust. If Rockefeller and his colleagues were tempted to sigh in relief, Tarbell disabused them of that notion. The next month, in the most successful act of literary revenge in American history, she published a two-volume book, *The History of the Standard Oil Company*, which resuscitated all her charges against the firm. Her innuendos were visceral and hardly unbiased. Her hatred of Rockefeller had become an obsession, as intense as Henry Folger's obsession with Shakespeare. More than any other executive at the company, Folger knew how one book could change history. Tarbell had set into motion forces that would, over the next seven years, alter the destinies of Standard Oil, John D. Rockefeller, and, with them, Henry Folger.

In 1904, Folger was promoted to assistant manager of Standard Oil Works and he continued to collect First Folios at almost the same pace he had the previous year. In March, he purchased a copy for $1,100 (W 92, F 34) and in April he paid $2,625 for another (W 78, F 20). The first copy, bound in "crushed crimson morocco" by Bedford, a renowned English binder, was purchased from London booksellers Pickering & Chatto. During conservation, several damaged leaves were removed and saved. The copy was trimmed closely at the head margin, making it one of the shortest copies Folger owned. The second copy included the very desirable genuine portrait, in state two, but removed from another First Folio and inlaid in the title page. It is a made-up copy, containing leaves from one or two fragments of First Folios. Folger offered booksellers Maggs Bros. £515 for the copy, which they declined, having offered it to another American for £665. Apparently that sale did not happen, and Folger received the book from Maggs "on approval" for £550. In what would become a classic Folger move, Henry wrote out a nitpicky list of the copy's imperfections, and pointed them out to the dealer. They ultimately agreed to a price of £525. In July, on his annual summer trip to England, he acquired another copy for $1,254 (W 115, F 57). He saw it in Sotheran's shop in London in sheets, and asked that it not be bound. Hundreds of leaves had been replaced from another copy, pages had been remargined, and all the preliminaries were in facsimile. One of the previous owners had handwritten a list of characters appearing in *The Merry Wives of Windsor*. In November, he purchased from New York bookseller George H. Richmond his last folio of the year for $1,850 (W 104, F 46). One of the quirks of old books is that they may contain remains or traces of items belonging to previous owners. This copy contains the rusty outline of a pair of eyeglasses, once long ago left between the pages.[1] Their modest prices alone reveal that none was a spectacular copy. By now Henry knew that if he limited himself to buying only the best copies, he would end up with a very small collection of First Folios indeed. Compared to other iconic books such as the Gutenberg Bible, the survival rate of the First Folio was high. Only eighteen percent of the Gutenberg print run had survived, while more than thirty percent of the First Folio print run had survived. But that number was deceptive. Of more than two hundred First Folios, fewer than thirty-five copies are complete with the title page/portrait, all other preliminaries, and all text leaves.

The next year began with the emergence of another great Shakespeare rarity, one as exciting, in its own way, as the Vincent First Folio. On Wednesday, January 11, a brief story in the *New York Times* grabbed Henry Folger's attention. The headline proclaimed in boldface capital letters: "A SHAKESPEARE DISCOVERY." It was an era when papers followed news from the literary and rare book worlds with an interest nonexistent today. One never knew what amazing finds the newspapers might herald—an important presentation copy of the First Folio, a rare Shakespeare autograph, a hitherto unseen quarto, or the Holy Grail, a manuscript of a poem or play in the master's own hand. Folger's eyes raced to the follow-up headline: "Hitherto Unknown Edition of 'Titus Andronicus' Found in Sweden." So it was a quarto. The story was brief, just eight lines: "LONDON. Wednesday, Jan 11.—The Morning Ledger's Copenhagen correspondent reports the discovery at Lund, Sweden, of a book containing the text of Shakespeare's 'Titus Andronicus,' printed in London in 1594. The oldest edition hitherto known is the 1600 quarto." Henry cut the announcement from the paper and studied the little 1.5-by-2-inch clipping. If the story was true, this was an earthshaking discovery—the first printing of Shakespeare's first play. The existence of this 1594 quarto edition had been reported in the 1600s, but because no example had ever been found, it had been dismissed as lost or apocryphal.

The discovery attracted worldwide attention. Two days later in London, *The Standard* published more details in a long article headlined: "ROMANCE OF A SHAKESPEARIAN QUARTO. EXTRAORDINARY FIND IN SWEDEN." The story revealed that the book had been discovered in the house of a "countrywoman," which later gave rise to the myth that the quarto had been rescued from a Swedish peasant's cottage. The discovery was less romantic. A Swedish postal clerk in Malmö, Petrus Johannes Krafft, had inherited it.

"It is a find," reported *The Standard*, "that the most level-headed bibliophile can be excused for raving over, for no single copy of this first edition has ever been known to exist." The quarto's owner had placed it in the temporary care of the librarian of Lund University, who had alerted an English bibliographer to its existence. That man, so the story said, had offered £100 for it, which was refused. Then he offered £300. *The Standard* scoffed at these lowball offers: "But it would probably fetch much more—anything between £600 and £1,000." Quoting the unnamed bibliographer, the story warned readers that this cultural treasure might not find a home in Shakespeare's land: "Will it come to England? Yes, I expect so; but, I fear, not to stay. It will probably be put up at Sotheby's and find a home in America. It is a dreadful pity, but the British Museum can't afford to buy it at a high price."

The next day, on January 14, an article in another London paper followed up *The Standard*: "THE SHAKESPEARE DISCOVERY. THE 1594 QUARTO. PROBABILITIES OF PURCHASE." This story speculated that the discovery "will lead to careful search for further copies on the Continent, and stimulus given to inquiry by this discovery now it is hoped, have some valuable results." The article lamented that England had been picked clean of her Shakespeare treasures, by Americans no doubt, and that Europe was a better hunting ground: "Great Britain has been so thoroughly investigated by book collectors of late years that the Continent is now the likeliest place to reward the quarto hunter."

From the instant that Henry Folger read the *New York Times* story, he coveted the *Titus* quarto. Although he had focused on First Folios, as a careful Shakespeare student he was well aware of the importance and rarity of the various quartos. Quarto editions of some of the plays—including the first Quarto of *Hamlet*—existed in only one or two copies.[2] Over the last 311 years, no copy of the 1594 *Titus* quarto had ever turned up. This would be, Folger reasoned, his first and probably only chance to acquire one. But he was at a disadvantage. Sweden was thousands of miles away. He had no contacts there. At this moment, he guessed, European book dealers were already converging on Scandinavia. The book might already have been sold. His only hope was the London dealer who had, two years earlier, performed a miracle for him—the purchase of Coningsby Sibthorp's First Folio. If anyone could capture *Titus Andronicus*, it was Sotheran and Company.

Unbeknownst to Folger, Sotheran had already mustered its forces on his behalf. On January 14, Mr. Sotheran dispatched a letter to New York: "You will have doubtless ere this have heard in America of the find in Sweden of the First Quarto 1594, of Titus Andronicus. We enclose the cutting from the 'Standard' of yesterday which was the first public announcement." Sotheran had cabled the librarian at Lund University, asking if the book was still in his care, and if Sotheran might send someone to inspect it, in the hope of possibly buying it. "We have had no answer up [to] this present mail-time," he wrote Folger. The firm would stand by to rush a representative to Sweden. It was possible that another dealer had gotten there first, but Sotheran was not willing to concede defeat: "If, as we fear, the book is already in London you may trust us to lose no effort to obtain it; and we should not hesitate to go up to £3000 on your behalf. We beg to remain, Your faithful servants. H. Sotheran." Sotheran did not know that one of his London competitors, Pearson and Co., had already made an offer of £500, which was declined, and had then made a second offer of £650.

On the same day, at 9:40 AM, Sotheran cabled Folger one sentence: "What utmost offer will you make for 1594 Titus wanting only ten words." The book was in good condition, had suffered only minor damage, and had lost just ten words of the printed text. By "utmost offer," Sotheran meant that he would have one chance to make his best, highest offer. There was no time for Henry to indulge in complicated negotiations of the sort that had nearly cost him the Vincent First Folio. Folger would have one chance.

Later, Henry recalled the day he made his offer for *Titus*. He was, in 1905, or so he claimed, "an enthusiast whose means did not match his interest." That description, coming from the man who two years before had paid almost $50,000 for the Vincent Folio, the most expensive book in history up to that time, was an absurd understatement. But it confirms that Folger had not forgotten the frugal habits of his early, lean years. "It took [me] three hours of tramping over city streets to clarify a bewildered mind sufficiently to cable the answer, 'Two Thousand Pounds.'"

Sotheran responded the same night to Henry's offer: "Are doing our best for quarto letter follows."

Folger also received messages from other dealers. "During the next week," he reported, "another London dealer cabled he was about to offer me a superb Shakespeare gem, and a third dealer wrote he would soon submit the lost *Titus* of 1594."[3] Folger had no way of knowing whether they had beaten him to the volume.

After a few days of silence, Sotheran cabled Henry again at 11:12 AM on January 19: "Representative now in Sweden may need cash tomorrow when will cable doubtful two thousand enough." The owner had quoted a price of £3,000 to £4,000, but the Sotheran man whittled that down to £2,000 by promising immediate cash payment. Rival dealers were not prepared to back up their offers with instant cash. The next day, Sotheran cabled the outcome to Folger: "Bought cable immediately two thousand pounds direct to account of Jos Kraftt Riksbanken Malmo Sweden money must be paid today." Folger paid at once, transferring $9,762.25 to Brown Brothers of New York in exchange for their making the payment of £2,000. Sotheran congratulated Folger on his bargain: "There is no doubt it would have fetched a remarkable price . . . at auction." Henry knew it was true. A few months later he was offered three times what he had paid, and at one point he wrote, "Ten times Two Thousand Pounds would not be too much to expect should the treasure be now put on the market." If Sotheran had acted in its own interests, it could have purchased *Titus* on speculation for its own stock, and marked it up by a few thousand pounds before offering it to Folger, or another wealthy American. If pressed, Folger might have paid a fantastic sum, perhaps £5,000 or more, for the little book wrapped in soft gray paper covers. Instead Sotheran sent Folger an itemized bill for cable messages, telegrams, registered mail, and insurance fees for shipping the quarto to New York, plus traveling expenses to Sweden. This time Sotheran did not invite Folger to fix the sales commission: the firm billed him £150—7.5 percent—for its services.

Sotheran warned Folger that there would be publicity over the sale because Swedish sources had been talking to the press. And indeed, on January 27, a headline in *The Globe* broke the bad news to the people of England: "A SHAKESPEARE TREASURE FOR AMERICA." The British press lamented the loss of the unique first printing of Shakespeare's first play: "The copy of the first edition of 'Titus Andronicus,' 1594, recently discovered in Sweden, has been purchased by Messrs. H.C. Sotheran and Co. . . . and is now, unfortunately, on its way to America." The next day *The Standard* attempted to verify "the statement that . . . 'Titus Andronicus' . . . was now on its way to America." A newsman, the story revealed, had "communicated with . . . Sotheran . . . but could obtain no information as to the ultimate destination of the volume, the reply being—'We are not at liberty to give any further information on the subject whatever.'" To conceal Folger's identity, a spokesman for the firm lied to the press and claimed that the book had been bought for "stock."

The *Titus* episode taught Henry that not all publicity was bad—it could sometimes lead to good things. It was a newspaper article about Henry's recent and well-publicized purchase of the so-called Shakespeare Bible that caught the eye of a postal clerk in Sweden, and that prompted him to take a second look at an old English pamphlet in his possession. Maybe, the Swede speculated, it was worth something.

Today, looking back more than a century, Henry Folger's acquisition of the sole surviving quarto of *Titus Andronicus*, the first of Shakespeare's plays ever printed, stands as one of the greatest triumphs in his collecting career, and possibly as the greatest bargain he ever enjoyed. It was the first—and to this day the last—copy ever found. Henry described his coup as a "delightfully romantic literary rescue." And he waxed about his treasure:

> It proved to be a veritable nugget. It is in immaculate condition, clean, perfect, and in the original bluish-gray, soft paper covers, just as such plays were offered to the playgoers at the theaters for a few pence. How it ever reached Sweden will probably never be known, but its migration to America might never have occurred had there been a delay of even a few hours in the race to secure it.[4]

If *Titus* were to come on the market now, it might fetch several million dollars—as much as a fine First Folio of thirty-six plays. The *Titus* triumph alone would have made Henry's year, but he did not allow 1905 to pass without acquiring *any* First Folios. In March, he paid $1,350 for his twenty-second First Folio (W 89, F31), purchased from Sotheran, and then $7,250 (W 77, F 19) in November for another.[5] The latter copy had been given the name "the Tweedmouth Copy" after two of its former owners, the First Lord Tweedmouth, who had been a brewer, director of the East India Company, and a Member of Parliament, and his son, who had been a Member of Parliament and First Lord of the Admiralty in the late nineteenth and early twentieth centuries.

This same year also brought one of Folger's greatest controversies when, in a spectacular public struggle, all of England seemed to rise against him in an attempt to thwart his buying one of the nation's most cherished and historic First Folios. No other episode in Henry's collecting life better illustrates the Anglo-American cultural war over England's literary treasures. The controversy began when one Gladwyn Turbutt brought a copy of the First Folio to Oxford to show it to Falconer Madan, sublibrarian at the Bodleian Library. The binding had suffered unusual damage, and Turbutt might have wanted advice on repairing or rebinding the book. Gladwyn's father, Gladwyn M. R. Turbutt of Ogston Hall, Derbyshire, had discovered the volume in his family's library no later than 1902, where it had languished for 150 years. The senior Turbutt had reported its existence to Sidney Lee two weeks after the bibliographer had published his *Census* of 1902. Lee added the information to his files, but nothing about this particular copy seemed especially interesting.[6]

At the Bodleian, Oxford's expert on bindings, Strickland Gibson, examined the Turbutt Folio. The binding aroused his curiosity. It was very old, probably dating to the early 1620s, and thus appeared to be original to the book. That alone qualified this First Folio as rare and important. Gibson observed the odd damage to the cover—a long time ago the fore edge of the top board had been marred by a deep, unsightly gouge, as though something once attached to the cover had been ripped off. Gibson concluded that an iron clasp or staple had once been mounted there, and that the staple had been secured to a chain. In the 1600s it was common for libraries, including the Bodleian, to chain a volume to a bookcase to prevent theft. Such a chain was long enough to permit the reader to place the book on a shelf below and to read it while sitting on a fixed bench. It took Gibson only a few minutes to recognize certain idiosyncrasies in the binding—the techniques used to craft it, the color of the calfskin, the type of waste paper used to line the inside of the boards and spine—that identified it as the work of the master seventeenth-century Oxford bookbinder William Wildgoose. It was as obvious as if Wildgoose had stamped his own name on the cover. There was one more thing—in the 1620s, Wildgoose had bound a number of books for the Bodleian. Indeed, as Gibson examined Turbutt's folio, identical Wildgoose bindings sat on the Bodleian's shelves. The evidence pointed to one conclusion. The Turbutt First Folio had once been the property of the Bodleian Library. And if that were true, the book must be stolen property.

But had the library ever owned a First Folio? If so, how did it land in the hands of the Turbutt family? Falconer Madan dug into ancient records and discovered a handwritten entry in the Bodleian Binder's Book of 1624 proving that William Wildgoose had bound and returned to the library a copy of Shakespeare's First Folio. Madan also consulted the printed 1635 appendix to the Bodleian catalogue, which confirmed the presence of a First Folio in the collection. It was obvious how this folio had arrived in Oxford. In 1602, Sir Thomas Bodley founded the library that bears his name. By 1610, he had arranged for the London Stationers' Company to deposit with the library one copy of each book printed by its members, much like copyright law requires publishers to deposit copies of all books published in America. He declined to add plays to his shelves, describing them in 1612 as "idle books, and riff-raffs."[7] Sometime before his death in 1613, however, he must have relaxed that rule. In 1623, Jaggard sent one set of unbound sheets of the First Folio to the Bodleian. The library delivered them to Wildgoose, who bound them in 1624. According to Bodleian custom, the copy was then chained to a bookcase.

Falconer Madan discovered something else. A later Bodleian catalogue from 1674 did *not* include a First Folio, listing only the Third Folio of 1664. That evidence supported an inference that sometime between 1635 and 1674, a vandal had torn the First Folio from its iron chain and made off with the Bodleian deposit copy. If true, then the library might invoke the law to reclaim its long-lost, stolen property. But was theft the only plausible explanation for the folio's disappearance? Madan dug deeper and excavated a fact that supported a different conclusion. The Turbutt First Folio had not been stolen from the Bodleian Library at all. Instead, the library had judged it worthless and sold it. In 1664, upon their receipt of a deposit copy of Shakespeare's Third Folio, Bodleian curators branded their First Folio inferior and obsolete and sold it off in a group lot of other "superfluous" and unwanted books. Perhaps they reasoned that the Third Folio, which contained more plays, was superior to the First. The buyer, Richard Davis, bought the discarded copy for £24. Then the First Folio vanished from sight for almost two and a half centuries. Sometime in the 1700s, the book, its history long forgotten, came into the possession of the Turbutt family. Now, 241 years later, it had returned home.

A jubilant Falconer Madan brought the volume to the February 20, 1905, meeting of the Bibliographical Society, where it was publicly displayed for the first time since 1664. The years had taken their toll, and the folio showed signs of heavy use. Countless Oxford undergraduates had read the book in the forty years it had been chained to its case. Judging from the comparative damage to individual leaves, the most read and popular plays included *Julius Caesar*, *The Tempest*, *Henry IV Part I*, *Macbeth*, and *Cymbeline*. Suffering more wear and tear than any other work in the folio were the leaves of one play: *Romeo and Juliet*. And the most well-worn page of that play—indeed the most heavily damaged page in the entire folio—was the one facing the balcony scene in Act II, Scene ii. For decades, students enchanted by that romantic moment had rested their hands or elbows on the facing page and had actually rubbed through the paper. In condition, the Turbutt Folio was far from perfect. In romance, it was irresistible. Madan discussed his research, and proved to the satisfaction of all in attendance that this was indeed the missing Bodleian deposit copy of William Shakespeare's First Folio. His announcement caused a sensation. Only the Augustine Vincent Folio boasted such an ancient provenance. Indeed, of all the other known copies of the First Folio, none but Vincent and Turbutt could be traced back to their original owners in 1623. Four days after the meeting, *The Athenaeum* published the news.

It was not wise of Falconer Madan to publicize his discovery. His excitement had trumped his prudence. He was desperate to obtain the book for the Bodleian. Chief librarian E. W. B. Nicholson wanted the book back and offered to purchase it, but the Turbutts were not inclined to sell, hoping to keep it as a family heirloom. Furthermore, the library did not possess the funds to purchase the folio, which consensus opinion seemed to value at about £1,000, or about $5,000. No one knew that two years earlier Henry Folger had paid ten times that for the Vincent Folio. Coningsby Sibthorp had kept his word, and had not disclosed the sale or the price. No one in England—save Sibthorp and Sotheran—could imagine how valuable a special First Folio could be, or how much Henry Folger might pay for one. Madan's work had enhanced the value of the Turbutt Folio and had advertised the discovery all over the world, but he had failed to secure the book for the Bodleian. It would have been better to acquire the folio first, and only *then* publicize it. Madan would come to regret his naïve enthusiasm.

When news of the rediscovered Bodleian First Folio reached Folger, he decided that it would make a perfect mate to his precious Vincent Folio. Henry knew that if he could buy it, he would own the only two First Folios in the world that could be associated with their original owners. Folger suspected that the Bodleian must have already tied up rights to its former property. Still, it was worth inquiring.

Again, Folger turned to Sotheran, writing to declare his interest. Sotheran learned that the book was no longer in Turbutt's possession. It was still at Oxford. He had not sold it yet, but had left it at the Bodleian during meandering discussions about a possible sale to the library. In October 1905, perhaps reluctant to offend officials at the library, Sotheran called on Falconer Madan to assess the situation and gather intelligence about his intentions before making an offer on the book. To the firm's surprise, the Bodleian did not seem "keen" to pursue the folio. So Sotheran contacted Turbutt, who allowed them to call upon him. In the meantime, the firm advised Folger to prepare to make a high bid, adding that they hoped to acquire the book for a price "as low as possible." Henry cabled an offer of £3,000, close to $15,000, which Sotheran considered sufficient. Turbutt declined, but revealed that, although he had granted the Bodleian the first right of refusal on the folio, Sotheran's impressive offer had given him second thoughts.

On October 23, the firm cabled Folger that Turbutt would take one month to consider his offer. Sotheran believed—and advised Henry— that it would be difficult for the Bodleian to match his price. Folger agreed to wait until November 23, the day on which his agents had led him to believe he could quietly purchase the Turbutt Folio.

In mid-November, an article in the London *Standard* took Sotheran by surprise. The Bodleian had gone public. The story revealed that the library hoped to raise money to buy back its old folio, but editorialized that the cause seemed hopeless. On November 15, Sotheran mailed Folger a copy of the article. Near the end of the month, Turbutt informed Sotheran that he wanted to give the Bodleian more time to raise the funds, and declined to sell the folio on the agreed upon date of November 23: "I wish the Bodleian to become the possessor, or failing them, your client." Henry was furious. He dashed off an angry cable to his agents: "Offer for folio made for immediate acceptance cannot extend time cancel if not accepted." Henry, having second thoughts, followed with another cable on the same day: "Do not cancel if you think unwise." But Sotheran had already threatened Turbutt, receiving no reply. Then, on December 1, Sotheran reported outrageous news to Folger. Turbutt had extended the November 23 deadline for four months and given the Bodleian until March 31, 1906, to raise the £3,000. "This is regrettable and is doubtless owing to Mr. Turbutt's son being at present an undergraduate at Magdalen and mixing in literary circles at the University." Then Sotheran gave what would turn out to be fateful advice: "We doubt if a higher offer at this stage would be advisable."

Sotheran was wrong. This was precisely the moment when Folger should have dispatched the kind of cable he dictated when the Vincent copy was at stake: "Buy without fail even at ten thousand cash." A new offer of £5,000 or £10,000 might have compelled Turbutt to succumb. Instead, Henry heeded his agent's advice and did nothing.

Sotheran wrote again on January 6, 1906, giving Folger the good news that the library was nowhere close to raising the money. The Bodleian had less than three months left. On February 19, the *Lancashire Evening Post* reminded readers that the folio would set sail for America in less than two months, at the end of March. The article had little effect. Then, in a masterpiece of propaganda, librarian E. W. B. Nicholson reframed the Bodleian's predicament into a referendum on British patriotism by publishing a public appeal in the *Times* of London:

> Unless [the Bodleian copy] can be recovered there will be an indelible blot on our scutcheon. At present about £1300 has been received or promised in hundreds of subscriptions . . . but I do not think that they can raise the total to £2000. That after two and a half centuries we should have the extraordinary chance of recovering this volume, and should lose it because a single American can spare more money than all of Oxford's sons or friends . . . is a bitter prospect. It is the more bitter because the abnormal value put on this copy by our competitor rests on knowledge ultimately derived from our own staff and our own registers. But from so cruel a jibe of fortune this appeal may perhaps yet save us.

Nicholson tried to shame donations from Oxford men by taunting them that "*Cambridge* men have asked leave to contribute and so have men and women from *no* University" (italics added). Nicholson's appeal worked. On March 6, the *Times* of London printed an indignant letter from one Mr. Edmund Gosse: "Who is this millionaire? Why does he offer a sum three times larger than has hitherto been the market value of the book? Is he a private person? Is he a tradesman? Is he a syndicate? Does he offer his prodigious sum that he may add a treasure to his personal collection, or that he may sell again at a profit?" It was bad enough to lose the folio. But God forbid, Gosse implied, that this impertinent American be "in trade."

Snobs like Gosse and Sidney Lee might have asked why American collectors like Folger, Perry, and Morgan were so successful at buying English books. At public auction, books went to the highest bidder. Anyone could bid against the Americans. And the London dealers would have been happy to sell books to wealthy Englishmen. Henry Folger was hardly the richest man in the world. Many English gentlemen were wealthier, but not one of them devoted his resources to outbid him or the other top American collectors. Indeed, few Englishmen could be bothered to rally to the Bodleian's cause. The slow progress of Nicholson's fund-raising drive was excruciating, and many an Englishman who could have single-handedly saved the First Folio "in one fell swoop" sat on the sidelines in a studied pose of disinterest. In all of Great Britain, not one man or woman volunteered to put up the £3,000 necessary to ransom the Bodleian First Folio and save a national treasure. It was a national embarrassment. Because the English wealthy did nothing to interrupt the one-way, transatlantic trade in rare Shakespeariana, Lee proposed that the government intervene in the free market and provide the money that English gentlemen refused to give. But he was like a zealot preaching to an indifferent congregation.

Still, the Bodleian's cause acquired momentum among smaller donors. On March 13, 1906, the *Western Daily Press* echoed Nicholson's plea: "On every ground of national sentiment and literary expediency the volume that is now on the market should not be allowed to quit this country." Even in America, the *New York Times Book Review* attacked the "reprehensible American millionaire" who coveted this British national treasure.

Folger had never seen a campaign like this before. His most important previous purchases had been transacted in private, without public attention or pressure. Some of the English papers had groused about his purchase of *Titus Andronicus*, but the chatter did not amount to much, given that he was taking the book out of Sweden, not England. This was different. It was the time for Folger to confound his foes with a stunning cash offer, impossible to match. But on March 16, Sotheran reassured him that the campaign against him "up to to-day . . . had apparently not succeeded." The firm prepared to inform Turbutt that its offer was good until Monday, April 2.

On March 17, the *Morning Leader* newspaper went to battle and published a contemptuous cartoon depicting a nameless—and faceless—Henry Folger, dressed in a fancy suit and silk top hat, crawling on his belly in pursuit of the Bodleian First Folio. Surrounded by sacks of money, a fat roll of bills, and gold coins strewn upon the ground, the undignified American slithers through his spoils of English treasures—paintings and sculptures—as he grasps for the Bodleian's pride. Captioned with the boldfaced demand "WHO IS THIS MILLIONAIRE?" the cartoon reprinted from the *Times* Edmund Gosse's imperious questions about what kind of man dared to bid for England's prize.

By March 24, the Bodleian had collected just £1,967 in donations and pledges. Nicholson resorted to the London *Times* for a last appeal: "When this book is on the way to America, which I apprehend will be on April 2, some of you will agree with your paper that 'a grave scandal' has befallen, and will regret a mistaken confidence in other people's promptitude hindered them from averting it." He stated that it was too late now for small donations. Only gifts "from many men who can give hundreds [of pounds] without missing them" could ransom the folio in time.

On Thursday, March 29, the *Morning Post* published a notice that should have alarmed Sotheran. Folger's opponents were closing the gap:

> The fund to restore to the Bodleian Library, Oxford, its First Folio of Shakespeare has reached £2594. A London resident (not an Oxford man) has guaranteed £300 for himself and relatives. Just over £400 must now be guaranteed by the librarian by Saturday to save the volume for Oxford and this country.

It was an emergency, but Sotheran failed to cable a warning to Standard Oil headquarters in New York City. Instead, Sotheran asked Henry to cable only £3,000 to London so the firm would be ready to close the sale on Monday, April 2.

But on Friday, March 30, the *Times* of London announced a stunning reversal of fortune. A notice headlined "SHAKESPEARE AND THE BODLEIAN" carried a triumphant message from E. W. B. Nicholson: "The Shakespeare is saved." A handful of pledges, including £200 from Turbutt himself but foremost £500 from Donald Alexander Smith, Lord Strathcona and Mount Royal, High Commissioner of Canada, had put the Bodleian over the top. Nicholson admitted that not all the cash was on hand: "Nearly £1000 of the total is in promises, some of them running in terms which render payment a matter of uncertainty." But the Bodleian had done it.

Back in New York, Henry Folger knew nothing of these developments. He waited out the weekend assuming that Monday would bring a cable from Sotheran telling him that he had won the Turbutt Folio for £3,000. Just as he expected, a cable arrived on Monday, and he tore open the sealed envelope to read the good news: "Regret owner sold to Bodleian their subscription completed at last moment." Sold? How could this be? Sotheran had assured him that the situation was under control. The words stunned Folger. Perhaps, he murmured, the Bodleian did not deserve to get its copy back. It was the library employees' own foolishness centuries before that had led to the loss of the book in the first place. There was only one thing to do: apply more pressure. He sent an urgent cable to London: "Offer Turbutt 5,000 if transfer is not finally closed." He had just raised his offer from almost $15,000 to almost $25,000.

No further word came from Sotheran, so Folger retired on the night of April 2 not knowing whether his new offer had won the prize. The news came by cable the next day: "Transfer final." He had lost the book without having had his best offer laid on the table. And whose fault was that? Sotheran had underestimated the library's campaign and Folger had suffered the loss of the book. Few things can infuriate an obsessive collector more than losing a coveted object not because he could not afford it, but because a rival had outmaneuvered him. It was now in Sotheran's interest to convince Folger that his quest had been impossible from the start. After the Vincent Folio and *Titus Andronicus* triumphs, they knew they had disappointed him. They did not want to lose him as a client. The odds had always been against him, the firm explained in a letter of April 4. Remember, the firm told him, Turbutt was "an old Oxford man with his son present at Magdalen College"—the Bodleian was their sentimental favorite. And "with Lord Strathcona in reserve the Bodleian was bound to win." Sotheran tried to appease

Henry by suggesting that they had already obtained for him the best folio in existence, the Vincent copy: "The present matter leaves your own immeasurably finer and more interesting copy absolutely unique in the world."

Sotheran's consolations failed to assuage Folger's frustration. He wanted the Turbutt Folio and refused to accept defeat. On April 9, he cabled his agents to propose a bizarre scheme: "See librarian and offer 1500 pounds cash for privilege of having book in my collection during my life to be completely protected thus relieving subscribers making sacrifices. If I had purchased I would have willed book to Bodleian. Wrote you fully Saturday."

It was a strange cable. Sotheran had never seen Folger go to such fevered lengths to obtain a book. The cable concluded with an even odder concession: "If necessary book may remain permanently stored in London." In other words, Folger would not even demand that the folio be sent to him in America. He would be satisfied with the knowledge that he "owned" the book in the abstract without ever having it in his possession. This was a psychological portrait of the mind of an obsessive collector.

Sotheran called upon Nicholson, who rejected any arrangement with Folger. The librarian had the upper hand now, and he enjoyed playing it. He refused Sotheran the courtesy of examining the book, and would not even take it off the shelf. According to Sotheran, "He said that the Bodleian had determined to have the book six months before our offer, and . . . he had resolved to guarantee *any* necessary amount himself out of his private pocket." That was big talk for a man who just a few days before had not publicly pledged one pound of his personal funds to save the folio. Nicholson's "private pocket" was not as deep as Folger's, and an offer of five or ten thousand pounds would have exposed the librarian's false bravado.

Sotheran advised Folger to forget about this folio: "You can at least feel that everything possible has been done, but the fact that the matter has been made a national one would have stood in the way of an even larger offer." But Folger would not stop writing to the firm. His persistence caused Sotheran to send him its final letter on the subject:

"As I said in my previous letter, I fear we really never had a chance, even at the highest possible price, owing to its being considered a national matter." Folger came to his senses, realized that it was hopeless, and abandoned his pursuit of the Bodleian First Folio.

The *London Standard* assailed the gravitational force that American wealth exerted over Shakespeare rarities. When Sidney Lee spoke at an annual banquet commemorating the playwright's birthday he rejoiced that the Bard was more popular than ever "in the life of the nation" and that his fame "was one of rapid and triumphant advance." But Lee had detected a "discordant undertone," and the next day the *London Standard* reported his warning—the Americans were spoiling everything. "On the adverse side of the account must be set the recent triumphs of American collectors in stripping this country of rare early editions of Shakespeare's plays and poems—editions which had long been regarded among its national heirlooms."

Lee recited a roll call of lost prizes: "The unique first quarto of *Titus Andronicus*, which had lately been discovered in Sweden, was promptly secured at an enormous price by an American enthusiast." Indeed, England was losing entire collections:

> More lamentable was the sudden flight to the shop of a bookseller in New York of the surprisingly rich library of the late Mr. Locker-Lampson, of Rowfant. At one fell swoop the country has been deprived by this transaction of as many as twenty-seven copies of the lifetime editions of Shakespeare's plays, with much else of almost equal rarity and interest.

The Americans operated by stealth, Lee complained:

> Never in the history of English book collecting had this country lost suddenly and secretly such a treasure of Shakespeareana. . . . Before the officers of any public institution like the British Museum or the Bodleian Library, before any British private collector had any suspicion of their impending fate, these Rowfant volumes crossed the Atlantic never in all probability to return.

Lee was honest enough to point the finger of blame in the right direction—at wealthy Englishmen who had done nothing to save England's heritage:

> While we admired the superior enterprise of the American collector, we could not but grieve over the insensibility of our own rich men who allowed these heirlooms to leave our shores without making any effort to retain them here. One smaller and more flickering shadow had been cast across the brilliant page . . . of Shakespeare's fame.

Henry Folger's inability to acquire the Bodleian copy was the first time that anyone in England had ever defeated him in pursuit of a First Folio, and even then he had been outmatched, but not outbid.

Chapter 9

❧❦❧

"Do . . . Devise Some Way to Get the Books"

—HENRY CLAY FOLGER

NINETEEN HUNDRED and six was a slow year for Henry Folger's Foliomania. He bought only one First Folio. It was made up from several copies, and it came as part of a set that included copies of the Second, Third, and Fourth Folios. He acquired it through the Boston dealer Charles F. Libbie in February 1906, at $6,500 for the set (W 101, F 43). Such a pedestrian example offered little to compensate for his failure to seize the illustrious Bodleian copy.

For consolation, Folger turned to Shakespeare himself. For most of his life, whatever his circumstances or state of mind, Henry found in the plays relief, catharsis, pleasure, humor, and perspective. He kept a volume or two as almost everyday companions, and he was a faithful reader. He and Emily also loved live performances. Beginning in 1906, and for almost the next quarter century, her plain green buckram-covered diary—PLAYS I'VE SEEN—recorded more than one hundred of the performances that she, and sometimes Henry, attended. The diary provides a glimpse into the theatrical world of the late nineteenth and early twentieth centuries. Perhaps inspired by Samuel Pepys's diary of seventeenth-century London, her theater journal is a gifted amateur's record of the thespian scene, particularly Shakespearian, at the turn of the century in New York City and its environs. She did not limit her attendance to Shakespeare plays; many others, including *Peter Pan*, appear in her handwritten notes. She included her impressions as well as her husband's—"Henry did not applaud," she recalled one night. At a performance of *Hamlet* at the Garden Theatre in New York City, she found the play "well-acted & well put on as to costume & scenery to next to nobody in that barn of a theatre. . . . The audience was so small that one can expect, we fear, only a short run of the Shakespearian parts promised. . . . The Avenue and Street were filled with autos, taxis & hansoms for the Horse Show."[1] She made other observations too. Did the actors make good eye contact? Or an odd one, asking whether or not the actors were "lispers." Emily was keen on visuals and production values, and her diary teems with related questions: Were the costumes historically accurate? Were the theater acoustics adequate? Was the scenery "elaborate"? The final entry in the diary, dated February 5, 1930, mentions not a live performance but a film—the "talkie" *Taming of the Shrew*, starring Mary Pickford as Katherine and Douglas Fairbanks Sr. as Petruchio. It was the dawn of a great age to come for Shakespeare in the cinema. As always, Emily noted her companion for the evening: "[went] with Dick and self." (She was using her affectionate nickname for her husband.) Emily Folger found the film to be a bargain: "It is not Shakespeare, but . . . amazing what can offer for 35 cents per!"

Henry loved the culture and history of theatergoing. So he became an obsessive collector not only of the most rare and valuable books but also theatrical memorabilia, from Shakespeare's time to his own. He accumulated an enormous hoard of ephemera—advertisements, diaries, scrapbooks, cast lists, ticket stubs, broadsides, playbills, and more. Indeed, his staggering collection of playbills, none of them worth more than a few dollars each at the time he acquired them, includes more than half a million examples. This collection preserves a now priceless history of live Shakespeare performance over time. The material ranges from eighteenth-century pieces advertising some of the earliest performances of Shakespeare in America, to a glorious broadside announcing a one-night-only performance in New York City of *Julius Caesar* starring the three Booth brothers, Edwin, Junius, and John Wilkes.

The reappearance of one of Henry Folger's self-declared foes also made 1906 an inauspicious year. Sidney Lee published an updated version of his First Folio *Census*. This revised edition located an additional fourteen newfound copies, increasing the total from 158 to 172 as of May 24, 1906. He also amended for accuracy some of the entries in his 1902 volume. Henry Folger had escaped Lee's scrutiny in the late 1890s and early 1900s, but by 1906, Lee knew exactly who Henry was and must have grasped that he was collecting multiple copies of the First Folio. Indeed, Lee's 1906 *Notes and Additions to the Census of Copies of the Shakespeare First Folio* outed both Marsden Perry and Henry Folger. "Mr. Perry and Mr. Folger, are now the keenest collectors of Shakespeareana in the world. Mr. Folger is to be congratulated on having acquired in the last few years as many as eight copies of the First Folio in all—a record number for any private collector."[2] Lee was only half right. No other person *or* institution in the world possessed so many. America was a magnet for rare Shakespeariana, which worried Lee. His 1906 census warned, "The American demand for First Folios, which has long been the dominant feature in their history, has shown during the last three years no sign of slackening. It will therefore surprise no one to learn that [the] thirteen English copies [remaining in private hands] are now reduced to eight. Five of them have crossed the ocean during the past three years."[3] After such wistfulness, Lee groped for positive news. Thus, he could not resist sniping that "it is perhaps a matter of congratulation that, despite the recent activity of American buyers, the most interesting of recently discovered copies still remain in this country." Lee could have had only two copies in mind: the Bodleian and Sibthorp/Vincent copies. As far as Lee knew, Coningsby Sibthorp still stood watch over his copy at Canwick Hall. Indeed, crowed Lee, "only one of the 'new' copies which have lately found homes in America has any title to be considered of first-class rank." When Henry Folger read Sidney Lee's new census, the bibliographer's ignorance must have amused him. "The most precious book in the world," Augustine Vincent's First Folio, had been Henry's for three years.

Lee scored the competition like a cricket match, noting that Great Britain led the game with 105 folios, compared to America's sixty-two. But he detected an ominous trend. Between 1902 and 1906, eleven of Great Britain's First Folios had "suffered" passage across the Atlantic to new homes in the United States. Lee called the game for the Americans and predicted Great Britain's rout: "If the tide continue[s] running so strongly towards the West, the present ratio . . . will not be long maintained . . . of seventy-three copies which still remain in private hands on this side of the Atlantic . . . probably half . . . are destined during the next generation to adorn the shelves of private collectors in America." Lee guessed that by 1915, Great Britain and America would own eighty-three First Folios each, followed by the inevitable shift to American superiority: "No diminution of the American demand during the next quarter century looks probable at the moment. The chances are that at the close of that epoch the existing ratio of American and British copies, sixty-two to one hundred and five, will be exactly reversed." Time would prove Lee right. But in his wildest dreams, he could never have guessed that one man, almost single-handedly, would be responsible for the British reversal of fortune.

Folger was not amused when he read Lee's latest declaration of war against American collectors. It was that very sentiment that had deprived Henry of the Bodleian Folio he coveted. But Lee was oblivious to Folger's injury, and to the consequences of his disparagement of American collectors. During Lee's decades-long quest from 1900 through the 1920s to locate all surviving First Folios, he wrote to Henry several times, asking him to please reveal the number he owned and to complete census questionnaires for each one—he expected the American to help him. Folger, scoffing at the bibliographer's impudence, ignored every request. Without access to Folger's collection, Lee's third attempt at an accurate census, published in 1926, was fatally flawed. He estimated that Henry owned twenty-five copies. By that time, he owned more than seventy. Sidney Lee went to his grave in March 1926 never having seen Folger's collection, nor knowing how many copies it contained. At least three copies of Lee's questionnaire—all blank— repose in the Folger archives, as does a copy of an evasive and noncommittal letter from Folger to Sidney Lee's assistant, explaining why he had not yet replied.

In the summer of 1906, during Henry and Emily Folger's annual trip to England, they visited St. Paul's Cathedral. Emily, playing tourist, was fascinated that "anybody can see the crypt with tombs of Wellington and Nelson . . . and the hole where coffins are let down."[4] It was not the last time she contemplated how the English honored their heroic dead.

The year 1906 may have been one of Folger's worst periods for collecting First Folios, but a key acquisition in another field of Shakespeariana redeemed the year. A footnote published in Lee's revised census caught Folger's eye.[5] The Bishop of Truro, Dr. John Gott of Trenython, possessed a First Folio that he had inherited from his father, William Gott of Wyther Grange, Yorkshire. That was not the exciting news. In addition, Gott owned a choice collection of Shakespeare quartos as part of a magnificent library he had inherited from his family, wool traders from Leeds. "The bishop also tells me," Lee revealed in his proud footnote, "that he possesses a large number of original . . . quartos, including 'Hamlet,' 1611; 'Love's Labour's Lost,' 1598; 'Romeo and Juliet,' 1599; 'Midsummer Night's Dream,' 1600 (the two editions); 'Merchant of Venice,' 1600 (Roberts' 4to); 'Henry V,' (3rd edition), 1608; 'King Lear,' 1608, with some other volumes hardly less valuable."[6] Sidney Lee should have known better. His footnote sent Henry Folger on the hunt.

Folger asked Sotheran to send a representative to Truro at once to inspect the quartos. But, replied the dealer, they were not for sale. "This did not satisfy the eager American," Sotheran recalled after the episode. So he requested the dealer "to please send someone to sit on the Bishop's doorstep until he was admitted. In America such obstacles would be treated lightly, or ignored." Sotheran cautioned that English gentlemen did not conduct business that way. Folger scoffed at the idea that the dealer could not, in the collector's words, "without a letter of introduction, hope to see the books of a Bishop, and certainly not expect an interview with the great man himself." Perhaps the quartos were not for sale because no one had ever thought to ask the bishop to sell them. Folger, perhaps recalling the success of his fevered pursuit of Coningsby Sibthorp and the failure of his restrained tactics when chasing the Bodleian Folio, persisted. He urged the dealer to concoct a way to discuss the matter with the bishop. "Do," Folger wrote, "send someone at my expense, and devise some way to get the books."[7] Reluctant to approach Gott himself, the dealer broached the subject with the bishop's son-in-law. With his help, Sotheran was able to persuade the divine to sell eighteen precious quartos, closing the deal the day before the bishop died. Had the negotiations taken one more day, the quartos would have become entangled in Gott's estate, tied up in valuation, and not fallen into Folger's hands promptly, if at all. The Bishop of Truro episode reminded Folger that in collecting, time was often of the essence. As it turned out, the Gott estate called upon Sotheran to sell the rest of the bishop's collection.

Later in 1907, the firm's enormous, 120-page catalogue, *Bibliotheca Pretiosa*, described 595 items. Lot number 369, priced at £7,000, was a set of First, Second, Third, and two Fourth Folios "finely and uniformly bound in red morocco . . . by C. Lewis," a renowned nineteenth-century London bookbinder. Sotheran also listed a group of Shakespeare quartos, with eighteen of them designated as "sold" before the catalogue was mailed. These were the very ones secured for Folger by private treaty before the bishop's death. The preface to the catalogue mourned the diminishing availability of collections of such caliber, stating, "It is within the range of probability that the era will have come to an end."[8] The set of folios failed to sell, either through the catalogue, or in 1908 through the first of the Sotheby's auctions at which the remaining items from the collection were dispersed. Bidding did not reach the £3,850 reserve. Folger did not like it when dealers tried to tie the sale of a First Folio to a so-called set that included the three later folios. Describing the four editions as a "set" was a misnomer—they had not been published together, and were never a set in the first place. It was just a dealer's trick. Folger wanted Gott's First Folio, but not the later editions. He had already bought a four-volume "set" in February 1906. This time he sat on his hands. He would encounter the book again.

In 1907, during their annual trip to England, the Folgers went to Westminster Abbey, where they visited the tombs of famous actors and, no doubt, poets. Emily wrote in her diary: "Looked again and saw [Henry] Irving's tablet—small and square—by [David] Garrick's. His ashes are underneath."[9] Henry and Emily made a ritual pilgrimage to the final resting place of Shakespeare's Queen: "Saw Queen Elizabeth's tomb again," Emily noted in her diary. "Dick says it's worth dying to be buried in Westminster Abbey."[10]

That June, Henry paid $750 for an unremarkable First Folio, and in July, he paid $245 for another, remarkable only for its reprehensible state. It was one of the two least complete copies he would ever buy (W 90, F 32; W 124, F 66) with sixty percent of the leaves missing.

Also in 1907, taking advantage of a worldwide financial panic that J. P. Morgan tried to stem in a famous conference convened in the library of his New York City mansion, Folger purchased treasures from the collection of one of his rivals, Marsden J. Perry, the Rhode Island millionaire. It would not be the last time Folger pillaged Perry's collection.[11]

Meanwhile, Folger's career kept progressing. In June 1908, he was elected to the board of Standard Oil of New Jersey and appointed assistant treasurer. In this position, he prepared the company's annual financial report. Later that year, he was elected to the executive committee, which met daily to discuss company successes, problems, and policy. Folger's annual salary was now $50,000. In February 1909, he was elected a director of the Standard Oil Company of New York. That year, Henry began a two-year run during which he acquired a startling ten First Folios. In February 1909, be bought one for $3,500 (W 85, F 27). In March, he paid $2,200 each for a pair of copies that had belonged to Lord Jeffrey Amherst, namesake of his alma mater (W 83, F 25; W 84, F 26).

✺ By Henry's first year as a director, the federal government's anti-trust action against Standard Oil had worked its way through the lower courts and climaxed in a three-day oral argument at the Supreme Court on March 14, 15, and 16, 1910. The very name of the case—*Standard Oil Co. of New Jersey v. United States*[12]—irked Folger. On March 30, he replied to an encouraging letter from his favorite sea captain, John Robinson: "We get many communications like yours, hoping for a sat-isfactory outcome of the contest with the U.S. Government." Folger criticized the U.S. Court of Appeals for ruling against the company: "It seems to us that the decision of the lower Court, from which appeal is now being taken, was most unreasonable, not being at all sustained by the evidence and ignoring the position which the Standard attorneys took in its defense." He briefed Robinson on the inner workings of the case, suggesting that the March oral argument had been a waste of time because, due to illness, one justice had been absent from the proceedings, and another had died suddenly less than two weeks later, leaving seven justices and not a full court of nine to decide Standard's fate. Folger predicted that a shorthanded Supreme Court would not want to decide a case of this importance: "The Court undoubtedly had had no opportunity of studying the Standard's case, and certainly had reached no conclusions. This leaves the situation quite complicated, and it is not at all unlikely that the Court may ask for re-argument, and have it take place when the nine judges have again been put upon the bench."

Despite a titanic and distracting legal battle taking place between the government and Standard Oil, Henry found time in 1910 to pur-chase seven First Folios—the most he had ever acquired in one year. He started small with a $450 copy in April (W 107, F 49), and then a $3,060 one in July (W 116, F 58). That month, he also acquired the well-known "Hargreaves" copy for $10,200 (W 71, F 13), which he considered a bargain given the figure at which it had been offered to him three years earlier. On May 31, 1907, the Abel Buckley copy had sold at Sotheby's to London bookseller Bernard Quaritch for £2,400

($12,000). In August 1907, on one of his trips to London, Folger ex-
amined the copy, noting the book was "sound and unwashed." Quaritch priced it at £3,000 ($15,000), and Folger passed. Quaritch sold it
to Colonel Hargreaves in October 1907 for £2,850. He did not keep
it long. Sotheby's auctioned "The Property of Colonel Hargreaves" on
July 11, 1910, at which time Quaritch bought the copy back, this time
for just £2,000. Folger purchased it from Quaritch that month for
$10,200. By waiting three years, he had saved almost $5,000.

Ten days later, on July 21, 1910, Folger bought the Bishop of Truro's First Folio, removed from its set with the later folios, for $9,260
(W 67, F 9). Twice before, John Gott's copy had failed to sell, first in
1907 in Sotheran's catalogue and then in 1908 at Sotheby's. Packaging
it as part of a set had deterred buyers. The set of four folios was split
up for individual sale and the Gott copy came to the Sotheby's auction
block again, this time by itself. Quaritch won it for £1,800 ($9,000),
and passed it on to Folger the same month for $9,260. While conclud-
ing the sale to Folger, Quaritch told him "the Gott folio at £1800 . . .
is not so fine as the Buckley-Hargreaves copy, which I think you got
cheaply."[13]

Henry's acquisition of the Hargreaves and Gott copies taught him
the virtue of patience when pursuing some First Folios. It was not always necessary—or wise—to dash off in headlong pursuit of every de-
cent copy that came his way. No other collector was buying multiple
copies in bulk, and he could wait out the seller of an overpriced lesser
copy with little fear of serious competition. But if a spectacular specimen in superb condition, or one possessing an alluring provenance,
became available and attracted the attention of one of his rivals—J. P.
Morgan, Marsden Perry, Alexander Smith Cochran, Joseph Widener,
or Henry E. Huntington—Folger had to take immediate, decisive, and
expensive action. Even then he possessed a competitive advantage—no
other collector in the world knew to what lengths Folger would go to
obtain a First Folio that he coveted. Yes, he was obsessed with all copies
in degrees of mania. But his rational side managed to maintain control
over his checkbook. When Folger abandoned himself to the thrall of
a superior copy, however, as he had with the Vincent Folio, he was

beyond control. He was fortunate that no other collectors, dealers, or auctioneers, none of whom believed that a First Folio could be worth more than $15,000, discovered that he had paid $50,000 for one.[14]

Nineteen eleven was a landmark in the history of book collecting, the fortunes of Standard Oil, and the life of Henry Folger. The Supreme Court called for reargument in Standard's ongoing antitrust case. The arguments, lasting four days that January, were an epic moment for Standard Oil, and the destiny of American capitalism.[15]

In April, the world of rare books witnessed an epic event of its own. The great Hoe collection, one of the finest hoards of rare volumes ever assembled, went up for auction. It was the kind of ultra auction that bibliophiles feel lucky to see once in their careers. And the auction would take place not in London, traditional home of the most prestigious sales, but in New York City. It symbolized the shifting balance of power between English and American buyers. The April 24 auction attracted all the book-hunting luminaries of the day: Joseph Widener; Henry Widener; Beverly Chew; Belle da Costa Greene, the exotic personal librarian to J. Pierpont Morgan; the Maggs Brothers, the famous London dealers; George D. Smith, New York bookseller and Henry Huntington's operative; and Henry Folger. This cast of stars would never gather together in one room again. Soon disaster, death, the specter of the First World War, and changing times would bring this magical era in the prewar Anglo-American bibliophilic scene to an end.

At the Hoe sale, American buyers trounced their English cousins in the competition for the choicest lots. Indeed, noted the *New York Times,* "Few prizes went to London." Folger collected a prize for himself, a First Folio for $14,300 (W 65, F 7). The high point of the auction was Henry Huntington's purchase of a precious and most rare variant of the Gutenberg Bible, printed not on paper but vellum, for an astonishing sum. The *New York Times* of April 25 considered it worthy of a headline: "GUTENBERG BIBLE SOLD FOR 50,000." Newspapers around the world touted that the California millionaire had just paid $50,000 for the iconic volume—the highest price in the world ever paid for a book, so the stories claimed. Henry Folger knew better.

———

Three weeks later, on May 15, the Supreme Court made its own astonishing announcement. The nine justices, including Oliver Wendell Holmes Jr., filed into the Old Senate Chamber in the U.S. Capitol and took their seats behind their big, rectangular wood bench. Speaking for the court, Chief Justice Edward White announced that the justices had reached a decision in the case of *Standard Oil Co. of New Jersey v. United States*. Then, for nearly an hour, he read aloud the court's opinion.[16]

Seven men and a corporate machine have seized unlawfully the second greatest mineral product of this country, and are converting it into mountainous private fortunes. For the sake of the Republic, we now declare that this dangerous conspiracy must be ended by November 15.[17]

It was devastating.[18] The court found that Standard Oil's actions had been against the public interest, concluding that "the very genius for commercial development and organization . . . soon begat an intent and purpose to exclude others . . . from their right to trade." As a remedy, the court did not impose a massive fine, nor did it order the company to change its practices. Instead, it meted out the most extreme punishment: the Supreme Court sentenced the Standard Oil Company to death. It ordered the company to dissolve within six months, an absurdly short deadline for the breakup of the largest business in history.

In 1911, Standard Oil transported eighty percent of all oil produced in Pennsylvania, Ohio, and Indiana. It refined more than seventy-five percent of all crude produced in the United States. It owned more than half of all tank cars. It marketed more than eighty percent of all kerosene sold in the United States and exported more than eighty percent of the kerosene that went abroad. It sold to the railroads more than ninety percent of their lubricating oils, and owned seventy-eight steamships and nineteen other sailing vessels.[19]

Henry Folger rejected the flawed economic rationale underpinning the Supreme Court's opinion. "My own observation, which has been close, and has covered a long series of years," Folger wrote, "has satisfied me that the aim of the organization is to do its business in a straight-forward and strictly upright manner. It of course strives to build up its trade, and in doing so has to meet competition, but it has always both built up the trade and met competition in an honorable, business-like way." Folger had the insight that inefficient firms manipulated antitrust law to cripple their more efficient and successful rivals, thus serving their own interests, not those of consumers. Folger argued that govern-ment officials hoped to advance their careers by taking Standard's scalp: "Of course . . . the attacks [against us] have been largely occasioned by the ambitions of politicians, who hoped to gain favor in this way, and then by unsuccessful competitors who strive to cover up their lack of success by charging unfair methods by the Standard."[20]

Rockefeller was confronted with the most difficult business prob-lem of his life. How could he slice his company into pieces in a way that did the least possible harm and still comply with the Court's order? Folger, with his vast knowledge of all aspects of Standard's far-flung operations, was an important voice, second only to Rockefeller's, in determining how the company should be split up into thirty-four new ones. The dissolution of the Standard Oil Company, an embarrass-ing disaster for Rockefeller, presented a great opportunity for Folger. In a time of crisis, Henry Folger proved himself calm and indispensable. Henry Folger signed the announcement of the breakup on July 28. Later that year, he was appointed president of the second largest of the new companies, the Standard Oil Company of New York.

Acting as Rockefeller's cat's paw and funded with a loan from Stan-dard Oil, Henry Folger, acting in concert with other Standard officers, acquired controlling interests in Texas refining firms including the Na-varro Refining and Magnolia Petroleum companies. The purpose of these acquisitions was to circumvent scrutiny by a federal grand jury and the state attorney general of Texas of Standard's activities in Texas oil country. Through a convoluted series of complex legal and financial transactions designed to conceal this activity, Folger and Standard were able, at least temporarily, to shield the company from liability. As a result, Folger reaped a windfall: earning more than $650,000 per year in Magnolia dividends, and even more in capital gains when, in 1918, Standard began to acquire Magnolia stock from Folger. Eventually, an indictment was handed down, seeking to prohibit Magnolia from doing business in Texas and seeking damages, including $8.15 million from Folger. Ultimately, Henry walked away from the scheme without suffering any harm, and having netted hundreds of thousands in dividends, and even more in capital gains, all of which he deployed to finance his collection.

The monumental events of 1911 did not dampen Henry Folger's Foliomania. The only disruption to his collecting seems to have involved his annual summertime pilgrimage to England. On July 17, in a letter to Captain Robinson, he revealed, "We have had to give up our usual trip to London, as I did not wish to be away in view of the work to be done on the Standard Oil [matter]."[21] He still managed to buy five First Folios that year.

That fall, Henry planned to be a major bidder at a Sotheby's sale of the famous Huth collection, which included many fine lots of Shakespeariana. He and Emily combed through and annotated the thousands of pages of the auction catalogues printed for the occasion. In a masterstroke, an anonymous American intervened before the auction and made an offer for the best Shakespeare lots, an offer that proved too good for the seller to refuse. Hopeful bidders who arrived at the auction with their presale catalogues found, to their dismay, the coveted lots withdrawn. The *New York Times* reported the exciting news in a November 11 page-one story: "Shakespeare Rarities Sold, American May Have Bought Editions Withdrawn from Huth Auction." The *Times* revealed that "the Shakespeare Folios and quartos, numbered 1,187 to 1,228 in the catalogue of the Huth Library, have been disposed of by private treaty, and consequently will not be included in the sale at auction announced for November 24." The story teased readers with an air of mystery: "Both the name of the purchaser of the Huth Shakespeare folios and quartos and the price paid are at present a matter of speculation, but the general idea is that they will go to America." It was a secret move worthy of Henry Folger, but Alexander Smith

Cochran, not Folger, had staged the coup.[22] Alexander Smith Cochran, the America's Cup defender, had inherited thirty million dollars upon the death of his uncle, the carpet maker Warren B. Smith, allowing him to acquire his collection through the famed London book dealer Bernard Quaritch. The Huth sale continued in 1912.[23] Rare book collecting was front-page news, and the papers covered the competition the way they covered horse racing on the sports pages. After Cochran bought the Huth Shakespeare lots privately, *en bloc*, the *New York Times* offered its readers not just the story but a detailed, bibliographic catalogue listing every item in the collection. Despite being beaten out at the Huth auction, Folger bought two more First Folios that December, one for $2,500 (W 109, F 51), and a copy that had been owned by Thomas Hanmer, the eighteenth-century Shakespeare editor, for $6,650 (W 74, F 16).

In 1911, Henry's Shakespeare mentor Horace Howard Furness tried to tease his protégé into revealing his great secret: the number of First Folios he possessed. "Tell me," he wrote to Folger, "that I may have it in black and white, how many First Folios you have. I long to be pea-green with envy." When the scholar learned that Folger had forty, he nicknamed his favorite collector "Forty Folio Folger."[24]

By the end of the year, Henry Folger had achieved two landmark accomplishments. As a collector, he had reached the milestone of forty First Folios. His success would have stunned the literary world and possibly given Sidney Lee heart failure. But of course he kept it secret. All of England possessed just ten more copies than Folger alone. Nineteen eleven also marked a career milestone for Folger as a businessman. Now, as president of Standard Oil of New York, he commanded an important business enterprise. He took his place onstage with the other leading magnates of the age.

It was a time of great industrial fortunes built upon steel, oil, coal, railroads, banking, and manufacturing. When Mark Twain coined the expression "The Gilded Age" with his 1872 novel, he did not mean it as a compliment. Instead, he suggested that a paper-thin veneer of shimmering gold leaf camouflaged an underlying structure of crass, grasping corruption. It was a time of conspicuous consumption and dazzling displays of wealth. It was not enough to be rich; one had to burnish one's wealth with class, taste, and refinement—and material possessions. And so it was a time when larger-than-life American millionaires— Cornelius Vanderbilt, Henry Clay Frick, Andrew Carnegie, Benjamin Guggenheim, Isaac D. Fletcher, Elbridge T. Gerry, J. Pierpont Morgan, and others—built magnificent New York City mansions, summered at palatial seacoast cottages, and ravished the European continent for her cultural treasures. But by the time of Folger's rise, the first Gilded Age had passed, supplanted by a second era of wealth. In the 1890s, John D. Rockefeller, in a time of depressed land values, purchased four hundred acres in Pocantico Hills, a one-hour train ride north of New York City along the Hudson River. In 1893, he and his son John Jr. began to build and landscape a compound and small golf course on the property. The house, called Kykuit, Dutch for "lookout," overlooks the Hudson. John Pierpont Morgan (1837–1913), known as Pierpont, founded the United States Steel Corporation and J. P. Morgan & Co. investment banking institution. His son, John Pierpont Morgan Jr. (1867–1943), called J.P. or Jack, inherited the collection and made a public institution of the Morgan Library in New York.

The castles lined Fifth Avenue. William Henry Vanderbilt constructed the grandest mansion in New York City, at Fifty-First Street and Fifth Avenue. Elbridge T. Gerry, who collected thirty thousand rare law books, hired the famed architect Richard Morris Hunt to design his French fantasy at Fifth and Sixty-First. Isaac D. Fletcher collected Rembrandts and built a French Renaissance–style mansion at Seventy-Ninth and Fifth. Andrew Carnegie, steel magnate, purchased property a mile north of most of his colleagues, where land was less expensive. There, far from the concentrated development downtown, he had the firm of Babb, Cook & Willard build him a huge Georgian-style country house with spectacular gardens. Henry G. Marquand, who collected Van Dyck paintings, Roman bronzes, and Chinese porcelains, built a château at Madison Avenue and Sixty-Eighth. Henry

Clay Frick, Carnegie's partner and supplier of coke for the steel furnaces, collected all types of European art treasures, and in a physical expression of his symbiotic, competitive, and envious relationship with Carnegie, constructed a beautiful limestone mansion at Fifth and Seventieth that he is alleged to have vowed would make the steel magnate's home "look like a miner's shack."

Their foremost wealthy counterparts on the West Coast—publishing magnate William Randolph Hearst, railway and real estate magnate Collis Huntington, and his nephew Henry Edwards Huntington—also built magnificent homes and joined in the chase for treasures across the ocean: art, books, culture. Many other industrialists whose names are no longer familiar to us—sons of jewelers, carpet manufacturers; Marsden Perry, for example—also quietly built magnificent libraries, including some rival Shakespeare collections. Ocean liners departed English and French ports laden with the finest objects money could buy: paintings, sculptures, tapestries, furniture, arms, armor, entire period rooms, even entire buildings—some churches—taken apart stone by stone for reassembly in the States. And, of course, rare books and manuscripts; some of the finest English book collections ever sold went up for sale in those first twenty years of the century.

By 1911, Henry may have joined the world of the super-wealthy, but he was not like them. *They* built opulent Fifth Avenue mansions to advertise their success and announce their importance to the world. Folger and his wife lived modestly in a rented house in Brooklyn. *They* bought jaw-dropping works of art to show off their good taste and culture. Some bought rare books and built or purchased magnificent collections *en bloc*. Folger bought rare books that appealed not simply to the eye but to the mind. *They* displayed their collections in their mansions to awe their inner circle of elite guests. Folger showed off his collection to no one save his wife, and kept most of his treasures hidden—even from himself—in storage. *They* carried themselves larger than life. Folger went his way modestly. *They* reveled in their fame. Folger eschewed personal publicity. To *them*, amassing and displaying their hoards was the whole point of the game. To Folger, it was the beginning of a dream. *They* became case studies for Thorstein Veblen and his theories of conspicuous consumption and the leisure class. Folger stood apart as an outlier.

It was also a time of social change: the invention of the wireless, the mass production of the automobile, the rise of Teddy Roosevelt and the Progressive movement, and the sailing of the wonder of the age, that unsinkable luxury liner the *Titanic*. It was a time of fevered European nationalism, the First World War, and the explosion of American power when, for the first time in history, American armed forces set foot upon European shores to fight. And it was the time of the influenza pandemic of 1918, millions dead from war and disease, the Bolshevik revolution, labor unrest, and the triumph of industrialization in Europe, in North America, and around the world.

Henry James, the most astute interpreter of this luxurious age, a wealthy American riding the early wave of post–Civil War transatlantic tourism, was an observer of the differences between European and American experience. In his novels he wrote about the nexus of wealth and culture, commerce and taste, consumption and display. His brother, the philosopher and psychologist William James, understood what it meant to be an accumulator of beautiful, coveted things. He theorized that the impulse began in childhood:

> In education, the instinct of ownership is fundamental, and can be appealed to in many ways. In the house, training in order and neatness begins with the arrangement of the child's own personal possessions. In the school, ownership is particularly important in connection with one of its special forms of activity, the collecting impulse. An object possibly not very interesting in itself, like a shell, a postage stamp, or a single map or drawing, will acquire an interest if it fills a gap in a collection or helps to complete a series. Much of the scholarly work of the world, so far as it is mere bibliography, memory, and erudition (and this lies at the basis of all our human scholarship), would seem to owe its interest rather to the way in which it gratifies the accumulating and collecting instinct

than to any special appeal which it makes to our cravings after rationality. A man wishes a complete collection of information, wishes to know more about a subject than anybody else, much as another may wish to own more dollars or more early editions or more engravings before the letter than anybody else.[25]

In 1912, Folger purchased two more First Folios. In February, for $7,500, he acquired a copy from Alexander Smith Cochran that contained a rare proof page from *Henry IV* with corrections (W 108, F 50). That April, the sinking of the *Titanic* claimed one of Folger's competitors, Harry Elkins Widener, but not in time to prevent Widener from buying New York stockbroker William C. Van Antwerp's choice, complete, tall copy of the First Folio. Widener had engaged the famous Philadelphia collector, scholar, and dealer in books and manuscripts Dr. A. S. W. (Abraham Simon Wolf) Rosenbach to purchase the First Folio for him at Sotheby's on March 22, 1907. Rosenbach, aboard ship en route to the sale in London, had eliminated the competition posed by dealer Bernard Quaritch by engaging *him* to bid on Rosenbach's behalf, up to £5,000 ($25,000) for the volume.[26] Quaritch purchased it for £3,600 ($18,000) and Rosenbach sold it to Widener for $20,000.[27] After the *Titanic* went down on April 15, 1912, Widener's bereaved mother donated her son's literature collection, including the First Folio, to the Harvard Library.

A few months later, in July, Folger purchased a noteworthy First Folio for $13,750 (W 60, F 2). This fine copy contains the Droeshout portrait in state one, one of only three surviving examples in the world of that variant. It also has the last page of *Romeo and Juliet* crossed out by the printer. In 1913, Folger purchased four First Folios. In March, for $4,970, he bought a copy with a provenance dating back to the seventeenth century (W 110, F 52). In April, he acquired one that Sidney Lee described as "shabby, unrepaired" (W 81, F 23). Folger had first seen this copy at Pickering & Chatto booksellers in London in August 1907. In a letter, Henry expressed doubt about the authenticity of two leaves, but was in the end reassured by Pickering, and he bought the volume six years later for $4,850. On July 15, 1913, a copy sold at auction at Christie's for £273 and Folger bought it later that month for $3,950 (W 112, F 54).[28] In December, he bought a cheap copy for $255 (W 117, F 59), lacking the play *Troilus and Cressida*. The copy has a Plymouth Public Library bookplate in it with the handwritten note "7 days" crossed out and "not to circulate" in its place, implying that even as late as 1829 the library did not think the volume so valuable that it could not be checked out by readers.[29]

In the summer of 1914, a month before the outbreak of the First World War, the *New York Times* published a boastful headline: "England's Rarest Books Being Bought by Americans." The New World was maturing, and was stripping England—indeed, all of Europe—of its heritage. The culture that Europeans believed Americans were incapable of creating, they were buying. Wealthy American women, daughters of industrialists, were marrying titled but penniless princes and counts. One by one the best English private libraries—the fourth Earl of Ashburnham's, Henry Huth's, and so on—fell to the Americans. "The cream of those great English libraries dispersed within the last twenty years has come to this country," reported the *New York Times*.[30] European culture was for sale, and Americans were stocking up. Henry Folger continued to take advantage of the situation.

Throughout his time as an employee at Standard, Henry continued to buy the company's stock, which paid generous dividends. But that was often not enough. To finance his purchases, Henry frequently borrowed money from Charles M. Pratt, from John D. Rockefeller, and from numerous banks that Standard Oil did business with. The Folgers did not use these loans to support an extravagant lifestyle. They lived a frugal life in their rented Brooklyn home. A visitor there found it modest, but filled with "books, books, books!" They disliked crowds and turned down most social invitations and public events. But the Folgers were not recluses from their own families. Twice a year, Thanksgiving and New Year's, they held a kind of open house for extended family members. Henry had great affection for his siblings and, over time, arranged employment for three of his brothers at Standard Oil.

Henry Folger did not have the field of collecting Shakespeare to himself. And he was not the wealthiest collector—Henry E. Huntington and J. Pierpont Morgan, who spent a million dollars a year each on rare books, were far richer. But Henry Folger was single-minded in his pursuit of Shakespeariana. Other millionaires might want a high spot or two—a fine First Folio, a collection of the First through Fourth Folios, a group of trophy quartos—but Folger wanted it all, and related to Shakespeare only. Folger was not the richest, but he was the most single-mindedly Shakespearian, and he and his like-minded wife, Emily, were the only collectors who sought to dominate the First Folio trade. Folger's chief rivals were Huntington, Cochran, and, until he quit the game, Perry. When Huntington's agent, George D. Smith, bought most of the Earl of Pembroke's library at auction in London, it was a tough blow for Folger.

In 1914, Folger purchased two First Folios. That March, he directed Quaritch to buy one at the Sotheby's auction of the A. B. Stewart library. Henry paid £1,263, including the usual five-percent commission, plus £3 for expenses (W 118, F 60). The same month, the *New York Times* trumpeted a triumph by Henry Huntington that must have pained Folger: "HUNTINGTON TAKES DEVONSHIRE BOOKS."[31] This magnificent library, one of the most famous and prized in England, contained four thousand volumes, including one of each of the four editions of the folio and fifty-seven quartos. For decades, envious collectors and dealers had considered the Duke's collection unattainable. Indeed, in 1903, when Folger sent Sotheran a checklist of First Folios he hoped to acquire, the dealer told Henry to forget about it—the famous noble, rest assured, would never sell. Huntington paid an estimated $1 million to $1.2 million for the collection, causing the *New York Times* to speculate that the Californian's Shakespeariana would "now rival Folger," whose collection had "long been considered the best in the world."

In April 1914, Folger bought another folio for $15,500 (W 69, F 11).

This copy, the Beaufoy copy, bound in 1780 by the prominent binder Roger Payne, contained an invoice from Payne detailing the work he completed to rehabilitate the volume, at a total cost of £4 13s 9d.[32] That summer, Henry circulated word around Standard Oil that on August 11, he would receive an honorary doctorate from Amherst. It was to recognize his achievements in business. At the awards ceremony, Folger did not boast of his success or give advice on how to succeed in commerce. Instead, he touted his collection and advised the audience to study the Bard: "Collect Shakespeare, and you will soon find yourself in the very best company." From Rockefeller's home in Pocantico Hills, New York, came a letter addressed to Folger at Twenty-Six Broadway, dated July 25, 1914:

> Thank you for your letter . . . regarding the degree conferred upon you by Amherst College. I congratulate you upon receiving the degree, and that your connection with a great and useful business organization did not detract from your high standing. It begins to look as though it may not always be regarded as a crime in our country to be engaged in honorable business callings, even though the business is conducted upon a large scale.

Three years later, the titan still smarted from the Supreme Court ruling against his company.

In 1915, Folger, motivated perhaps by Huntington's Duke of Devonshire coup, concocted a scheme to extract more First Folios from English private libraries. Conventional wisdom had been that Devonshire would never sell. American cash had shattered that conceit. If a man in such a high place as the Duke was willing to sell, then, Henry decided, *any* Englishman could be induced to sell. Folger, as he had done many times at Standard Oil, drew up a detailed battle plan. In this case, it was to acquire additional fine, or not so fine, copies. He had managed to keep secret that he already owned forty-nine copies of the First Folio when, in May 1915, he wrote to A. H. Mayhew, formerly of Sotheran's, swearing him to secrecy, and requesting he make inquiries of thirty-five private owners of First Folios—whose identities had been exposed by the two Lee censuses—to determine whether they were willing to part with their copies. Folger still required a dealer to preserve his anonymity; as an American, and as an extremely wealthy man, his name might rankle British pride and drive up prices. Folger hoped to cut out the auction houses and other dealers, and minimize the competition he might face from other collectors if these copies became available on the open market.

May 17, 1915
Mr. A. H. Mayhew
56 Charing Cross Road
London, W.C.

Dear Sir:

I need one more First Folio to bring my collection where I wish it, and will be very glad if you can make some inquiries looking to securing another copy for me. If we cannot obtain a copy that is in pretty good condition, then I would be satisfied with two copies in poorer condition.

I give below a list of owners of First Folios, most of which are in rather poor condition, and will you please write each one of these owners and ask whether his copy is for sale, and if so what value he puts on it. As they are all described in the Sidney Lee Census it is not necessary perhaps to ask them to describe the copy, although it might be well to try and get some general idea of the defects in each case. This, however, may keep many from answering, so I would not make it too emphatic. In other words, let them say whether their copy is for sale and give a price for it, then, if they are disposed to do so, add something about the condition of the copy.

I of course will be glad to reimburse you for any expense you incur in this correspondence, or further inquiries you may think advisable, and would like to have for my files the answers you receive.

Earl of Carysfort, Elton Hall, Peterborough
Earl of Crawford, Haigh Hall, Lancashire

Alfred Law, Esq., Honresfield, Littleborough

William Phelps, Esq. Chestel, Dursley, Gloucestershire

R. J. Walker, Esq., St Paul's School, London

The Marquis of Bath, Longleat, Wiltshire

Francis Alexander Newdegate, Esq., Arbury, Nuneaton, Warwickshire

John T. Adams, Esq., Snathfield, Ecclesall, Sheffield

The Misses Williams Llandaff House, Pembroke Vale, Clifton,
Bristol

Sir Thomas Brooke, Bart. Armitage Bridge House, Hudders-
field

Mrs. Margaret Bulley Marston Hill, Fairford

The Rev. Sir. Richard Fitzherbert Dent, Tissington Hall, Derbyshire

W. C. Lacy, Esq. 52 North Side, Wandsworth Common SW

Sir Edwin Durning Lawrence, Bart., M.P.

Lord Leigh, Stoneleigh Abbey, Warwickshire.

John Murray, Esq., 50 Albemarle St. London

The Duke of Newcastle, Clumber House, Worksop.

Mrs. J. W. Pease, Pendower, Newcastle-upon-Tyne.

Major General Frederick Edward Sotheby, Ecton, Northamp-
tonshire

Michael Tomkinson, Esq., Franche Hall, Kidderminster

E. E. Harcourt Vernon, Esq., Grove Hall, Retford.

The Rev. Fulford Adams, Little Faringdon Vicarage, Lechlade

W. Hughes Hilton, Esq., Woodlands, Sale Cheshire

The Marquis of Northampton, Castle Ashby, Northampton

Alexander Pickover, Esq., L.L.D., Bank House, Wisbech

Lord Zouche of Parham

John Clause Danbury, Esq., Killian, Truro

Lord Forester, Willey Park, Broseley, Shropshire

T. E. Watson, Esq., Newpoet [sic], Monmouthshire

Frederick Haines, Esq., Boreham House, Hampstead

The Duke of Leeds, Hornby Castle, Yorkshire

Panlin Martin, Esq., Clock House, Abington-on-Thames

W. L. Martin, Esq., Ayton, Abernethy, N.B.

R. H. Wood, Esq., Sidmouth, Devonshire

Sir Everard Philip Digby Pauncefort Duncombe, Brickhill
Manor, Bletchley

It was a breathtaking, ambitious, and even audacious scheme. But audacity had conquered the Duke of Devonshire. Why, on smaller scale, could it not work for Folger? Three months later, Mayhew reported the results of the quest: complete failure. Not one soul had agreed to sell his or her First Folio. Not even the First World War, which had raged in Europe for the last year and drained Great Britain of men and treasure, could dislodge one. Henry, expressing his disappointment in a letter dated August 16, 1915, asked the dealer not to give up.[33]

With each letter Mayhew had included a blank penny postcard on which the recipient could dash off a typed or handwritten reply. In the course of time, Mayhew received no encouraging answers, only negative responses, which he forwarded to Folger. Many of the returned postcards contained only three words, "Not for Sale." That summer, a parson, the Reverend W. Fulford Adams, replied to Mayhew's inquiry. He had inherited a First Folio from his aunt in 1890. On one side of the postcard was Adams's return address, Weston-sub-Edge Rectory, Broadway, Worcestershire. On the reverse he had written, "Sir I have no intention of selling my First Folio Shakespeare." The small-town vicar was not about to part with his treasure. The reply, like all the others, frustrated Folger. But Henry Folger would never dispute what the vicar wrote next. "It is something," wrote Adams, "to have one."[34]

Chapter 10

"The False Folio"

THE "MAYHEW PLAN" had been an utter failure: It had resulted in no acquisitions. However, Folger was more successful the following year when in 1916 he purchased six First Folios: one for $870 (February, W 98, F 40), a pair for $3,000 each (in April and summer, W 120, F 62; W 97, F 39), one for $3,500 (W 121, F 63), another for $6,000 (March, W 119, F 61), and one for $6,050 (May, W 100, F 42). In 1916, a German submarine sank RMS *Arabia*, taking with it a precious cargo en route to Folger: twenty-five handwritten letters by David Garrick.[1]

Nineteen sixteen should have been a landmark year for Folger. That April, Great Britain and America commemorated the three-hundredth anniversary of Shakespeare's death with books, articles, pamphlets, dealer catalogues, lectures, performances, and exhibitions. Dr. A. S. W. Rosenbach, by now a famous bibliophile and dealer and not publicity-shy, crammed the display windows of his Philadelphia bookshop with Shakespeariana. The tercentenary unleashed an unbridled celebration of the playwright and the Anglosphere that he had come to represent. For the British Empire, mired for the past two years in the trenches of the Western Front, and mourning tens of thousands of her slaughtered sons, the anniversary served as a reminder that the civilization that had produced William Shakespeare was worth defending.

It was the perfect moment for Folger to come out from the shadows and claim his crown as the greatest Shakespeariana collector in the world. Instead, he observed the tercentenary by pretending that it wasn't happening. He stayed in hiding, determined to preserve the anonymity he refused to admit he had forfeited years earlier. He might have considered the anniversary a nuisance that threatened to distort the rare book market by raising the demand and prices of Shakespeare rarities. So he declined to participate in any tercentenary events. Henry gave no public talks, wrote no articles, and displayed no treasures from the warehouses where his collection was stored. He could have displayed a selection of rarities in the lobby of Twenty-Six Broadway, locked behind protective plate-glass floor cases under the eyes of Standard Oil watchmen. Or he could have lent a few of the highlights from his collection to a major exhibition at a museum or library. He received one loan request from an institution in his own city, the New York Public Library. He said no. In 1916, Henry and Emily honored Shakespeare with but a single gesture—a cash donation to help finance the conversion of an existing garden in Central Park to one dedicated to plants mentioned in Shakespeare's plays. It was the same public space that the three Booth brothers had sought, more than fifty years earlier, in 1864, to mark with a Shakespeare sculpture. Emily, enamored with all the plants and flowers mentioned in the plays, preferred a living memorial.

In the early twentieth century, Admiral Sir John Fisher tried to "Wake Up England!" to the threat of German naval expansion and superiority. During the war, he continued to urge First Lord of the Admiralty Winston Churchill to convert the British naval fleet from coal to fuel oil, emphasizing the advantages conversion would bring: smaller crews, lower costs, increased maneuverability, and a greater radius of action because warships could be refueled at sea. Churchill agreed to the conversion. The refining industry no longer produced just a valuable consumer good. It was now essential in providing a reliable source of fuel oil for Allied shipping. Oil had become a strategic military commodity. In 1916, Standard Oil launched the tanker SS *H. C. Folger* to transport fuel to Europe. The sinking of the Cunard liner *Lusitania* by a German U-boat in May 1915 helped propel the United States into the First World War. The mobilization of a large American army to sail across the Atlantic and fight a land war in Europe, using trucks, ambulances, tanks, airplanes, and other mechanized equipment, called upon the resources of Standard Oil of New York. The war effort added to Henry Folger's responsibilities, and in 1917 he purchased no First Folios. By March 1918, American troops had begun to arrive in France in sufficient numbers for the Allied Powers to arrest the momentum of Germany's last great offensive. By November, "the war to end all wars" was over. Historical events had not dissuaded Folger from collecting. The Panic of 1907 had not deterred him. The 1911 breakup of Standard Oil had resulted in a promotion for him and increased, not diminished, his wealth. Through 1914, Henry continued to purchase books in England, and indeed in 1916, the year of the Battle of the Somme, he purchased six First Folios. In 1918, he bought three more: a copy for $2,500 in April (W 99, F 41); one in June for $11,000 (W 80, F 22), one of the ten most expensive copies he ever purchased; and for $75 in November an incomplete set of loose leaves (W 123, F 65). The war had inconvenienced Folger in only a minor way: he had to pay for special insurance against the risk that steamships carrying his books from England to America might be sunk by German submarines.

In 1919, the war was over but the combatant nations remained in turmoil. The punitive Treaty of Versailles stripped Germany of its pride, its monarch, its military power, its colonies, and its prewar borders, thus setting the stage for the meteoric political rise of an unknown German army corporal and a second world war more destructive than the first. The Russian Revolution degenerated into civil war, "the Great Influenza" spread around the world and killed millions, and German society collapsed amid economic depression, strikes, civil unrest, and nihilism. But for Henry Folger, positioned in New York City at a safe remove from Europe's troubles, 1919 was one of his best years. He found no First Folios, but he was presented with the opportunity to acquire one of the greatest Shakespeare treasures of all time, one that rivaled in importance even the incomparable Vincent First Folio.

Folger's principal collecting rivals at the time were Marsden Perry and Henry Huntington. Neither one challenged Henry's supremacy as king of First Folios or attempted to acquire more than a few choice copies of that book. But in the field of rare Shakespeare quartos and other important English books, they threatened Folger's dominance. Huntington was newer to the game than Perry or Folger, but his appetite for quartos, combined with his almost unlimited financial resources, established him at once as a serious buyer. Soon he would spend on average one million dollars a year on rare books. By the time Huntington got into the game, Perry had already squirreled away some choice quartos.

Marsden J. Perry, financier and utilities and interurban electric trolley transportation magnate, was known by the nickname "Utility King."[2] Beginning his collection in the 1870s, Perry aspired to build the finest Shakespeare library in America. In 1891, by the time Perry was forty-one, he possessed a collection of Shakespeariana sufficient to warrant a "Preliminary List" of one thousand titles.[3]

In the late nineteenth century, Perry purchased a small Providence bank, and by 1894 had transformed it into the Union Trust Company of Providence. In 1897, he purchased the great Halliwell-Phillipps collection, which Folger had coveted, but could neither afford nor persuade John D. Rockefeller to buy. In 1901, when Perry built the Union Trust Company Building, he rerouted the trolley cars of his Union Street Railroad Company of Providence to the corner of Dorrance and Westminster, bringing "all of Rhode Island to the Union Trust's doorsteps."[4] As Perry became wealthier, his collection grew, fueled by, in the words of one observer, "obsession, challenge and competition." But the financial panic of 1907 hurt his interests, and he was forced to sell, through the offices of Sotheran and Co., the Halliwell-Phillipps copy of the First Folio. The buyer was Henry Folger. But Perry did not dispose of his best pieces, nor did he quit collecting. He viewed the events of 1907 as a temporary setback. For a number of years prior to 1919, Perry, like Folger and other collectors, had coveted the fifty-seven Shakespeare quartos owned by the Duke of Devonshire. They were Perry's Holy Grail. But in 1914, Huntington had acquired them all when he bought a major portion of the Duke's library. Crushed by this defeat, Perry announced that, without the Devonshire quartos, "My collection can never now achieve top rank and I think it time to sell it." Perry brooded over the loss: "If I can't have the Devonshires . . . I will give up collecting. I will not take second place."[5] What neither Perry nor Folger knew was that Huntington had a goal of his own in mind: the Devonshire quartos would make his collection of plays rival that of the British Library.

In 1919, Perry's failing health following a stroke, plus his continued disappointment over the lost Devonshire quartos, prompted him to sell the rest of his collection. He chose not to offer it at auction, which might have netted him the best prices. He could have also sold it *en bloc* to another collector with the hope of achieving close to its retail value. But Perry did not offer his library to Henry Huntington, Henry Folger, or any other private collector. Instead, in July, he sold it at a discount to the dealer Rosenbach for about half a million dollars.[6] The bookman gloated over his good fortune: "I [had] purchased the then finest collection of Shakespeare books in America." He was in the catbird seat to play Folger and Huntington against each other for ownership of Perry's best books.

The legendary Philadelphia bookseller Dr. Abraham Simon Wolf Rosenbach became "perhaps the only bookseller that has ever interrupted a meeting of the Executive Committee of the Standard Oil Company." Folger had been an "old and faithful customer" since 1903, when he became Rosenbach's "first customer."[7] Folger respected Rosenbach's intelligence and knowledge and the two shared a sympathetic enthusiasm for Shakespeare. The committee met at ten AM every day to discuss Standard business. Rosenbach was eager to find out which of the Perry treasures Folger was interested in acquiring. The dealer, informed by Standard underlings that the meeting could not be interrupted, proffered a card on which he wrote the news, and which was taken to Folger: "I have just purchased the library of Marsden Perry. Can you see me for a minute?" Folger, no doubt fearing the competition he might face from Huntington and others, rushed out of the meeting and asked Rosenbach, "Will you give me the first choice?"[8]

Rosenbach recognized that he had Folger at his mercy. For years, the oilman had quibbled over Rosenbach's high prices, often demanding discounts or refusing to buy at all. Now Rosenbach would offer Folger a Shakespeare treasure so exquisite that he knew that Henry could not refuse it. For this item, Rosenbach decided, he would charge Henry the highest price that had ever been paid for a book. He tantalized Folger with several of Perry's choicest items, and then offered what he described as "the greatest prize of the Perry collection." It was the earliest known compilation of Shakespeare quartos: the legendary Pavier Quarto—the notorious, pirated "false folio" published in 1619, and whose publication had been suppressed by the King's Men. The quartos had been assembled and bound at the time of their publication in a "charming fat little volume in plain brown calf, with the name of a well-known seventeenth-century book-buyer Edwin Gwynn, stamped in gold, on the covers."[9]

Folger responded to the offer exactly as Rosenbach had expected. Henry coveted this volume. He knew all about it—how Jaggard had printed these nine plays just three years after Shakespeare's death, four years prior to the publication of the First Folio; how the King's Men had enlisted the help of the Lord Chamberlain to prevent the publication of the Pavier Quarto; and how it was the first attempt in history to print a collection—albeit incomplete—of the plays of William Shakespeare. Folger also knew that the volume was one hundred times more rare than a First Folio—only two copies of the Pavier "false folio" had survived the vicissitudes of censorship and three centuries. It would, he decided, join the Vincent First Folio as one of the two most precious items in his collection. Folger was savvy enough to know that the dealer had him in the palm of his hand. Whatever stratospheric price the dealer asked, Henry would have to pay it. It was too dangerous to haggle. If Folger refused Rosenbach's price, Huntington would meet it.

The dealer informed Henry that of course the book was "priceless." Then he delivered the bad news: $100,000. The figure astonished Folger. It was nearly twice the amount that he had paid in secret in 1903 for the Vincent Folio. It was double the $50,000 that Huntington had paid in 1911 for a Gutenberg Bible printed on vellum, setting the public record for any book. It was the highest price ever asked for any item of Shakespeariana—for any rare book in any field. Rosenbach was shooting for the moon.

The price was so high that under different circumstances Folger would have haggled, using his favorite tactics of disparaging the price, making a series of counteroffers, and engaging in protracted correspondence. But there was no time. Henry Huntington, a far wealthier rival, lurked in the shadows. On July 21, Folger mailed payment to Philadelphia: "Enclosed please find check for $100,000.00 as agreed. You certainly did good work in putting the deal through, and are to be congratulated." For the second time in his life, Henry Folger had set the world-record price for a book. It was the most expensive thing he had ever bought.

On July 23, 1919, Rosenbach wrote to Folger, vacationing at the Homestead, in Hot Springs, Virginia, acknowledging receipt of $100,000 on account, against his bill of $128,500 for a total of fifty-seven items he purchased from the Perry collection. No price was recorded for the Pavier Quarto alone. On July 28, Folger wrote a second check, this one for $28,500, to the book dealer. Rosenbach, in his typical obsequious language, congratulated Folger for "obtaining, what I consider, the FINEST SHAKESPEAREAN VOLUME IN EXISTENCE, and upon which no price can be placed, namely the GWYNNE VOLUME of 1619."[10]

A week later, on August 1, Rosenbach courted his other major Shakespeare client by wiring Henry Huntington that he had just "purchased for stock" the Perry library. Rosenbach dangled before Huntington the "first offer of Shakespeare quartos not in your collection" which included "three of the earliest known published in 1591 and 1592."[11] Rosenbach, conjuring the illusion that Huntington would get the pick of the litter, insisted on secrecy as the Perry collection's sale was not yet public knowledge. "Please consider Perry purchase confidential," he requested.

Rosenbach, without revealing that he had already sold the single best item in Perry's collection to Folger, along with a number of other books, warned Huntington that time was of the essence: "Telegraph me at once as would like to give you first opportunity before offering elsewhere," he wrote to Huntington.[12] Rosenbach advised the railroad magnate that he was traveling to California, and asked whether he could visit him and show him a suitcase packed with treasures. On August 19, Huntington purchased eleven quartos from the Perry collection for $121,000.[13] Rosenbach also sold other items from the collection to collectors William Andrews Clark Jr. of Los Angeles and Joseph Widener of Philadelphia, who bought Perry's First Folio.[14]

Folger intended to keep secret his purchase of the Pavier Quarto, just as in 1903 he had suppressed all publicity surrounding his purchase of the Vincent Folio. Through the summer and fall of 1919, he kept his acquisition of the "false folio" out of the news. Then, on October 28, the *New York Times* surprised him with an unexpected headline: "FOLGER PAID RECORD PRICE. Standard Oil President Gave $100,000 for Unique Shakespeare Edition." The *Times* knew everything: "The Shakespeare collector, who paid the Rosenbach Company of Philadelphia . . . the record price . . . for the only known copy of the first collected edition of the famous dramatist's works, is Henry Clay Folger, Jr., President of the Standard Oil Company, of New York." The newspaper even added a bibliographic description of the book: "It contains nine quarto plays of Shakespeare and was printed in London in 1619, for Thomas Pavier by William Jaggard, who in 1623 printed the first folio." Then the *Times* revealed Henry's whole collection: "He owns what is regarded as the finest library of Shakespeareana in America, comprising more than 20,000 volumes." The publicity outraged Folger. Only one man in the world could have been the source of the story: Rosenbach.

One of the most compelling figures in the history of the rare book trade, Rosenbach had at least two personalities. He was a brilliant scholar of breathtaking range who had mastered the intellectual content and historical importance of rare books and manuscripts in many fields. The breadth of his knowledge allowed him to pounce upon treasures that had gone unrecognized or underappreciated by other dealers or collectors. He possessed an uncanny ability to recognize the connections that linked apparently unrelated books, an almost occult talent at discovering Shakespeare's printed sources and allusions to him. When dealing with wealthy collectors, Rosenbach adopted the persona of a charming, professorial, and obsequious courtier. He loved associating with captains of industry and enjoyed the splendors of their world, where he proved himself a delightful social companion and conversationalist.

Rosenbach had another side. To those he considered lesser beings he could be imperious, rude, bullying, or condescending. He ignored colleagues whom he dismissed as unworthy of his time, and scorned collectors whose resources did not equal the first rank of American bibliophiles. He possessed an American brashness that offended his British peers. He thrilled at placing exorbitant and unprecedented prices on the choicest items, believing that anything he consecrated should have special value simply because he said so. On one occasion, he bribed Henry Huntington's personal secretary to conceal from the millionaire a confidential list of the prices Rosenbach had paid for items he had inadvertently included in a shipment of books to California, fearing that his exponential markup would infuriate the railroad magnate. Like many dealers of the era, Rosenbach was not immune to exaggerating or on occasion even misstating the significance or condition of an item. Rosenbach was vainglorious and boastful, and he coveted publicity. As soon as Henry Folger read the *New York Times* story, he knew that Rosenbach had sold him out. As a client, Folger could not have been more different from Rosenbach. Folger wished to keep his purchases private, but Rosenbach could not restrain himself from bragging about the record prices he had received for the Perry treasures. Rosenbach was determined to make his handling of the Perry collection a historical event in the annals of bookselling. An article about the details of the sale would announce his success as a scholar-dealer, able to sell the most valuable parts of the Perry collection for more than $350,000 within three short months of purchasing it.[15]

According to Rosenbach's biography, one man, the wrong man, happened to read the leaked newspaper account of the $100,000 book. Rosenbach claimed that Folger recounted to him a cautionary tale. John D. Rockefeller, who on the golf course usually forbade all discussion of business, money, or philanthropy, cornered Folger on the links, admonishing him: "Henry, I see from the papers that you just paid a hundred thousand dollars for a book."[16] Folger demurred, claiming that the newspapers were prone to exaggeration. "Well, I'm glad to hear you say that, Henry," Rockefeller replied. "We—that is, my son [John D. Jr.] and I and the board of directors—were disturbed. We wouldn't want to think that the president of one of our major companies would be the kind of man foolish enough to pay a hundred thousand dollars for a book!" That was just a fraction of his total purchases from the Rosenbach firm alone. In fact, over a period of ten years he spent $1,388,990 with Rosenbach: $421,705 at auctions, and the rest from stock. The story may be embellished or apocryphal. It cannot be traced back to any original writings of Rockefeller or Folger. Moreover, it would be out of character for Rockefeller to have said such a thing, given his close relationship with Henry. Long before 1919, Rockefeller had absolute trust in Folger's character, prudence, and talent. He knew all about his protégé's Foliomania, having abetted it more than once with loan guarantees and personal banking references. It is unlikely he would have insulted Folger's business acumen based on his purchase of a rare book—whatever the price.

The *New York Times* was not finished publicizing what Folger considered his private affairs. Two months later, in an article published on December 18, it revealed Folger's involvement in the record-breaking auction of rare quartos at Sotheby's: "Henry E. Huntington said yesterday that it was for himself that [the dealer] George D. Smith paid $75,000 at the Britwell Court library sale at Sotheby's in London . . . for the fourth quarto edition of Shakespeare's 'Venus and Adonis,' bound with 'The Passionate Pilgrim.'" The *Times* reported that it was the highest price ever paid in England for a book, and exposed Henry as the underbidder: "His principal competitor . . . was Henry Clay Folger, who owns one of the finest collections of Shakespeareana in the world." The newspaper reminded readers that Folger still held the world record: "Henry Clay Folger, President of the Standard Oil Company, recently paid the Rosenbach Company of Philadelphia $100,000 for the first collected edition of Shakespeare's plays, dated . . . before the first folio of his works appeared."[17]

The coverage embarrassed Folger, and he denied its veracity. When a fellow Amherst alumnus, W. B. Mossman, wrote to Folger and enclosed a clipping of an article about his purchase of the Pavier Quarto, Folger lied about the price. On December 2, 1919, he dispatched a letter to "Dear Mossman": "Thank you for your notes with the clipping from the Transcript of Saturday last; I had not seen it. I did buy the book referred to, but paid only a fraction of the price named—as you doubtless had guessed, knowing me as you do. It hardly pays to deny such newspaper statements, as I find very few people notice them." Folger accused Rosenbach of exaggerating the price. In a sentiment unworthy of him, Henry blamed the confusion on Jewish merchants: "I have bought the book out of a collection which is being sold by a Philadelphia firm with some Hebrew members, who apparently think the only way they can justify the prices they are asking for other items they are trying to sell is by advertising this, which happened to be the best item in the library."

But the publicity would not die down. In the December 28, 1919, issue of *The World Magazine*, Stuart Baldridge mocked Folger's purchase:

> The price of books is evidently going up. But if any ambitious young author wishes to command fame by having his works sold at some figure above the famous $100,000, let him destroy all but one copy of his work . . . then die, moulder in his grave, and bid his soul be patient. For though he may starve in a garret while he lives, some future generation is sure to consider him "curious" enough to pay the price.

From the fall of 1919 through the winter of 1920, newspapers around the world circulated stories about the American collector who had paid $100,000 for a book. Even Folger's own college newspaper reported his purchase. *The Amherst Student* of February 9, 1920, head-lined the story "Mr. Folger, '79, pays record price for Shakespeare" and added that "Henry Clay Folger, Jr., '79, is the Shakespeare collector who paid . . . the record price of $100,000 for a unique copy of the first collected edition of the famous dramatist's works."

The April 10, 1920, issue of *The Literary Digest* criticized the pur-chase and damned what it called "bibliophilism"—"people who love books not for the literature but for love of title-pages, imprints and colophons."

Henry did not care what others thought. The newspaper publicity, and the chuckling in some circles that he was a fool to pay so much for a single book, did not cause him to question his judgment. He could always make or borrow more money. But he could never find another Vincent First Folio, a first quarto of *Titus Andronicus*, or a Pavier "false folio" again. Folger might agonize over a high price, and he was not too shy to bargain, but once he had a choice purchase in hand, he didn't second-guess himself, and never regretted paying too much. He regretted only the occasions when he had offered too little for a great rarity and, by failing to act decisively, had lost the book to a competitor. Although Henry hated the limelight, publicity offered certain benefits. After he became famous as the man who had paid the highest price in the world for a book, no canny seller in the world would offer a Shake-speare rarity for private sale without contacting him.

Oil and Shakespeare were not Henry Folger's only passions. He had a third one, which he shared with John D. Rockefeller: golf. Henry took up the sport as early as 1899. Glen Cove, on Long Island's Gold Coast, was the locus of many Standard Oil executives' homes, includ-ing the Pratts—*père et fils*—with whom the Folgers socialized. Henry and Emily joined the Nassau Country Club in 1899. In 1903, Folger won the Adams Cup in a member golf tournament. In 1926, he won a tournament at the Homestead in Hot Springs, Virginia.

Rockefeller played golf often as he began to step away from day-to-day operations of the company. He invited Folger to play Mondays at 10 AM, mostly at the Apawamis Club in Rye, New York, a short trip from the titan's compound in Pocantico Hills, near Tarrytown. Henry also played at Nassau on Saturday mornings, and eighteen holes in the afternoons. Rockefeller had the habit of rewarding accomplishments by friends and strangers with shiny dimes—when Henry sank a difficult putt, for example. Rockefeller presented the coins to tire mogul Harvey Firestone and to President Herbert Hoover. Henry and Emily saved a fistful of the dimes, and she had them fashioned into a silver bracelet watchband.

Folger played golf with the same quiet, understated determination that he applied to his business life. A small and slight man, he focused his attention on his short game. He invented a new kind of putter, and perhaps the highlight of his golf avocation was his appearance on the cover of the October 8, 1921, issue of *American Golfer*, which pictured Folger in his odd, signature stance, preparing to putt using a croquet stroke. Henry declared, "I've tried 'em all, and this is the best way."[18]

The private correspondence between the two oilmen reveals their love of golf, and their friendship. In a note to a messenger who would see Henry in person, Rockefeller wrote: "Please say to Mr. Folger, [that] Mr. Ferris and I just played Mr. Murphy and Mr. Inglish. We had a splendid game and beat them out of their boots. Hope the day will be pleasant and that we shall see you Saturday morning. Wish you could come tomorrow morning." Rockefeller often wrote letters to Henry telling him that he wished they were together. In a letter to Folger written from the links in Ormond Beach, Florida, in January 1919, Rockefeller said, "I wish you were here for a game of golf this morning. . . . I am just starting out." The last sentence of the note shows how much business authority Rockefeller had delegated to Henry and is shocking in its deferential understatement: "May I ask what the result of last year was, how much cash you have on hand, and if there is anything especially new?"

The month before Henry Folger bought Marsden Perry's copy of the Pavier Quarto, he discovered what he believed was another great treasure. In June 1919, he received from the venerable London bookseller Maggs Bros. catalogue #377, *The Drama and Music*. Scanning the booklet, Henry made note of several interesting but not spectacular books that he considered adding to his library. Then he spotted item 594. It was a First Folio. At first glance, it sounded like a humdrum copy. Maggs, a careful bibliophile, had described a number of condition defects, and the dealer also noted several missing leaves—important ones at the beginning and end of the book—that had been supplied in facsimile. From the description, it was obvious to Folger that many of his First Folios were superior to this copy in both condition and completeness. The price was cheap—only £850—and there was no apparent reason to buy such an inferior copy. Except one.

Despite this folio's imperfections, the Maggs catalogue described it as "a Copy of special interest, as probably it originally belonged to Samuel Gilburne, one of the celebrated group of Original Shakespearian Actors, as his name is written next to his printed name on the leaf 'Names of the Principall Actors.'" Indeed, the preliminaries of the First Folio did include a page that listed "*The Names of the Principall Actors in all these Playes*," including John Heminges and Henry Condell. On this page, the first name at the top of the second column of this list is Samuel Gilburne. We know little of him other than that he was an apprentice to, and was mentioned in the will of, Augustine Phillips, who is listed as the fourth of the "principall actors."

In this copy of the First Folio, in pencil beside Gilburne's printed name, someone had written "Samuel Gilburne" in an early—possibly seventeenth-century—hand, leading Maggs to speculate, based on the writing alone, without any supporting provenance, that the copy had belonged to Gilburne and bore his autograph. The tantalizing association excited Folger. He had a weakness for any object that could be associated with someone who knew Shakespeare, and he coveted any First Folio that could be traced back to its original owner in the 1620s. The Gilburne copy promised both. Only two copies in the world enjoyed the elite status of a provenance that reached back to the very year of publication in 1623: the Vincent Folio that Folger had acquired in 1903 and the Bodleian Folio that had eluded his grasp in 1906. *If* the Gilburne inscription was the actor's authentic signature, then this folio was the *ne plus ultra*—the only copy in the world that could be identified as having been once owned by one of the King's Men and one of Shakespeare's friends. Without the inscription, Folger might have dismissed the volume as unworthy of his collection. With it, he was willing to overlook its imperfections.

He cabled Maggs at once, placing an order for the so-called Gilburne Folio. He did not even try to knock down the price. Eight hundred fifty pounds—reflecting the poor condition of the book—was cheap enough. Indeed, Henry Folger considered it a bargain for a First Folio that had been owned by one of the King's Men. Maggs replied with bad news: the book had already been sold. The catalogue, which Henry did not receive until June, had been printed in May, and slow surface mail had delayed its prompt arrival. Someone else had received the catalogue first, and had already bought the Gilburne First Folio. It was not the first time this had happened, and it irritated him whenever it did. No matter, Folger resolved. More money should do the trick. He wrote a letter to Maggs on July 2:

I am very sorry indeed to lose lot 594 from your catalogue 377. I cabled as soon as the catalogue was received. A first Folio is directly in the line of my collecting. Can I get you to try to buy it back for me from the purchaser, even at a considerable advance in price? If it happens to have been bought by an American dealer kindly let me have his name and I will negotiate with him.

Maggs was happy to help such an important collector, and not reluctant to make an extra profit by buying and selling the book a second time. The firm replied on July 18: "We are making inquiries to ascertain if we cannot yet get it to offer you." Maggs failed, and in October, the book dealer told Henry that they had informed the buyer of his interest, and that "we are asking him to write direct to you."

On October 7, 1919, the New York City book dealer Gabriel Wells wrote to Folger, revealing that it was he who had bought the Gilburne Folio. Unfortunately for Henry, Wells had ordered it for a client, not for stock. Unbeknownst to Folger, Wells had acquired the volume for an American collector in Buffalo, New York, Colonel Charles Clifton, president of the Pierce-Arrow Motor Car Company. The book was already in the customer's possession.

In a letter dated November 11, 1919, Folger tried to buy it by disparaging its quality:

> As First Folios go it is a poor copy, as you doubtless know, having a number of leaves at the beginning and at the end in facsimile, but I think it has some special interest for my collection, so that I feel like still making an effort to secure it. Could you induce your client to let me have it for, say, $6000.00, which must be more than it cost him, and really much more than the volume is worth to anyone else.

Henry flattered Wells by telling him that he trusted his "judgment and expertise" on how best to get the book. He also offered to pay Wells "the usual 10% commission, of course," but Wells, hoping to curry favor with a millionaire collector and place Folger in his debt, demurred: "If it is in my power you shall have the Folio. . . . I would willingly waive any compensation for my efforts as I am anxious to please you."[19]

In January 1920, Wells offered Folger a "fine perfect copy" of the First Folio for $11,500 less ten percent. Henry seized on the offer as a way to get the Gilburne Folio. Suggest to Clifton, Henry told Wells, that *he* buy the perfect First Folio. Folger would pay $7,350 for the Gilburne copy, and if its owner put up just another $3,000, he could replace the Gilburne with a much finer copy.[20]

Wells wrote back, warning Folger that there was a psychological dimension to a transaction like this. "I shall do my best to secure it; but you know how people are when they are approached about giving back something which they bought. They at once get an exaggerated idea of value, and so the matter must be handled in a very diplomatic way."[21]

In March, Folger wrote to Wells about another copy that the dealer had offered him:

> Thank you very much for letting me see the Borden First Folio, it is a fine copy. Can we not make use of it to secure for me the

First Folio from the Maggs catalog. . . . This is certainly a very much better copy, and I should think a collector should prefer to have it. . . . I am willing to pay up to $6500 for the [Gilburne] copy, and if the owner were to use this sum towards buying the Borden copy he would have to pay only $2300 more to get an admirable volume. Can you not arrange this for me?[22]

Wells replied that now was not the time: "The gentleman has a serious illness which causes him to remain in the South until he recovers his health. You realize that it would not do to write him about this matter, and that the best way is to take it up with him personally."[23]

Then, on May 21, Folger received a telegram from Wells: "Folio exchange made. Sending volume tomorrow." Henry thanked the dealer for enduring months of pestering: "I am greatly obliged to you for the trouble you have taken, and the patience shown, in getting me the First Folio. . . . I enclose a check." It had taken almost one year, but once again, Henry had gotten his way. He believed that he now owned another great treasure—one of only three association copies of a First Folio in the world, and the only one alleged to be associated with a member of Shakespeare's King's Men.

Or was it? In 1920, when Folger acquired it, there existed no other known specimens of Gilburne's signature or handwriting. Thus, it was impossible to authenticate the signature in the book by comparing it against another example. The evidence supporting Gilburne's association was circumstantial at best. And the list of actors was an odd place to locate an ownership signature. Such a mark would more likely be expected on the first leaf, and not several leaves deep into the preliminaries. To this day, no other examples of Gilburne's handwriting have been discovered, making it impossible to verify that his own hand penciled his name in this First Folio. Indeed, there is no evidence that Gilburne was literate; many actors of the time could not read or write, and memorized their parts by hearing them read aloud. Today most scholars, skeptical of the evidence, doubt that the "Gilburne" Folio ever belonged to Samuel Gilburne. If not, then Henry Folger had made a huge mistake. In his zeal to obtain the copy, he had sacrificed a far superior First Folio to obtain an inferior one whose story was better than the book itself. Without that story, the book loses its magical resonance and falls to earth as just another flawed volume. The book still reposes in Henry's collection. Perhaps one day some new discovery will validate his high hopes for the volume's provenance.

Chapter 11

۞

"I Am an American"

—Henry Clay Folger

In the summer of 1920, Henry Folger turned sixty-three years old. He had worked more than forty years in the oil industry. He had begun his fourth decade of collecting. He looked ahead with excitement to the 1920s and to the next stage of his life. He could retire. Or he could spend the next decade doing what he had done since the turn of the century—advancing his stellar business career and pursuing his Shakespeare obsession. He was in good health. He could still work, and he possessed the skills and competitive drive capable of advancing him to the presidency and even the chairmanship of Standard Oil. And he still possessed the collector's insatiable appetite for more. He had already built a spectacular stockpile. Despite his penchant for secrecy, he was the most famous Shakespeare collector in the world. He possessed many more First Folios—fifty-nine—than any institution or individual, along with an overwhelming hoard of thousands of other rare books and manuscripts. If he stopped collecting then, his collection would still rank as the finest private collection of Shakespeariana in history. But there were always more treasures to pursue. Even the $100,000 Pavier Quarto, which many bibliophiles would have treated as the capstone acquisition of their careers, had only whetted Folger's appetite for more.

Henry Folger prepared for the final push that would propel him to the peak of his career and anoint him as a captain of American industry, and also secure his legacy as a great Shakespeariana collector. He saw a future filled with opportunities for even greater wealth and more exquisite books. But by 1920, he decided that in addition to his ongoing pursuits, it was time to act on something he had been thinking about for a long time. Henry Folger considered the future of his collection. What, he wondered, should he do with his vast and priceless hoard?

By combining his passion and wealth with three decades' worth of ingenuity, perseverance, and patience, Henry Folger had built the greatest collection of First Folios in the world, plus a spectacular literary and historical library of books, manuscripts, maps, broadsides, art objects, and ephemera from Shakespeare's time. And he was not finished. But now what? His friend Horace Howard Furness had pleaded with him to build a first-class home library: "Would that this taste of putting your books to their befitting use would induce you to stop piling up any more hard food for Midas. Build yourself a fine library wherein you and Emily may ensconce yourself into a corner, like a couple of industrious mice, and nibble at the contents of your treasures and let the rest of the world share in your pleasures."

Unlike other major American collectors, Folger had never built the monument expected of a man in his position: a grand Manhattan mansion with dozens of rooms and, of course, a spectacular library. Thus, Henry Folger had never enjoyed the collector's privilege of seeing all his books shelved together in one place. His eyes had never danced from spine to spine, shelf to shelf, and case to case, beholding in one sweeping, exquisite moment the sum of what he had achieved. It was the secret pleasure known to only the greatest collectors—that rapturous sensation when one experiences for the first time the joy of the *tout ensemble*, that instant when one realizes that the climax of a lifetime's passion has exceeded the sum of its parts—that you did this, and that no one, no matter how wealthy or determined, can ever duplicate your singular triumph.

Folger possessed the books, but no physical library to hold them all.

That unified library was an abstraction existing only in his imagination, and on the countless pages of his catalogues and inventories. Once Henry and Emily had stuffed the rooms and closets of their modest home full of Shakespeariana, they had to banish the bulk of their treasures to warehouses, perhaps never to be seen by them again. It would have required several thousand feet of shelf space to keep just their books at home, to say nothing of paintings, sculptures, tapestries, and more. Folger knew what he possessed, he could summon a mental picture of his books, but he had never seen all of his possessions together. But he had seen what could become of collections unanchored to a permanent place in the world once their owners died.

A man like Henry Folger was more than a serious collector. He lived through his collection. Such a man wants to possess his hoard forever, and he does not wish to part with it, even in death. The collection is a living thing that has its own demands. Folger knew what could happen if he died without a plan. The collection might be sold and dispersed. What he had devoted much of his lifetime to build, an auctioneer would dish out over a few days in public sales, serving as undertaker and gravedigger. Like Henry, the collection would die. His life's work would be obliterated. Death, taxes, need, greed, reversals of fortune, and familial apathy had eviscerated some of the finest art, antique, and book collections in history. Indeed, had Henry not benefited countless times by taking advantage of such calamities and feasting on the carcasses of many fine, once-loved libraries?

If Emily survived him, her passion, as profound and expert as his own, would carry on the collection. But with neither children nor a trusted protégé to succeed her, what would happen to the collection after *her* death? Henry had thought about the problem as early as 1910, when he was in his early fifties, after envisioning what kind of collection he hoped to assemble. Perhaps one day, he mused, he would build a library to hold all his books.[1] It would not be a private library in his home, but an incomparable resource, a public institution for scholars—a center of Shakespeare studies. In the years that followed, the Folgers mulled over the idea of what kind of library to build, and where they would locate it.

The two young couples: Charles M. Pratt (standing) and wife, Mary, and Henry Folger with wife, Emily (in dark dress). Henry and Emily's friendship with the Pratts lasted a lifetime.

Henry Folger at the height of his power.

24 Brevoort Street, Brooklyn, New York. Henry and Emily Folger lived in this house in Bedford-Stuyvesant while they amassed the world's greatest collection of Shakespeare's First Folios.

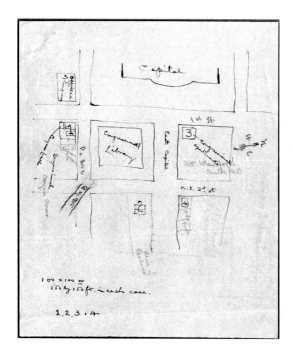

Henry Folger sketched a map of several possible Capitol Hill locations for the Folger Library. The United States Capitol and the Jefferson Building of the Library of Congress are prominent.

The *Morning Leader*'s "cartoon of the day" demanded to know what millionaire, with bags of money at his side, sought to outbid the Bodleian Library for the prodigal First Folio it hoped to purchase and return to its shelves.

Henry Folger, later in life, in a miniature portrait painted on ivory.

It took nine years and $317,000 for Henry Folger to acquire all fourteen houses on Grant's Row, just East of the United States Capitol building, which is visible in the background. The townhomes were soon demolished to make way for the Folger Shakespeare Library.

Henry Folger's unusual putting stance was apparently effective. Henry frequently played golf with his boss, John D. Rockefeller.

The Board of Directors of Standard Oil presented this engraved gold Tiffany bowl to Henry Folger upon his retirement. The quotation "Thy truth and thy integrity is rooted in us, thy friends" is from *Henry VIII*.

One of the nine John Gregory high-relief sculptures lining the front of the Folger Shakespeare Library. It depicts King Lear, the Fool, and Kent on the Heath. This is the only one of the Gregory sculptures Henry Folger saw before his death.

Looking east through the exhibition gallery at the Folger Shakespeare Library.

View from behind Brenda Putnam's Puck statue at the Folger Shakespeare Library. The United States Capitol is visible in the background.

Emily Folger in the Old Reading Room, gazing at the Salisbury portrait of Henry Folger. Henry holds the Pavier "false folio."

Exterior of the Folger Shakespeare Library, 1949, looking east along East Capitol Street. The John Gregory high-relief sculptures are visible along the front of the building.

A view from the balcony of the Old Reading Room at the Folger Shakespeare Library, circa 1949. The plaster bust of Shakespeare is visible on the far wall, and the Salisbury portraits of Henry and Emily Folger flank the niche in which their ashes repose.

Eighty-two copies of Shakespeare's First Folio—42 percent of the known existing copies—rest on shelves in the chilly subterranean vault at the Folger Shakespeare Library.

Sentiment could not be the only determining factor. Money would influence the choice too. Henry did not possess unlimited resources. He would always have to be much more careful with a dollar than John D. Rockefeller, Henry Huntington, or J. P. Morgan. Such a project would call upon Henry's business expertise: careful, hands-on management, a strict budget, and long-range financial planning. More than any other factor, the availability and price of real estate would dictate Folger's options. The location of the library was in no way predestined, and he considered a number of locations, weighing where his dollar would go further. In Amherst, Massachusetts, he noted, the real estate he needed would cost only $25,000. He also considered Nantucket, the ancestral family home of Peter Folger. The new University of Chicago, financed in 1892 by John D. Rockefeller, offered to construct a building to house the Shakespeare treasures if Folger agreed to donate the collection to the city.

Folger even considered Stratford-upon-Avon, Shakespeare's birthplace, but ultimately decided against repatriating his collection. "I am an American," he concluded. Perhaps it was a delicious retort to all the Englishmen who had for years scorned rich American collectors for pillaging Great Britain of her literary treasures. After all the trouble and expense Folger had gone to get them *out* of England, he wasn't going to send them back. He had not forgotten the Bodleian brouhaha, and its insulting newspaper articles and the accusatory "Who is this millionaire?" cartoon. Nor had he forgotten the lobbying campaign of that English pest, Sidney Lee, to prevent First Folios from falling into his hands. Returning his hard-won collection to England—as a gift, no less!—would be an admission that the critics were right, that America was not good enough for these treasures. No, Folger might have reasoned, England did not deserve to have them back.

After eliminating several locations, Henry focused on New York City. Sentiment favored the location—it was his birthplace and his home. Manhattan was a practical choice, too. It was a convenient and accessible destination for scholars, and New York was fast becoming a cultural center for museums and libraries. Manhattan also offered Folger unrivaled personal convenience. He could supervise the project from his Standard Oil office at Twenty-Six Broadway, and if he built his library close enough, he could make frequent trips to the construction site. But New York presented formidable obstacles; in no other American city would land prove more difficult and expensive to obtain.

In Henry Folger's private papers, undated holographic notes document his frustrated inquiries about Manhattan real estate. Most of the prime locations had already been developed. And few single lots were large enough to accommodate the size of library that Folger had in mind. He needed a parcel one city block long and half a block deep. That meant he would have to assemble a large parcel by purchasing multiple lots from individual owners of some of the priciest real estate in the country, assuming they were even willing to sell. Then he would have to demolish the existing structures, some of them tall commercial buildings, and break ground for the library.

Folger wrote detailed notes about several locations in Manhattan.[2] The most expensive, at $550,000, comprised a group of properties at Eighty-First Street and Fifth Avenue, across the street from the Metropolitan Museum of Art, and a short walk north on Fifth Avenue from coal magnate Henry Clay Frick's mansion, and also a short walk south from steel magnate Andrew Carnegie's recently completed Fifth Avenue palace.

Folger engaged brokers to attempt to assemble parcels on Fifth Avenue between Eighty-First and Eighty-Third Streets. His hand-drawn map of the layout of the avenue documents his attention to detail. Gould House is prominently marked on the map drawn in his own hand. Less than a mile down Fifth Avenue from the Carnegie Mansion, and a short walk from Frick's, was the mansion of the son of scion Jay Gould, one of the Gilded Age's barons of business who controlled Western Union Telegraph, the New York Elevated Railroad, and the Union Pacific Railroad. He was as despised an industrialist as Rockefeller. If Folger could acquire the property, he would not live in the home that stood there. He would do what Frick had done to the Lenox Library: tear it down and replace it with something bigger, more suited to his purpose.

But every New York location that Folger considered suitable suffered from the same defect: the real estate was too expensive. He had hoped to spend no more than one million dollars on the entire project, and that figure included not just construction but the land, too. He knew that he could never spend half a million or more on land and still build the library of his dreams for just $450,000 or $500,000. Folger gave up—New York City was too expensive.

Where should he look next? Folger had eliminated the three senti-mental favorites—Amherst, Nantucket, and New York—and had not been moved by appeals for Chicago or Stratford-upon-Avon. Henry wrote a list of potential locations for the library and crossed off un-suitable candidates. Emily described her husband's thinking. "As time passed," she said, "he came to favor Washington. That city is the com-mon capital of the whole United States; it belongs to all the people. It is advantageously situated, it is beautiful, and it constantly is grow-ing in cultural significance. Since the collection was to be given to the whole people, it seemed fitting that it should be placed in the District of Columbia."[3]

In 1918, the Folgers had enjoyed an impromptu visit to Washington, D.C., that later helped them choose the home for the library. "Dur-ing the World War, Henry and I," Emily remembered, "journeying to Hot Springs, found ourselves delayed by dislocated railroad schedules, and used the time walking about the city in the rain, viewing possible sites."[4] They walked through the white marble great hall at Union Sta-tion, pushed through the bronze revolving doors, gazed up Delaware Avenue, and saw it, looming straight ahead, three blocks away—the great dome of the U.S. Capitol. They decided to go for a walk. Drawn by the gleaming, white, cast-iron dome, they continued south. When they were halfway to the Capitol and they crossed Constitution Av-enue, they saw, if they glanced to their right, the shiny marble exterior walls of the Russell Senate Office Building, site of the recent 1912 hearings on the *Titanic* disaster.

The Capitol was stunning. It was a mountain of marble—outer walls of thick slabs; wide, white steps cascading down from the East Front like the sculpted tiers of a wedding cake; and tall columns. Everything was white. What was not natural white marble—like the great iron dome—was painted white. Emily was familiar with the city. She had spent her early childhood in Washington. Her fondness and familiarity with the city had, no doubt, a positive effect on the choice of Washington as the location for their library. Perhaps that was the moment Henry Folger said for the first time, "Yes, someday I will build mine of white marble, too."

Later, one of the Folgers' advisors suggested that they choose Capitol Hill as the site for their Shakespeare library. Henry was inclined to agree. He drew maps of the area east and southeast of the U.S. Capitol, and evaluated at least four different locations on the Hill, varying in total cost between about $125,000 and $300,000, according to his handwritten notes and estimates that he scribbled on stationery from the Raleigh Hotel, at Twelfth and Pennsylvania, his base of operations during scouting. A trusted advisor told the Folgers to look at East Capitol Street.

As Henry and Emily stood on the eastern edge of the Capitol grounds, they looked east, just across First Street, at another beautiful structure, the Jefferson Building of the Library of Congress. A triumphant edifice of the Beaux-Arts style, completed in 1897, it radiated American optimism and confidence. In the mid-1840s, when Abraham Lincoln first came to Washington as a newly elected congressman, he lived in a boarding house that had once occupied part of the site. The Folgers crossed First Street, walked east on East Capitol Street, and, passing the Jefferson Building on their right, continued to the corner of East Capitol and Second Street. They were now in Washington's historic Capitol Hill district, one of the city's oldest residential neighborhoods. There, on the south side of East Capitol between Second and Third Streets, they beheld a block-long stretch of beautiful nineteenth-century brick row houses—"Grant's Row," the developer had called it—that had seen better days. It was a historic street. From where they stood, their view of the great dome was unobscured and unsurpassed. The Library of Congress—that architectural confection—was only a block away. It might be desirable to have two great libraries in complementary locations.

After searches, inquiries, and comparisons, the Folgers chose the place to build their Shakespeare memorial library. It would be Washington, or not at all. Henry Folger loved the Grant's Row location, but he confronted the same obstacle that had defeated him in New York. The fourteen houses on Grant's Row were private property—each structure and lot belonged to a different owner. He would have to acquire them individually, without letting the group of owners know what he was doing, and then tear them down all at once. If word got out that a millionaire was buying up the properties, then holdout owners could demand exorbitant prices for their lots. It was not difficult for the president of Standard Oil to solve this problem. He would buy the parcels in secret. Front men acting on his behalf would negotiate with the owners and buy all the land. Only then, once he controlled the whole block, would Folger reveal his plan.

The land was cheaper than in New York, so Folger went forward and undertook the task of assembling a property of sufficient size, with the help of real estate agents, who kept Folger's name and his plan out of the public eye. As early as 1918, Folger was corresponding with Washington, D.C., real estate agents about property acquisition. Perhaps in an attempt to maintain secrecy, Henry dealt with several of them to conceal from any one of them his real purpose. His correspondence supports the idea that he wanted to make discreet inquiries without anyone knowing what he was doing.[5] To one trusted real estate agent he sent a hand-drawn map of the area east of the dome, with properties marked by Folger: "Inquire very cautiously indeed, to learn in a general way what each would probably cost." Folger offered to pay the agent's expenses, instructing him to "get what money you need from Mr. Welsh." Alexander G. Welsh was Folger's secretary and Man Friday at Standard Oil. For years, he had performed many confidential financial tasks for Henry: depositing his dividend checks, sending to Henry's father his Standard Oil dividends, and handling some of the massive paperwork and personal correspondence Folger conducted with hundreds of book dealers over the years. Welsh was also charged with picking up valuable shipments and delivering them to Folger, and to storage.[6]

Through the early 1920s, the Folgers read up on the city that they had adopted for their library. They crammed one file with newspaper clippings and another with magazine articles about Washington as a cultural capital, including the entire June 1923 *National Geographic*, a special issue devoted to Washington, D.C., and containing articles like "The Capitol, Wonder Building of the World," "Washington, the Pride of the Nation," and "The Sources of Washington's Charms." The same folder contains Henry Folger's holographic notes on publications and brochures he gathered about other libraries.

Planning the library would require Folger to make major readjustments in the way he lived. From now on, he would have to hold significant assets in reserve for land and construction. He would have to discipline his collecting habits and, as difficult as that might be, make fewer and less grand purchases. If he hoped to build a library, he could not buy any more $50,000 or $100,000 books. The price he had paid for the Pavier Quarto alone would finance ten percent of the anticipated cost of the library project. Of course, he could not stand on the sidelines for long. It was still only a question of when—not if—he would open his checkbook again for some extravagant new acquisition.

But for now, beginning in 1920, Folger seemed to bow to the new austerity of the times and revised his collecting strategy. For the next year and a half, between January 1920 and May 1921, he did not buy any First Folios, not even inexpensive, imperfect, or inconsequential copies. But it did not take long before he broke his short streak of fiscal restraint. In May 1921, no longer able to resist, he purchased a First Folio for $13,000 (W 76, F 18). He also continued to purchase large quantities of inexpensive books. These were not collector's prizes, but they were valuable as research and reference titles, and essential for the kind of library that Folger had in mind. The correspondence between Henry and Rosenbach between May and July 1921 is evidence of the level of attention that the collector gave to even these lesser purchases. On May 21, Folger wrote to the dealer about acquiring more items from Marsden Perry's collection:

> Probably you have gone through the package of cards for the Perry books, so that you know how many there are, and what a task it is to examine them all. I have put in a good many hours, and am sending you by registered mail to-day, the cards of the books which appeal to me, although I think the number will be increased as I study the rest of the cards. Those describing books I already have I am putting to one side and will return to you promptly for such other use as you may wish to make of them.

Folger, always the careful buyer, did not ask Rosenbach to name a group price for those dozens of cheap titles. He wanted to know what the dealer proposed to charge him for each individual book. "What I would like to know, first of all, is the price asked for each one of these items. If you think I should see them be good enough to put in any books you send over the cards belonging with them . . . as [the cards] are of value in suggesting why the books are put into a Shakespeare Library."

On July 6, 1921, Folger wrote to Rosenbach at his New York office at 273 Madison Avenue. This letter, perhaps more than any other that Folger sent the dealer, reveals the meticulousness he exhibited in even the smallest transactions, even at the height of his wealth and power. "There may be a few of the items, which, for one reason or another I will not wish, but I think I will need nearly all of them." Folger bought additional items from the Marsden Perry collection. On July 22, Rosenbach sent him a receipt for $922.50—including a credit of $270 for returns. The original inventory of this purchase, typed on acidic paper, now aged brown and brittle, lists each item and its price, and contains, in Folger's tiny handwriting, checks and marks indicating the purchases and returns. Even at this advanced stage of his business and collecting careers, Henry Folger handled all the details personally, without the help of a librarian or staff. The same man who had purchased the most expensive book in the world spent hours inspecting cartons of inexpensive books and hand-selecting the ones he would keep. He had ordered on approval $1,192.50 worth of books from the Perry collection, and had returned $270 worth, including a $12 item— a group of pamphlets. Henry Huntington would have bought these inexpensive books sight unseen, inspected none of them personally, and left it to his staff to deal with the petty details. But to Folger, every book—whatever its value—was worthy of his personal attention. And no amount of money—no matter how little—was too small to save.[7]

Around the same time, Rosenbach, the chatty publicity hound who had divulged the secret of the Pavier Quarto and the last person Henry would take into his confidence, and who had no idea of Henry Folger's long-range plans for his collection, suggested that Folger might consider building a library. Rosenbach had mastered the power of suggestion and had made an art of hinting to his major collectors what course they should follow. It was a method by which the dealer obtained information about their plans. On June 3, 1921, Rosenbach wrote to Henry about an important artwork: "Mr. Joseph Widener has kindly consented to send in from his home, Lynnewood Hall, the famous original drawing of Cruikshank: The Birth of William Shakespeare, and I am sending it for your inspection to our place in New York." Folger, an enthusiastic if indiscriminate buyer of art related to Shakespeare, coveted the piece. Two weeks later, Rosenbach sent a black-and-white photograph of the Cruikshank taken in Marsden Perry's home, when it was still part of that collection: "Perhaps if you erect a library building some day it will have the place of honor, the same as in Perry's. I enclose a photograph showing how it looks in the latter's home." Little did Rosenbach know what plans Folger had already set into motion.

By the end of 1921, Henry Folger had accomplished the first two steps of his grand philanthropic mission—he had chosen the home city for his Shakespeare library, and he had started buying the lots to assemble the parcel where it would be built. He was looking forward to the next steps: gaining complete control of the block, demolishing

Grant's Row, designing his library, and breaking ground. That, he anticipated, might take several years. In the meantime, in 1920 and 1921, he remained unsatisfied as a collector. He had not bought a major First Folio in a few years. He had acquired the Gilburne copy, but its desirability was exclusive to its romantic, if unproven story. There were other great First Folios still out there, in private hands not his own. One of them, one of the best and most elusive of all, had been on his "want list" for more than twenty years. He had made provision for an endowment to finance the operating expenses of the library. In his judgment, he could afford to open his checkbook again and renew his hunt for all First Folios, great and small.

In early 1922, Folger went on a First Folio buying binge. He bought a fine one in January for $22,750 (W 129, F 71), a weak copy in February for $3,450 (W 62, F 4), and a third in March for $9,130 (W 79, F 21). In April, he received an unexpected letter that took him back almost twenty years. It was from Rosenbach and it was about a First Folio. Somehow the dealer had obtained a copy of a letter dated November 1, 1902, from Coningsby Sibthorp, the former owner of the Vincent Folio, to Sidney Lee, the bibliographer. It was the very letter in which Sibthorp had quoted, for the first time, a price of £10,000 for the Vincent copy.

Now, nineteen years later, Rosenbach had discovered Sibthorp's letter to Lee and sent it on to Folger: "Enclosed herewith find a letter relating to the famous Coningsby Sibthorp first folio edition of Shakespeare, which please accept with my compliments. Are you the American gentleman referred to therein? The letter was written to Sidney Lee just before his departure to America in 1902."[8] Ignorant of Folger's epic chase for the book, he had always wondered what had happened to it. Rosenbach could not resist asking Folger if he owned the Vincent copy.

In May 1922, Folger learned of an opportunity to acquire one of the most desirable First Folios in private hands—the celebrated Burdett-Coutts volume. The English Baroness Angela Burdett-Coutts owned an exceptional copy in excellent condition with all of its original leaves. She had purchased it in July 1864 at the auction of the famous library of George Daniel, paying the then-record sum of £716. Daniel, a writer, poet, and book collector, also had a penchant for theatrical relics. In addition to owning a copy of each of the four Shakespeare folios, he acquired two prized possessions belonging to David Garrick. The first was a cane, the second a cassolette—a carved casket made from the mulberry tree purported to have been planted by Shakespeare.[9] The First Folio from his collection was a beautiful and very tall copy, sold in the year of the three-hundredth anniversary of Shakespeare's birth. The price was a high-water mark at the time. Its distinguished provenance included the Roxburghe library sale in 1812. Folger's contemporary, the bibliographer Seymour de Ricci, praised it as one of the "choicest copies in private hands."[10] The Baroness, perhaps inspired by the cassolette owned by George Daniel, stored the book in a gorgeous, elaborately carved wooden casket. This book chest was not made from any ordinary tree. Queen Victoria had presented Burdett-Coutts with a gift of wood taken from Herne's Oak, a famous tree dating to Shakespeare's time, and mentioned by him in *The Merry Wives of Windsor*. The Baroness had used it to fashion the casket. The elaborate carvings on the box depict characters from *The Merry Wives of Windsor*, Shakespeare's initials, and symbols of the Globe Theatre. It was an important work of art in its own right. She also owned a second, less impressive copy of the First Folio that was nevertheless interesting as it contained the rare canceled first page of *Troilus and Cressida*.[11]

Henry Folger had known about her two copies of the Folio for years, and as early as 1903, during his pursuit of the Vincent copy, he had written about them to Railton at Sotheran, when he sent the firm a "want list" of First Folios he hoped to acquire. Sotheran advised him that a quest for the fine Burdett-Coutts copy was hopeless. The book was considered an English treasure, and of course, the dealer reported, such a titled and wealthy family would *never* sell it. How many times had Folger heard that line? And how many times since then had he snapped up rare books that experts had advised would never come on the market?

Now, after almost two decades of waiting, he would have his chance. Christie's announced that the Baroness's library would be sold at auction. Rosenbach entered the race for the Burdett-Coutts copies, suggesting to Folger that there might be a chance to buy the books privately before they were sold by Christie's . . . if the price was high enough. Folger replied by cabling "£12000 FOR TWO FOLIOS SEEMS EXCESSIVE." He changed his mind the next day and cabled "IF NECESSARY PAY £12000." Then he sent a final cable that stated "WISH FOLIOS." That was all Rosenbach needed to know. In Folger's vocabulary, those two words signaled the dealer to spend whatever was necessary.

In the end, there would be no long courtship, no opportunity to negotiate an advantageous price, and no private sale. The heirs preferred to take their chances on the auction block. The highest bidder would claim the prize. On May 15, Henry took the finer copy for $52,070 (£8,600) (W 63, F 5). It was the new world-record price for a First Folio, surpassing by a few thousand what Henry had paid in 1903 for the Vincent copy, though almost no one knew it. The mercenary auctioneer had separated the book from its custom-made casket, hoping to attract bidders for the Herne's Oak relic alone. Without the book, no one wanted its empty box—customized with a compartment to fit this particular First Folio—so Folger won it for a few hundred pounds. He also purchased in a separate lot the voluminous scrapbooks assembled by Burdett-Coutts on the history of the volume. That was not the end of the sale for Henry. He also took home the second copy (W 68, F 10) for $32,400 (£5,400), and a fanciful chair once owned by David Garrick.

England mourned the loss of this historic First Folio. The May 24, 1922, issue of *Punch* published a full-page cartoon depicting an American millionaire named "Autolycus, U.S.A." looting England's treasures.[12] Autolycus, a character from Greek mythology who possessed skills of theft and trickery, is also a character in Shakespeare's *The Winter's Tale*, a roguish "snapper-up of unconsidered trifles" (Act IV, Scene iii). But no matter. The Bodleian affair had been England's last major victory in the folio wars. Folger had bought the Burdett-Coutts folios. Not one English patriot had seen fit to top his high bid. He had won the war of the books that the English press had declared against him years prior. Indeed, Folger, along with other Americans like Huntington, had routed their critics. As a symbol of his triumph, Folger bought the original artwork for the *Punch* cartoon and added it to his collection. In that year, Folger's salary was $100,000.

That was not the only work of art that Folger bought in 1922. He continued to buy important artworks related to Shakespeare. One of the Fuseli oil paintings from the long-defunct Boydell Shakespeare Gallery found its way into the collection of Sir Herbert Beerbohm Tree and in December 1922, through the London bookseller Maggs Bros., it went to Folger.

With five new First Folios—including the two Burdett-Coutts copies—and a major oil painting among his acquisitions, it had been a great year for Henry Folger. He inaugurated the New Year by opening a heartfelt letter from John D. Rockefeller dated January 1, 1923: "I would not be out-done in appreciation of your companionship, and the delightful associations of the long years, and notably of these later years, as the ranks of the older associates are thinning out and we of the Old Guard draw closer together." The letter foreshadowed things to come. Henry did not know it yet, but the titan had bigger plans for him.

Henry's plans did not include the ever-persistent Sidney Lee. Folger had stonewalled him for years, and he offered no assistance for Lee's amended First Folio *Census* of 1923, the latest—and third—edition of his original work published in 1902. By 1923, according to Lee, Henry Folger owned thirty-five copies of the First Folio. In fact, he already owned sixty-six.[13]

At the end of the year, Folger divulged one of his best-kept and longest-held secrets—his hitherto anonymous ownership of the Vincent First Folio. The article that he published in *The Outlook* shortly after he acquired "the most precious book in the world" had created suspicion in bibliophile circles that he owned the book, but he did not admit ownership in the article, and in the years since he had never acknowledged possession of it. By 1923, Folger was such a famous collector—the purchase of the Marsden Perry Pavier Quarto in 1919 and the Burdett-Coutts First Folios in 1922 had spoiled what little remaining anonymity he still possessed—that he saw no harm in confessing that he owned the best First Folio in the world. On December 23, 1923, Folger wrote to Yale professor of English C. F. Tucker Brooke, who had founded the Yale Shakespeare edition of the plays. What had once been an obsessive secret became a casual admission:

> I have just finished reading, with great satisfaction, your article on the Folio of 1623 in the October Yale Review. In the interest of having the record of Shakespeare Folios as accurate as possible, I venture to call attention to the last paragraph of your article, in which you speak of the Augustine Vincent presentation copy from Jaggard as "lately in the possession of Mr. Charles C. Sibthorp Coningsby." This copy belonged to Charles C. Sibthorp, but some fifteen years ago he sold it to me, and since that time it has been in my possession.[14]

Nineteen twenty-three marked another important milestone in Folger's business career. He was elected chairman of the board of Standard Oil of New York. He would retain that position until his retirement from the company. The new position and the new economic opportunities it offered were good for Henry's career and collection.

Folger devoted most of 1924 to business, not collecting. His agents continued to negotiate for the purchase of the fourteen lots on Grant's Row. Folger and Rockefeller held identical opinions on how a great business should be run, shared the same values on business ethics and stewardship, disdained personal greed that displaced a higher duty, and, as members of what Rockefeller had called the "old guard," possessed unmatched knowledge of the history of the oil business and an unrivaled expertise in all elements of its operation. And to the extent their expertise and talents combined to increase the value of the company, the shareholders, including Rockefeller and Folger, benefited tremendously. In April, he bought an unexceptional First Folio for $7,400 (W 125, F 67). In December, he began an eight-month run of major purchases with the acquisition of a fine copy for $37,000, one of his five most expensive copies (W 126, F 68). He bought another copy for $32,000 in March 1925 (W 127, F 69), and that August, he paid $19,500 for another (W 128, F 70). That year, he also acquired a valuable and exotic curiosity—a copy of the Geneva Bible of 1569 once owned by Edward de Vere, the Earl of Oxford, the man Anti-Stratfordians proposed as their candidate for alternative author of Shakespeare's plays. Henry Folger dismissed the claim as absurd, but was happy to have de Vere's Bible.

All through 1924 and 1925, Henry engaged in active correspondence with the real estate agents he had enlisted in his East Capitol Street scheme. After purchasing several of the houses, he encountered an obstacle—a couple named Newhauser were holdouts in negotiations over their Grant's Row house, refusing to sell for less than $100,000. Folger's real estate agent, who thought the price outrageous—which it was—suggested that Henry paint the other houses and raise the rents. The advice suggests that this real estate agent did not fully know what Folger had in mind. Folger demurred, writing, "I am rather inclined to think that any appearance of putting the property in better condition may encourage the [holdouts] to delay their decision."[15] To put the holdout demand in context, another real estate agent had suggested that he should be able to acquire *all* fourteen properties on the south side of East Capitol between Second and Third Streets for just $260,000. He had already been at it for several years, and it would take him nine years, in total, to acquire all fourteen parcels. In the end, he would pay $317,000 for the houses on the fifty-thousand-square-foot tract.

Chapter 12

❧❦❧

"Portrait of a Collector"

—A. S. W. ROSENBACH

ROM THE mid-1920s onward, Henry Folger's purchases of First Folios, especially expensive ones, became routine. And his relentless pursuit of First Folios continued to drive market prices higher. His plans for a library were becoming real, and he collected with renewed urgency. In January 1926, he bought a copy for $6,050 (W 61, F 3); in June, he paid $6,075 for another copy missing two of the plays (W 132, F 80). The following month, he purchased two copies, one for $9,900 (W 131, F 73), and a fine, expensive one for $41,000 (W 130, F 72).

Once he had become known as an important collector, Folger often received letters from booksellers, librarians, or curators seeking to examine or exhibit this treasure or that, from bibliophiles and scholars pleading for access to his collection for their various research projects, and from bibliographers like Sidney Lee inquiring about his inventory. In January 1923, Lee, by now president of the Shakespeare Society, complained about the inaccessibility of Folger's collection: "He seems to think First Folios ought to be put in a bin in cellars like fine vintages." Lee hoped that "now that America has gone dry, other American collectors will not attempt to fill their empty bins with First Folios."[1] Henry ignored most of the requests, but in July 1927,

223

he received one request he could not. Belle da Costa Greene wrote
to Folger on behalf of a scholar who hoped to make use of some of
his books. Greene, whom Morgan had hired in 1905, had become a
legendary society figure in her own right, and Folger owed her at least
the courtesy of a reply. Even to Greene, however, Folger replied that
it would be impossible for him to help her: "I hope, at some time in
the near future, to have a proper place for storing my collection, so
that it will be accessible to all who wish to make use of it. At present
it is all packed up in some 1700 cases and put away in several warehouses."[2]

"The near future" that Folger mentioned to Greene was getting
close enough that it was time to commission oil portraits of him and
Emily to hang in the library they would build. Many businessmen
of similar status to Folger had ordered such portraits early in their
careers to display in their residences. Henry was too modest for that,
but it would not, he felt, be inappropriate to display in his Shakespeare
library token reminders of the husband and wife who had built the
collection.

He chose the artist Frank Salisbury. Salisbury, recommended by Folger's friend Dr. S. Parkes Cadman, was a society, political, and court
painter who specialized in portraits of leading figures of the Anglosphere
on both sides of the Atlantic. His subjects included King George V and
various British coronation scenes; presidents Calvin Coolidge, Franklin
Roosevelt, and Harry Truman; John D. Rockefeller Jr. and J. P. Morgan;
British Field Marshal Bernard Montgomery; and, strangely, Italian dic-
tator Benito Mussolini.

Salisbury recalled his introduction to Folger:

> One day in New York I was rung up by the private secretary of
> a man who wished to be unknown but asked if I would paint two
> portraits. He turned out to be Henry Clay Folger, President of the
> Standard Oil Company, but better known as the founder of the
> marvelous Shakespeare Library at Washington, which was then
> coming into being. He wanted portraits of himself and his wife
> which could be hung in the building.[3]

Salisbury asked Henry to choose a favorite object to feature in the painting: "At one sitting . . . I said I should like him to be holding something in his hands." Folger considered the matter. Whatever single book he selected would symbolize the meaning of his whole collection, of his life's work. One candidate seemed obvious—the Vincent First Folio, "the most precious book in the world." But the obsessive collector of First Folios decided to pose without a copy of his trademark book. Salisbury described what he brought instead: "Wrapped up in newspaper, [was] a precious Shakespeare quarto published before the First Folio, for which he had paid thousands of pounds and refused half as much again." Henry had chosen his copy of the Pavier Quarto. Salisbury marveled at the characteristic, understated way Folger handled the book: "Coming to the studio that day, he carried it in a newspaper wrapping and came by the subway, alone." It was a routine trip for a man who had for years taken the streetcar across the Brooklyn Bridge as part of his daily commute to Twenty-Six Broadway.

When Emily Folger sat for her portrait, Salisbury was struck by the appearance of her hands: "What a noble memorial he and Mrs. Folger have left the world, a heritage for all generations! Mrs. Folger's right hand was crippled with writer's cramp through cataloguing the collection, but what of that? Altogether the collection has seventy thousand volumes by or about Shakespeare and his contemporaries. No wonder Mrs. Folger's hands were crippled in cataloguing them."

Henry's choice of Salisbury attests to his indiscriminate taste in art. In the field of rare books, Folger's taste was splendid. In the field of art, it was miserable. The murky portraits, while serviceable likenesses of Henry and Emily, are dominated by brown, green, and yellow tones, and appear dark and muddy. The history of art has left the workmanlike Salisbury behind as a forgotten footnote. In the 1980s, when his home and studio were broken up and his paintings dispersed at auction, they brought pitifully low prices, and today, his works have almost no commercial value. But the Folgers were delighted with their portraits, and they had black-and-white photographic copies made, which they autographed and distributed to friends.

Henry was too modest to hang the portraits at home while he

waited to commence construction of his library: "As the library was not completed when they were finished" in 1927, Salisbury recalled, "the portraits were put into a case and stored for years in a depository with Mr. Folger's collection."

In 1928, Henry bought four more First Folios, two of them at some of the highest prices he had ever paid: $47,500 (W 133, F 75) and $68,750 (W 134, F 76); indeed, the latter was the highest dollar figure he would ever pay for a First Folio. This was also among the last copies he purchased.[4] These purchases, in addition to other books he acquired in 1928, suggest that he was neither slowing down nor cutting back on his collecting in anticipation of breaking ground for his library.

Then, in the same year, Henry Folger made a major and unique purchase. It was something that throughout his adult life he had neglected to acquire. He bought a home. It was in Glen Cove, Long Island, at Eleven St. Andrews Lane, across the street from his beloved Nassau Country Club, close to the homes of Charlie Pratt and Pratt's siblings. In his retirement, he would play golf, plan the library, and continue to collect.

Despite expensive First Folios, his ongoing shipping of crates of other books from England, and the purchase of a home, Henry Folger's chief preoccupation in 1928 was the land on which he planned to build his library. He now owned more than seventy-five copies of the First Folio. By January 1928, Folger had purchased all fourteen of the East Capitol Street lots, at a cost of $317,000, and he had cause to celebrate. It had taken eight years to assemble the parcel, much longer than it would take to actually build the library, if all went according to plan. He was eager to demolish the buildings, hire an architect, approve plans, and begin construction. He reviewed his finances and his Standard Oil stock holdings to confirm that he would have easy access to the $750,000 he expected his library to cost. Unbeknownst to him, another party wanted that land, one that had the power to take it, even from him. For some time, the federal government had been scouting Capitol Hill for real estate to expand the overcrowded Library of Congress. Once that library selected the spot for its new annex building, the United States government, using its power of eminent domain, would condemn the land and seize it from its owners. Just one block east of the Library of Congress, along East Capitol Street, ran a one-block stretch of brick row houses that seemed very tempting to library officials. It was Grant's Row. Buried in Henry Folger's private archives is a handwritten note he scribbled in haste on a scrap of paper: "Gov. going to take property."

That January, Folger learned from a newspaper article that the Library of Congress planned to expand, and that Congress was about to seize the entire block bordered on the north by East Capitol Street, on the south by Pennsylvania Avenue, on the east by Third Street, and on the west by Second Street. Half of that block included his Grant's Row properties. He did not have long to act. Some men, faced with opposing Congress, might have conceded defeat. Henry decided to fight. But how? He could tap his wealth, connections, and the name of Standard Oil to battle Congress head-on. Brute force might prevail—Henry could try to compel New York's senators and congressmen to bend to his will and derail the legislation—but such a blatant political play risked provoking other members who hated Standard Oil and who might do anything to spite its chairman. Folger mustered his businessman's savvy. His job had always been to solve difficult problems. Throughout his career he had tried to do that through cooperation, not intimidation.

He decided on another approach. No government official stood to gain more from taking Henry's land than Herbert Putnam, the Librarian of Congress. If Folger could persuade Putnam that it was not in his best interest to seize Grant's Row, then Folger might turn the librarian into an ally. Henry sat at his desk at Twenty-Six Broadway and drafted a personal, confidential note to Putnam. In a brilliant move, Folger decided not to threaten him, but to entice him.

First, he revealed that it was he who owned the land. He explained what he planned to do with it, unless Congress interfered. He would build a structure and institution that "would harmonize with the Library [of Congress]" and would house his "library of Shakespeareana," which was "finer than anything that has ever been acquired." He revealed that it was his ambition "to help make the United States a center for literary study and progress." He had considered other sites, in the United States and abroad, but he "preferred to consider Washington as its permanent home, being satisfied that it is of sufficient value and importance to add to the dignity of your City."

Henry expressed shock that the federal government planned to seize his land: "Until I saw this newspaper mention of the Library expansion it had never occurred to me that the site I had selected might be considered within the zone of possible Government territory."

Of all people, the Librarian of Congress needed no introduction to Henry Folger or his fabulous collection. Bibliophiles had long wondered what Folger planned to do with his hoard. And now Putnam was the first outsider to be let in on the secret. The news thrilled him, as Henry knew it would. Now, Folger brought up the subject that he counted on to terrify the librarian: "This all leads up to my question: should I give up my thought of making Washington the choice for a location? The plan I am perfecting includes an adequate and proper building and a considerable endowment to care for the library and to add to it."

Without threatening Putnam, and in the politest way possible, the chairman of Standard Oil dictated his terms: if the government takes away his land, then he will take away his library.

Putnam snapped at Folger's bait. He telegraphed an immediate reply: "Your letter of yesterday is of extraordinary interest and supreme importance." He wanted to see Folger as soon as possible. "May I confer with you on some day of next week at place and hour convenient to you?" Putnam was so excited that he lacked any patience to await a reply. He told his secretary to telephone Twenty-Six Broadway at once, but he could not reach the chairman. Putnam followed up his telegram with a longer letter telling Folger what a wonderful idea it was to build his Shakespeare library in Washington: "Your letter of yesterday opens a prospect more thrilling (I am frank to say) not merely for the National Capitol, but for the cultural interests of this country, than anything that has happened for Washington since the establishment of the Freer Gallery."

Putnam would be happy to defer to Folger's project. Attracting this new and major Shakespeare library to Washington was more important to the Librarian of Congress than building an annex for his own institution:

Any governmental project involving the two squares to the rear of the Library [of Congress] would assuredly be subordinated to yours (for the utilization of the northern strip which you control). With your intention made definite, the governmental undertaking (as respects the remainder of the area) would then become complementary and auxiliary to yours. Indeed, were your structure in existence, the government should acquire the remainder of the area (to Pennsylvania Avenue) in order to assure it a dignified background.

Putnam promised to keep Folger's plans secret, but suggested that it was in their interest to take into confidence the influential congressman Representative Robert Luce of Massachusetts, chairman of the House Committee on the Library, who held sway over the legislation that would enable Congress to confiscate the Grant's Row property for use by the Library of Congress.

Folger read the draft legislation, dated January 16, 1928, which was to become H.R. 9355, introduced in the first session of the Seventieth Congress. Section two contained the provision that targeted Folger's property. Something would have to be done, and quickly.

Folger replied to Putnam: "Your telegram and letter were duly received, relieving my great concern about our plans." Indeed, Putnam's response reassured Folger. The Librarian of Congress had embraced the idea of a Shakespeare library within the shadow of his own Jefferson Building, and had agreed to subordinate his plans to Folger's. Not only that, but Putnam offered to act as Henry's unpaid advocate to influence Luce. Luce had the power to delay action on the bill, and then revise its language to exempt Folger's property from its reach. That was perfect, replied Folger, for "my hope has been to locate [my library] where it would be undisturbed for many years." Henry demurred on agreeing to an immediate appointment to see Putnam, explaining that he was "not quite ready to present in detail what we are trying to work out." He promised to drop in on the librarian soon, the next time he was in Washington. He also reassured Putnam that he would not compete with the Library of Congress. He would keep his library within narrow limits, not "to go outside Shakepeariana and Elizabethan literature."

Putnam repeated his request for a meeting. To avoid any interference with the Shakespeare library, Putnam wrote, "The pending bill should be modified" as soon as possible. Before that can happen, he informed Folger, "The Committee will naturally expect to have before it some expression of your interest which will explain the modification." Henry authorized Putnam to show his original letter describing his plans to the House Committee. "After working on the Grant Row properties for eight or nine years," he added, "I was only recently [able] to secure the last house. I was on the point of giving up the effort, as the delay was so disheartening. . . . My concern now is, will the location be left undisturbed in this use of it?"

Folger's delay in coming down to Washington worried Putnam. Yes, "the site is perfect to the purpose as none other could be," the librarian purred, but no action would be taken on Henry's behalf until he made his case in person. "Come here and make known to the committee in general terms what you have in mind," Putnam urged, "but come within the month!"

Before Henry Folger could travel to Washington, he had other important business to take care of in New York City. On February 9, 1928, he announced his resignation as chairman of Standard Oil of New York, effective in one year. Folger presented his letter to the president of Standard Oil of New York (and half brother to Charles M. Pratt), Herbert Pratt, and to the company's board of directors: "I have been so happy in my position, and my fellow-workers in Socony [Standard Oil Company of New York] have made the work so easy, that the years have slipped by almost unnoticed. I owe them all a deep debt of gratitude and love." Henry Folger had devoted half a century to the oil industry, and when he left, it was "amid the universal regret of his associates."[5]

Business had been his first love. And it was the success of Standard Oil that had made his great collection possible. But now it was time, Henry concluded, to devote himself to another dream, building his Shakespeare library. The board tendered an affectionate reply, their words printed large and illuminated on vellum pages bound into a beautiful book presented to Folger. They knew he would appreciate this homage to his bibliomania.

The illuminated manuscript lavished praise upon Henry's "thorough knowledge of every phase of the oil business, his long experience and unerring good business judgment." The board recognized him as a titanic figure in the history of American industry: "[H]is business life has been contemporaneous with the great development of the oil industry; he has been actively and prominently identified with it practically since its inception." And now, as Folger's career came to a close, the board honored him with the words: "He is the last of the great pioneers of the industry to retire."

Along with the book, on February 29, 1928, the board presented to him a beautiful Tiffany & Company eighteen-karat, three-legged golden bowl, engraved with a phrase from *Henry VIII*, "Thy truth and thy integrity is rooted in us, thy friends," spoken by King Henry to Archbishop Cranmer. Two legs of the bowl are engraved with stylized logos symbolizing the two enterprises in which Folger had served and the dates of his service: SONY (1911–1928) (Standard Oil of New York) and SONJ (1879–1911) (Standard Oil of New Jersey); the third leg was engraved with his initials, HCF. The gift harked back to the seventeenth century, when upon Shakespeare's death he left to his daughter Judith a great silver bowl. But Shakespeare's bowl was only silver; Folger's was crafted of gold.

It was a bittersweet time. Letters from younger Standard employees reacting to Henry's retirement poured into his thirteenth-floor office at Twenty-Six Broadway. Representative of them is a touching letter from F. S. Sales:

> I confess I am thinking tonight more of my own personal loss than anything else. . . . My feeling of gratitude to you for your

sympathetic and kindly help is far greater than I can express. I shall miss greatly the privilege of conferring with you, which I have done so often when the waters seemed troubled. We ought to be able to keep the old ship on an even keel with our years of training under your guiding hand but I wish you might be on the bridge forever, charting our course for us. You are practically the last of the original builders of our great company. Much of its success in all of its ramifications is due to your foresight and planning. . . . After nearly fifty years of faithful service, you certainly have earned a rest but I hope our paths may cross frequently and that you will continue to consider old "26" as your headquarters.

John D. Rockefeller had already sent a sentimental letter to Folger on January 2, 1926: "These long and delightful business relations mean to us inexpressibly more than the gold and silver that came from their great prosperity."[6] Rockefeller later wrote:

I of course regret to have you retire from the responsible position you have held in connection with our business interests for such a long time. I wish it might have been delayed a little to give the younger men the benefit of your long experience and steadying and quieting influence, and even now I am hoping you will continue to have the same sympathetic interest in the business as ever . . . [W]e shall not be separated far. We shall see to it that the pleasant paths in which we have walked together with such genuine enjoyment shall continue to the end.[7]

On February 16, 1928, one week after Henry Folger announced his retirement, he wrote again to Herbert Putnam, explaining that he preferred to have the legislation modified quietly, without publicity or newspaper coverage. As before, secrecy served his interests best. Did he really have to come to Washington to appear before the House Committee? Couldn't Putnam get the job done quietly, with Folger's letter alone? He appealed to Putnam:

I have persistently avoided all publicity, feeling that book buying could be done more cheaply and successfully if there were no advertising. And that is still true, so I shrink from making public any of our plans until it is absolutely necessary. Just at the moment I am negotiating for some twenty Shakespeare books of the very first rank, each unique, or practically so, to secure any one of them would be an event, and to obtain a score at one time is a stroke of almost incredible good-fortune. But I need not tell an experienced collector like yourself that in such matters the Friar's counsel to Romeo is very opportune, "Wisely and slow; they stumble that run fast."

On February 18, Putnam gave in. Henry's letter would suffice. But he warned Folger that the report of the House Committee accompanying the bill "will of course have to explain the omission." But the reason could be vague. "I think," wrote Putnam, "that the explanation can be merely in general terms to the effect that the area omitted is to be developed in a project that will not merely not interfere with the utilization of the residue of the two squares for library use, but be fully consistent with it, and indeed prove cooperative with the larger purposes of the Library as an institution." Putnam met with Congressman Luce the same day and, after presenting him with a redacted copy of Folger's letter, cautioned Luce that should Folger not get his way, "He would feel constrained to abandon not merely the site, but the selection of Washington itself." Luce agreed to implement the librarian's scheme.

A month later, on March 15, Luce submitted an amended report of the committee on the library. As promised, this report, *Acquisition of Additional Land for the Library of Congress*, never mentioned Henry Folger. But it did include, on page three, an interesting revision:

As introduced, the bill provided for the acquisition of the whole of square 760, as well as square 761. *As reported it omits lots 1 to 14 inclusive, to the alleyway, constituting slightly more than one half of square 760.* The omission is recommended upon information, received by the committee since the introduction of the bill, that the area omitted (the entire northern portion, fronting on East Capitol Street) is to be developed in a project that will not merely not interfere with the utilization of the residue of the two squares for library uses, but be fully consistent with it, and indeed prove cooperative with the larger purposes of the library as an institution [italics added].

The vague explanation for the carve-out had come straight from Putnam's pen. He mailed the report to Folger on March 16, noting that the bill was now on the legislative calendar and would not attract attention until it was up for passage. If at that point it did provoke scrutiny, Putnam warned, "It is very desirable that this should not seem to be evaded." In other words, he and Luce would have to identify Folger and his collection if the newspaper correspondents who covererd Congress started asking questions. Henry hoped it would not come to that. On March 23, Putnam reported that he had given the press a vague but "authoritative statement which would preclude erroneous gossip." The librarian expected Washington and New York papers to publish the news soon.

Congressman Luce wrote to Folger on April 19, 1928, telling him that the bill would probably pass. Some members liked it because the omission of Henry's land had reduced the total payout from $760,000 to $600,000, which meant less expenditure by Congress. Luce congratulated Henry and was not shy to remind him who deserved some of the credit:

Such a structure as you contemplate and such a gift to the scholarship of the nation make all of us who have any share in their acknowledgment grateful for the opportunity. Furthermore we are particularly pleased because your project promises still further adornment of the surroundings of the capitol and betokens impetus to the progress making toward creating here what in time will be the most beautiful Capital in the world.

On April 22, the *New York Times* broke the news in a story headlined: "GREAT FOLGER LIBRARY TO HAVE ITS OWN HOME—Shakespeare Collection . . . Will Be Housed in Washington, Contains Among Its Treasures One-Fourth of the World's Stock of the Folios." It was a huge, three-column article measuring 6.5 by 21.5 inches, and containing more than three thousand words. It was the longest story that had ever been written about Folger's collection, and it underestimated the number of First Folios he owned. There was no hiding it now. The unprecedented publicity must have horrified Henry. But even the *New York Times* feature could not persuade him to abandon his reflexive compulsion for secrecy, by now a hopeless cause.

The *Times* assigned the story to the bibliographer George H. Sargent, who proved himself a careful student of Folger's activities and purchases. Sargent greeted the endeavor with unqualified praise:

> Recent announcement that Henry C. Folger was to erect a building near the Library of Congress . . . to house his magnificent Shakespearean library has its greatest significance in the fact that material heretofore unavailable will be made accessible to scholars. Whether the title is vested in the Library of Congress, the people of the United States or in trustees is of no consequence. The doors of the greatest Shakespearean library in the world are to be thrown open.

Sargent compared Folger's trophy hunt against that of some of his competitors and ranked him as the winner: "The Henry E. Huntington Library presents a magnificent array of twenty-nine folios, four of which are the First. The New York Public Library has eighteen folios, with four Firsts. The Folger Library contains more than fifty copies of the various folios, including . . . no less than thirty of the First." Henry must have smiled when he read that. Sargent had made a colossal mistake. Folger did not own thirty First Folios; he possessed more than seventy.

Folger noticed that few of the highlights of his collection had escaped Sargent's attention. Yes, the Vincent, Burdett-Coutts, and Hoe copies of the First Folio; *Titus Andronicus* and other precious quartos; the Pavier false folio—"said to have cost more than $100,000"—they were all there. But Sargent was far off the mark when he estimated that the collection held only 25,000 items. Only Henry and Emily knew that the true number—unknown even to them—dwarfed that guess. Sargent was right in his assessment of the library's importance: "Works by and about Shakespeare fill 232 pages of the British Museum catalogue, and the Folger Library rivals this. No one man will ever live long enough to read all the Shakespearean books in the Folger Library. Nor can any living man hope ever to accumulate another such collection."

On May 8, Putnam notified Folger of great news: "The bill passed by unanimous consent." On May 10, Folger finally invited Putnam to visit him at Twenty-Six Broadway, in his new office on the twenty-fifth floor. Henry told him he expected to be at work there three or four days a week, and that his door would always be open. They agreed to meet on May 21. The next day, President Calvin Coolidge signed H.R. 9355. Henry had saved his land from confiscation. Now he could build his library.[8]

Henry had retired not to rest, but to work. All of his energy was directed toward the library and collecting. He admitted, "I find it so engrossing that I cannot undertake anything outside of it." Starting in 1928, he brought to bear on his library project everything he had learned in fifty years at Standard Oil. During his long and spectacular rise at the greatest industrial enterprise yet known to man, Folger had been at the center of the action. He had seen it all: oil fields clogged with sticky mud and black crude; leaky barrels strapped to wagons pulled by straining horses; steam engines dragging railroad tank cars groaning with tons of oil; hitherto volatile and explosive kerosene tamed by Standard's refining processes; the epochal changeover from lighting fuel to gasoline; the transition to electric lighting; the invention of the internal combustion engine; and the proliferation of automobiles and airplanes. Henry Folger had mastered every aspect of the petroleum industry—he could calculate the cost of a barrel of oil down to a fraction of a penny, and then recite off the top of his head the scientific process used to refine it. Knowledge was the source of his power.

Over the next couple of years, his work on the Shakespeare library would showcase all the characteristics—intense concentration, meticulous attention to detail, an iron grip on expenses, dedication to quality, expertise in several fields, making important decisions personally, cultivation of a self-deprecating collegiality—that marked his tenure at Twenty-Six Broadway. He served as the unofficial general contractor for his own pet project. He involved himself in all matters, whether aesthetic or practical. From stained-glass windows to coal-heated boilers, Henry Folger was interested in the details, and usually had something to say.

The construction of the library involved several phases. The first thing Folger needed was an architect. After the April 22, 1928, *New York Times* article had revealed his plans, he was inundated with letters and proposals. Shreve & Lamb, who built Twenty-Six Broadway, hoped they had an inside track in becoming the architects for the new project. Dozens of letters from architects, stone quarries, and real estate agents (oblivious that Henry had already bought his land) poured into Folger's office. Folger did not want a fuss. Nor did he want to stage an architectural competition of the kind that newspaperman Colonel Robert McCormick had held in Chicago for his new Tribune Tower. A contest would create publicity and might even result in the premature publication of the winning design. Henry wanted to keep the project under wraps—the fewer people who knew any details, the easier he could guard its secrecy.

Besides, no group of architects, now matter how famous or talented, knew what ideas already percolated in Folger's mind. Without his input, their designs could never match the library of his dreams. No, Folger thought, better to make discreet inquiries among people he trusted. Henry already knew Alexander Trowbridge, a consulting architect who acted as a project manager specializing in all matters—large and small—in bringing buildings to completion. In 1897, Trowbridge had married into the extended Pratt family (his wife was George Pratt's sister-in-law). In 1913, his company, Trowbridge & Ackerman, built "Killenworth" in Glen Cove for George Dupont Pratt, half brother to Charles M. Pratt. The large house was a Tudor, with thirty-nine paneled rooms, more than a dozen bathrooms, a dozen fireplaces, a tearoom, and a swimming pool. The house was made of seamed faced granite, ranging in color from gray to gray-green.

Trowbridge advised Folger to hire Paul Philippe Cret. Born in France in 1876, Cret had studied at the École des Beaux-Arts in Lyon and Paris, the influential art school with a history dating back to 1648. After serving in the French army in the First World War, he moved to the United States, where for more than thirty years he would teach in and later head the architecture department at the University of Pennsylvania. Cret's first important project (1908–10) was the Pan American Union Building (now the headquarters of the Organization of American States) in Washington, D.C. Other projects included the National Memorial Arch (1914–17) at Valley Forge National Historical Park, and the original Barnes Foundation (1923–25). Folger liked what he saw and made a quick decision, hiring Cret on Trowbridge's recommendation, and then engaging Trowbridge as consulting architect.

Chapter 13

꙰Y꙰

"Thou Art a Moniment, Without a Tombe"

—BEN JONSON

$\mathcal{E}$ARLY ON, Henry and Emily Folger revealed their overall vision for the building. More than three thousand miles and three hundred years removed from Shakespeare's place and time, one block away from the U.S. Capitol, and across the street from the Library of Congress, the idea of erecting a gigantic English cottage would have been out of place, so despite their love of all things Elizabethan, they wanted a modern but classical exterior, not the half-timber and whitewashed plaster ubiquitous in Renaissance England.

Trowbridge and Cret envisioned a modern building, too, designed with a streamlined aesthetic, pared down to classical forms. The architects proposed a two-story rectangular structure clad in white Georgia marble, without columns or excessive external adornment, accented with stylish Art Deco touches, including railings, decorative window grilles, and doorways all fashioned from aluminum.

Cret and Folger reached a happy compromise. The library would become two different buildings, one concealed within the other. The architect's vision would rule the exterior design, but the Folgers' Shakespearian taste would dominate the interior. On the outside, Cret's design would harmonize with its surroundings: the Capitol, the Library of Congress, the Russell Senate Office Building, and the soon-to-be-built

Supreme Court Building. Inside, Folger's library would indulge his Elizabethan tastes with a riot of dark wood wall paneling and high beams, stone blocks, ornate and exquisite carvings, elaborate stained-glass windows, huge chandeliers and torchieres, and a Great Hall complete with a gigantic hearth and massive sixteenth- and seventeenth-century-style furniture. The Great Hall was designed as a high-ceilinged public exhibition hall, filled with glass cases of Folger treasures on display. The Folger Library would be an institution with two personalities. To passersby, the exterior would suggest the federal buildings of twentieth-century Washington. To those who ventured inside, the interior would, in an instant, transport visitors back more than three hundred years to Elizabethan or Jacobean England. Like a play within a play, the architecture of the Folger Library contained secrets.

Letters and memos preserved in Folger's private files reveal the degree to which his library was the product of his singular imagination. He valued Cret's talent, and deferred to the architect's broad vision, but on issues involving specific decorative elements for the exterior, Folger's proposals prevailed. Henry also suggested additional rooms, not included in Cret's original renderings, and almost every visible decorative element. The collector looked to Trowbridge to interpret and implement his dreams. Henry and Emily wanted the library's interior to mesmerize visitors with words, signs, and symbols. Emily wrote that they intended the library to represent "the First Folio, illustrated." Thus, Henry would call for stained-glass windows, crests, floor tiles, quotations cut in stone, and symbols—including the ubiquitous Tudor rose—carved in wood. He chose every design element to communicate a specific meaning—many of them sophisticated and obscure. The symbols, images, and sayings formed a silent composition that only he and Emily could hear. In balance, they created a harmonic resonance that conjured up the spirit of Shakespeare's England. Folger exercised great care in choosing them, specifying their exact spelling and punctuation, preserving archaic forms. In the realm of these secret words and signs, only a time traveler or a scholar could comprehend and decode them. The documents that Folger left behind show his profound influence on his library. Indeed, almost everything there today has its origins in a letter or memo signed by Henry Folger. These papers, uncatalogued and forgotten, are echoes of Folger's fervid and passionate state of mind during the two years he was in the grip of his last obsession—building his treasure house.

At the beginning, he tried to give his architects an idea of the true scope of his collection, and how he envisioned the library might operate. After outlining the sheer bulk of the books and printed materials that would need to be housed, Henry turned to the Shakespeare-themed art he had accumulated. He informed Trowbridge "there must be a thousand or more water-color drawings . . . [including] Cruikshank's *Birth of Shakespeare,* which is famous and was the center of attraction in the Marsden Perry Library." Folger added that there were oil paintings, too. "We have never tried to buy paintings or other Shakespeare illustrations . . . but when paintings were offered, not too costly and they seemed worth while, we have taken them and put them away in storage." In looking over his checklist, Folger admitted, "They are more in number than I had supposed." Folger enclosed with his letter an inventory of more than two hundred oil paintings, including seventeen portraits of Shakespeare. Predictably, he warned that this information was secret. "I would like to ask that this list be used by you for your private, personal information, as I do not feel ready yet to give out any announcements about the size or character of the collection."[1]

And still, Henry was not finished buying paintings, if the price was right. On one occasion Folger refused a set of drawings based on *The Winter's Tale* that Rosenbach offered him. "I buy illustrations only when they appeal to me as being very cheap. I do not doubt that the price you name is a fair one, still it is not low enough to tempt me."[2] In October 1928, one "case of paintings" and one "box of four paintings" arrived in New York. In November, he purchased two First Folios for $22,500 (W 136, F 78) and $5,375 (W 137, F 79). The first contained replacement pages from a copy of the Second Folio, including the title page, mounted and altered to make it look like one from a First Folio title page. It also contained juvenile drawings on several of the preliminary pages. The second copy, with brittle pages, lacked all the preliminaries.

These two additions brought his collection to eighty-two copies. They were the last two copies that Henry ever bought.

Folger could not afford to keep collecting unless he kept careful watch over his construction budget. A month after spending more than $75,000 on the two books, he wrote Trowbridge that the library was starting to look too expensive:

> The cost seems to total more than I had hoped would be shown for the structure. I had been carrying in my mind a total cost of, say, $750,000, so that the cost of the building and land would be about $1 million. We wish the structure to be fitting both to the location and to the material to be housed, so we do not wish to cramp it. If necessary we can take some funds from the Endowment, or can extend the time of construction, postponing a part of the actual expenditure.[3]

When Folger saw some of Cret's preliminary drawings for the library's principal public space, a huge rectangular room that ran three-quarters of the length of the building, he feared that the architects had misunderstood his wishes. Folger had in mind that the reading room would be a harmonious mixture of a Tudor-style great hall with a trussed roof but with "the warm atmosphere of a private home."[4] In a long letter to Trowbridge dated December 20, 1928, Henry set down in writing for the first time how he expected his library to function:

> Studying the attractive drawings of the ground plans for the Washington Library leads me to think I might do well to give you and Mr. Cret some idea of how we expect the Library to be used. Sketch "A" has in the body of the main room five tables, and Sketch "B" eight tables, giving the impression that the room is to be used as a reading-room. But I doubt if this will be the case. It will not be a reading room in the way reading-rooms are used generally, nor even as a room for study, because our Library is too special in its character, and the contents are so costly and limited in scope.

Folger reminded Trowbridge that the "main room" did not require so many tables and chairs because few people would ever be allowed to set foot in it:

> You once spoke of having the general effect intimate, rather than imposing. This would be more in keeping with the limitation of the collection. The Lenox Library, which stood on the Fifth Avenue property now occupied by the Frick Home, was restricted to Americana and Shakepeariana. Admission was secured only by ticket, which had to be obtained a day or two before and named not only the day but also the hour for admission. The visitors were treated as guests and were made at home by the custodian. The result was that only those who had real business at the library came to see it. That, of course, carried the limitation to an extreme, but our collection should not be offered freely to all comers, and the Library should not be looked upon as a reading-room nor a comfortable rest-room.

In the New Year, Folger turned to the library's single grandest decorative element—a huge stained-glass window set in the west wall of the reading room. It would be visible only from inside, and its theme was of vital importance to Henry. His original concept was to replicate the window in the rear of the chancel in Holy Trinity Church, where Shakespeare is buried. He modified that idea, asking that each panel of the tracery window depict a phase from Jaques's "Seven Ages of Man" speech from *As You Like It*. Its universal truth appealed to Folger, and he typed out the quotation for Cret:

> All the world's a stage,
> And all the men and women merely players.
> They have their exits and their entrances,
> And one man in his time plays many parts,
> His acts being seven ages. At first the infant . . . ,
> Then the whining schoolboy . . . then the lover . . .
> Then, a soldier, . . . And then the justice, . . .

The sixth age . . . [then the] Last scene of all,
That ends this strange, eventful history,
Is second childishness and mere oblivion,
Sans teeth, sans eyes, sans taste, sans everything.
(Act II, Scene vii, lines 139–142, 146, 148, 152, 156, 162–165)

Folger also proposed oriel stained-glass windows—popular in Tudor architecture—in the south wall of the room. They would illustrate the coats of arms of those instrumental to the performance and publication of Shakespeare's plays: King James I, James and Richard Burbage, John Smethwick, William Aspley, and William Jaggard.[5]

Throughout the project, Henry's attention shifted back and forth between aesthetic and practical questions. In February 1929, he instructed his architects that he wanted visitors to be able to drive up to the library in their cars: "There will be need of some way of coming up to the building in an automobile, for protection at night and in stormy weather." And did Cret and Trowbridge expect the library staff to carry boxes of books up and down the stairs? "As yet we have seen no provision for an elevator, which would seem to be needed to move books and other heavy parcels from the street level, or the basement, to the upper floors."[6] Folger also wondered whether an exhibition hall—a long hall parallel to the main reading room—was practical:

> In your letter of the 23rd, you express for us our own views about the Shakespeare Gallery. The proportions and design are so well done that we cannot find fault. Still our enterprise is first of all a Library, not a Museum. And the setting may be . . . more beautiful than the contents. We have only a few real Museum Pieces. Most of our items are interesting because they are Shakepeariana rather than artistic.[7]

Despite his reservations, Folger accepted the proposal.

Cret and Trowbridge had been pressuring their client to allow them to publicize their role in the project. Future commissions depended on their ability to showcase their work. It was only fair, they suggested, that they inform colleagues and potential clients of their talents. Predictably, Folger refused, complaining that if dealers learned of his plans, they would "advance the prices" of items he wished to purchase. It was an unreasonable posture. Book dealers in Europe had been "wise" to Folger's not-so-secret obsession for years, they had already read about the library from the April 1928 *New York Times* article, and additional publicity about the project would only confirm what they already knew.

Henry's consulting architect would not relent. In a letter dated March 7, 1929, Trowbridge suggested language for what he described as a "booklet containing an explanation of my particular form of service as advisory architect and I wish to include in it some reference to the Folger Shakespeare Foundation." Professing sensitivity to Folger's fretting about publicity and its potential harm to his book-hunting escapades, the architect added, "If this is not the sort of thing you would like to have stated, I will be very much appreciative if you will give me suggestions. I do not think this booklet will bring about real publicity, as it is going to individuals and not to newspapers or magazines, or other publicity mediums."

Henry surprised Trowbridge by capitulating two days later: "[O]f course feel free to refer to the Shakespeare library in your booklet if you think it may help you. And the paragraph you quote is all right, except that I would prefer to have omitted the line 'said to be the finest collection of its kind outside of the British Museum.'"[8] Perhaps Henry believed his collection to rival that of the British Museum? That month, Trowbridge published his booklet, a small, four-by-six-inch pamphlet bound in gray wrappers. He deleted the objectionable line about the British Museum.

After studying Cret's plans, Folger proposed the addition of two spaces within the building. Henry looked forward to using his library, and he imagined spending long hours there with Emily poring over catalogues, handling their treasures, and enjoying themselves. But they could hardly sit at a table in the main book room, in full view of visitors and employees—they were too reticent for that. Henry had another idea, which he proposed to Trowbridge in a letter mailed from the Homestead in March 1929:

Don't you think it might be well to consider providing in the Shakespeare Building a room or two for social purposes, where we can meet business callers and friends informally? I will hope to spend some time, myself at the Library, quietly, away from the working force and visitors. I suggest two rooms with a lavatory. The rooms should have good light and air, with a fireplace, but not, necessarily, an outlook.[9]

Cret designed a two-room suite—a reception room and a private room—for his patron. Given that the Folgers lived in New York and were not planning to relocate to Washington, it was surprising that Henry did not call for a small private apartment to be built inside the structure. But he did ask for something larger and much more daunting. By April 1929, Folger concocted a scheme to include a theater inside his library, to be located at the east end of the building, on the Third Street side. Folger considered copying a lesser-known Elizabethan theater, but then settled on the Globe. He explained to Trowbridge in a letter in late April: "[W]e had better do what we can to make the Theatre a reproduction of the Globe. . . . [Shakespeare's] reputation was made by what he accomplished at the Globe." But Cret could not make the design work. Perhaps it was better, Folger wrote, to "construct a theatre which will suggest the several Elizabethan theatres, in a general way, rather than try to copy simply one of them."[10] Folger's plan was eccentric. He requested no dressing rooms, and had no plan to put on plays. The playhouse would exist merely to evoke an Elizabethan mood, and serve as a venue for academic lectures.

In the spring of 1929, Folger's concerns swung again from artistic to practical. He knew that once his books were concentrated in one place for the first time, a fire or other disaster could destroy his entire collection. As long as his books remained dispersed in storage units scattered throughout New York City, a fire at any one warehouse would endanger only a portion of his collection. "[M]any of the items," Henry cautioned Trowbridge, "are unique, so that if they are damaged or destroyed they cannot be replaced."[11] He questioned whether using so much wood—furniture, paneling, beams, and more—might "detract from a perfect fire-proof construction, as is necessary for the library books. I suppose there are several ways of avoiding this. I enclose a sketch of asbestos, which may be suggestive." He enclosed a newspaper clipping that included a photo of a home library, with the caption "Panels of Asbestos are now used to simulate ancient oak."[12] In the end, however, Folger approved fitting out the library with Appalachian oak.

He also had practical concerns about lighting, wondering if enough natural light would pass through the giant "Seven Ages of Man" stained-glass window to illuminate the main room. He asked Trowbridge: "Do you think that the chandeliers sketched into the reading-room are in keeping with the plan of the room? Might it not be better to try having hanging lanterns, suspending them from the end of the arches, and supplementing them, where necessary, with torches coming up from the floor, giving, as far as possible the Elizabethan atmosphere."[13] In the end Folger chose both types of illumination.

By late summer 1929, Folger focused on what he considered the three most important decorative elements of the exterior: sculptures, quotations, and a fountain. Henry viewed the long, East Capitol Street façade as the "front" of the library. He located two entrance doors there, and decided to decorate the middle stretch of the wall with nine marble panels bearing relief sculptures depicting characters and scenes from nine of Shakespeare's plays. In a letter to Cret, Folger revealed his choices: Titania with fairies, from *A Midsummer Night's Dream*; Shylock and Portia, from *The Merchant of Venice*; Falstaff and Prince Hal, from *Henry IV Part I*; Richard and the two young princes from *Richard III*; Romeo and Juliet in the balcony scene; Julius Caesar in the "Et tu, Brute?" scene; Macbeth and the weird sisters; Hamlet and his mother, Gertrude; and King Lear and the Fool. Folger also specified the act and scene numbers for the scenes.[14]

In October, Folger urged Cret that they speak to the American artist Frederick William MacMonnies, a disciple of the great Augustus Saint-Gaudens, "before coming to a conclusion about the nine sculptures on the East Capitol Street front of the Library." Always the bargain hunter, Folger suggested that they might get a good deal. "I am told that he is in financial straits, and, therefore, eager to secure work, and will make a reasonable charge."

Folger also visited the sculptor John Gregory at his studio. He discovered that the artist was a sympathetic book collector, and the two hit it off. According to John Harbeson, one of Cret's architects who accompanied Folger to meet the sculptor, "The two men were immediately at ease with each other, completely understood one another. When we came out of Gregory's Studio Mr. Folger said 'We need not visit any others; I am entirely satisfied to go ahead with Gregory. You fix up the contract, and bring it to me to see.'" The penny-pincher in Folger was pleased that Gregory seemed eager for the work. Later, when Henry visited the artist to look at studies for the high-relief sculptures, he liked what he saw, but in a letter to Cret, he suggested changes to the King Lear relief in progress. The Lear was too old, and the Fool too young. He should be "made a little more muscular," Henry wrote, "to seem more vigorous." Folger also thought that Lear's expression should reflect his state of mind. "And I think he might be a little more distraught, because, as you know, he was already on the verge of madness. And yet, whatever changes are made will have to be very slight so as not to go too far."

Folger wanted to erect a fountain featuring a freestanding marble sculpture of the sprite Puck from *A Midsummer Night's Dream* on the west side of the library that faced Second Street, the Library of Congress, and, beyond it, the Capitol. He considered engaging sculptress Rachel Hawks or Harriet Hosmer, who had previously executed a sculpture of Puck. Trowbridge favored another sculptor, Brenda Putnam, who, not coincidentally, was the daughter of the helpful Librarian of Congress Herbert Putnam. In a wise concession, Folger deferred to Trowbridge. Later Henry told his consulting architect how pleased he was with the idea: "We are under great obligations to Dr. Putnam, and for that and other reasons will be glad to see the name of his daughter associated with our project." But Brenda Putnam's special status did not exempt her from Folger's artistic direction. He said that he wanted the figure of Puck to appear more or less "embowered in shrubbery." He got what he wanted: oak branches carved in the marble base of the sculpture create the impression of being in the forest where the trick-ster Puck gamboled.

In the summer of 1929, as Henry started considering the words he wanted carved on the exterior walls of what he called his "Washington venture," he changed the name of his institution. He no longer liked its first one, "Folger Shakespeare Memorial." Instead, he wrote, "[L]et us, then, put on the building 'FOLGER SHAKESPEARE LIBRARY.' After all our enterprise is primarily a library, and all other features are supplemental." He ordered that the word *SHAKESPEARE* be carved on the East Capitol Street façade in letters slightly larger than *Folger* and *Library*.

He chose three quotations to be carved on the wall facing East Capitol Street, typing them exactly as he wanted them to appear.

This therefore is the praise of Shakespeare,
That his drama is the mirrour of life.

SAMUEL JOHNSON

His wit can no more lie hid, than it could be lost. Reade him, therefore; and again, and again.

JOHN HEMINGE
HENRIE CONDELL

Thou art a Moniment, without a tombe,
And art aliue still, while thy Booke doth liue,
And we have wits to read, and praise to give.

BEN IONSON

Folger supplied these inscriptions to Cret, along with one quotation from *Love's Labour's Lost* for the west wall facing Second Street—"For Wisdomes sake, a word that all men loue [love]"—with the admoni-tion that they be large enough to be easily read from the street, and that "the spelling and punctuation should be followed exactly." Just to be sure, Folger wrote to him a second time to emphasize the importance of the spelling and punctuation of the quotations. To ensure that Cret did not think that his instructions contained any typographical errors, Folger was precise: "In the First Folio Ben Jonson appears twice in the preliminary pages. The leaf just before the title page, facing the title page, is signed B.I.—meaning Ben Jonson. The page from which our quotation is taken is likewise signed Ben:Ionson. There seems to be another reason: There is no letter that runs below the line, unless the J is used in Jonson. Using the I would not only be fitting, but would be harmonious with the rest of the lettering." Henry Folger's library would perfectly reflect his vision. No detail was too small for him.

He asked Cret to tell him what kind of heating boilers would be used, adding that if they were coal-fired, provisions must be made for a room to store emergency stockpiles of the fuel. Or perhaps, Henry speculated, he could buy heat from the Library of Congress and obtain it via underground steam pipes.

The attention that Henry gave the library never prevented him from buying more books. Shipments of new acquisitions arrived often. In just one example, on September 24, 1929, a letter from the customs house brokers Tice & Lynch, Inc., informed Folger of the arrival of a "Box of Books from [Bernard] Quaritch, Ltd. London," that had come in on the RMS *Aquitania* and for which five dollars was due for duty and cartage.

Thursday, October 24, 1929, the banner headline of the *Brooklyn Daily Eagle* read, "WALL STREET IN PANIC AS STOCKS CRASH." The following Monday, the value of the New York Stock Exchange fell thirteen percent and billions of dollars of stock market wealth were lost. It marked the end of almost a decade of increases in the Dow Jones Industrial Average and the end of the optimism of the Roaring Twenties. Less wealth meant less buying for cash-strapped book collectors.

Cret, Trowbridge, and Folger had been planning the library on paper for more than a year. Soon, it would be time to break ground and begin construction. But before that could happen, Folger needed to hire a general contractor to pull down the houses on Grant's Row. Trowbridge recommended civil engineer James Baird, who had directed the erection of the Flatiron Building, the iconic, steel-framed skyscraper in New York City. In Virginia, Baird had supervised the construction of the Tomb of the Unknown Soldier at Arlington National Cemetery, the Lincoln Memorial, and the Freer Gallery of Art in Washington, D.C. Cret advised that they should salvage some of the "brick in these old residences, which could be used in the construction of the walls as a backing for the marble exterior." Folger must have loved that economy. He agreed on the choice, and in November, Trowbridge wrote that as soon as he received the estimates he was expecting from Baird, the contracts could be negotiated and signed. The first brick was removed from the first house to be torn down on November 11, Armistice Day.

On December 3, 1929, with serious demolition about to commence, Folger informed Trowbridge that he wanted no publicity associated with the tearing down of the houses: "[W]e would very much prefer, for the present at any rate, to have no sign, or other description, put up in connection with the dismantling for the Shakespeare Library, as suggested by the Baird Company. We are not seeking any advertising—in fact we are doing our best to avoid calling attention to the enterprise." This was to be expected from a man who, one of his classmates said, lived by three rules: "Never tell what you've done, what you are doing, or what you are going to do." Again, it was a pointless charade. Sign or no sign, everyone knew who owned Grant's Row and what he planned to do with it.

That month, Folger met with Rosenbach to examine a group of Elizabethan rarities that were for sale. Folger returned to the dealer all the items save one, noting that he must be "economical in buying books, for a time at least." The only book he kept from the lot was a copy of Greene's *Groatsworth of Wit.* The stock market crash and the continuing expenses of building the library limited his acquisition fever.

After more than a decade of planning, 1930 promised to be the pivotal year. If all went well, Henry would see construction begin in earnest. Demolition of Grant's Row was under way, and the site was being cleared in preparation for excavating the foundation. Then, through the summer and fall of 1930, he could watch his Shakespeare palace rise. Baird might finish the job by the end of the year, but if not then, certainly in 1931. It would not be long, Folger believed, before he could reclaim the oil portraits of himself and Emily from storage and hang them in the library. Indeed, by the end of January 1930, he had already chosen the exact spot for their display—the screen at the east end of the reading room, below a replica of the Shakespeare memorial bust at Holy Trinity Church in Stratford-upon-Avon. He had even consulted the portraits' artist, Frank Salisbury, who approved. Henry did not know how significant that spot in the library would soon become.

In the meantime, he had many more important decisions to make. On February 4, 1930, Henry wrote to Trowbridge about the cost of the building's systems:

> I am just in receipt of a copy of Mr. Cret's letter to the Baird Company, Feb. 1st, approving a sub-contract for Heating, Plumbing and Ventillating, to the Standard Engineering Co., $150,000. Was the estimate, upon which the total figures of cost were based, as large as this sum for Heating, Plumbing and Ventillating? It is a satisfaction to find the work progressing, but as the totals grow I am concerned to learn whether we are going to keep within our figure of total expenditure.

It was Folger's habit to read every single work order, invoice, and approval connected to the project, and a week later, he asked Trowbridge to clarify something he did not understand: "May I trouble you to send just a line, for information, as to what is meant by the expression 'Air-Conditioning,' in Approval #20, sent the James Baird Co. February 11. I presume it is something in connection with the ventilation." Trowbridge explained that it was a new process to cool the air and reduce the temperature inside a building. Folger was curious and wrote back:

> Thank you for your letter of the 14th, explaining the contract for "Air-Conditioning"; but I am surprised that anyone will undertake, in a building of that size, in Washington, to secure a temperature of 85° in the Summer with a 50% humidity. We will

certainly have a popular room if this is accomplished. What cooling medium are they planning to use? Knowing the conditions in Washington in Mid-summer we had supposed it might be necessary to close the building for several weeks.

In May, Cret informed Folger that soon it would be time to lay the cornerstone. It was the usual custom to mark the occasion with a ceremony. Did Henry want to plan one? No, he replied, "our preference is to postpone any ceremony until the dedication of the building at its completion. And we think a stone, with the date, 1930, but without a box [a time capsule], will be the best. Let it go into the structure whenever convenient, without ceremony."

Folger was more interested in selecting the final quotations and symbols for the library's interior than in what he believed was a premature ceremony. And, of course, such an event would certainly involve dreaded publicity. Henry Folger acquired a booklet, *A Complete Collection of the Quotations and Inscriptions in the Library of Congress.* He did not wish to copy any of them, but was keen to see how another institution had adorned itself. Then he made a list of the inscriptions he wished to have in his own library, planning each one, and again instructing the architect not to change the archaic spelling or punctuation of the words. He chose passages about Shakespeare and by his acolytes, from Ralph Waldo Emerson, David Garrick, Victor Hugo, Johann Wolfgang von Goethe, and others.

In Folger's last letter about the inscriptions, he gave Cret a quotation that summed up the meaning of both the whole enterprise and Henry's genial character. Henry asked that it be carved above the door in a vestibule that led into the exhibition hall. Anyone who entered the building there would, even before they approached the reading room, see these words. It was the shortest of all the quotations to be inscribed anywhere inside the library or on its exterior walls. And, of course, it was by Shakespeare: "I shower a welcome on ye. Welcome all."

Having finished with the inscriptions, Henry selected the final symbols. He wanted crests—lots of them. He wrote Cret instructions to place the crests of England and the United States, at opposite ends of the exhibition hall, facing each other. He also wanted the crests of Shakespeare's two monarchs, Queen Elizabeth I and King James I. To these he added those of Shakespeare patrons the Earl of Southampton, the Earls of Pembroke and Montgomery, and the Earl of Warwick. And, of course, Folger wanted these symbols to appear exactly correct: "It seems to me that all these crests can well be colored, as used by their owners. We doubtless can find, and send to you, copies in colors, of all." William Jaggard, Isaac Jaggard, and Edward Blount are also commemorated in stained glass in the reading room.

Three months after Folger's first correspondence in February about air-conditioning, he still had not made up his mind. On May 2, he wrote Trowbridge that he would be satisfied if limited air-conditioning were used only for the "book stacks and the vaults—that they were making no attempt to 'Condition' any other part of the building. I was quite satisfied that they would not be able to accomplish any satisfactory results if they attempted to Condition the Main Library itself." Then, three days later, he wrote again, wondering if they should bother with any air-conditioning at all: "It seems that this is the first Library installation which they have secured, and I am inclined to think it will be better for us to let some other Library do the pioneer work, and later, if it is successful, consider installing it in our building."

Henry Folger complained to his contractor, James Baird, that a newspaper had published a front-page photograph of the construction in progress. He did not want that kind of attention. By this point, his paranoia about publicity was utterly absurd. Baird pointed out the obvious in a letter to Folger's secretary, A. G. Welsh: "[T]he building [is] rapidly rising, and [anyone can] take their own photographs and publish them whenever they pleased." He repeated a request from Trowbridge to allow photographs and information about the project to be made available. "The building is taking shape," Baird reminded his patron, "and the thousands who pass the site every day can see it in plain view, and it is a very difficult matter, and going to become [an] even more difficult matter, to maintain secrecy about the project, for it is in plain view and occupies one of the most prominent sites in the city." What Baird wrote was rational. But Henry's instinctual abhorrence of publicity sometimes clouded his otherwise rational and brilliant mind.

In late May, Henry left his home in Glen Cove, Long Island, and entered St. John's Hospital in Brooklyn for what he and Emily believed would be a minor operation. After prostate surgery, performed under local anesthesia, he was confined to bed. While Folger was recuperating in the hospital, Rosenbach visited him, bringing him grapes he had brought across the Atlantic from his recent trip to England. In a temporary arrangement, his secretary Welsh took over Folger's correspondence. On May 28, 1930, Welsh wrote to Trowbridge informing him that Henry had just signed the agreement with Brenda Putnam to commence the Puck sculpture: "I have forwarded the contracts with Miss Putnam to Mr. Cret, duly signed by Mr. Folger. Mr. Folger is still laid up, in bed, but I am able to take important matters up with him." On June 5, Welsh informed Trowbridge that Henry was still not well: "For your information, personally, Mr. Folger has been confined to bed for the last three weeks, or more, and, outside of the Library, there are few matters I can take up with him. But, for the Library, he wants me to keep in touch with you." That did not stop Henry himself from writing to Trowbridge the same day. As so often over the past two years, it was about the little details. Folger inquired what the "special allowance 'G' [for] Lighting Fixtures . . . covers?"

Trowbridge answered on June 10, explaining the charges for the fixtures and adding that he was "sorry to hear of your illness." It is the last letter in Folger's personal files on the construction of his library. Henry Folger would never reply to this letter.

His doctors determined, three weeks after the first operation, that he needed a second. He had survived the first, but could not bear the strain of another, and on June 11, he succumbed to a pulmonary embolism. He was a week shy of his seventy-third birthday. What would Folger's death mean for the future of his library? Would laborers show up on schedule the next morning at East Capitol Street, and would work go on? Would it ever be finished? And if the building were completed, would it ever open its doors as a library? How badly had the October 1929 stock market crash affected his investments? Perhaps his estate no longer possessed sufficient assets to complete the building, establish the library, and endow its future. Perhaps the collection would have to be sold at auction. Henry Folger *was* the Folger Shakespeare Library. In the aftermath of his death, who would carry on?

The obituary in the next day's *New York Times* summed up his life in four efficient headlines: "H. CLAY FOLGER DIES AFTER AN OPERATION/ Resigned as Head of Standard Oil of New York to Plan a Shakespeare Memorial/ HAD RARE BOOK COLLEC-TION/ Proposed to Make Works of Dramatist and Poet Available to Students of Literature." It must have quenched Rosenbach's thirst for publicity to see that he made an appearance in Henry's obituary: "In 1919 [Folger] paid the Rosenbach Company . . . $100,000 for the unique Gwynn volume of nine plays, published in 1619." The *Times* made no further mention of the future of the Folger Shakespeare Library. Soon Rosenbach would write a substantial monograph on Henry as a collector.

The funeral was held in Brooklyn on June 13 at 8 PM, in the chapel of the Central Congregational Church on Hancock Street, near Franklin Avenue. Its pastor and Henry's close friend, the Rev. Dr. S. Parkes Cadman, presided. After the service, Emily Folger did not bury her husband of almost forty-five years. She chose to cremate his remains. But she did not scatter the ashes. She had a special place in mind for Henry. It would, she vowed, be ready soon.

Chapter 14

❧❦❧

"It Is the Key to Our Hearts"

—Emily C. J. Folger

*H*ENRY'S SUDDEN death after two minor surgeries shocked Emily Folger. His retirement from Standard Oil and total involvement in all aspects of the construction of the library had brought out in him the energy and enthusiasm of a much younger man. He had loved every moment he spent working on the project, relishing every detail from the mundane—toilets and heating—to the sublime—stained glass and marble sculpture. For weeks after his death, books Henry had purchased continued to arrive at Twenty-Six Broadway. Emily instructed Alexander Welsh to return those that had been sent on approval but not yet purchased.

Despite Henry's death, Emily had no doubt that the library would be completed. She knew that even before experts came in to analyze his will and tally his assets, and even while America was experiencing a severe economic downturn—and who knew how long that would last?—there would be enough money, whether the final bill was $750,000, as Henry had hoped, or double that. She also knew that Henry's will established a generous endowment to cover the library's operating costs for years to come.

But how seriously had the stock market crash reduced the value of Henry's estate? He did not possess major cash reserves. His principal assets, aside from the Shakespeare collection, were his investments, and of these holdings the most valuable by far were his shares in the Standard Oil companies. He had scrimped and borrowed for decades to accumulate them and they were the major assets upon which the long-term future of the library depended. Henry's estate could afford to build it, but without his stock portfolio, Emily could not afford to perpetuate it.

Regardless, she vowed to continue, even if she had to spend all her own assets. "On June 11, 1930," she reminisced, "I was left alone to carry on his work. It was a grave responsibility. But we had been together so long and had been so much at one in our thought that I knew what he desired and was prepared to take up the task in his name."[1] It was as though Emily Folger sought to fulfill the lover's promise in *Measure for Measure*: "What's mine is yours and what is yours is mine. So, bring us to our palace; where we'll show what's yet behind, that's meet you all should know."

On June 24, 1930, the *New York Times* made public the terms of Henry Folger's will: "$10,000,000 TO AID SHAKESPEARE STUDY/ Fund Set Aside in H.C. Folger Will to Finish and Maintain Library at Washington. BUILDING COST $2,000,000/ Edifice to House World-Famed Collection of the Oil Man." It was a huge amount of money, especially during the Great Depression. Ten million dollars in 1930 would be the equivalent of one hundred million today. The *Times* continued: "Henry Clay Folger, former chairman of the board of the Standard Oil Company of New York, who died before realizing his ambition to establish a memorial home for his world-famous Shakespearean collection for the use of students of Elizabethan drama, made provision in his will for its completion and maintenance, it was learned yesterday." Folger left specific bequests to his sister, two brothers, a nephew, and five nieces totaling $300,000. He dictated that an endowment fund for the library be maintained in an amount no less than $10 million to be administered by the trustees of Amherst College. One-quarter of the annual income from the fund would be paid to Amherst, with a floor of $100,000 and a cap of $250,000 per year. The remaining three-quarters would go to the library. Emily would receive an annuity of $50,000 per year during her lifetime.

On Halloween, 1930, Emily Folger transferred the deed to the library and title to the collection to the trustees of Amherst. She paid off the $104,000 mortgage on the library, and agreed not to demand of the estate immediate payment of the $1.5 million in promissory notes that had accumulated as Henry had borrowed money from her to buy items for the collection.

Henry's instructions regarding the library were plain:

> Within three years from the date of my death said trustees shall install and establish my Shakespeare collection . . . as a permanent library in a building in Washington, D.C., said library to be known as the "Folger Shakespeare Memorial," [Folger's will predated his decision to change the word *memorial* to *library*] and shall thereafter maintain said library and all additions thereto as a separate and distinct library . . . for the promotion and diffusion of knowledge in regard to the history and writings of Shakespeare.

Up to this point, the text of his last will and testament was strictly business, and spoke in the dry language of the law. Then Henry added a sentimental bequest—it was more of a tribute—for Emily:

> My wife, Emily C. J. Folger, has from the beginning aided me greatly with her advice and counsel, and has shared in developing my plan . . . and has assisted me in the selection and care . . . of my collection. I therefore request that the trustees . . . will permit my . . . wife to borrow books and other items from said collection freely and without restriction and that they consult her in the case of all plans of the . . . library and all regulations and expenditures pertaining to the same.

To this day, Emily remains the only reader ever to have enjoyed the privilege of borrowing a book from the Folger Shakespeare Library. She was his silent partner, his equal in their calling. He knew it, which explains why, of course, the name *Henry* is not carved in wood or stone anywhere in the library. Instead, the walls bear only the name they shared, *Folger*.

Henry's death did not delay the construction. "Architects and builders," Emily wrote, "went on with their duties. Again and again we met to discuss developments as they occurred. I lost myself in the work, and . . . was happy." Indeed, the day after the *New York Times* story appeared and only fourteen days after Henry died, the "Daily Reports" from East Capitol Street on Wednesday, June 25, record a busy scene: "Temperature 76 degrees at 7:30 a.m., skies clear. 122 men employed for carpentry, brickwork and concrete. An additional 36 men employed by sub contractors for plumbing, heating, and ventilation." Three days later, on June 28, twenty flights of iron stairs were installed.

Work continued through the summer and fall of 1930. Emily corresponded with Cret about a new decorative element she wanted to install in the reading room, in a niche not far from where the Salisbury portraits would hang—a bronze tablet honoring her husband. On October 21, Cret asked her to approve the design of the engraved and enameled memorial he had fashioned. Cret wrote to Emily on February 29, 1931, to thank her for selecting him as their architect: "Now that the building is from week to week taking better shape, I feel still more my deep obligation to Mr. Folger and you who gave me the opportunity to be interpreter of your thoughts in honoring genius." She had one more idea, she confided to Cret; it was something that Henry did not request. In a modest, even tentative voice, her letter asked whether the architect thought it might be appropriate to commission a marble bust of her husband, to be placed on permanent exhibit somewhere in the library. Of course, Cret replied, and he could suggest several places for it, including the exhibition hall. Emily engaged John Gregory, who was still busy sculpting the nine high reliefs for the East Capitol front of the library, to create a white marble bust of Henry.

Baird's construction crew put in a hard season of work in the summer of 1931, bringing the library almost to completion. From time to time, Emily Folger took the train down from New York to watch the building rise. "By the autumn of 1931," she observed, "the outer shell of the library was complete, and the interior well advanced. It was a busy scene . . . as the marble rose around the steel armature, I spoke of the building as being like a pearl, and The Pearl became a common synonym for the Library." As Henry had foreseen, 1931 turned out to be the critical year.

He had not predicted another milestone—the settlement of his estate. On September 23, 1931, the *New York Times* announced the news: "$13,719,635 ESTATE LEFT BY H.C. FOLGER/ Former Head of Standard Oil Owned Securities Valued at $9,005,020 in Appraisal/ $4,355,373 LOST IN SALE." The article explained that, to date, $12,781,599 had been paid out of the estate. Folger's largest holdings were 151,167 shares of Standard Oil of New York valued at $5,077,521, 25,340 shares of Standard Oil of New Jersey valued at $1,843,485, plus other stocks. The Shakespeariana collection was valued at $4,265,000.[2]

The value of Henry Folger's stock portfolio had decreased by half between October 1929 and the time of his death. What did this mean for the library? He knew the stock market had crashed, and that the money he had provided in his will for the library's ongoing operations might not be enough to support the institution he was building. He included in his instructions to the trustees at Amherst that if the endowment's value fell below $10 million, the income from it was to be used only for operations, not acquisitions. Henry need not have worried. Emily shored up the library's finances, donating money as well as hundreds of thousands of dollars in IOUs she held against Henry's estate at the time of the library's opening.

On September 23, the same day the *New York Times* published its article about Henry Folger's estate, William A. Slade, who had been hired with Emily's approval as the Folger Library's first librarian, wrote an important letter to Emily: "The furnishings are in. . . . The actual moving in of the collections will now begin in only a few days . . . [we will soon] start the first lot of material."[3] Slade's excitement was premature. Before all the books could be moved, they had to be found.

On October 21, 1931, the *Times* announced: "FOLGER BOOKS MOVED BY ARMORED TRUCK/ Five guards take First Lot of

$4,265,000 Shakespeareana to New Capital Library." On Monday, October 19, an armored car from the United States Trucking Corporation had driven the first shipment of Henry's books from New York to Washington. The vehicle carried a small lot of just 350 titles, a tiny portion of Folger's vast collection, but this grouping included some of his most rare and valuable books. They were the easiest ones to find because Henry had stored his best volumes in bank vaults, instead of scattering them in warehouse storage rooms all over New York. The *Times* story named several of them: "The Vincent Folio of 1623 . . . the most precious book in the world" and worth $100,000; "'Venus and Adonis' from 1599 and valued at $75,000"; the *Titus Andronicus* of 1594, "valued at $45,000, and the Pavier Quarto from 1619 and valued at $100,000."[4] If anything happened to that truck, the library could lose more than half a million dollars' worth of Folger's most famous and valuable treasures in an instant. The armored car departed New York at 10 AM. The drive took twelve long hours—almost three times what it would take today via modern highways and bridges—and it was not until 10 PM that night that the truck rolled into the curved driveway at Second and East Capitol Street.

There was no single "moving day" on which Folger's entire collection was brought from New York to Washington. His vast holdings made the logistics of that impossible. The first armored car kicked off what can only be described as "moving season"—a period of six months, from the fall of 1931 through the spring of 1932, when the collection was transported to Washington. And it took time to find all the books. In New York, multiple storage rooms in several commercial warehouses disgorged their crates of treasures. Henry Folger's intricate, hand-drawn plans—like a pirate's treasure map—traced pathways through the labyrinthine storage vaults and marked the locations of individual crates. Without Henry's meticulous record keeping, some of his collection might have been lost. By the end of 1932, the warehouses in Brooklyn and Manhattan had surrendered 2,109 crates of books, artworks, manuscripts, furniture, and other objects. No one save Emily knew exactly what the boxes contained. Rosenbach was sure there would be revelations as the materials were unpacked: "There will be surprises innumerable. Hidden in the profound depths of this collection there will be, I am sure, much new material."[5]

The records of just one warehouse reveal the staggering scale of the Folgers' storage system. The first store room they rented was at Eagle Warehouse, and if they kept it until the library was ready to open—and all indications are they did (there are invoices paid by Henry from as late as September 1929 and it is likely that the next invoice for storage was paid for by the estate, then by the trustees of Amherst College under the terms of Henry Folger's will)—then they occupied this storage room for thirty-four years, from 1897 to 1931. The rent was $4 a month for four years, $12 per month for the next eight years, and at least $16 a month for the next twenty-two years; $5,280 is the low estimate for the charges for thirty-four years just *for that one room.* And the Folgers had rented several other rooms in that one warehouse. And more rooms in other warehouses. Most of these storage rooms had gone undisturbed for decades.

The task of locating every single crate of Henry's hoard and driving it to Washington was difficult enough. But once the containers arrived at the library, they had to be unpacked, their contents catalogued, and the books shelved. This would take thousands of hours. Until it was done, the building on East Capitol Street would be a library in name, not in fact. How thrilled Henry would have been to watch the first volumes placed on their shelves, breathing life into the library.

It is easy to picture him plunging his hands into crates that he had sealed twenty or thirty years before, unpacking books, removing their protective paper wrappers, holding them tight, and greeting them like old friends. He would have loved it. He had lived without them for so long, possessing only his typewritten lists of what each carefully labeled case contained.

The resurrection of Folger's long-buried books brings to mind Ben Jonson's invocation "My Shakespeare, rise!" Day after day, for six months, the library staff unpacked and began to catalogue the world's largest collection of Shakespeare's printed works, the largest assembled collection of *each* of the Folios, First through Fourth,[6] one-third of the known surviving copies of the First Folio, a magnificent collection of

Elizabethan and Jacobean works, Shakespeare's primary sources (what would have been available in the grammar school curriculum in Elizabethan England—Ovid, Seneca, Raphael Holinshed's *The Chronicles of England, Scotland, and Ireland*, Sir Thomas North's translation of Plutarch's *Lives of the Noble Greeks and Romans*), allusion works (works that mention Shakespeare, or, as in Christopher Marlowe's 1598 *Hero and Leander*, works Shakespeare "borrowed" from,[7] and Renaissance books, manuscripts, and objects related to all subjects: history, science, economics, politics, religion, law, theater, and the arts. Two hundred fifty-six thousand books; 60,000 manuscripts; 200 oil paintings; 50,000 watercolors, prints, and photographs; dozens of sculptures; half a million playbills; plus theater programs, musical instruments, costumes, and more. Each book, artwork, and artifact spoke to the others in a magical resonance that recreated the spirit of Shakespeare's age.

Rosenbach marveled at what Folger had accomplished. Even this important dealer who kept close watch on his clients' purchases was astonished by the size of the collection: "At first the mass of it alone seems overwhelming. It does not seem possible that in the short span of a lifetime one could gather so much. It must not be forgotten that every piece in this collection whether it was a book, manuscript, costume or picture was handled directly by him. He examined carefully every piece before it was packed away for the future use of scholars."

On Henry's behalf, Emily Folger bore witness to it all. She experienced the joy of watching their collection fill up the bookshelves, vaults, niches, and walls of the library. An undated photograph captures her in a moment of contemplation standing in the reading room, gazing up at Henry's portrait hanging next to hers. But the completion of the library did not end her quest. She wanted to buy *more* treasures, and proved to be as insatiable as Henry. In March 1931, she purchased the Ashbourne portrait, which she believed to be of Shakespeare.[8] She continued to collect and advise on library acquisitions. And she wanted more First Folios. "Every page of a First Folio is precious is it not," she asked one of her librarians in her dispassionate assessment of a copy on the market, "but as a copy of a book the one offered is surely a sad cripple. It ought to be acquired at a low price indeed; according to your findings."

Emily Folger and the trustees of Amherst College chose April 23, 1932, William Shakespeare's 368th birthday, as the official dedication day of the library. Emily came down from New York for the great event, which was attended by numerous dignitaries, including members of Congress; the ambassadors of England, France, and Germany; justices of the U.S. Supreme Court; Amherst president Arthur Stanley Pease and George Arthur Plimpton, chairman of the board of trustees of Amherst; leaders of numerous other colleges and universities; and President Hoover and his wife. King George V sent a cable from Windsor Castle in honor of the man who had, more than three centuries before, known and entertained two monarchs who once sat on his throne. Also in the audience were the architects Cret and Trowbridge, the builder Baird, and some of the construction workers. The *Washington Post* reported, "The service was attended by as distinguished an audience as ever gathered in Washington for any cultural reason." Emily, Pease, Plimpton, and President and Mrs. Hoover took their places on the stage of the Elizabethan Theatre, which was filled to capacity. A schedule of the day's events survives. The event was broadcast across the country on AM radio. Dr. Pease presided. After an invocation by the Rev. Dr. S. Parkes Cadman, who had also delivered Henry Folger's funeral eulogy, a reading from Ralph Waldo Emerson followed in homage to the author who had first inspired young Henry's great interest in Shakespeare.

At the climax of the ceremony, Emily Folger rose from her chair and handed the key of the library to George Plimpton, who accepted it on behalf of the trustees of Amherst College. Then she spoke. "Her voice shaken with emotion," the *Washington Post* noted, "[she] offered the key . . . as the symbol of the respect and love of her husband and herself towards Shakespeare's memory." Emily spoke just two sentences, including a line from *Henry IV Part 1*: "Shakespeare says for Mr. Folger and me, 'I would you would accept of grace and love' this key. It is the key to our hearts" (Act IV, Scene iii, lines 114). The *Post* reporter observed that at this moment, "tears glistened in the eyes of many in the room."

After Plimpton's brief remarks, a musical interlude, played on period instruments owned by the Folger Library—treble viol, viola da gamba, and clavichord—preceded the principal address by Dr. Joseph Quincy Adams, the library's research supervisor. Entitled "Shakespeare and American Culture," it was a full-throated celebration of the Anglosphere. Adams compared the importance of the Folger Shakespeare Library with that of the Lincoln Memorial and the Washington Monument:

> In its capital city a nation is accustomed to rear monuments to those persons who most have contributed to its well-being. Amid . . . Washington D.C., three stand out conspicuous above the rest: the memorials to Washington, Lincoln and Shakespeare. They stand out as symbols of the three great personal forces that have moulded the political, the spiritual and the intellectual life of our nation.

Although Shakespeare, Adams argued, was English and not American, the poet exerted on American language and life an influence that preserves English culture among a "people who now occupy a domain vaster than the Elizabethans dreamed of."[9]

After Cadman's benediction, Emily left the stage and welcomed the attendees. "The list of guests following the dedication was both lengthy and notable. I stood in the Founder's Room to greet old friends and new. They passed in a long line, each with a word of kindness and congratulation." That night, she returned to the Hay-Adams Hotel, overlooking Lafayette Park and the White House. "Back in my room alone I knew that the dream had come true at last. I was humbly grateful."[10]

The Folger Shakespeare Library may have opened, but it would take years to catalogue the collection. The enormity of the task was staggering. Henry and Emily had spent most of their time acquiring materials, not sorting or cataloging them. Unaided by a librarian, and with only the help of Henry's Standard Oil secretary, Welsh, they were unable to stay current with the backlog of their acquisitions, even for the books

Emily had catalogued; it would take years to replace the sixty drawers full of her handwritten and typed four-by-six cards with a library
catalogue. It took months for the staff to unpack and organize enough
materials to even open the doors to scholars.

Emily's first research project was not Shakespearian, but biographical. Henry Folger had planned to write a book titled *Ventures and Adventures in Collecting*. But building the library had occupied so much
of his attention that he never sat down to draft the memoir. All he left
behind were a few unfinished pages from a manuscript he never completed. It was no more than a summary of his triumphs as a collector.
This roll call of books reads more like a press release than the introspec-
tive insights of a driven bibliophile. But, brief as it is, it remains the
longest surviving piece of writing that he ever set down about himself
or his collection: "A study of the check lists of the Folger Shakespeare
Library soon to be installed in its own building in Washington, D.C.,
show it to be much larger, and extremely more interesting and valuable, than even those who have helped in assembling it had supposed,"
Henry began. Then followed, one after another, a long list of his greatest acquisitions. He never finished it.[11]

Emily was impressed by a long *Washington Times* article that praised
the library's architecture and decoration. She engaged its author, Frank
Waldo Fawcett, to undertake Henry's biography, but nothing ever
came of it. Fawcett performed some desultory research, contacting a
few of Henry's business acquaintances and relatives to extract personal
observations and reminiscences. An envelope marked in Emily's hand
with the name "Waldo Fawcett" on it contains all that remains—and
that was perhaps ever done—for this aborted project: just ten typed
pages of notes.

In 1932, Emily received an honorary doctorate from Amherst College. Citing her as the "enthusiastic, tireless, and discriminating companion of Henry Clay Folger in the collection of a unique library of
the works of Shakespeare; generous benefactress of Amherst College
and of the lovers of letters throughout the whole world; the degree
which 18 years ago Amherst College appropriately bestowed upon
your husband it now, with the same hood as symbol, confers upon

you"—transferring from Henry to her the responsibility of carrying the library forward.

By mid-1932, the work on the library's north façade was still not quite done. In April, on dedication day, only six of the bas-relief sculptures had been in place. In July 1932, John Gregory reported to Emily that he and his carvers had just finished the seventh (*Richard III*) and eighth (*Romeo and Juliet*) panels. The high reliefs were carved by the Piccirilli Brothers, who carved in marble Daniel Chester French's Lincoln Memorial sculpture, the lions Patience and Fortitude that flank the entrance to the New York Public Library on Forty-Second Street and Fifth Avenue, and the Tomb of the Unknowns at Arlington National Cemetery.

Late in December 1932, Gregory gave Emily Folger a wonderful Christmas present. He sent a letter informing her that he had just completed his marble bust of Henry, and it awaited her approval. For a sculpture not done from life, but from the artist's memory refreshed by photos, it was a remarkable likeness.

By 1933, the reading room was fully opened to scholars. The first years were haphazard, with tens of thousands of items uncatalogued and inaccessible. Researchers could not make use of materials that could not be found.

In 1935, another white marble palace rose within sight of the Folger Shakespeare Library. In 1929, the Chief Justice of the United States, former president William Howard Taft, lobbied Congress to give the Supreme Court its own building one block east of the Capitol. At that time, the justices were neglected stepchildren with an inadequate home within the U.S. Capitol. The cornerstone of the new courthouse was laid in October 1932 and the building completed in 1935. In a great irony, the Supreme Court built its bigger palace next to the one built by the chairman of Standard Oil. Thus, the Folger Library stands forever in the shadow of the Supreme Court—an eternal reminder of the blow that the Court struck against Standard in 1911. Henry never beheld it, but he knew it was coming. Today, when you exit the Folger, and step onto East Capitol Street, the first thing you see is the back of the Supreme Court. Henry might have preferred that his library cast a longer shadow.

Emily Folger enjoyed her regular trips to Washington: "When I visit the Library today I find it a happy place, and I think of Henry being present there, rejoicing in its completion. . . . I think, too, of how the Library expresses his ideals, his personality, his thought, his hope, his faith."

By 1936, her health was in decline, and she knew it. Her correspondence early that year reveals that she was unwell. "I cannot write clearly because I am not clear," she wrote to librarian William Slade on January 24, 1936.[12] She died a month later, at home, at 6:30 AM on February 21, 1936. She was seventy-seven, and had outlived Henry by six years. Her funeral was held in Glen Cove, New York, the following Sunday.[13] After her death, she made two final contributions to the library. The first was a generous sum of cash to secure its future. Her other bequest was very strange.

Epilogue

I N T H E decades following Emily Folger's death, the Folger Shake-speare Library prospered. Indeed, it became a bigger and better institution than Henry and Emily might ever have hoped. What began as a single-mindedly Shakespearian effort evolved into a time capsule of the whole culture and history of early modern England and Europe. The 1938 purchase of Sir Robert Leicester Harmsworth's massive collection of 8,000 books printed between 1475 and 1640 was the tipping point. The Folger has grown into one of the greatest private libraries in the world. Even for scholars with no interest in Shakespeare or English literature, the Folger Library is a repository of indispensable materials—books, manuscripts, broadsides, objects, musical instruments, artworks, and more—for the study of music, art, law, science, economics, and politics of Europe during the reigns of Elizabeth I and James I. In many ways the library still reflects the personalities of its founders. In an unintentional tribute to the Folgers' chaotic buy-now-and-catalogue-later ethos, the library still has not, to this day, catalogued the entire original Folger collection. Several hundred thousand playbills await digitization. Thousands of documents in Henry's personal archives have never been individually catalogued. As recently as 2012, the librarian was unable to even estimate how many loose, orphaned First Folio pages reside in the collection, or what plays they are from. It is possible that Henry Folger bought enough unbound pages to assemble one or two more complete First Folios. In the catalogue room's stacks of wood drawers—the Folger still uses catalogue cards, in addi-

tion to computerized files—readers can find old-fashioned typed catalogue index cards. In the archives are the index cards that Emily wrote
out by hand more than one hundred years ago.

The Folger Library maintains the culture of modesty and secrecy established by its founders. Although the exhibition hall and the theater
are open to the public throughout the year, the rest of the building—
the two reading rooms, the Founders' Room, the underground hidden
book stacks, and the treasure vaults—are off-limits to all but staff and a
select group of "readers" whose scholarly credentials have earned them
a place in the institution's inner circle. Once a year in April, on the
Sunday closest to Shakespeare's birthday, the public is invited for a
peek inside the library and to an Elizabethan festival—complete with
costumed Queen Elizabeth—of games, music, and theatrics. In April
2012, to celebrate the eightieth anniversary of the library's dedication,
a pair of Henry and Emily look-alikes welcomed visitors to the exhibition hall.

There have been many changes since Henry and Emily's era, many
of which they would have approved. In the early 1980s, a second reading room, the New Reading Room, was built adjacent to the old one.
And the air-conditioning system that so confused Henry has long
since been extended throughout the building. In the summer months,
it cools the reading rooms well below Henry's target of eighty-five
degrees to an Arctic chill more comfortable for books than humans.
A state-of-the-art conservation laboratory ministers to bookbindings
and works on paper. Outside, on the west wall near the Puck Fountain, the small magnolia tree from which Emily plucked a fresh leaf in
1932, on dedication day, has grown into a sprawling giant that blocks
the once-splendid view of the Capitol dome from the executive offices.
Although the tree symbolizes the longevity of the library, Henry, who
fought so hard to secure the site and its spectacular view, might today
order it to be cut down.

Other changes would please Henry. Before he died, he worried that
the Great Depression might interfere with his plans to complete construction of his library and to give it the lifeline of a proper endowment
to secure its survival. Today the Folger Library is on sound financial

footing, and ranks as the second-best-endowed private library in the world. And it would delight Henry to learn that his library accomplished one of the dreams that prompted him to collect so many First Folios in the first place: the complete collation of all eighty-two of his copies in a page-by-page comparison to detect the unique fingerprint of each volume. A mechanical visual device invented after the Second World War—the Hinman collator—enabled the human eye to examine two First Folios side by side and discern even the most minute textual or typographic differences between them. Folger would have been disappointed that, even with the postwar technology of the Hinman collator and its updated computer equivalent, collation of copies of the First Folio did not result in the discovery of any momentous textual discrepancies. A word here, a line there, a misspelling—these differences were not, as it was hoped, enough to reveal the "true text of Shakespeare." What Henry could not have known was that collation would permit inference about how—and in what order—the plays in the First Folio were printed.

Two other changes would disappoint Henry. In the almost eighty years since Emily's death, the Folger Library has made a prodigious number of important acquisitions for its collection. The sheer quantity, quality, variety, and research value of these materials would thrill Henry. But, in an era of high prices and limited budgets, there is one book that the library will never buy again. Since Henry's death, the Folger Library has never bought another copy of Shakespeare's First Folio. This has not been for lack of opportunities. Between 1930 and 2013, almost eighty copies have come to market. Meisei University in Japan purchased twelve of them. In 2006, when Sotheby's auctioned one of the finest examples in the world, the Dr. Williams copy, Henry would have been smitten. The description of the folio in the sixty-page auction catalogue was mouthwatering: "A tall and exceptional copy . . . no loss of text other than a few letters, has suffered little damage, is uncleaned and has not been repaired . . . [N]o other such textually complete copy of the First Folio in a mid-seventeenth century binding is known to survive in other than institutional hands."

In condition alone, this volume equals any of Folger's best ten First

Folios. But its alluring history would have caused Henry to prize it above all of them save one, the Vincent copy. The volume offered by Sotheby's had been owned by only two individuals since the 1600s: Dr. William Bates (1625–1699) and Dr. Daniel Williams (c. 1643–1716). Since 1729, the folio had been in the collection of the Williams library, which specialized in the history of nonconformist theology. One sentence in Sotheby's description would have tantalized Henry beyond measure: "It has therefore the longest uninterrupted ownership of any copy in the world." If the Dr. Williams copy *had* come up for sale during Henry's lifetime, he would have given his ultra-command, reserved for only the rarities that stirred his soul: "Buy without fail." The Williams copy sold for $5.2 million, the world-record price—so far—for a First Folio.

At the library that bears his name, there is little remembrance or recognition of Folger's other life, the one that paid for it all. A few years ago, an exhibition catalogue published by the Folger Library made a vague and reluctant acknowledgment that Henry had once "worked for an oil company." That was was like saying Steve Jobs or Bill Gates had once worked for a computer company. Another library publication notes that "Folger . . . made [his] money in the hard-driving days of American industry, on the backs of . . . oil workers."[1] That misguided statement reveals a sad misunderstanding about economics and the founder, and a disdain for his business.

In a library filled with signs and symbols that evoke the age of Shakespeare, there is none that evokes the industrial age of Henry Folger. Had Henry foreseen that a library built by petroleum would one day suffer amnesia about its origins and about him as a man of commerce, he might have commissioned John Gregory or Brenda Putnam to sculpt an oil derrick, refinery, railroad tanker car, or gasoline pump—adorned with Tudor roses—to stand beside the bas-relief of Lear or the Puck Fountain. Henry Folger was a brilliant, ethical American businessman. He was an unapologetic industrialist. And the Folger Shakespeare Library is a triumph of American capitalism and philanthropy.

The Shakespeare Library is Henry Folger's great monument, but other landmarks to his life and quest survive in the United States and in England. In New York City, in Bedford-Stuyvesant, Brooklyn, a modest home still stands at 212 Lefferts Place. In 2010, when the house was placed on the market for a little more than a million dollars, the real estate agent's listing failed to note that it was once the rental residence of the most famous Shakespeariana collector in America, or that millions of dollars in rare books and manuscripts had once passed through its door. On the Gold Coast of Long Island, the only home that the Folgers ever owned still stands on a two-acre parcel.

In Manhattan, Henry's old office building at Twenty-Six Broadway still stands, but the former headquarters of Standard Oil no longer dominates the skyline, and its illuminated beacon no longer sparkles above the harbor, a short walk away. The lobby looks almost as it did in Folger's day, with the names of John D. Rockefeller and several of his partners, including Charles Pratt and Henry Flagler, still embedded in decorative tiles in the walls. The old clock still tells time with metal hands cast in the shape of the logo SONY—for Standard Oil of New York. In a nod to its former life as an epicenter of American capitalism, Twenty-Six Broadway now overlooks a plaza dominated by the enormous Charging Bull sculpture made famous in Merrill Lynch advertisements. Nearby, the old Cunard building remains, but the line's great vessels no longer transport America's elite—or Europe's treasures—on Atlantic crossings.

In London, several of the venerable booksellers patronized by Henry Folger, including the great Sotheran and Maggs firms, are still in business. The former recently celebrated its 250th anniversary. But the London firms no longer maintain a brisk trade in rare Shakespeariana, and it has been a long time since one of them offered an example of a fine First Folio. The Americans, in particular Henry Folger and Henry Huntington, largely depleted England's reserves of First Folios, choice quartos, and other rarities long ago.

Near St. Paul's Cathedral, rebuilt after the Great Fire of 1666, you can stand at the old wall that once surrounded London. You can walk to the intersection of the Barbican and Aldersgate Street, just beyond

Cripplegate, at the northwest corner of the wall, and, at the old sign of the Half Eagle and Key, you can visit the birthplace of the First Folio. Here, in 1623, stood the shop of its printer, William Jaggard. No plaque or monument marks the spot.

But not far away, in the churchyard of St. Mary Aldermanbury, there stands one of the most unusual monuments in all of London: an open book carved of stone, set against a pink-and-gray granite plinth, and crowned with a large bronze bust of William Shakespeare. Set above the book is a stone scroll bearing the legend FIRST FOLIO. The left-hand page represents the title page, and cut into it is the full name of the volume and the place and date of publication. Cut into the right-hand page is an excerpt from the preliminary leaves, containing the message to the reader from Heminges and Condell. Set into the face of the plinth is a tall, rectangular bronze plaque that sings the praises of the two men who created the First Folio and rescued from oblivion the Shakespeare we know today:

TO THE MEMORY OF
JOHN HEMINGE
AND
HENRY CONDELL
FELLOW ACTORS
AND PERSONAL FRIENDS
OF **SHAKESPEARE**
THEY LIVED MANY YEARS IN THIS
PARISH AND ARE BURIED HERE

TO THEIR DISINTERESTED AFFECTION
THE WORLD OWES ALL
THAT IT CALLS **SHAKESPEARE**
THEY ALONE
COLLECTED HIS DRAMATIC WRITINGS
REGARDLESS OF PECUNIARY LOSS
AND WITHOUT THE HOPE OF ANY PROFIT
AND GAVE THEM TO THE WORLD

It is the only monument in the world dedicated to a book and its editors. There is little doubt that Henry Folger once journeyed to this place. In his archives, in a cardboard folder of documents pertaining to his trips to England, there is a small scrap of paper bearing a single note in his tiny handwriting: "St. Mary Aldermanbury." The church is long gone, destroyed first by the Great Fire of London, rebuilt and destroyed again on December 19, 1940, during the height of the Blitz of World War II. Only the graves and the monument, erected in 1896, remain.

When a lonely little old man hoards thousands of pounds of stacked newspapers and trash, we call him compulsive and crazy. When a multimillionaire industrialist squirrels away tons of rare books, manuscripts, artworks, and memorabilia, we call him a great collector and a man of exquisite taste. Henry Folger manifested few of the visible hallmarks that characterized the notorious, hoarding Manhattan brothers, Homer and Langley Collyer. Often the personal lives of the great collectors are not fully known; the collection can be the most interesting thing about them.

On the surface, Henry Folger's normalcy might appear unexciting. It might even seem disappointing that he was kind, humorous, and unpretentious, and that he was well liked and inspired loyalty. His was a selective and singular madness. It did not manifest itself in odd behavior. Folger never murdered a rival, never seduced a young librarian, never stole a rare book, never concocted a fraud, never forged a manuscript, and never squandered a fortune. Neither did his outward appearance or behavior give any indication of the obsession that roiled within him. His compulsion never turned him into a madman. His preoccupation with secrecy never twisted him into a paranoid recluse. Throughout his life, he was a highly functional professional who thrived at the highest level of American business. But for almost forty years, he led a double life. Like Faust, he was a prisoner of a notion not his own.

Henry Folger succeeded in channeling his energies into a socially acceptable pursuit. In so doing, he served his own deepest psychological needs while also benefiting society. In the context of other famous

American pack rats, the signs, symptoms, and psychology of Henry Folger's collecting located him within the spectrum of sanity.

Folger recognized the great irony that confronts every devoted collector. Compulsive hoarders are fighting a battle against time, death, and oblivion. By accumulating objects that will last forever, or at least for centuries, the collector merges his identity with the collection and attempts to make time stand still. If he becomes one with his possessions, he can somehow live forever. That is one of the classic delusions of an obsessive personality.

Henry Folger escaped that trap by recognizing his mortality. The only way to keep his collection intact forever was to let it go, and to donate it in toto to a monument of his own creation. And so in his will he passed on his treasures to a custodian that would outlive him and generations to come: the Folger Shakespeare Memorial, which he renamed the Folger Shakespeare Library.

In *Julius Caesar*, Shakespeare wrote that the good men do is "oft interred with their bones." Perhaps it was that verse that gave Emily Folger a most unusual idea. At the east end of the main reading room hang the two Salisbury oil portraits of Henry and Emily Folger. Between the paintings is a passageway that leads to hidden, twin staircases that rise to the wraparound balcony overlooking the Old Reading Room. Upon entering that passageway, you will find yourself face-to-face with a large, rectangular brass plaque. The inscription engraved upon it reads: FOR THE GLORY OF GOD AND THE GREATER GLORY OF SHAKESPEARE. But the plaque is more than a decorative device. It is a door meant to seal shut the opening to a niche embedded behind the wall. In that niche lie the mortal remains of Henry and Emily Folger, who preside together over their palace. After Emily placed her husband there, she arranged that upon her death she would join him. They remain the only American philanthropists ever entombed within their creation. If they haunt the halls of the library, they are benevolent ghosts.

Henry Folger defied the truism that you can't take it to your grave. His library *is* his grave. At the end of each day, when the lights go down and the staff and security guards go home, Henry Folger stays behind.

In the stillness of the night, amid the hundreds of thousands of books, manuscripts, and other treasures he loved in life and that now rest quietly on their shelves, he, too, abides in silence.

As long as the name of Shakespeare lives, Henry Folger will never be forgotten. As long as the Shakespeare Folger Library lives, Shakespeare's great books will never be lost. Both men live on through the collection. And that collection will never be broken up. Solid financial footing ensures that no future bibliomaniacs will lay claim to Folger's First Folios or will defile his pyramid.

The spiritual center of the Folger Library is not, however, the tomb of its founders. Instead, the holy of holies is the network of underground fireproof vaults that house the library's collection of First Folios and its other most precious books, including the unique *Titus Andronicus* and the Pavier Quarto. Few people ever enter this sanctuary. The folios are not shelved vertically, standing side by side. Conventional shelving would place too much weight on fragile bindings and gravity would cause the pages to sag. So each volume lies flat. Many of these First Folios have never left the vault for public display. Once, during the Second World War when it was feared the nation's capital might come under attack, thirty thousand of the Folger treasures were removed from the library and transported in a sealed train car to Amherst College for safekeeping.

When you go to the library today, you can lose your bearings. It is easy to lose sight of the line that divides past from present. The theater is a time machine that transports audiences back to the stages of old London. The vast Old Reading Room, with its enormous stone fireplace, looks like a Cecil B. DeMille Hollywood fantasy set of Queen Elizabeth I's feasting chamber. The exhibition hall, nearly a city block long, evokes the treasure room of some nobleman's country house. The leaded glass windows, stripped in 2013 of thick coats of paint that had for several decades blocked out natural sunlight and afternoon shadows, now admit them. Only the electric lights provide a tenuous, visible connection to the twenty-first century. A portion of the collection—and always one First Folio—is displayed in this room. High overhead, resting on a little shelf set into the south wall, is a snow-white marble bust of Henry Folger. In the Old Reading Room, the other great chamber that lies parallel to the Great Hall, a polychromed bust of William Shakespeare—a copy of the seventeenth-century original that reposes in Stratford—sits on a shelf above the Folger tomb and gazes across the room to the monumental stained-glass window of the "Seven Ages of Man."

The subjects of these sculptures seem so different from each other: an English playwright from the Elizabethan Age and an American industrialist from the Gilded Age, two men divided by vastly different cultures separated by a wide ocean and three centuries of history. But how alike they are. Both remain mysterious. Shakespeare is one of the most famous names in history. But his private life is obscured from us forever because the original sources have vanished. In contrast, Folger's private papers are voluminous, but he remains little known. Neither man was born to wealth or greatness. Commoners both, they discovered their natural talents and rose in their respective worlds of art and commerce. Both were democratic men. William Shakespeare, whether writing about gravediggers or kings, divined the profound commonality of man, and empathized with humanity's frailty and brevity. Not an intellectual or cloistered scholar, Shakespeare wrote to entertain the people.

In one of the greatest understatements in the history of collecting, Henry's wife noted that he "rather specialized in First Folios." But, she added, he was also motivated by a "sense of responsibility to God and man. He did not feel that he had been sent into this world merely to live and prosper to himself alone." Folger stood apart from the millionaires of his time who sought to legitimize themselves by buying the cultural trappings of Western civilization. He wanted to liberate the First Folios that slept on the dusty, forgotten shelves of Europe's privileged elites and bring them to the New World as a gift to the people. Folger's ultimate goal was not the ownership of priceless books as vulgar trophies to impress his friends. To Folger, the First Folio was a magical text, "one from which we . . . draw . . . our faith and hope."

In the end, neither Shakespeare nor Folger lived to see his legacy secured. The poet wrote acclaimed plays, became a theatrical entrepreneur, and earned handsome profits. The industrialist made his fortune, and amassed an acclaimed collection. But Folger died before he saw his library built and his tens of thousands of books arrayed on the shelves for all to see. Shakespeare died before he saw his works preserved and his plays collected between the covers of one book for all to read.

In hindsight, though, Shakespeare's eighty-first sonnet seems prophetic: "Your monument shall be my gentle verse, / Which eyes not yet created shall o'er-read." Folger instructed his stonecutters to carve the words of that "gentle verse" into the center wall of his library's reading room. Verse becomes monument, and monument becomes verse.

Before his death, Henry Folger seemed to project a knowing serenity about what he had accomplished, not in words, but in his appearance. You can almost see it on his face. In a gorgeous, miniature portrait painted on ivory late in life, Folger resembles, in outward appearance, a typical businessman of his era. Handsome, of medium height and build, he wears a dark, conservative wool suit, vest, white shirt, and tie. His snowy hair is groomed into a conventional, neatly trimmed beard and mustache. But it is in the eyes. Bright, alert, they twinkle in a bemused and inviting way. This image is not at all like the intimidating, glowering portraits that Huntington, Rockefeller, and Morgan left us. The corners of Folger's mouth are just beginning to wrinkle into a generous smile. Oddly, the painting is reminiscent of another work of art executed almost four hundred years ago—the engraved portrait of Shakespeare on the title page of the First Folio. Together, side-by-side, creator and collector smile at us across time, united by that book, and by the treasure house that, thanks to Folger, reunited more copies of the book than any place in the world.

If William Shakespeare could travel from his age to ours, he would marvel at his apotheosis. He had a fascination with the passage of time and the endurance of memory. In the plays, he used tricks of time to curse, haunt, redeem, promise, comfort, resurrect, or immortalize his characters. In some, the players step outside the boundaries of time to experience miraculous, even supernatural, reversals of fortune. The unpredictability of the future is one of Shakespeare's great, recurring themes. "What's to come is still unsure," he wrote in

Twelfth Night. Looking back across the centuries, he would relish the drama of his own improbable tale. Time has performed many conjuring tricks, but few so fantastic as the making of the First Folio, and the making of the great library that preserves it. Shakespeare went to his grave a mortal man destined to fade from memory. Four hundred years later, he reigns forever in the library that bears his name. The greatest tribute to Henry Folger is this: If Shakespeare could visit the Folger Library, he would not, based on what he found there, believe that he had journeyed to some future time. He would believe that he was at home in his own.

In the First Folio, Ben Jonson wrote William Shakespeare's truest epitaph: "He was not of an age, but for all time!" So, too, are Henry Clay Folger and his magnificent obsession.

Finis

Acknowledgments

✿❦✿

I WROTE *The Millionaire and the Bard* under the watchful and encouraging eyes of my husband, James L. Swanson, a *New York Times* bestselling author and an obsessive collector of rare books, documents, and artifacts. Years of knowing him and observing his collecting habits provided insight into the thought processes of Henry Folger, and vice versa. To a first-time author, he gave priceless advice: "Write about something you love." I thank him for getting me started on this project, helping me along the way, and for putting the final pieces of the puzzle together with me. This book would not exist without his help.

A team of talented people at Simon & Schuster shepherded me through the journey of writing, editing, and publishing the book, and were vital to its becoming a reality. Thanks to Marysue Rucci, the book found a home at S&S. Jonathan Karp was kind enough to spend a long afternoon over lunch offering suggestions on how to tell this story. My editor, the incomparable and discerning Jofie Ferrari-Adler, improved the manuscript in countless ways. He has an unerring instinct for how to move a narrative forward without getting bogged down in details.

I am privileged to have several friends who are specialists and experts in different aspects of the stories I have related. Anthony James West, from our first meeting, provided fruitful directions for me to pursue, answered countless questions, and shared my enthusiasm for tales of First Folio acquisitions. I value his insight, his expertise, and his friendship. His *magnum opus*, *The Shakespeare First Folio: The History of the Book*, three volumes and counting, was an essential part of my research. All other students of the First Folio must stand on his shoulders. David Bevington, Shakespeare scholar extraordinaire and professor emeritus at the University of Chicago, read the manuscript and offered gracious encouragement and kind words. David helped launch this project when he sponsored my application to become a reader at the Folger Library. I also thank Christopher Vizas, all-around Renaissance man and former chairman of the library's finance committee, for bringing me into the Folger's fold.

My agent, Richard Abate at 3 Arts Entertainment, deserves high praise for his encouragement and ability to remain calm whatever the circumstances. I value his friendship, patience, and diplomatic skills.

David Lovett, Washington, D.C., attorney, historian, and obsessive bibliophile, provided invaluable assistance in hunting down obscure sources for my notes and bibliography. His lifelong quest to assemble a complete collection of books related to the assassination of President John F. Kennedy has made him an incomparable guide in the labyrinth of bibliography. I thank him for his friendship and enthusiastic and generous contributions.

Research for this book required the expertise of archivists in several locations, and in particular I thank the Folger Shakespeare Library, the Library of Congress, the Rockefeller Archives, and the Standard Oil Archives at the Ransom Center at the University of Texas at Austin. Betsy Walsh, Head of Reader Services at the Folger, and Head Research Librarian Georgianna Ziegler, together with the Folger Reading Room staff, provided hours of patient and cheerful assistance as I requested box after box of documents, artifacts, engravings, and books. On one magnificent and unforgettable morning, Steven Galbraith, former Andrew W. Mellon Curator of Books at the Folger took me on a tour of treasures, patiently showing me the First Folios, quartos (including the unique quarto of *Titus Andronicus*), and other confections chilling in the underground vaults at the Folger. Former director Gail Kern Paster, current director Michael Witmore, and former head librarian Stephen Eniss welcomed me and made my time doing research at the Folger productive and memorable. Matthew Darby at Ransom Center Standard Oil Archives provided able assistance. Thanks to

Clark Evans, former Library of Congress specialist, I spent a memorable day examining the institution's two copies of the First Folio. That day had a surprise ending when Clark brought out a dozen exquisite Elizabethan rarities for me to examine.

The Folger Library staff and readers mingle every afternoon at 3:00 PM when tea is served in the in the basement lounge. I found the conversations and exchange of ideas invigorating and inspiring. I thank the staff and many readers, especially Stephen Grant, Folger biographer, for their encouragement and insights over cups of tea too numerous to count.

Ronald K.L. Collins and Michael F. Bishop, Jr. were my first readers; they were helpful and patient souls, undaunted by tight deadlines. Each made suggestions that improved the narrative immeasurably.

Finally, to the people who supported me day by day so that I could pursue this project: my teenage sons, Cameron and Harrison, who accompanied me on research trips far and wide; my mother, Rosemarie Greb, who cooked innumerable meals for all of us; my sister, Joanne Becker for her moral support and calming influence; and patient friend and reader extraordinaire, Chuck Stender. I could not have finished this book on time without you.

Andrea E. Mays
Long Beach, California
February 1, 2015

A Note on Sources
֍֍֍

*T*HE LITERATURE on William Shakespeare is vast. It is, to borrow a phrase associated with biblical heretic John Wyclef, "as wide as the waters" of the ocean sea. I do not pretend to catalogue it here. The complete bibliography, which no scholar has ever compiled, contains tens of thousands of books, pamphlets, journal monographs, newspaper articles, and various ephemera. Any attempt to cite every item with conceivable relevance to this book, when I could never read them all, seemed pointless and useless to a reader who wanted a starting point from which to learn more. The bibliography that follows is hardly comprehensive and represents, with few exceptions, little more than a selective shelf list of the several hundred titles I used while researching and writing *The Millionaire and the Bard*. These are the books and articles that I found most helpful in several subtopics of Shakespeariana.

The paucity of source material on Shakespeare's life has not discouraged a number of authors from attempting biographies of the Bard. Most of them, recognizing the limitations placed on them by the thin historical record, have constructed their narratives from the outside in rather than from Shakespeare's inner life, about which very little is known but about which much is inferred. Thus, many books about Shakespeare are about his context—the life, culture, commerce, agriculture, literature, theater, and arts of Elizabethan England and the Jacobean era. They may not be able to reconstruct Shakespeare's life, but they can recreate the world that surrounded him. Other books try to extract Shakespeare the man—or at least his opinions, nature, and influences—from his plays and poems, but these efforts are more properly the province of literary criticism, not biography. That said, there are several excellent and enjoyable books about Shakespeare. Anyone wanting to read a first book on the subject would do well to begin with any of the following: Peter Ackroyd's *Shakespeare: The Biography*, Bill Bryson's *Shakespeare: The World as Stage*, Stephen Greenblatt's *Will in the World: How Shakespeare Became Shakespeare*, or Stanley Wells's *Shakespeare: For All Time*. Ron Rosenbaum's *The Shakespeare Wars: Clashing Scholars, Public Fiascoes, Palace Coups* details the skirmish over how Shakespeare should be performed and is the best book I have read on the subject. Irvin Lee Matus's *Shakespeare in Fact* is an invaluable collection of material. For encyclopedic coverage, see the three-volume *William Shakespeare: His World, His Work, His Influence*, edited by John F. Andrews.

Often overlooked by modern readers, the preliminaries to the First Folio remain vivid testimonials from Shakespeare's contemporaries, who speak to us across time. Ben Jonson's "To the Memory of My Beloved, Mr. William Shakespeare and what he hath left us" shimmers with the greatest tribute of all, praising Shakespeare as the "Soule of the Age," then declaring "he was not of an age, but for all time!" In their appeal to "The great Variety of Readers," editors John Heminges and Henry Condell warrant that the plays in this book will "draw, and hold you." Thus, we must "Reade him, therefore; and againe, and againe." The same must be said about the preliminaries. No one should read one of Shakespeare's plays without reading them first.

The best short introduction to William Shakespeare is David Bevington's delightfully erudite 105-page introductory essay that appears in Bevington's sixth edition of the plays, *The Complete Works of William Shakespeare*.

Regarding the plays themselves, I recommend the Folger Library editions of the individual plays, published by Simon & Schuster. For a single-volume collection of all the plays, I recommend David Bevington's *The Complete Works of William Shakespeare*, not only for the annotations, but also for his thoughtful and imaginative introductory essays to each play. Bevington's edition is my personal favorite, but there are other fine, single-volume collections of all the plays.

To read about the London fire, see Neil Hanson's *The Great Fire of London: In that Apocalyptic Year, 1666* and Adrian Tinniswood's *By Permission of Heaven: The True Story of the Great Fire of London*. For actor David Garrick's grand folly and Shakespeare fantasia, see Christian Deelman's *The Great Shakespeare Jubilee*. For John Boydell's quixotic art project, see Wilfred H. Friedman's *Boydell's Shakespeare Gallery*. For Shakespeare in America, see Michael D. Bristol's *Shakespeare's America: America's Shakespeare*, the museum exhibition catalog *Shakespeare in American Life*, edited by Virginia Mason Vaughan and Alden T. Vaughan, and their book *Shakespeare in America*. Also see *Shakespeare in America: An Anthology from the Revolution to Now*, edited by James Shapiro. For the most notorious Shakespeare event in America, see Richard Moody's *The Astor Place Riot* and Nigel Cliff's *The Shakespeare Riots: Revenge, Drama, and Death in Nineteenth Century America*.

For the history of the First Folio, Peter Blayney's brief but comprehensive forty-page study, *The First Folio of Shakespeare*, and *Foliomania: Stories Behind Shakespeare's Most Important Book*, edited by Owen Williams and Caryn Lazzuri, are fine and informative introductions. To go back to the beginning and read the plays as they appeared when collected for the first time, see *The First Folio of Shakespeare: The Norton Facsimile*, especially the second edition containing Peter Blayney's introduction. Also, for a detailed description of a fine copy of the First Folio, see the Sotheby's auction catalog, *The Shakespeare First Folio, 1623: The Dr. Williams Library Copy*. For early, incomplete efforts to create a census of First Folios, see the census of 1902 and the census of 1906 by Sidney Lee, Henry Folger's nemesis and lifelong literary irritant.

For more on Standard Oil, John D. Rockefeller, and the business to which Henry Folger devoted his prodigious business talents and stellar professional life, one must contend with Ida Tarbell's landmark two-volume *The History of Standard Oil*. The culmination of her obsessive, one-woman assault against the man she demonized as the "world's oldest living mummy," Tarbell's work carved in stone a stereotype of

Rockefeller and Standard Oil that survives in the popular mind to this day. A more balanced approach than Tarbell's can be found in Allan Nevins's two-volume *John D. Rockefeller: The Heroic Age of American Enterprise* and in his one-volume follow-up, *John D. Rockefeller, Industrialist and Philanthropist*. Also essential is *History of the Standard Oil Company (New Jersey)*, a three-volume study published between 1955 and 1971. Especially useful are volume one, *Pioneering in Big Business, 1882–1911*, by R. W. Hidy and M. E. Hidy; and also volume two, *The Resurgent Years, 1911–1927*, by G. S. Gibb and E. H. Knowlton. Ron Chernow's *Titan: The Life of John D. Rockefeller* is the best modern biography. More recently, Steve Weinberg's *Taking on the Trust: The Epic Battle of Ida Tarbell and John D. Rockefeller*, while it captures the fevered antibusiness temper of the times, accepts too many of Tarbell's claims at face value and ultimately presents too sympathetic a portrayal of the crusader herself. The full book arguing Rockefeller's side of the 1911 case with the insights of law and economics and modern antitrust jurisprudence remains unwritten.

For more on Henry Folger, the memorial book published after his death, *Henry Folger: 18 June 1857–11 June 1930*, contains valuable essays, including "Henry Folger as a Collector" by the great dealer A. S. W. Rosenbach and "Biographical Sketch" by George E. Dimmock. Stephen Grant's biography, *Collecting Shakespeare: The Story of Henry and Emily Folger*, offers a detailed account of their private life together and brings Emily out of the shadows.

For more on the history of the Folger Library, see *The Folger Shakespeare Library: Washington* and also Joseph T. Foster's 1951 *National Geographic* article "Folger: The Biggest Little Library in the World" and Marie Severy's 1987 *National Geographic* article "Shakespeare Lives at the Folger." Stanley King's *Recollections of the Folger Shakespeare Library* and Louis B. Wright's *The Folger Library, Two Decades of Growth: An Informal Account* are valuable works by library insiders.

Last, and deserving of a singular category devoted to them alone, are the works of the great First Folio scholar Anthony West: *The Shakespeare First Folio: The History of the Book, Volume I; An Account of the First Folio Based on its Sales and Prices, 1623–2000* and *The Shakespeare First*

Folio: The History of the Book, Volume II; A New World Census of First Folios. Reading these books, one cannot help but notice that Anthony West's energy and determination in pursuit of the First Folio equal those of Henry Folger. A third volume, *The Shakespeare First Folio: A Descriptive Catalogue* by Eric Rasmussen and Anthony James West, extends the series. The three volumes (with more to come) contain an amazing, sometimes mind-boggling, amount of factual information about all known copies of the First Folio. If one wants a detailed narrative or technical description of a particular copy—provenance, binding, sales history, prices, defects, marginalia, size, and more—West's books are indispensable.

Bibliography

❧✿❧

Manuscripts and Primary Source Material, in the Folger Shakespeare Library, Washington, D.C.

Documentary Files (one file for each of the seventy-nine copies of the First Folio), stored in the Library's Catalogue Department:

Copy 19: Henry Clay Folger, letter to John Camp Williams, December 1905.

Copy 58: Bernard Quaritch, letter to H. C. Folger, July 29, 1910.

Case Files 1999:

Henry Clay Folger, letter to A. H. Mayhew, bookseller, Charing Cross Road, May 17, 1915.

Lady Durning-Lawrence, letter to A. H. Mayhew, June 11, 1915.

The Revd Fulford Adams, postcard to A. H. Mayhew, 1915.

Folder 1 (one of thirteen folders at the back door marked "Correspondence Folios and Quartos" in dark green filing cabinet in closet 2 in the Catalogue Office as of September 1992):

Printed letter from Sidney Lee, 108 Lexham Gardens, Kensington, London W., February 1901, accompanied by his two-page questionnaire, "Schedule of Particulars of the Shakespeare First Folio" (along with cover note).

Letter from Sidney Lee, May 9, 1902, presumably to Henry Folger.

Folder 2:

Labeled "First Folio, F2, F3, F4" (Folger's Price List).

A typed document (not dated) with the heading "Collected Works: First Folio: 1623," with a note added "Copies from Mr. Folger's list in his priced catalogue (Mr. Slade's copy)."

Tin Box in Catalogue Department:

"Copy of S. de Ricci Note Book—First Folios . . . made before his 1932 visit to the [Folger Library]"—a series of typewritten slips, one for each folio copy with occasional handwritten notes.

Also:

A. C. R. Carter, his handwritten notes in his own copy of Lee's *Census*.

Henry Clay Folger, his handwritten notes in his own copy of Lee's *Census*.

George Stevens to I. Reed 1777–1800 (bound volume) from the Shakespearean Library of Marsden J. Perry: George Stevens, letter to I. Reed, October 5, 1790.

Several letters and other documents in Boxes 21, 23, 28, 29, 33, 37, 56, 57, and 58.

Shakespeare's First Folio

Baldwin, Thomas Whitfield. *On Act and Scene Division in the Shakespeare First Folio*. Carbondale: Southern Illinois University Press, 1965.

Bartlett, Henrietta C., and Alfred W. Pollard. *A Census of Shakespeare's Plays in Quarto, 1594–1709*. New Haven, Connecticut: Yale University Press, 1916 (revised, 1939).

Bate, Jonathan, and Eric Rasmussen, eds. *RSC Shakespeare: The Complete Works*. (Includes "The Case for the First Folio" by Jonathan Bate.) New York: Palgrave Macmillan, 2007. Also found on the Royal Shakespeare Company (RSC) Shakespeare Companion website (Palgrave Macmillan), 2007. http://www.rscshakespeare.co.uk/pdfs/Case_for_Folio.pdf.

BBC Four (British Broadcasting Corporation). *The Secret Life of Books*. Episode 2 of 6, "Shakespeare's First Folio." (30 minutes.) http://www.bbc.co.uk/programmes/b04gv5zy. The complete broadcast can be found at: https://www.youtube.com/watch?v=6U7WpTQdr0g.

Blayney, Peter W. M. *The First Folio of Shakespeare*. Washington, D.C.: Folger Shakespeare Library, 1991.

————. "Report on the Condition of the Two Copies of the Shakespeare First Folio" (now Meisei 8 and 9), unpublished, May 1985.

Cole, George Watson. "The First Folio of Shakespeare: A Further Word Regarding the Correct Arrangement of Its Preliminary Leaves." *Proceedings of the Bibliographical Society of America* 3 (1908): 65–83 (also self-published by author with corrections, New York, 1909).

Collins, Paul. *The Book of William: How Shakespeare's First Folio Conquered the World.* New York: Bloomsbury, 2009.

_____. "Folio, Where Art Thou?: One Man's Conquest to Track Down Every Copy on the Planet." *Smithsonian* 37, no. 6 (September 2006): 67.

Dawson, Giles E. "A Bibliographical Problem in the First Folio of Shakespeare." *Library* 22 (1941–1942): 25–33.

De Ricci, Seymour. *A Nobel Fragment, Being a Leaf of the Original First Folio of William Shakespeare's Plays, Printed in 1623; with a Bibliographical Essay.* New York: Dingwall-Rock, 1926.

Flatter, Richard. *Shakespeare's Producing Hand: A Study of His Marks of Expression to Be Found in the First Folio.* London: W. Heinemann, 1948.

_____. "Some Instances of Line-Division in the First Folio." *Shakespeare Jahrbuch* 92 (1956): 184–196.

Fleming, William H. "Bibliography of First Folios in New York City." *Shakespeariana* 5 (1888): 101–117.

Folger, Henry C., Jr. "A Unique First Folio." *Outlook* 87 (November 23, 1908): 687–691.

Folger Catalog of First Folios. Research Libraries Information Network, DCFG91 or 2.

Greg, W. W. "The Bibliographical History of the First Folio." *Library* (second series) 4 (February 1903): 258–285.

_____. *The Shakespeare First Folio: Its Bibliographical and Textual History.* London: Oxford University Press, 1955.

Gregory, Dan. "Devil in the Details." *Fine Books and Collections* 6 (July/August 2008): 27–31. https://www.ilab.org/eng/documentation/171-devil_in_the_details.html.

Hinman, Charlton. "Cast-off Copy for the First Folio of Shakespeare." *Shakespeare Quarterly* 6 (1955): 259–273.

_____. "'The Halliwell-Phillipps Facsimile' of the First Folio of Shakespeare." *Shakespeare Quarterly* 5, no. 4 (Autumn 1954): 395–401.

_____. *The Printing and Proof-Reading of the First Folio.* 2 volumes. Oxford: Clarendon Press, 1963.

_____. "Variants and Reading in the First Folio of Shakespeare." *Shakespeare Quarterly* 6 (1955): 279–288.

Horrox, Reginald. "Tables for the Identification and Collation of the Shakespeare Folios." *Book Handbook* 1 (1947–1950): 105–176.

Howard-Hill, Trevor H. *Ralph Crane and Some Shakespeare First Folio Comedies.* Charlottesville: University Press of Virginia, 1972.

Ireland, W. H. *An Authentic Account of the Shakespearian Manuscripts.* London: Printed for J. Debrett, 1796.

Jaggard, William. *Shakespeare Bibliography: A Dictionary of Every Known Issue of the Writings of Our National Poet.* Stratford-on-Avon, U.K.: Shakespeare Press, 1911.

Kiffer, Selby. "Collecting the Book That Breaks the Rules: The Shakespeare First Folio at Auction." A Folger Shakespeare Library Podcast given by a senior specialist for books and manuscripts at Sotheby's as a part of the lecture series to accompany the Folger exhibition, *Fame, Fortune, and Theft: The Shakespeare First Folio,* June 29, 2011. http://www.folger.edu/template.cfm?cid=3861.

Kiffer, Selby, et al. "The First Folio: A Four Hundred Year Obsession." A 6 minute 45-second promotional video for the Folger Shakespeare Library exhibition *Fame, Fortune, and Theft: The Shakespeare First Folio,* 2011. https://www.youtube.com/watch?v=WicxFbaSxgE.

_____. *Notes and Additions to the Census of Copies of the Shakespeare First Folio.* London: Henry Frowde; Oxford University Press, 1906. Reprinted from *Library* 7 (April 1906): 113–139 and then revised May 1906.

_____. *The Shakespeare First Folio: Some Notes and a Discovery.* New York: Macmillan, 1899. First appearance in *Cornhill* (new series) 6, no. 34 (April 1899): 449–458.

Lee, Sir Sidney, ed. *Shakespeares Comedies, Histories, & Tragedies: Being a Reproduction in Facsimile of the First Folio Edition, 1623, From the Chatsworth Copy in the Possession of the Duke of Devonshire, K.G.* Oxford: Clarendon Press, 1902.

_____. *Shakespeares Comedies, Histories, & Tragedies: A Supplement to the Reproduction in Facsimile of the First Folio Edition (1623), From the Chatsworth Copy in the Possession of the Duke of Devonshire, K.G., Containing a Census of Extant Copies With Some Account of Their History and Condition.* Oxford: Clarendon Press, 1902.

Maggs Bros. *Shakespeare and Shakespeareana: A Catalog Issued in Commemoration of the Tercentenary of the First Folio Shakespeare, A.D. 1623–1923.* Catalog 434. 1923.

NPR (National Public Radio). "Fingering Shakespeare's First Drafts." *Weekend Edition,* November 28, 2009. Interview with Paul Collins and Folger Shakespeare Library, Gail Paster. http://www.npr.org/templates/story/story.php?storyId=120909124.

The Original Bodleian Copy of the First Folio of Shakespeare (The Turbutt Shakespeare). Oxford: Clarendon Press, 1905.

Otness, Harold M., comp. *The Shakespeare Folio Handbook and Census.* New York: Greenwood Press, 1990.

Pollard, Alfred W. *The Foundations of Shakespeare's Text.* London: Oxford University Press, 1923.

————. *Shakespeare Folios and Quartos: A Study in the Bibliography of Shakespeare's Plays, 1594–1685.* London: Methuen, 1909.

Rasmussen, Eric. "The Secrets of the Shakespeare First Folio." *Forum/Stratford Festival,* 2014. One hour and thirty minute video lecture at the Studio Theatre, Stratford, Ontario https://www.youtube.com/watch?v=sUEd6kee57I.

————. *The Shakespeare Thefts: In Search of the First Folios.* New York: Palgrave Macmillan, 2011.

Rasmussen, Eric, Anthony James West, and Donald L. Bailey, et al. *The Shakespeare First Folios: A Descriptive Catalog.* New York: Palgrave Macmillan, 2012.

Rhodes, R. Crompton. *Shakespeare First Folio: A Study.* Oxford: B. Blackwell, 1923.

Scheide, William H. "The Earliest First Folio in America." *Shakespeare Quarterly* 27 (1976): 332–333.

Schroeder, John W. *The Great Folio of 1623: Shakespeare's Plays in the Printing House.* Hamden, Connecticut: Shoe String Press, 1956.

Shakespeare, William. *Mr. William Shakespeare Comedies, Histories, & Tragedies.* London: Isaac Jaggard and Ed. Blount, 1623. The very first printing of the First Folio.

Shakespeare, William. (Charles Hinman, ed.) *The First Folio of Shakespeare: The Norton Facsimiles.* New York: W. W. Norton, 1996. Especially Peter W. M. Blayney's introduction to the second edition.

Shakespeare Association (Great Britain). *1623–1923: Studies in the First Folio Written for the Shakespeare Association in Celebration of the First Folio Tercentenary and Read at Meetings of the Association Held at King's College, University of London, May–June 1923.* London: H. Milford, Oxford University Press, 1924. Includes "A Survey of First Folios" by Sir Sidney Lee; "The First Folios and Its Publishers" by W. W. Greg; "The Task of Heminge and Condell" by J. Dover Wilson.

Shakespeare Stolen and Reclaimed: The Story of the Durham First Folio. The Grolier Club of New York, March 31, 2011. One-hour-and-30-minute presentation with moderator Stephen C. Ennis and panel members Richard Kuhta and Stephen C. Massey. http://vimeo.com/23048931.

Smith, Robert M. "Why a First Folio Shakespeare Remained in England." *Review of English Studies* 15, no. 59 (July 1939): 257–264.

Sotheby's. *The Shakespeare First Folio, 1623: The Dr. Williams Library Copy.* July 13, 2006. Research by Peter Selley and Dr. Peter Beal. The special hardcover edition of Lot 95, printed in addition to the regular auction catalogue.

Spielmann, M. H. *The Title-Page of the First Folio of Shakespeare's Plays: A Comparative Study of the Droeshout Portrait and the Stratford Monument.* London: H. Milford, Oxford University Press, 1924.

Stealing Shakespeare. True North Productions for the BBC, 2010. One hour video on the Durham theft and the recovery of the First Folio.

Walker, Alice. *Textual Problems of the First Folio.* Cambridge: Cambridge University Press, 1953.

Weingust, Don. *Acting from Shakespeare's First Folio: Theory, Text, and Performance.* New York: Routledge, 2006.

Werstine, Paul. "More Unrecorded States in the Folger Shakespeare Library's Collection of First Folios." *Library* 2 (1989): 47–51.

West, Anthony James. "How Many First Folios Does the Folger Hold?" *Shakespeare Quarterly* 47, no. 2 (Summer 1996): 190–194.

_____. "In Search of Missing Copies of the Shakespeare First Folio." *Book Collector* 43 (1984): 396–407.

_____. "A Model for Describing Shakespeare First Folios, with Descriptions of Selected Copies." *Library* (6 series) 21 (1999): 1–49.

_____. "The Number and Distribution of Shakespeare First Folios, 1902 and 1995." *Analytical and Enumerative Bibliography* 9 (1995): 1–23.

_____. "Ownership of Shakespeare First Folios over Four Centuries." *Library* 10, no. 4 (2009): 405–408.

_____. "Proving the Identity of the Stolen Durham University First Folio." *Library* 14, no. 4 (December 2013): 428–440.

_____. "Sales and Prices of Shakespeare First Folio: A History, 1623 to the Present." *Papers of the Bibliographical Society of America* 92, no. 4 (1998): 465–528, and 93, no 1. (1999): 74–142.

_____. *The Shakespeare First Folio: The History of the Book, Volume I; An Account of the First Folio Based on Its Sales and Prices, 1623–2000.* New York: Oxford University Press, 2001.

_____. *The Shakespeare First Folio: The History of the Book, Volume II; A New World Census of First Folios*. New York: Oxford University Press, 2003.

_____. "Why Is the First Folio So Important?" A short video for the Folger Shakespeare Library exhibition *Fame, Fortune, and Theft: The Shakespeare First Folio*, 2011. https://www.youtube.com/watch?v=Iv3WqPVIcYA.

Williams, Owen, and Caryn Lazzuri, eds. *Foliomania: Stories behind Shakespeare's Most Important Book*. Washington, D.C.: Folger Shakespeare Library, 2011.

Williams, Roger M. "The Great First Folio Caper." *Amherst* (Spring 2011). https://www.amherst.edu/aboutamherst/magazine/issues/2011spring/firstfolio.

Williams, W. P. "The Shakespeare 'First Folio': The History of the Book, vol. 1; An Account of the First Folio Based on its Sales and Prices, 1623–2000." *Notes and Queries* 49, no. 2 (2002): 117–118.

Willoughby, Edwin Eliott. *A Printer of Shakespeare: The Life and Times of William Jaggard*. London: F. Allan, 1934.

_____. *The Printing of the First Folio of Shakespeare*. Oxford: Oxford University Press, 1932.

Wilson, Frank P. "The First Folio of Shakespeare." *Times Literary Supplement* 5 (November 12, 1925): 756.

_____. "The Jaggards and the First Folio of Shakespeare." *Times Literary Supplement* 5 (November 1925): 737.

Wood, E. R. "Cancels and Corrections in *A Discovery of Error*, 1622." *Library* (5th series) 13 (1958): 124–127. Accuracy of Jaggards printing.

The Life, Times, and Works of Shakespeare

Ackroyd, Peter. *Shakespeare: The Biography*. New York: Nan A. Talese, 2005.

Allibone, S. Austin. *A Critical Dictionary of English Literature and British and American Authors, Living and Deceased, from the Earliest Accounts to the Latter Half of the Nineteenth Century*. Philadelphia: J. B. Lippincott, 1859 (numerous editions and supplements).

Anderson, Mark. *"Shakespeare" by Another Name: The Life of Edward de Vere, Earl of Oxford, the Man Who Was Shakespeare*. New York: Gotham Books, 2005.

Andrews, John F., ed. *William Shakespeare: His World, His Work, His Influence*. 3 volumes. New York: Charles Scribner's Sons, 1985.

Bate, Jonathan. *The Genius of Shakespeare.* New York: Oxford University Press, 1998.

_____. *Shakespearean Constitutions: Politics, Theatre, Criticism, 1730-1830.* Oxford: Clarendon Press, 1989.

_____. *Soul of the Age: The Biography of the Mind of William Shakespeare.* New York: Random House, 2009.

Bate, Jonathan, and Dora Thorton. *Shakespeare: Shaping the World.* London: British Museum, 2012.

Beal, Paul. "The Burning of the Globe." *Times Literary Supplement* (June 20, 1986): 689–690.

Beauclerk, Charles. *Shakespeare's Lost Kingdom: The True History of Shakespeare and Elizabeth.* New York: Grove Press, 2010.

Bevington, David. *Shakespeare and Biography.* New York: Oxford University Press, 2010.

_____. *This Wide and Universal Theater: Shakespeare in Performance, Then and Now.* Chicago: University of Chicago Press, 2007.

Bevington, David, ed. *The Complete Works of William Shakespeare.* 6th edition. New York: Pierson/Longman, 2008.

Bloom, Harold. *Shakespeare: The Invention of the Human.* New York: Riverhead Books, 1998.

Bohn, Henry G. *The Biography and Bibliography of Shakespeare.* London: privately printed, 1863; reprinted New York: AMS Press, 1972.

Bristol, Michael D. *Shakespeare's America: America's Shakespeare.* New York: Routledge, 1990.

Brown, Ivor, and George Fearon. *The Shakespeare Industry: Amazing Monument.* New York: Harper and Brothers, 1939.

Bryson, Bill. *Shakespeare: The Illustrated and Updated Edition.* New York: Atlas Books, 2009.

_____. *Shakespeare: The World as Stage.* New York: Atlas Books/HarperCollins, 2007.

Cartwright, Justin. *This Secret Garden: Oxford Revisited.* London: Bloomsbury, 2008.

Chambers, E. K. *The Elizabethian Stage.* 4 volumes. Oxford: Clarendon Press, 1923.

_____. *A Short Life of William Shakespeare: With the Sources.* Oxford: Clarendon Press, 1946.

_____. *William Shakespeare: A Study of Facts and Problems.* 2 volumes. Oxford: Clarendon Press, 1930.

Churchill, Reginald Charles. *Shakespeare and His Betters: A History and Criticism of the Attempts Which Have Been Made to Prove That Shakespeare's Works Were Written by Others.* Bloomington: Indiana University Press, 1958.

Chute, Marchette Gaylord. *Shakespeare of London.* New York: E. P. Dutton, 1949.

_____. *Stories from Shakespeare.* Cleveland: World Press, 1956 (and revised editions).

Cliff, Nigel. *The Shakespeare Riots: Revenge, Drama, and Death in Nineteenth-Century America.* New York: Random House, 2007.

Connell, Charles. *They Gave Us Shakespeare: John Hemings & Henry Condell.* Boston: Oriel Press, 1982.

Cooper, Tarnya. *Searching for Shakespeare.* New Haven, Connecticut: Yale University Press, 2006.

Deelman, Christian. *The Great Shakespeare Jubilee.* London: Michael Joseph, 1964.

De Lisle, Leanda. *After Elizabeth: The Rise of James of Scotland and the Struggle for the Throne of England.* New York: Ballantine Books, 2005.

Dobson, Michael. *The Making of the National Poet: Shakespeare, Adaptation and Authorship, 1660–1769.* Oxford: Clarendon Press, 1992.

Dugas, Don-John. *Marketing the Bard: Shakespeare in Performance and Print, 1660–1740.* Columbia: University of Missouri Press, 2006.

Duncan-Jones, Katherine. *Ungentle Shakespeare: Scenes from His Life.* London: Arden Shakespeare, 2001.

Enmondsen, Paul, and Stanley Wells, eds. *Shakespeare beyond Doubt: Evidence, Argument, Controversy.* Cambridge: Cambridge University Press, 2013.

Fisher, Paul. *A House of Wits: An Intimate Portrait of the James Family.* New York: Henry Holt, 2008.

Fleay, Frederick Gard. *A Chronicle History of the Life and Work of William Shakespeare, Player, Poet, and Playwright.* New York: Scribner & Welford, 1886.

Folger, Mrs. Henry C. *Did Not Shakespeare Write Shakespeare, Read before the Meridian Club, November 9, 1923.* Privately printed, 1923.

Friedman, Wilfred H. *Boydell's Shakespeare Gallery.* New York: Garland Publishing, 1976.

Fripp, Edgar Innes. *Shakespeare, Man and Artist.* 2 volumes. London: H. Milford, Oxford University Press, 1938.

Garber, Marjorie. *Shakespeare After All.* New York: Pantheon Books, 2004.

Gibson, H. N. *The Shakespeare Claimants: A Critical Survey of the Four Principal Theories Concerning the Authorship of Shakespearean Plays.* London: Methuen Publishing, 1962.

Grebanier, Bernard D. M. *The Great Shakespeare Forgery: A New Look at the Career of William Henry Ireland.* New York: W. W. Norton, 1965.

Greenblatt, Stephen. *Will in the World: How Shakespeare Became Shakespeare.* New York: W. W. Norton, 2004.

Gurr, Andrew. *Playgoing in Shakespeare's London.* New York: Cambridge University Press, 1987 (numerous revised editions).

_____. *The Shakespearean Stage: 1574–1642.* Cambridge: Cambridge University Press, 1970 (numerous revised editions).

Halliday, F. E. *The Cult of Shakespeare.* New York: T. Yoseloff, 1960.

_____. *The Shakespeare Companion: 1550–1950.* New York: Funk & Wagnalls, 1952. Revised edition, *The Shakespeare Companion: 1554–1964.* New York: Schocken Books, 1964, along with subsequent printings.

_____. *Shakespeare in His Age.* London: G. Duckworth, 1956.

Halliwell-Phillipps, J. O. *The Last Days of Shakespeare.* London: Chiswick Press, 1863.

_____. *Outlines of the Life of William Shakespeare.* 8th edition, 2 volumes. London: Longsman, Green, 1889.

Hanson, Neil. *The Great Fire of London: In That Apocalyptic Year, 1666.* New York: John Wiley, 2002.

Hawkins, Ann R., and Georgianna Ziegler, co-curators. *Marketing Shakespeare: The Boydell Gallery (1789–1805) and Beyond.* Folger Shakespeare Library, September 20, 2007–January 5, 2008. http://www.folger.edu/Content/Whats-On/Folger-Exhibitions/Past-Exhibitions/Marketing-Shakespeare/.

Headley, Joel Tyler. *The Great Riots of New York, 1712–1873: Including a Full and Complete Account of the Four Days' Draft Riot of 1863.* New York: E. B. Treat, 1873 (numerous revised editions).

Heylin, Clinton. *So Long As Man Can Breathe: The Untold Story of Shakespeare's Sonnets.* Philadelphia: Perseus Books Group, 2009.

Holden, Anthony. *Shakespeare: The Man behind the Genius.* Boston: Little, Brown, 2000.

Honan, Park. *Shakespeare: A Life*. New York: Oxford University Press, 1998.

Honingmann, E. A. J. *Shakespeare: The Lost Years*. Manchester: Manchester University Press, 1985.

Kastan, David Scott. *Shakespeare and the Book*. Cambridge: Cambridge University Press, 2001.

Kermode, Peter. *The Age of Shakespeare*. London: Weidenfeld & Nicolson, 2004.

Leasor, James. *The Plague and the Fire*. London: George Allen & Unwin, 1962.

Lee, Sir Sidney. *A Life of William Shakespeare*. New York: Macmillan, 1898.

———. *Stratford-on-Avon: From the Earliest Time to the Death of Shakespeare*. London: Seeley, 1885.

Lynch, Jack. *Becoming Shakespeare: The Unlikely Afterlife That Turned a Provincial Playwright into the Bard*. New York: Walker, 2007.

Marder, Louis. *His Exits and His Entrances: The Story of Shakespeare's Reputation*. Philadelphia: J. B. Lippincott, 1963.

Marino, James J. *Owning Shakespeare: The King's Men and Their Intellectual Property*. Philadelphia: University of Pennsylvania Press, 2011.

Matus, Irvin Leigh. *Shakespeare in Fact*. New York: Continuum, 1994.

McManaway, James G. *The Authorship of Shakespeare*. Washington, D.C.: Folger Shakespeare Library, 1962.

McManaway, James G., and Jeanne Addison Roberts. *A Selective Bibliography of Shakespeare: Editions, Textual Studies, Commentary*. Charlottesville: for the Folger Shakespeare Library by the University of Virginia Press, 1975.

Moody, Richard. *The Astor Place Riot*. Bloomington: Indiana University Press, 1958.

Mortimer, Ian. *A Time Travellers' Guide to Elizabethan England*. New York: Viking Press, 2012.

Murphy, Andrew. *Shakespeare in Print: A History and Chronology of Shakespeare Publishing*. Cambridge: Cambridge University Press, 2003.

National Geographic. *Shakespeare of Stratford and London*. Produced in association with WQED, Pittsburgh, and in cooperation with the Shakespeare Birthplace Trust, Stratford-upon-Avon, 1978.

Nicholl, Charles. *The Lodger: Shakespeare on Silver Street*. London: Allen Lane, 2007.

Nunzeger, Edwin. *A Dictionary of Actors and Other Persons Associated with the Public Representation of Plays in England before 1642.* London: H. Milford, Oxford Universitiy Press, 1929.

Palmer, Alan, and Veronica Palmer, eds. *Who's Who in Shakespeare's England.* Brighton, Sussex: Harvester, 1991.

PBS. *In Search of Shakespeare: Hosted by Michael Wood.* 2 DVDs, 2005. 4-part series, 240 minutes, first broadcast on BBC2.

Pierce, Patricia. *The Great Shakespeare Fraud: The Strange True Story of William-Henry Ireland.* Gloucestershire: Sutton Publishing, 2004.

Potter, Lois. *The Life of William Shakespeare: A Critical Biography.* Malden, Massachusetts: Wiley-Blackwell, 2012.

Pritchard, R. E., ed. *Shakespeare's England: Life in Elizabethan & Jacobean Times.* Stroud, Gloucestershire: Sutton Publishing, 1999.

Quennell, Peter. *Shakespeare: A Biography.* Cleveland: World Publishing Company, 1963.

Reese, M. M. *Shakespeare: His World and His Work.* New York: St. Martin's Press, 1953.

Ritchie, Fiona, and Peter Sabor, eds. *Shakespeare in the Eighteenth Century.* Cambridge: Cambridge University Press, 2012.

Rosenbaum, Ron. *The Shakespeare Wars: Clashing Scholars, Public Fiascoes, Palace Coups.* New York: Random House, 2006.

Sams, Eric. *The Real Shakespeare: Retrieving the Early Years, 1564–1594.* New Haven, Connecticut: Yale University Press, 1995.

Schoenbaum, Samuel. *Shakespeare and Others.* Washington, D.C.: Folger Shakespeare Library, 1985.

_____. *Shakespeare: A Documentary Life.* Oxford: Clarendon Press, 1975 (numerous revised and edited editions).

_____. *Shakespeare, the Globe & the World.* New York: Oxford University Press, 1979.

_____. *Shakespeare Lives.* Oxford: Clarendon Press, 1970 (and revised edition 1990).

Shakespeare's England: An Account of the Life & Manners of His Age. 2 volumes. Oxford: Clarendon Press, 1911.

Shapiro, James. *Contested Will: Who Wrote Shakespeare.* New York: Simon & Schuster, 2010.

_____. *A Year in the Life of William Shakespeare; 1599.* New York: HarperCollins, 2005.

Stern, Tiffany. *Making Shakespeare: From Stage to Page*. London: Routledge, 2004.

Stewart, Doug. *The Boy Who Would Be Shakespeare: A Tale of Forgery and Folly*. Cambridge, Massachusetts: Da Capo Press, 2010.

————. "To Be . . . or Not: The Greatest Shakespeare Forgery; William-Henry Ireland Committed a Scheme So Grand That He Fooled Even Himself into Believing He Was William Shakespeare's True Literary Heir." *Smithsonian* 41, no. 3 (June 2010): 72.

————. "To Be or Not to Be Shakespeare." *Smithsonian* 37, no. 6 (September 2006): 62–66, 68–71.

Sutherland, Kathryn. *Electronic Text: Investigations in Method and Theory*. Oxford: Clarendon Press, 1997. Includes the article by Peter S. Donaldson, "Digital Archive as Expanded Text: Shakespeare and Electronic Texuality."

Taylor, Gary. *Reinventing Shakespeare: A Cultural History, from the Restoration to the Present*. New York: Weidenfeld & Nicolson, 1989.

Thompson, A. Hamilton, ed. *William Shakespeare, His Family and Friends, by the Late Charles Elton*. New York: E. P. Dutton, 1904.

Tillyard, E. M. W. *The Elizabethan World Picture*. London: Chatto & Windus, 1943.

Tinniswood, Adrian. *By Permission of Heaven: The True Story of the Great Fire of London*. New York: Riverhead Books, 2003.

Vickers, Brian, ed. *Shakespeare: The Critical Heritage*. 6 volumes. London: Routledge & Kegan Paul, 1974.

Wells, Stanley. *Shakespeare: A Dramatic Life*. London: Sinclair-Stevenson,1994.

————. *Shakespeare: For All Time*. New York: Oxford University Press, 2003.

————. *Shakespeare & Co.: Christopher Marlowe, Thomas Dekker, Ben Jonson, Thomas Middleton, John Fletcher, and the Other Players in His Story*. New York: Pantheon Books, 2010.

Wells, Stanley, Gary Taylor, John Jewett, and William Montgomery. *William Shakespeare: A Textual Companion*. Oxford: Clarendon Press, 1987.

Williams, George Walton. *The Craft of Printing and the Publication of Shakespeare's Works*. Washington, D.C.: Folger Shakespeare Library, 1985.

Wilson, John Dover. *The Essential Shakespeare: A Biographical Adventure*. Cambridge: Cambridge University Press, 1932.

Wood, Michael. *Shakespeare*. New York: Basic Books, 2003. Published to accompany the 2003 BBC 2 broadcast, *In Search of Shakespeare*.

Wright, Louis B. "The Britian That Shakespeare Knew." *National Geographic* 125, no. 5 (May 1964): 613–665. Includes the Shakespeare's Britain Map pull-out supplement.

_____. *Middle-Class Culture in Elizabethan England*. Ithaca, New York: for Folger Shakespeare Library by Cornell University Press, 1958.

Standard Oil and John D. Rockefeller

Chernow, Ron. *Titan: The Life of John D. Rockefeller, Sr.* New York: Random House, 1998.

Hinton, Diana Davids, and Roger M. Olien. *Oil in Texas: The Gusher Age, 1895–1945*. Austin: University of Texas Press, 2002.

History of Standard Oil Company (New Jersey). New York: Harper & Brothers, 1955–1971. 3 volumes: *Pioneering in Big Business, 1882–1911*, by R. W. Hidy and M. E. Hidy; *The Resurgent Years, 1911–1927*, by G. S. Gibb and E. H. Knowlton; and *New Horizons, 1927–1950*, by H. M. Larson, E. H. Knowlton, and C. S. Popple)

Holbrook, Stewart H. *The Age of Moguls*. Garden City, New York: Doubleday, 1953.

Howarth, Stephen. *A Brief History of Mobil*. New York: Mobil Corporation, 1997.

_____. *One Hundred Twenty-Five Years of History: ExxonMobil*. Irving, Texas: ExxonMobil Corporation, 2007.

Nevins, Allan. *John D. Rockefeller: The Heroic Age of American Enterprise*. 2 volumes. New York: Charles Scriber's Sons, 1940.

_____. *Study in Power: John D. Rockefeller, Industrialist and Philanthropist*. New York: Charles Scribner's Sons, 1953.

Rundell, Walter, Jr. *Early Texas Oil: A Photographic History, 1866–1936*. College Station: Texas A&M University Press, 1977.

Satterlee, Herbert L. *J. Pierpont Morgan: An Intimate Portrait, 1837–1913*. New York: Macmillan, 1939.

Singer, Jonathan. *Broken Trusts: The Texas Attorney General versus the Oil Industry, 1889–1909*. College Station: Texas A&M University Press, 2002.

Standiford, Lee. *Meet You in Hell: Andrew Carnegie, Henry Clay Frick and the Bitter Partnership That Transformed America*. New York: Crown, 2005.

Strouse, Jean. *Morgan: American Financier*. New York: Random House, 1999.

Tarbell, Ida M. *The History of Standard Oil.* 2 volumes. New York: McClure, Phillips, 1904 (numerous later printings).

Wallace, Charles B. *Nine Lives: The Story of the Magnolia Companies and the Antitrust Laws.* Dallas: by author, 1955.

Weinberg, Steve. *Taking on the Trust: The Epic Battle of Ida Tarbell and John D. Rockefeller.* New York: W. W. Norton, 2008.

White, Gerald Taylor. *Formative Years in the Far West: A History of Standard Oil Company of California and Predecessors through 1919.* New York: Appleton-Century, 1962.

Williamson, Harold F., and Arnold D. Daum. *The American Petroleum Industry: The Age of Illumination, 1859–1899.* Evanston, Illinois: Northwestern University Press, 1959.

Yergin, Daniel. *The Prize: The Epic Quest for Oil, Money, and Power.* New York: Simon & Schuster, 1991.

The Life, Career, and Collecting Activites of Henry C. Folger Jr, and the Folger Shakespeare Library

Burton, Katherine, and Louise Sanborn Gilford Perry. *Idolatry of Books: A Collected Edition of the Bibliolatrous Services.* Norton, Massachusetts: Periwinkle Press, 1939. Includes the essays "Henry Clay Folger: For I Am an American, Text and Press Work" and "Henry E. Huntington: 'This Library Will Tell the Story.'"

Crum, Alfred Russell, and A. S. Dungan, eds. *Romance of American Petroleum and Gas Vol. 1.* Oil City, Pennsylvania: Derrick Publishing, 1911. Early references to Henry Folger.

Dawson, Giles. "History of the Folger Shakespeare Library, 1932–1968." Unpublished manuscript, Folger Shakespeare Library.

DiPetro, Caryn, ed. *Bradley, Greg, Folger.* Great Shakespeareans, Volume IX. London: Continuum International Publishing Group, 2011. Includes Chapter 3, "Henry Clay Folger, Jr. (18 June 1857–11 June 1930)" by Michael D. Bristoll.

Ferington, Esther, ed. *Infinite Variety: Exploring the Folger Shakespeare Library.* Washington, D.C.: Folger Shakespeare Library, 2002.

Folger, Emily J. "The Dream Come True: The Story of the Library and of Henry Clay Folger." Corrected typescript of paper presented at the Meridian Club, 1933.

The Folger Library: A Decade of Growth, 1950–1960. Washington, D.C.: Folger Shakespeare Library, 1960.

Folger Shakespeare Library. *Catalog of Printed Books of the Folger Shakespeare Library, Washington, D.C.* 28 volumes. Boston: G. K. Hall, 1970.

Folger Shakespeare Library. *Catalog of Shakespeare Collection.* 2 volumes. Boston: G. K. Hall, 1972.

Folger Shakespeare Library. *The Folger Shakespeare Memorial Library Administered by the Trustees of Amherst College: A Brief Account.* Washington, D.C.: for the Trustees of Amherst College, c. 1947.

Folger Shakespeare Library. *The Folger Shakespeare Memorial Library Administered by the Trustees of Amherst College: A Report on Progress, 1931–1941, by Joseph Quincy Adams.* Amherst, Massachusetts: for the Trustees of Amherst College, 1942.

The Folger Shakepeare Library: Washington. Washington, D.C.: for the Trustees of Amherst College, 1933. Includes essays by Librarian Joseph Quincy Adams and Architect Paul Philippe Cret on the occasion of the opening of the library.

Folger's Choice: Favorites on Our Fifty-five Anniversary. Washington, D.C.: Folger Shakespeare Library, 1987.

Foster, Joseph T. "Folger: The Biggest Little Library in the World." *National Geographic* 3, no. 3 (September 1951): 411–424.

Goldscheider, Eric. "An Unlikely Love Affair." *Amherst* (Fall 2007). https://www.amherst.edu/aboutamherst/magazine/issues/2007_fall/shakespeare.

Grant, Stephen H. *Collecting Shakespeare: The Story of Henry and Emily Folger.* Baltimore: Johns Hopkins University Press, 2014.

————. "A Most Interesting and Attractive Problem: Creating Washington's Folger Shakespeare Library." *Washington History* 24, no. 1 (2012): 2–19.

Grolier Club. *Grolier 75: A Biographical Retrospective to Celebrate the Seventy-Fifth Anniversary of the Grolier Club in New York.* New York: Grolier Club, 1959. Includes the essay "Henry Clay Folger" by Louis B. Wright.

Grossman, Elizabeth Greenwell. *The Civic Architecture of Paul Cret.* Cambridge. Cambridge University Press, 1996.

Grover, Harriet. *Highlights of the Folger Family with a Brief Genealogy.* Berkeley, California: Privately printed, 1939.

Harrison, Robert L. "The Folgers and Shakespeare: A Long Island Story." *Nassau County Historical Society Journal* 61 (2001): 11–18.

Henry Folger: 18 June 1857–11 June 1930. New Haven, Connecticut: privately printed, 1931. Includes "Prayer and Discourse by Dr. S. Parkes Cadman at

Mr. Folger's Funeral," "Biographical Sketch by George E. Dimmock," "Resolutions by Pratt Institute Adopted at a Trustees' Meeting, June 26, 1930," "The Significance of the Folger Shakespeare Memorial: An Essay Toward an Interpretation by William Adams Slade," "Henry C. Folger as a Collector by A. S. W. Rosenbach," and "Letters to Mrs. Folger."

Holland, Leicester B. "The Folger Shakespeare Library." *American Magazine of Art* 24, no. 3 (March 1932): 183–190.

Kane, Betty Ann. *The Widening Circle: The Story of the Folger Shakespeare Library and Its Collections*. Washington, D.C.: Folger Shakespeare Library, 1976.

King, Stanley. *History of the Endowment of Amherst College*. Norwood, Massachusetts: Plimpton Press, 1950.

_____. *Recollections of the Folger Shakespeare Library*. Ithaca, New York: for the Trustees of Amherst College by Cornell University Press, 1950.

Love's Labor: How Henry and Emily Folger Built a Library. GVI Video Productions. Washington, D.C.: Folger Shakespeare Library, 2007. https://www.youtube.com/watch?v=XFS_q3jgqeI&index=41&list=PLvl8oT-pTXos6uXiV-cgxvP-UXYQlzcrq.

McManaway, James G. "Folger Library." *South Atlantic Bulletin* 6, no. 2 (October 1940): 1–4.

_____. "The Folger Shakespeare Library." *Shakespeare Survey* 1 (1948): 57–78.

_____. "The Folger Shakespeare Library in Wartime." *General Federation Clubwoman, American Home and Fine Arts* (December 1943).

Montague, W. L., et al. *Biographical Record of the Alumni of Amherst College, 1821– . . .)*. Amherst, Massachusetts: 1891–1901.

Parke-Bernet Galleries. *Georgian and Other Furniture and Silver; Shakepearian Memorabilia, Old English Porcelain, Paintings, Rugs; the Folger Shakespeare Library, and from Other Owners*. Public Auction, May 21 and 22. New York: Park-Bernet Galleries, 1984.

Paullin, Charles Oscar. "History of the Site of the Congressional and Folger Libraries." *Columbia Historical Society Records* 37–38 (1937): 173–194.

Pressly, William L. *A Catalogue of Paintings in the Folger Shakespeare Library: "As Imagination Bodies Forth."* New Haven, Connecticut: Yale University Press, 1993.

Rosenbach, A. S. W. *Henry C. Folger as a Collector*. New Haven, Connecticut: by author, 1931.

Salisbury, Frank O. *Portrait and Pageant: Kings, Presidents, and People.* London: J. Murray, 1944.

————. *Sarum Chase.* London: J. Murray, 1953 (enlarged and revised edition of *Portrait and Pageant*).

Schoenbaum, S. "The World's Finest Library Is This Side of the Atlantic." *Smithsonian* 13, no. 1 (April 1982): 118–127.

Severy, Marie. "Shakespeare Lives at the Folger." *National Geographic* 171, no. 2 (February 1987): 244–259.

The Shakespearian Theatre: Washington, DC. The Folger Shakespeare Library Prints. Washington, D.C.: Folger Shakespeare Library, 1935.

Slade, William Adams. "The Folger Shakespeare Library." *Library Journal* 57, no. 13 (July 1932): 601–607.

Sukert, Lancelot. "The Folger Shakespeare Library." *American Architect* (September 1932).

Vassar Encyclopedic Project (online). Includes the entry "Emily Jordan Folger" by Stephen H. Grant. http://vcencyclopedia.vassar.edu/alumni/emily-jordan -folger.html.

Vaughan, Virginia Mason, and Alden T. Vaughan. *Shakespeare in American Life.* Washington, D.C.: Folger Shakespeare Library, 2007. Includes "Duty and Enjoyment: The Folgers as Shakespeare Collectors in the Gilded Age" by Georgianna Ziegler, excerpted as "Origins of a Lifelong Passion" at: http:// www.shakespeareinamericanlife.org/education/everyone/library/origins.cfm.

Whicher, George F. "Henry Clay Folger and the Shakespeare Library," reprinted from the *Amherst Graduates' Quarterly* (November 1930): 2–16.

White, David G. "The Folger Shakespeare Library Architectural Woodwork of Appalachian White Oak." Brochure no. 7, Appalachian Hardwood Manufacturers, Inc., Cincinatti, Ohio, 1932.

Who We Are; Parts 1 and 2—Folger Shakespeare Library. Washington, D.C.: Folger Shakespeare Library, 2008. 8 minute and 10 minute videos. https://www .youtube.com/watch?v=3DWYG270gqE&list=PL9D58EF31D72082EC& index=2; https://www.youtube.com/watch?v=HZvdZgLYKjI&index=3&list =PL9D58EF31D72082EC.

Wolfe, Heather, ed. *The Pen's Excellence: Treasures from the Manuscripts Collection of the Folger Shakespeare Library.* Seattle: University of Washington Press, 2002.

Wright, Louis B. *The Folger Library, Two Decades of Growth: An Informal Account.* Charlottesville: for the Folger Shakespeare Library by the University Press of Virginia, 1968.

_____. "Huntington and Folger, Book Collectors with a Purpose." *Atlantic Monthly* 209, no. 4 (April 1962): 70–75.

The History of the Book, Bibliography, Bookbinding, Book Collectors, Collecting, and Booksellers

Ames, Joseph. *Typographical Antiquities: Being a Historical Account of the printing in England with Some Memoirs of our Ancient Printers, and a Register of the books printed by them, from the Year MCCCLXXI to the year MDC.* 4 volumes. London: W. Faden, 1749 (numerous reprints and editions, including London: for the Editor, 1785–1790.

Basbanes, Nicholas A. *A Gentle Madness: Bibliophiles, Bibliomanes, and the Eternal Passion for Books.* New York: Henry Holt, 1995 (and reprint edition).

_____. *Patience & Fortitude: A Roving Chronicle of Book People, Book Places, and Book Culture.* New York: HarperCollins, 2001.

Bearman, Frederick A., Nati H. Krivasty, and J. Franklin. *Fine and Historic Bookbindings from the Folger Shakespeare Library.* Washington, D.C.: Folger Shakespeare Library, 1992.

Bodmer, George. "A. S. W. Rosenbach: Dealer and Collector. *The Lion and the Unicorn* 22, no. 3 (1998): 277–288. http://muse.jhu.edu/journals/lion_and_the_unicorn/summary/v022/22.3bodmer.html.

Cannon, Carl L. *American Book Collectors and Collecting from Colonial Times to the Present.* New York: H. W. Wilson, 1941.

Carter, John. *ABC for Book Collectors.* New York: Alfred A. Knopf, 1953 (numerous later printings).

Catalogue of Shakespeare Reliques: Some Account of the Antiquities, Coins, Manuscripts, Rare Books, Ancient Documents and Other Reliques Illustrative of the Life and Works of Shakespeare. Brixton Hill, 1852. Also, the following supplemental booklets: *A Garland of Shakespeariana Recently Added to the Library and Museum of James O. Halliwell, Esq., at the Avenue Lodge, Brixton Hill.* (Brixton Hill, 1854), and *A Lyttle Boke Gevinge a True and Brief Accounte of Some Reliques and Curiosities Added of Late to Mr. Halliwell's Shakespeare Collection* (London, 1856).

A Catalogue of Shakespeareana. 2 volumes. London: for presentation only, Chiswick Press, 1899.

Craster, Edmund. *History of the Bodleian Library, 1845–1945.* Oxford: Clarendon Press, 1952.

Creasey, John. *Dr. Williams's Library: The Last Fifty Years.* London: Dr. Williams's Trust, 2000.

Currie, Barton. *Fishers of Books.* Boston: Little, Brown, 1931.

De Ricci, Seymour. *English Collectors of Books & Manuscripts, 1530–1930, and Their Marks of Ownership.* New York: Macmillan, 1930 (revised, Bloomington: Indiana University Pres, 1960).

Dibdin, Rev. T. F. *The Library Companion: Or, the Young Man's Guide, and the Old Man's Comfort, in the Choice of a Library.* London: Harding, Triphook, and Lepard, 1824 (and revised 2nd edition, 1825).

Dickinson, Donald C. *Dictionary of American Book Collectors.* New York: Greenwood Press, 1986.

_____. *Henry E. Huntington's Library of Libraries.* San Marino, California: Huntington Library, 1995.

Diehl, Edith. *Bookbinding: Its Background Techniques.* 2 volumes. New York: Rinehart, 1941.

Ettinhausen, Maurice L. *Rare Books and Royal Collectors: Memoirs of an Antiquarian Bookseller.* New York: Simon & Schuster, 1966.

Gibson, James M. *The Philadelphia Shakespeare Story: Horace Henry Furness and the Variorum Shakespeare.* AMS Studies in the Renaissance. New York: AMS Press, 1990.

Goldstein, Malcolm. *Landscape with Figures: A History of Art Dealing in the United States.* New York: Oxford University Press, 2000.

Gray, Victor. *Bookmen: London, 250 Years of Sotheran Bookselling.* London: Henry Sotheran, 2011.

Greg, W. W. *Catalogue of Books Presented by Edward Capell to the Library at Trinity College in Cambridge.* Cambridge: Trinity College University Press, 1903.

Halliwell-Phillipps, J. O. *A Calendar of the Shakespearean Rarities, Drawings, and Engravings, Preserved in the Hollingbury Corpse near Brighton.* London: for special circulation and for presents only, 1887.

_____. *A Catalog of the Warehouse of the Library of J. O. Halliwell-Phillipps.* London: J. E. Adlard, 1876.

The Huntington Library: Treasures from Ten Centuries. San Marino, California: Huntington Library, 2004.

Jones, Stephen Kay. *Dr. Williams and His Library.* Cambridge: for the Society by W. Heffer, 1948.

King, Edmund G. C. "Alexander Turnbull's 'Dream Imperial': Collecting Shakespeare in the Colonial Antipodes." *Script & Print* 24 (2010): 69–86.

Mandelbrote, Giles, ed. *Out of Print and Into Profit: A History of the Rare and Secondhand Book Trade in Britain in the Twentieth Century*. London: British Library, 2006.

McCormick, E. H. *Alexander Turnbull: His Life, His Circle, His Collection*. Wellington, New Zealand: Alexander Turnbull Library, 1974.

McKenzie, D. F. "Printers of the Mind: Some Notes on Bibliographical Theories and Printing-House Practices." *Studies in Bibliography* 22 (1969): 1–75.

McKerrow, Ronald B. *An Introduction to Bibliography for Literary Students*. Oxford: Clarendon Press, 1927.

Myers, Robin, Michael Harris, and Giles Mandelbrote, eds. *Books on the Move: Tracking Copies through Collections and the Book Trade*. London: British Library, 2007.

Newton, A. Edward. *The Amenities of Book-Collecting and Kindred Affections*. Boston: Atlantic Monthly Press, 1918.

————. *A Magnificent Farce, and Other Diversions of a Book-Collector*. Boston: Atlantic Monthly Press, 1921.

————. *This Book-Collecting Game*. Boston: Little, Brown, 1928.

Nicolson, Adam. *God's Secretaries: The Making of the King James Bible*. New York: HarperCollins, 2003.

The Penn Library Collection at 250: From Franklin to the Web. Philadelphia: University of Pennsylvania Library, 2000. Includes Chapter 3, "The Furness Memorial Library" by Daniel Traister. http://www.library.upenn.edu/exhibits/rbm/at250/furness/dt.pdf.

Perry, Marsden Jasael. *Marsden J. Perry Library of Shakespearean Library of Providence, R.I.* 1901.

Pollard, Alfred W., G. R. Redgrave, et al. comp. *A Short-Title Catalog of Books Printed in England, Scotland, & Ireland and the English Books Printed Abroad, 1475–1640*. London: by arrangement with the Bibliographical Society for B. Quaritch, 1926 (and numerous reprints).

A Preliminary List of Books and Manuscripts Relating to the Life and Writings of William Shakespeare Forming the Collection of Marsden Perry. Providence, Rhode Island, 1891.

The Redwood Library Guide to an Appreciation of Wm. Shakespeare, His Works, His Fame: Being a Few Explanatory Notes on an Exhibition of Books and Manuscripts Selected from the Collection of Mr. Marsden J. Perry. Providence, Rhode Island: Sign of the Standard, to be sold for the benefit of the Redwood Library in Newport, Rhode Island, 1916.

Rider, Sidney S. *A Bit of Shakespearean Bibliography: The Library of Marsden J. Perry Shakespearean Library of Providence, R.I.* 1901.

Rosenbach, A. S. W. *A Book Hunter's Holiday: Adventures with Books and Manuscripts.* Boston: Houghton Mifflin, 1936.

_____. *Books and Bidders: The Adventures of a Bibliophile.* Boston: Little, Brown, 1927.

_____. *The Unpublishable Memoirs.* New York: Mitchell Kennerly, 1917.

Rosenblum, Joseph. "The Booksellers and the Biographers: A. S. W. Rosenbach and Seymour de Ricci in the Interwar Period." *Book Collector* 49, no. 3 (Autumn 2000): 383–396.

Saltzman, Cynthia. *Old Masters, New World: America's Raid on Europe's Greatest Pictures.* New York: Viking, 2008.

Sherman, William H. *Used Books: Marking Readers in Renaissance England.* Philadelphia: University of Pennsylvania Press, 2008.

Smith, Robert M. "The Formation of Shakespearean in America." *Shakespeare Association Bulletin* 4, no. 3 (July 1929): 65–73.

Sotheran Firm, London Booksellers. *Bibliotheca Pretiosa: Being an Unusually Choice Collection of Books and Manuscripts in Exceptional Fine Condition . . .* London, 1907.

Sowerby, E. Millicent. *Rare People and Rare Books.* London: Constable, 1967.

Spurgeon, Selena A. *Henry Edward Huntington: His Life and His Collection; A Docent Guide.* San Marino, California: Huntington Library, 1992.

Steinberg, S. H. *500 Years of Printing.* London, 1955 (numerous revised and updated editions).

Thomas, Alan G. *Great Books and Book Collectors.* London: Weidenfeld and Nicolson, 1974.

Thorpe, James Ernest. *Gifts of Genius: Treasures of the Huntington Library.* San Marino, California: Huntington Library, 1980.

_____. *Henry Edward Huntington: A Biography.* Berkeley: University of California Press, 1994.

Towner, George. *The Elogant Auctioneers* (completed by Stephen Varble). New York: Hill & Wang, 1970.

Wernick, R., and J. McGrail. "The Bookseller Who Couldn't Stand to Sell His Books." *Smithsonian* 23 (April 1992): 106–113.

Willoughby, E. E. *The Classification of the Folger Shakespeare Library.* Chicago: University of Chicago Press, 1937.

_____. "The Folger Shakespeare Library." *Library World* 38, no. 442 (1936): 227–29.

Winterich, John T. "Dr. Rosenbach: The Tycoon of Rare Books." *Harper's Magazine* 212, no. 1270 (1956): 80–88.

Wolf, Edwin, II, and John F. Fleming. *Rosenbach: A Biography.* Cleveland: World Publishing, 1960.

Wright, Louis B. *Of Books and Men.* Columbia: University of South Carolina Press, 1976.

Ziegler, Georgianna, ed. *Shakespeare Study Today: The Horace Howard Furness Memorial Lectures.* New York: AMS Press, 1986. Includes her introduction and the article "Horace Howard Furness: Book Collector and Library Builder" by James M. Gibson.

Shakespeare First Folios (Digital Facsimiles Online)

Bodleian edition: http://firstfolio.bodleian.ox.ac.uk/.

Brandeis University Libraries edition: http://internetshakespeare.uvic.ca/Library/facsimile/book/Bran_F1/.

Brotherton edition: http://library.leeds.ac.uk/special-collections-shakespeare.

Folger Shakespeare Library, Copy No. 5: http://hamnet.folger.edu/other/folio/ShaF1B.pdf.

Folger Shakespeare Library, Copy No. 9: http://luna.folger.edu/luna/servlet/view/search?q=Call_Number%3D%22STC+22273+Fo.1+no.09%22+LIMIT%3AFOLGERCM1~6~6&pgs=250&res=2&cic=FOLGERCM1~6~6&sort=Call_Number%2CMPSORTORDER1%2CCD_Title%2CImprint.

Folger Shakespeare Library, Copy No. 68: http://luna.folger.edu/luna/servlet/view/search?sort=Call_Number%2CMPSORTORDER1%2CCD_Title%2CImprint&q=Call_Number%3D%22STC+22273+Fo.1+no.68%22+LIMIT%3AFOLGERCM1~6~6&pgs=250&res=2.

Furness Collection (University of Pennsylvania Library): http://sceti.library.upenn.edu/sceti/printedbooksNew/index.cfm?TextID=firstfolio&PagePosition=1.

Meisei University copy (one of 12, this one with unique annotations): http://shakes.meisei-u.ac.jp/e-index.html.

State Library at New South Wales edition: http://internetshakespeare.uvic.ca/Library/facsimile/overview/book/F1.html.

Stuttgart edition: http://digital.wlb-stuttgart.de/digitale-sammlungen/seiten

ansicht/?no_cache=1&tx_dlf%5Bid%5D=2103&tx_dlf%5Bpage%5D =1.

Walter Havinghurst Special Collections (Miami University of Ohio Libraries): http://doyle.lib.muohio.edu/cdm4/shakespeare/.

Useful Internet Sites

2016 ALA First Folio Tour: http://www.ala.org/programming/firstfolio.

British Shakespeare Association: http://www.britishshakespeare.ws/.

Folger Shakespeare Library: http://www.folger.edu/, specifically the First Folio landing page: http://www.folger.edu/template.cfm?cid=930.

Global Electronic Shakespeare Conference: http://shaksper.net/scholarly -resources/shakespeare-on-the-internet.

Internet Shakespeare Editions: http://internetshakespeare.uvic.ca/.

Shakespeare Association of America: http://www.shakespeareassociation.org/.

The Shakespeare Authorship Page ("Dedicated to the Proposition that Shakespeare Wrote Shakespeare"): http://shakespeareauthorship.com/.

Shakespeare Birthplace Trust: http://www.shakespeare.org.uk/home.html.

The Shakespeare Blog: http://theshakespeareblog.com/.

Shakespeare Online: http://www.shakespeare-online.com/.

The Shakespeare Society of Japan (English version): http://www.s-sj.org /?lang=en

Touchstone; Cooperation and Partnership among UK Shakespeare Collections: http://www.touchstone.bham.ac.uk/welcome.html.

World Shakespeare Bibliography Online: http://www.worldshakesbib.org/.

Appendix

Chronological Order of Henry C. Folger's Purchases
of the First Folio

Purchase Date	Simple Comparison Description[1]	West No.	Folger No.	Price Paid[2]
Bet. 1891 and 1893	very inferior copy	113	55	unknown
1896	Pope-Hoe—red morocco, binding by Francis Bedford	72	14	$4,500
1897	Warwick Castle collection (in group)— bound by Bedford	64	6	est. $2,500 to $4,000
1898	Hayes—inferior copy	102	44	$561
1900	Kalbfleisch—100% genuine with replacement pages from other First Folios	66	8	$9,000
1901	Frederickson-McKee—flawed and inferior	94	36	$892.50
1903	Vincent/Sibthorp—manuscript inscription	59	1	$48,732.50
1903	Jonas—proof sheet from *Othello*	105	47	$1,250
1903	Hilhouse—with composite title page	75	17	$2,250
1903	Sotheran—multiple leaves from different copies	114	56	$1,750
1903	Roberts—portrait inlay (copy used to make Chatto & Windus facsimile)	91	33	$825
1903	Spencer—very inferior copy	106	48	$400
1903	Dutton—very inferior copy	122	64	$220
1903	Tregaskis—leaves from First and Second Folio	103	45	$850
1904	Pickering—Bedford bookbinder, pages trimmed, morocco binding	92	34	$1,100

Purchase Date	Simple Comparison Description[1]	West No.	Folger No.	Price Paid[2]
1904	Lilly-Thorpe—some preliminaries in facsimile	93	35	$950
1904	Brodie—numerous imperfections	78	20	$2,625
1904	Duff—poor copy, mutilated	88	30	$2,205
1904	Sotheran—hundreds of replacement leaves	115	57	$1,254
1904	Richmond—outlines of eyeglasses	104	46	$1,850
1905	John Scott—all preliminaries in facsimile	89	31	$1,350
1905	Tweedmouth—facsimile first leaf	77	19	$7,300
1906	Denny—composite from other editions	101	43	$6,500
1906	Admiral Harvey—soiled and worn	86	28	$1,300
1907	Fitzgerald—unremarkable copy, some pages cut to border	90	32	$750
1907	Sotheby's—very incomplete copy	124	66	$245
1909	Ferrers—many leaves from other copies and trimmed	85	27	$3,500
1909	Lord Amherst—some leaves in facsimile and from Second Folio	83	25	$2,200
1909	Lord Amherst—imperfections in several leaves	84	26	$2,200
1910	Hawkins-Garnett—disbound in case	107	49	$450
1910	Sotheby's—mirror image of scissors	116	58	$3,060
1910	Bishop of Truro's (Gott)—bound in red goatskin	67	9	$9,260
1910	Buckley-Hargreaves—red morocco, gilded edges	71	13	$10,200
1910	Maggs—facsimile leaves and imperfections	87	29	$3,400
1910	Gaisford—misprint in *Hamlet*	73	15	$6,250
1910	Holham-Hilton—some imperfections	82	24	$2,100
1911	Crockett—many preliminaries in facsimile	95	37	$525
1911	Hoe—tall copy	65	7	$14,300
1911	Butler—crushed brown morocco binding	96	38	$660
1911	Mary Lewis—some preliminaries mutilated and in facsimile	109	51	$2,500
1911	Hanmer—stage directions in *Merry Wives*	74	16	$6,650
1912	Elizabethan Club—proof page from *Henry IV*	108	50	$7,500

Purchase Date	Simple Comparison Description[1]	West No.	Folger No.	Price Paid[2]
1912	Sabin—Droeshout portrait first state, last page of *Romeo and Juliet* crossed out	60	2	$13,750
1913	Brockett—shabby unrepaired copy	81	23	$4,870
1913	Vaughan—provenance to 17th century	110	52	$4,970
1913	Hutchinson—Histories annotated	112	54	$3,950
1913	Plymouth Library—lacking one play	117	59	$255
1914	A. B. Stewart library auction—red morocco binding by Francis Bedford	118	60	$1,263
1914	Beaufoy—Roger Paine binder	69	11	$15,500
1916	Leaves from various sources	98	40	$870
1916	Bulley—title page in facsimile	119	61	$6,000
1916	some imperfections	120	62	$3,000
1916	Smith—compilations, leaves of various sizes	121	63	$3,500
1916	Stevens—title page poorly reconstructed	100	42	$6,050
1916	Wilbraham—missing some preliminary leaves	97	39	$3,000
1918	Fitzwilliam—imperfections and mutilated	99	41	$2,500
1918	Vernon—imperfect title in facsimile	80	22	$11,000
1918	Leighton—bunch of loose leaves	123	65	$75
1920	Gilbourne—restored copy	70	12	$6,600
1921	Elliot-Baker-Wilbraham—facsimile and inlay, first leaf	76	18	$13,000
1922	Sabin-Wells—fine copy	129	71	$22,750
1922	Vernay—weak copy	62	4	$3,450
1922	Foster—genuine portrait, imperfect inlay title page	79	21	$9,130
1922	Daniel (Burnett-Coutts)—very fine copy	63	5	$52,070
1922	Sheldon (Burnett-Coutts second copy)—cancellation of *Romeo and Juliet* on last leaf	68	10	$26,730
1923	Wyndham—short, narrow, cropped copy	111	53	$1,275
1924	Fitzherbert—unexceptional copy	125	67	$7,400
1924	Earl of Kimberly—fine copy	126	68	$37,000
1925	Perkins—some imperfections	127	69	$32,000
1925	Landaff—manuscript additions	128	70	$19,500
1926	Stevens—original leaves and all preliminaries present	61	3	$6,050

Purchase Date	Simple Comparison Description[1]	West No.	Folger No.	Price Paid[2]
1926	Hellman—fine copy	130	72	$41,000
1926	Killigrew—some leaves missing and mutilated	131	73	$9,900
1927	Missing two plays	132	74	$1,739
1928	Wantage—manuscript additions	133	75	$47,500
1928	Ingleby—many leaves missing from *Cymbeline*	· 135	77	$13,200
1928	Hacket—juvenile drawings, replacement pages, title page from Second Folio	136	78	$22,500
1928	Toft Hall—brittle pages, no preliminaries	137	79	$5,375
1928	Bishop Perry, Earl of Caledon—some imperfections	134	76	$68,750

Folios 80, 81, 82[3]

[1]Shakespearian scholars have devoted hundreds of pages to describing fully the variations, marginalia, defects, facsimile, and replacement pages for the First Folios. This chart provides the reader with somewhat basic and very simplistic guidance to why Henry Folger paid exorbitant prices for some First Folios, and very little for others. For a complete catalogue and description of all First Folios, see Eric Rasmussen, Anthony James West, and Donald L. Bailey, et al., *The Shakespeare First Folios: A Descriptive Catalog* (New York: Palgrave Macmillan, 2012); and Anthony James West, *The Shakespeare First Folio: The History of the Book, Volume I; An Account of the First Folio Based on Its Sales and Prices, 1623–2000* (New York: Oxford University Press, 2001) and *The Shakespeare First Folio: The History of the Book, Volume II; A New World Census of First Folios* (New York: Oxford University Press, 2003).

[2]For more detailed price information on Henry Folger's purchases, see West, *The Shakespeare First Folio: The History of the Book, Volume I*, 101–104.

[3]West believes that any edition of this Shakespeare work that is more than fifty percent intact should be deemed a First Folio. Accordingly, Folger First Folios numbered 80, 81, and 82 fit into this category with some plays and fragments bound in leather. For a complete discussion of this topic, see West, *The Shakespeare First Folio: The History of the Book, Volume I*, 53–63 ("What to Count as a Copy and Copies 80 to 82 at the Folger's Library"). Folger 80 was purchased in December 1926 and Folger 82 in 1920. The price paid for the "fragment" 82 plus additional plays and leaves was £1,250.

Notes
꧁ॐ꧂

Prologue: "He Was Not of an Age, but for All Time!"

1. A. S. W. Rosenbach, *Henry Folger as a Collector*, privately printed, 1931, 76.
2. Ibid., 75.
3. The First Folio contains thirty-six plays and excludes *Pericles*. To bring the count to thirty-nine, two other plays that were published after 1623, *Two Noble Kinsmen* and *Cardenio*, collaborations with John Fletcher, with no copy of the latter surviving.

Chapter 1: "The Good [That Men Do] Is Oft Interred with Their Bones"

1. David Bevington, ed., *The Complete Works of Shakespeare*, seventh edition (New York: Longman, 2012), Act IV, Scene 5, lines 179–180.
2. James Orchard Halliwell-Phillipps, *The Last Days of Shakespeare* (London: Chiswick Press, 1863); David Cressy, *Birth, Marriage & Death: Ritual, Religion and the Life-Cycle in Tudor and Stuart England* (New York: Oxford University Press, 1999), 428–431.
3. Halliwell-Phillipps, *The Last Days of Shakespeare*, 11.
4. A famous example of iambic pentameter is: "Was this the face that launch'd a thousand ships, / And burnt the topless towers of Illium?" (Christopher Marlowe, *Dr. Faustus*, Scene 13). Shakespeare employed groups of five iambs or "feet," called iambic pentameter, which comes close to the sound of a natural speaking voice, to great effect: "But soft, what light through yonder window breaks?" *Romeo and Juliet* (Act II, Scene 2, line 2).
5. Charles Connell, *They Gave Us Shakespeare* (London: Oriel Press, 1982), 26.
6. Ibid., 25.
7. Marchette Chute, *Stories from Shakespeare* (New York: Meridian, 1987), 92.
8. S. Schoenbaum, *Shakespeare: The Globe and the World* (New York: Oxford University Press, 1979), 95.
9. James Shapiro, *A Year in the Life of William Shakespeare: 1599* (New York: Harper-Collins, 2005), 190–193. Also see the preface to Folger reprint of *The Passionate Pilgrim* (New York: Scribner, 1940), ix. Also see Bevington, *The Complete Works*, lxix.
10. Chute, *Stories from Shakespeare*, 92.
11. Schoenbaum, *Shakespeare: The Globe and the World*, 87, quoting Francis Meres's 1598 *Palladis Tamia, Wits Treasury*. Meres cites *Love's Labor's Won*. Meres's writ-

ings helped greatly with the establishment of the chronology of the writing of the plays.

12. The tally is thirty-nine by 1616 if you count *The Two Noble Kinsmen* and *Cardenio*, plays Shakespeare wrote in collaboration with Fletcher. And the count is zero if you don't believe he wrote any plays.

13. Jonathan Bate, *The Genius of Shakespeare* (New York: Oxford University Press, 1998).

14. Gary Taylor, *Reinventing Shakespeare: A Cultural History from the Restoration to the Present* (New York: Vintage, 1991), 96.

15. *A Midsummer Night's Dream*, in Bevington, Act V, Scene 1, lines 15–18.

Chapter 2: "Adieu . . . Remember Me"

1. Connell, *They Gave Us Shakespeare*, 3. Contemporary records spell their names, as well as Shakespeare's, in a multitude of ways—Hemings, Heminges, Hemmings, Hemminge, Heming, Condell, Condall, Cundell, Condy. Shakespeare himself refers to "my fellows John Hemynges and Henry Cundell." In a time where few people could write, orthography was not uniform. Even the spelling of Shakespeare's own name was not universally agreed upon. With the exception of the signature on his will, Shakespeare signed his name "Shakspere." On his will he spelled it "Shakspeare."

2. Ibid., 10.

3. Stanley Wells, *Shakespeare & Co.: Christopher Marlowe, Thomas Dekker, Ben Jonson, Thomas Middleton, John Fletcher and the Other Players in His Story* (New York: Vintage, 2008), 242–243. Footnote to *A Supplement to Dodsley's Old Plays*. http://www.archive.org/stream/asupplementtodo01hallgoog/asupplementtodo01hallgoog_djvu.txt.

4. This is part of the text of *A Sonnet upon the Pitiful Burning of the Globe Playhouse in London*, which, though listed in the Stationers' Register at the time, survives only in manuscript. See Peter Beal, "The Burning of the Globe," *Times Literary Supplement*, June 20, 1986, 689–90.

5. Excerpt from Anonymous, *A Funerall Elegye on the Death of the famous Actor Richard Burbage who died on Saturday in Lent the 13 of March 1619*.

6. Stationers' Company Court Book C, 110. Also in Charlton Hinman, *The Printing and Proof-reading of the First Folio of Shakespeare*, Volume 1 (Oxford: Clarendon Press, 1963), 27.

7. Butter Quarto 1608 and falsely dated Pavier Quarto 1608 (1610).

8. The manuscript, written by Eusebius Pamphilius, 260–340, Bishop of Caesarea, is *Historia Ecclesiastica*, translated by Tyrranius Rufinus, 640–650. The fragment was sold at auction to Sir Paul Getty.

9. Franklin Mowery, chief conservator at the Folger, uncovered the earliest manuscript written in England, bound as scrap paper inside the spine of a book that had been bound with printers' waste in 1578.

10. William Shakespeare, *Hamlet, First Quarto, 1603* (Menston, UK: Scolar Press, 1972).

11. Bevington, *The Complete Works*, 90–92, 1108.

Chapter 3: "Whatever You Do, Buy"

1. Charlton Hinman, *The Printing and Proof-reading of the First Folio of Shakespeare*, Volume 1 (Oxford: Clarendon Press, 1963), 17.
2. William Prynne, "To the Christian Reader," address in *Histrio-Mastix: The Players Scourge, or, Actors Tragedie* (London: Michael Sparke, 1632).
3. Epigrams 269 and 270, *Wits Recreations*, 1640. Also quoted in Herford and Simpson, *Ben Jonson*, 11 vols. (London: Clarendon Press, 1925), 13.
4. Ben Jonson, "To the Great Variety of Readers," dedicatory verse to Shakespeare's First Folio.
5. Peter W. M. Blayney, introduction to the second edition of *The First Folio of Shakespeare: The Norton Facsimile* (New York: Norton, 1996), xxxiii.
6. Prynne, "To the Christian Reader." This was the third dedication in the *Histrio-Mastix*, which was published at the time of the Second Folio in 1632. Prynne, a lawyer, author, and politician, expressed his opinion on all manner of subjects, from the ideal length of hair for men, to the desirability of state control over all matters religious.
7. Peter Blayney, *The First Folio of Shakespeare* (Washington, D.C.: Folger Shakespeare Library), 16–17, illustrates the corrected proof and corrected pages from *Othello*; W 105, F 47, contains the proof sheet of page 333 of the Tragedies, with the corrected state on the page opposite.
8. William Blades, *The Pentateuch of Printing with a Chapter on Judges* (Chicago: A. C. McClure, 1891).
9. Anthony James West, "The First Shakespeare Folio to Travel Abroad: Constantine Hugyens's Copy," in *Foliomania! Stories Behind Shakespeare's Most Important Book*, ed. Owen Williams (Washington, D.C.: Folger Shakespeare Library, 2010). This volume was published to accompany the Folger Shakespeare Library's 2010 First Folio Exhibition: *Fame, Fortune, and Theft: Shakespeare's First Folio*. To our knowledge, Shakespeare's image had not been preserved during his lifetime. No painting, no engraving, no likeness of him, has ever been found. Sometime between 1616 and 1623, a small bust of Shakespeare was placed along the north wall of the chancel in Holy Trinity Church in Stratford-upon-Avon. The sculpture is mentioned by the poet Leonard Digges in one of the prefatory poems to the First Folio. It is possible but not known that the sculptor, Gerard Johnson, knew William Shakespeare, at least by sight. The bust depicts Shakespeare in a red jacket, blue vest, and white collar and sleeves. The playwright holds a piece of paper in his left hand, a quill in his right. Above him is the Shakespeare coat of arms, hard won through the efforts of first John, then William Shakespeare. He is flanked by the figures of "Labor," holding a a shovel, and "Rest," holding a skull and torch. Inscribed under the figure of Shakespeare is:

"IVDICIO PYLIUM, GENIO SOCRATEM, ARTE MARONEM,
TERRA TEGIT, POPULUS MAERET, OLYMPUS HABET"

The first line translates as "A Pylian in judgment, a Socrates in genius, a Maro in art." The verse compares Shakespeare with Nestor, the wise king of Pylus, the

Greek philosopher Socrates, and the Roman poet Virgil, whose last name was Maro. The second line translates as "The earth buries him, the people mourn him, Olympus possesses him."

Below the Latin inscription is a poem in English:

STAY PASSENGER, WHY GOEST THOV BY SO FAST?
READ IF THOV CANST, WHOM ENVIOVS DEATH HATH PLAST
WITH IN THIS MONVMENT SHAKSPEARE: WITH WHOME,
QVICK NATVRE DIDE: WHOSE NAME, DOTH DECK YS TOMBE,
FAR MORE, THEN COST: SIEH ALL, YT HE HATH WRITT,
LEAVES LIVING ART, BVT PAGE, TO SERVE HIS WIT

10. An image of the frontispiece of Favyn's book has been transferred by contact with the tympan and is visible on one of the pages of W 123, F 65. This is illustrated in Blayney, *The First Folio*, 7.

11. Peter Blayney and F. P. Wilson, "The Jaggards and the First Folio of Shakespeare," *Times Literary Supplement* 5 (November 1927): 737. Also Anthony J. West, *The Shakespeare First Folio: The History of the Book* (London: Oxford University Press, 2001), Volume 1, 5, quoting Wilson.

12. By 1728, the last known manuscript, *Cardenio*, also known as *Double Falsehood*, a joint effort by Shakespeare and his junior, John Fletcher, survived only in an adaptation.

13. The full title is Windsor Herald of Arms in Ordinary. *Ordinary* in his title signifies a lifetime appointment. His duties included control over issuance of arms, participation in state parades and ceremonies, and preservation of heraldic records.

14. Thomas Moule, *Bibliotheca heraldica Magnæ Britanniæ. An analytical catalogue of books on genealogy, heraldry, nobility, knighthood & ceremonies* (London: Lackington, Hughes, Harding, Mayor and Lepard, 1822).

Chapter 4: "My Shakespeare, Rise"

1. Schoenbaum, *Shakespeare: The Globe and the World*, 191.

2. Justin Cartwright, *Oxford Revisited* (New York: Bloomsbury, 2008), 121.

3. James Leasor, *The Plague and the Fire* (London: George Allen & Unwin, 1962), 15.

4. Diary of John Evelyn, September 4, 1666.

5. Diary of Samuel Pepys, September 26, 1666. There were two main diarists of the era, John Evelyn and Samuel Pepys. Both of their diaries, in searchable form, are online.

6. Catalogues in the late seventeenth century listed the First Folio "under 'Miscellanies, viz. History, Philology, etc. in Folio,' on another it can only be under the 'Etc.'" West, *The Shakespeare First Folio*, 1:15.

7. Gerald Eades Bentley, "Shakespeare's Reputation—Then Till Now," in *William Shakespeare: His World, His Work, His Influence*, 3 vols., ed. John F. Andrews (New York: Scribner, 1985), III: *His Influence*, 705–716.

8. F. E. Halliday, *A Shakespeare Companion, 1564–1964* (Baltimore: Penguin, 1964), 148.

9. Gary Taylor, *Reinventing Shakespeare: A Cultural History from the Restoration to the Present* (New York: Weidenfeld & Nicolson, 1989), 114.

10. Brian Vickers, ed., *Shakespeare: The Critical Heritage*, 6 vols. (London: Routledge & Kegan Paul, 1974), 10.

11. Christian Deelman, *The Great Shakespeare Jubilee* (London: Joseph, 1964), 138–143, 214–215. The text of the ode can be found in Brian Vickers, *William Shakespeare: The Critical Heritage* (London: Routledge), 4:349.

12. Goethe's speech, "Shakespeare's Day," given at University of Duisburg, October 14, 1771.

13. Winifred H. Friedman, *Boydell's Shakespeare Gallery* (New York: Garland Publishing, 1976). Ann R. Hawkins and Georgianna Ziegler, curators, *Marketing Shakespeare: The Boydell Gallery (1789–1805) and Beyond*, at the Folger Shakespeare Library, September 20, 2007, through Janury 5, 2008.

14. West, *The Shakespeare First Folio*, 1:27.

15. Seymour de Ricci, *English Collectors of Books and Manuscripts (1530–1930) and Their Marks of Ownership* (Bloomington: Indiana University Press, 1960), 145.

16. The full title is *Catalogue of Shakespeare Reliques: Some Account of the Antiquities, Coins, Manuscripts, Rare Books, Ancient Documents and Other Reliques Illustrative of the Life and Works of Shakespeare* (Brixton Hill, 1852). Four to eighty copies were published. Also cited in de Ricci, *English Collectors of Books and Manuscripts*, 145. Phillips frequently sold his collections, and then started building fresh ones on new subjects. Sotheby's conducted an auction of his materials every year from 1856 through 1859. The 1857 auction lasted three days and "very high prices were realized." He sold quartos and other items that he used in editing his edition of the First Folio. See the entry for James Orchard Halliwell-Phillipps in the *Dictionary of National Biography*, Oxford: Oxford University Press, 118.

17. Thomas Carlyle, "The Hero as Poet," in *On Heroes, Hero Worship, and the Heroic in History* (London: Fraser, 1841). Also cited in West, *The Shakespeare First Folio*, 1:31.

18. Performances of plays were banned in some of the colonies beginning in 1700, and, with some reprieves, periodically thereafter through 1776.

19. Neil Harris, *Humbug: The Art of P. T. Barnum* (Chicago: University of Chicago Press, 1981).

20. Nigel Cliff, *The Shakespeare Riots: Revenge, Drama, and Death in Nineteenth-Century America* (New York: Random House, 2007).

Chapter 5: "Had I the Money, You Would Come . . ."

1. www.nha.org/history/hn/HNMooney-coffee.htm, accessed 1/3/2011. See also Summer 1997 issue of *Nantucket Magazine*.

2. Folger Shakespeare Library, Folger Collection, box 28.

3. Folger Collection, box 21, correspondence.

4. September 8, 1875, autograph letter signed, Folger archive, box 21.

5. October 24, 1875, autograph letter signed, Folger archive, box 21.

6. January 9, 1876, autograph letter signed, Folger archive, box 21.

7. January 12, 1876, autograph letter signed, Folger archive, box 21.

8. January 2, 1875, autograph letter signed, Folger archive, box 21.

9. January16, 1876, autograph letter signed, Folger archive, box 21.

10. January 22, 1876, autograph letter signed, Folger archive, box 21.

11. January 22, 1876, autograph letter signed, Folger archive, box 21.

12. November 7, 1875, autograph letter signed, Folger archive, box 21.

13. Letter to Henry C. Folger Sr., April 5, 1876. Folger archive, box 21.

14. Betty Ann Kane, *The Widening Circle: The Story of the Folger Shakespeare Library and Its Collections* (Washington, D.C.: Folger Shakespeare Library, 1976), 5.

15. Letter to Eliza Jane Folger, March 23, 1879, Folger archive, box 23.

16. *The Complete Works of Ralph Waldo Emerson* (Boston: Houghton Mifflin, 1904), XI, Miscellanies XXIII.

17. That ticket is on permanent display in the Founders' Room at the Folger Shakespeare Library.

18. *The Complete Works of Ralph Walso Emerson* (Boston: Houghton Mifflin, 1904), XI, Miscellanies, XXIII.

19. June 1879, Folger archives, box 21.

20. Autograph letter signed, to Eliza Jane Folger, Folger archive, box 21.

21. George F. Whicher, "Henry Clay Folger and the Shakespeare Library," reprinted from the *Amherst Graduates' Quarterly* (November, 1930), 2–16.

22. Ron Chernow, *Titan: The Life of John D. Rockefeller, Sr.* (New York: Vintage Books, 1998).

23. Allan Nevins, *Study in Power: John D. Rockefeller, Industrialist and Philanthropist*, 2 vols. (New York: Charles Scribner's Sons, 1953), 477, 652.

24. Although the cost savings enjoyed by Standard allowed it to expand its market, such savings did not enable it to control the retail market in the sense of being able to raise prices. Far from being an example of why antitrust law is necessary, the early Standard Oil history is a cautionary tale of how manipulation of the press, the legal system, and political influence can benefit small inefficient competitors at the expense of competition and consumer well-being.

25. Standard continually improved methods of production; in previous decades, by-products and residues of the refining process—including gasoline—were dumped, sometimes right into rivers and lakes. Kerosene lamps were smoky and prone to explosion, resulting in house fires and many deaths. Rockefeller invested in research and development that resulted in improvements in yields of refining lubricants, waxes, and eventually gasoline. The company found ways to make the product safer and less volatile. "And when customers found," Rockefeller boasted, "that they could buy for twenty or thirty or thirty-five-cents-a-gallon products that they had been made to believe were difficult to produce at seventy or eighty, they were not slow to avail themselves of the advantages offered by the Standard Oil Company." Rockefeller archive records to Henry C. Folger.

26. Rockefeller archive records, to W. P. Thompson, March 2, 1885. Rockefeller Archive Center, Sleepy Hollow, New York.

27. In 1870, a mere five years after entering the refining business, Rockefeller incorporated the Standard Oil Company with $1 million in capital. Though it was the largest refinery in Cleveland, it had just a four percent market share.

    Competition was alive and well in the oil industry. With a small investment, anyone could drill for oil and pump it out of the ground. With a small investment, anyone could build a small refinery. Rockefeller did not attempt to control all aspects of production, drilling, and refining. Indeed, in the absence of some barrier to entry by other potential competitors, he *could* not. With the cost advantage that came with being the largest refiner in the country, Rockefeller could deter entry by new competitors through price-cutting. If he could price below his competitors' costs, he could make it unprofitable for them to enter the refining business at all. He could also exploit his company's relationship with the railroads: Standard Oil would get the lowest shipping rates; its competitors paid higher rates, raising their costs relative to Standard's. In one ill-fated cartel plan that never actually went into effect, Rockefeller's company was to have received "drawbacks" from the railroads, a refund for every barrel of oil the railroads shipped for Rockefeller's competitors.

The story of his commercial success, however, did not end there. In an example of industrial expansion never seen before *or* since, in the first three months of 1872, Rockefeller increased the size of Standard Oil through dozens of mergers with competitors, increasing market share from around four percent to twenty-five percent of refining capacity in the United States. Rockefeller approached his many competitors—large and small—with an offer to sell out to or join his firm. He knew many of the firms were financially weak: three-quarters of the refiners were losing money. Total refining capacity in the United States was twelve million barrels per year and crude oil supplies reached just five million barrels per year; profit margins for refiners with excess capacity were squeezed between rising crude prices and falling prices of the final product. Refineries operating at such a small, inefficient scale were not able to compete head-to-head against Rockefeller: his refining and shipping costs were lower than theirs. Rockefeller approached the refineries' owners, showed them his company accounts, and invited them to join him, paying them—*their choice*—in cash or Standard shares. Some competitors, surprised by the efficiency of Rockefeller's operations, joined him right away. Many of the men who complained later that Rockefeller had not been fair with them had taken cash buyouts rather than stock and, when the price of Standard stock soared, regretted their choice. Most of those men who had chosen stock went on to become very wealthy.

Of course, there were also setbacks, and not all of Standard's actions were intended to benefit consumers. Rockefeller's company and most of its competitors participated in two failed attempts to form refiner cartels. The South Improvement Company Plan and the "Pittsburgh Plan" were both failed schemes that disproved the myth that Rockefeller "controlled" the price of kerosene. Each time refiners attempted concerted action to raise prices by limiting output and raising prices, sales fell and the refiners' excess capacity problem worsened. The solution for an industry with too much capacity was not higher prices, which encouraged yet more competitors to enter. And an agreement among so many competitors was bound to be plagued by cheating; there was incentive to participate in the scheme and simultaneously cheat on the side, offering price discounts to attract customers. To say that the plans were unpopular with independent oil producers would be an understatement. Three thousand men, wildcatter independent oil producers from western Pennsylvania, met in the Titusville Opera House, carrying banners denouncing the South Improvement Company Plan. The public and politicians added their voices to the tumult.

United and furious, the producers boycotted the refiners and railroads that had hatched the plan. The conspiring infant was strangled in its cradle; the plan was abandoned. Not a single barrel of oil was shipped under the South Improvement Company Plan.

Like the refining industry, railroads had a cost structure of very high initial expenditures—purchasing rights of way, laying track, purchasing locomotives and cars—with very low per ton-mile (marginal) costs. Once the track was laid between two cities, the cost of transporting an additional carload of oil along it was negligible. The low marginal costs experienced by all the railroads added to their tendency to overbuild, and gave competing railroads incentive to lure customers away from one another. Because their services were essentially identical, railroads competed based on price alone, periodically engaging in surreptitious price wars to attract large freight customers such as coal and steel producers. Discounts, kept secret to avoid overt price wars, were endemic throughout the industry and had been for decades. The largest shippers, like Rockefeller in the oil industry and Andrew Carnegie in the steel industry, negotiated the largest discounts, to the disadvantage of their competitors. The railroads suffered periods of what they termed "cutthroat competition"—bad for their profits, but good for the shippers and ultimately for the consumer.

Standard's large scale of operations, huge in relation to other refiners, allowed Rockefeller and his partners to negotiate preferential rates from the railroads because Standard was capable of lowering *the railroads'* costs. Standard guaranteed shipment of forty *carloads* of oil. Smaller independent refiners produced less and unpredictable volumes of traffic. By guaranteeing volumes, Standard lowered the railroads' cost of transportation by two-thirds, passing some of the savings on to Rockefeller through secret discounts.

28. *Manufacturing Book A*, 59, citing Rockefeller Records 1881–1886. R. W. Hidy and M. E. Hidy, "History of Standard Oil Company," vol. 1, *Pioneering in Big Business, 1882–1911* (New York: Harper & Brothers, 1955).

29. Charlton Hinman, "'The Halliwell-Phillipps Facsimile' of the First Folio of Shakespeare," *Shakespeare Quarterly* 5, no. 4 (Autumn 1954): 395–401. In June 1903, Folger purchased this volume also, now Folger 33.

30. John D. Rockefeller to Henry C. Folger, September 21, 1885, Rockefeller archive, Sleepy Hollow, New York.

31. Folger archive, letter to Amherst class historian, also cited in Dickinson, 120. Donald C. Dickinson, *Dictionary of American Book Collectors* (New York: Greenwood Press, 1986), 120.

32. Emily Folger autograph notes, Folger archive, box 33.

Chapter 6: "Had I the Means, I Would Not Hesitate . . . to Buy"

1. The text of the Sherman Act: "Every contract, combination in the form of trust or otherwise, or conspiracy, in restraint of trade or commerce among the several States, or with foreign nations, is declared to be illegal." Section 2 reads: "Every person who shall monopolize, or attempt to monopolize, or combine or conspire

with any other person or persons, to monopolize any part of the trade or commerce among the several States, or with foreign nations, shall be deemed guilty of a felony, and, on conviction thereof, shall be punished by fine not exceeding $100,000,000 if a corporation, or, if any other person, $1,000,000, or by imprisonment not exceeding 10 years, or by both said punishments, in the discretion of the court."

2. Prayer and discourse by Dr. S. Parkes Cadman, Henry Folger: 18 June 1857–11 June 1930 at Mr. Folger's funeral (New Haven: privately printed).

3. Throughout the text the notation for each copy of the First Folio is designated with a letter F, for Folger, followed by a number assigned by the Folger Library to indicate a particular copy. I have also included the W or West number assigned to each copy of the First Folio in West, *Shakespeare's First Folio: Volume I.*

4. Henry C. Folger to John D. Rockefeller, April 13, 1895, Folger archive, box 23.

5. Henry C. Folger to John D. Rockefeller, March 13, 1895, Folger archive, box 23.

6. Marsden Perry resold the collection in installments after the financial panic of 1907 and the disappointing loss of the Devonshire quartos to Huntington. Folger acquired many items from Perry's collection. Folger Shakespeare Library Marsden Perry correspondence file. Huntington purchased a significant portion of the remainder of the Perry collection.

7. Ralph Willard Hidy and Muriel Hidy, *History of Standard Oil Company (New Jersey): Pioneering in Big Business, 1882–1911* (New York: Harper, 1955), 342.

8. This is the sole copy attributed to Folger in Lee's 1902 *Census.* Folger actually owned six copies at the time. West, *The Shakespeare First Folio,* 2:160.

9. That year, he also purchased from bookseller George D. Smith at the bargain price of $12 a copy of the 1616 volume of Jonson's *Workes.*

10. Folger Shakespeare Library H. H. Furness correspondence file.

11. Rosenbach, *Henry Folger as a Collector,* 105.

12. "The new Earl, whose interests lay far more with hunting, shooting and fishing than with Shakespeare . . ." Victor Gray, *Bookmen: London: 250 Years of Sotheran Bookselling* (London: Henry Sotheran, 2011), 150–151. Based on Folger's correspondence with Railton, housed at the John Rylands Library, Manchester, U.K.

13. Rosenbach, *Henry Folger as a Collector,* 79.

14. Gray, *Bookmen,* 151.

15. Robert Cowtan, *Memories of the British Museum* (London: Richard Bentley and Son, 1872). Shortly thereafter, the museum required Harris to *sign* any pages he worked on for them.

16. Rosenbach, *Henry Folger as a Collector,* 104–105.

17. February 28, 1917, autograph letter signed Mrs. Godfrey, Folger archive, box 21.

18. Sidney Lee, "The Shakespeare First Folio: Some Notes and a Discovery," *Cornhill Magazine,* no. 34 (April 1899): 449–458, 452. Also cited in West, *Shakespeare's First Folio,* 1:137.

19. Sidney Lee, 1924, 105. Also quoted in West, *Shakespeare's First Folio,* 1:138.

20. West, *The Shakespeare First Folio,* 1:137.

Chapter 7: "The Most Precious Book in the World"

1. West, *The Shakespeare First Folio*, 1:103 note b. As the Warwick Castle copy was purchased in a lot with no specific value attributed to it, we do not have a specific price for it (W 64, F 6).
2. Ibid., 1:176.
3. A copy of the survey and Lee's letter of request for information are Appendix 4.1 in West, 1: 184–185.
4. Lee's *Census* says 160, but West says 158. Lee writes that two of the copies were stated to have been destroyed.
5. Even what was to be considered a "copy" was subjective and arbitrary. See West, *The Shakespeare First Folio*, 1:132–133, for a complete discussion of what constitutes a "copy."
6. By this time, he owned W 113, F 55; W 72, F 14; W 64, F 6; W 102, F 44; W66, F 8; and W 94, F 36.
7. *New York Times Saturday Review of Books and Art*, December 13, 1902, BR17.
8. Emphasis in original. A. B. Railton to Henry Folger, March 4, 1899, Folio file 1, Folger Shakespeare Library.
9. Railton to Henry C. Folger, April 1899. Folger folio file #1, Folger Shakespeare Library.
10. Lee, "The Shakespeare First Folio," 449.
11. Henry C. Folger Jr., "A Unique First Folio," *Outlook* 87 (November 23, 1908), 690.
12. Both the marked-up and corrected versions are illustrated in the ne plus ultra of facsimiles, *The Norton Facsimile*. See also Blayney, *The First Folio of Shakespeare*, 16–17.
13. Hinman, "The 'Halliwell-Phillipps Facsimile,'" 395–401, 396.

Chapter 8: "A Shakespeare Discovery"

1. Blayney, *The First Folio of Shakespeare*, 16–17, illustrates the First Folio page whose signature is Bb6v.
2. On the rarity of some of the quartos, a few of Shakespeare's plays in quarto size survive in only one or two known copies. There are but a half dozen known copies of *Hamlet* Q2 (1604), including the Howe copy at the Folger Shakespeare Library and the Devonshire copy at the Huntington Library. There are only two known copies of *Hamlet* Q1, neither complete—the British Museum copy lacks the title page and the Huntington copy lacks the last leaf. So when a facsimile edition of the Q2 was issued in 1969, the British Museum borrowed the title page from the Huntington Library. The Folger owns the world's *only* known copy of the 1594 *Titus* quarto.
3. Rosenbach, *Henry Folger as a Collector*, 81.
4. Ibid.
5. The Folger price list has $7,300. In a November 11, 1905, letter, Folger had offered the owner, John Camp Williams, $7,250 plus a copy of Lee's *Facsimile*. West, *The Shakespeare First Folio*, 2:164.
6. Sidney Lee, *Notes & Additions to the Census Copy of the Shakespeare First Folio* (London: Oxford University Press, 1906), 21.

7. Wheeler, "Letters of Sir Thomas Bodley to Thomas James, First Keeper of the Bodleian Library," (Oxford: The Bodleian Library, 1926).

Chapter 9: "Do . . . Devise Some Way to Get the Books"

1. Emily C. Folger theater diary entry, November 18, 1912, Folger archive.
2. Sidney Lee, *Shakespeares Comedies, Histories, & Tragedies, a Supplement to the Reproduction in Facsimile of the First Folio Edition (1623) from the Chatsworth Copy in the Possession of the Duke of Devonshire, K.G. Containing a Census of Extant Copies with Some Account of Their History and Condition* (Oxford: Clarendon Press, 1906), 30.
3. Lee, *Notes & Additions*, 13.
4. Emily Folger travel diary, *Places I've Been*, 48, 1906, Folger archive.
5. Lee, *Notes & Additions*, 19, footnote 1.
6. Ibid., 19, 20.
7. Rosenbach, *Henry Folger as a Collector*, 83.
8. Sotheran Firm, London Booksellers, *Bibliotheca Pretiosa: Being an Unusually Choice Collection of Books and Manuscripts in Exceptional Fine Condition*, 1907 (London).
9. Emily Folger, *Places I've Been*, 50.
10. Ibid.
11. "American Captures Shakespeare Prizes," *New York Times*, December 29, 1907.
12. The Supreme Court opinion is at 221 U.S. 1 (1911).
13. Folger documentary file for W 116, F 58. West, *The Shakespeare First Folio*, 2:156.
14. Folger faced little competition for the other three First Folios he purchased in 1910. He paid $3,400 for one (W 87, F29), $6,250 in November for another (W 73, F 15), and $2,100 in December for his last copy of the year (W 82, F 24).
15. On January 12, 13, 16, and 17, the company's legal team, led by Rockefeller's trusted chief counsel John Davis, advocated for the second time its best case in a grueling, four-day procedure.
16. The court articulated a new legal principle: henceforth evaluation of "restraints of trade" under the Sherman Antitrust Act would be conducted under a "rule of reason." That meant the court would enjoin and penalize only those restraints of trade that worked in opposition to the public interest. That was good news for Standard. Under the rule of reason, the company could not be found guilty of a per se—an automatic—violation of the Sherman Act simply because it restrained trade. Then Justice White announced the rest of the opinion. 221 U.S. 1 (1911).
17. *McClure's* 39 (May–October 1912), 409.
18. In Chief Justice Edward D. White's words: "on the one hand, with relentless pertinacity and minuteness of analysis, it is insisted [by the government] that the facts establish that the assailed combination took its birth in a purpose to unlawfully acquire wealth by oppressing the public and destroying the just rights of others, and that its entire career exemplifies an inexorable carrying out of such wrongful intents, since, it is asserted, the pathway of the combination, from the beginning to the time of the filing of the bill, is marked with constant proofs of wrong inflicted upon the public, and is strewn with the wrecks resulting from crushing out, without regard to law, the individual rights of others."

    He recognized the argument made by Standard: "On the other hand, in a powerful analysis of the facts, it is insisted [by Standard Oil] that they demonstrate that the origin and development of the vast business which the defendants control was but the result of lawful competitive methods, guided by economic genius of the highest order, sustained by courage, by a keen insight into commercial situations, resulting in the acquisition of great wealth, but at the same time serving to stimulate and increase production, to widely extend the distribution of the products of petroleum at a cost largely below that which would have otherwise prevailed, thus proving to be . . . a benefaction to the general public. . . ." 221 U.S. 1 (1911).

19. Daniel Yergin, *The Prize: The Epic Quest for Oil, Money, and Power* (New York: Simon & Schuster, 1991), 110.

20. Ibid.

21. Henry Folger letter to Captain Robinson, Folger archive.

22. *New York Times*, November 11, 1911, 1.

23. "Huth Library Sale Resumed on June 5, Part II of Auction Dispersal of Great Book Collection Contains 2,596 Lots," *New York Times*, May 19, 1912.

24. Later, when President William Howard Taft learned that Folger had reached forty-nine First Folios, more than the total number in all of England, he coyly reported, "We have the fiftieth at Yale," hoping to plant the seed for a possible donation from the Folger collection. Folger did not bite.

25. William James, *Talks to Teachers on Psychology and to Students on Some of Life's Ideals* (New York: Norton, 1958), Chapter 7.

26. West, *The Shakespeare First Folio*, 2:201.

27. Ibid., 2:210; A. S. W. Rosenbach, *Books and Bidders: The Adventures of a Bibliophile* (Boston: Little, Brown, 1927), 84–85.

28. West, *The Shakespeare First Folio*, 2:183.

29. Ibid., 1:111.

30. "ENGLAND'S RAREST BOOKS BEING BOUGHT BY AMERICANS," *New York Times*, July 12, 1914.

31. *Time Literary Supplement*, August 16, 1915.

32. The invoice is quoted in full in West, *The Shakespeare First Folio*, 1:24.

33. Folger archive. Also see West, *The Shakespeare First Folio*, 2:243, in describing West 187, Lee 108.

34. Ibid.

Chapter 10: "The False Folio"

1. Henry Clay Folger to Robert Bateman, December 12, 1916, Folger Shakespeare Library, Folger correspondence file B22.

2. Nicholas Basbanes, *A Gentle Madness: Bibliophiles, Bibliomanes, and the Eternal Passion for Books* (Owl Books, 1999), 197. See also redwoodlibrary.org/notables/perry.htm, accessed December 13, 2010.

3. Donald C. Dickinson, *Dictionary of American Book Collectors* (New York and London: Greenwood Press, 1986), 258. See also *A Preliminary List of Books and Manuscripts Relating to the Life and Writings of William Shakespeare, Forming the Collection of Marsden Perry*, Providence, Rhode Island, 1891, privately printed.

4. Patrick T. Conley and Paul Campbell, *Providence, a Pictorial History* (Norfolk/ Virginia Beach, Virginia: Donning, 1982), 118. The bank still exists today as Fleet National Bank.

5. Carl L. Cannon, *American Book Collectors and Collecting from Colonial Times to the Present* (New York: H. W. Wilson, 1941), 328. Also see 163, 326–328, 337.

6. Dickinson, *Dictionary of American Book Collectors*, 258.

7. Edwin Wolf and John F. Fleming, *Rosenbach: A Biography* (Cleveland: World Publishing, 1960), 341.

8. At the same time, Folger was after the famous Daniel Folio. "RESALE OF DANIEL FOLIO: HENRY C. FOLGER . . . £8600," *New York Times*, January 4, 1919.

9. *The Tradition of A. W. Pollard and the World of Literary Scholarship*, 1, http://sherpa .bl.uk/26/01/PollardSept1.pdf.

10. Emphasis in original. Wolf and Fleming, *Rosenbach*, 118. The total of $128,500 paid for the lot included the Pavier-Gwynne quarto, the only known copy in America of the 1594 *Henry VI Part II*, the only known fragment of the 1595 *Venus and Adonis*, a 1605 *Richard III*, Charles Lamb's copy of *Poems*, and other items.

11. Basbanes, *A Gentle Madness*, 196–198.

12. Ibid.

13. The eleven quartos he purchased included *King John First Part*, *King John Second Part* 1591, *Hamlet* 1676, and *Julius Caesar* 1684. Basbanes, *A Gentle Madness*, 196, 197.

14. See page 16 in the Rosenbach pamphlet prepared for the occasion of the donation of the four folios by the Widener daughters in memory of their father, January 22, 1945. This story is told in West, *The Shakespeare First Folio*, 2:235. Today Widener's four folios are at the Free Library of Philadelphia.

15. Wolf and Fleming, *Rosenbach*, 120–21.

16. Ibid.

17. "BOUGHT FOR HUNTINGTON," *New York Times*, December 18, 1919.

18. Folger Shakespeare Library folio file, Folger letter, January 12, 1920.

19. Folger Shakespeare Library folio file, Gabriel Wells letter, January 15, 1920.

20. Folger Shakespeare Library folio file, Folger letter, March 30, 1920.

21. Folger Shakespeare Library folio file, Gabriel Wells letter, March 30, 1920.

22. Folger Shakespeare Library folio file, Folger letter, June 4, 1920.

23. The Gilburne Copy—bound in "full morocco extra by Riviere," Maggs catalogue. See Peter W. M. Blayney, *The First Folio of Shakespeare* (Washington, DC: The Folger Shakespeare Library, 1991), 43–44. Also West, *The Shakespeare First Folio*, 2:157 re: W 70, F 12.

Chapter 11: "I Am an American"

1. Emily J. Folger, "The Dream Come True: The Story of the Library and of Henry Clay Folger," corrected typescript of paper presented at the Meridian Club, 1933. Folger archive, box 56.

2. Ibid.

3. Ibid.
4. Ibid.
5. One folder in Folger archive, box 56, contains letters from the Realtor/lawyer indicating that one row house owner has become aware that properties surrounding his on Grant's Row have been bought up, and he has become a holdout.
6. In 1930, Standard Oil employee Alexander Welsh wrote, "There has been no Librarian, nor a staff of any kind. With Mrs. Folger's and my help we have gotten through."
7. ALS, signed by A. S. W. Rosenbach, June, 16, 1921, Folger correspondence file.
8. A. S. W. Rosenbach writing from Philadelphia to Folger at the Homestead resort in Virginia, April 1, 1922, First folio files, folio 1.
9. Henry Folger had purchased a mulberry thimble from the Warwick Castle sale, and added several mulberry relics including a mulberry goblet of David Garrick's. Folger had reached his limit on purchases of mulberry objects purportedly fashioned from the tree planted by Shakespeare when he wrote, "I have many articles carved from the mulberry tree, so am not inclined to buy any more."
10. De Ricci, *English Collectors*, 148–149.
11. The book contains the cancellandum and the cancellans of the last leaf of *Romeo and Juliet*. Folger folios 2, 4, 59, 71, and 72 also contain the canceled leaf.
12. *Punch*, May 24, 1922. The Folger Library owns the original artwork.
13. West, *The Shakespeare First Folio*, 1:137.
14. Letter from Henry Folger to C. F. Tucker Brooke, Folger archive.
15. Letter from J. C. Weedon to Henry Folger, September 17, 1925, Folger archive, box 56.

Chapter 12: "Portrait of a Collector"

1. Wolf and Fleming. Also "U.S. Cellars for First Folios," *Brooklyn Daily Eagle*, January 23, 1926, 6.
2. Wolf and Fleming, *Rosenbach*, 200.
3. Frank O. Salisbury, *Sarum Chase: New and Enlarged Portrait and Pageant* (London: John Murray, 1953), 101.
4. West, *The Shakespeare First Folio*, 2:194, citing letter February 23, 1999; also Wolf and Fleming, *Rosenbach*, 293–294.
5. The *Lamp* in *Henry Folger: 18 June 1857–11 June 1930*.
6. Rockefeller correspondence folder, Folger archive, box 23.
7. Ibid.
8. Henry Clay Folger letter to Forsyth, January 11, 1929, Folger correspondence file.

Chapter 13: "Thou Art a Moniment, Without a Tombe"

1. Henry Folger letter to Trowbridge, October 19, 1928, Folger archive, box 57.
2. Henry Clay Folger letter to A. S. W. Rosenbach, April 29, 1929, Folger archive, folio correspondence file.

3. Folger letter to Trowbridge, December 17, 1928, Folger archive, box 57.

4. Henry Clay Folger letter to Trowbridge, December 20, 1928, Folger archive, box 57.

5. Henry Clay Folger letter to Trowbridge, January 7, 1929; February 11, 1929, Folger archive, box 57.

6. February 13, 1929, Folger archive, box 57.

7. Henry Clay Folger letter to Trowbridge, February 28, 1929, Folger archive, box 57.

8. Henry Clay Folger letter to Trowbridge, March 9, 1929, Folger archives, box 57.

9. Henry Clay Folger letter to Trowbridge, March 7, 1929, Folger archive, box 57.

10. May 20, 1929, Folger archive, box 57.

11. Ibid.

12. October 11, 1929, Folger archive, box 57.

13. Folger archive, box 57. Alas, Henry's torchières have been sold off. They were sold recently at auction and will illuminate a casino in Florida.

14. Folger personally chose the following quotations for inscription in the library.

Entrance from Theatre Lobby to Theatre:

As Plautus and Seneca are accounted the best for Comedy and tragedy among the Latines: so Shakespeare among the English is the most excellent in both kids for the Stage.

Meres, *Palladis Tamia*, 1598

East End Exhibition Hall:

Thrice happy the nation that Shakespeare has charm's.
More happy the bosoms his genius has warm's:
Ye children of nature, of fashion, and whim,
He painted you all, all join to praise him.

David Garrick

Entrance from Main Reading Room to Catalogue Room, under Church Window:

I do not remember that any book or
Person or event ever produced so great an
Effect on me as Shakespeare's plays.
I am astonished by their strength and
Their tenderness, by their power and
Their peace.

Goëthe

Next to it:

Shakespeare is fertility,
Force, exuberance, no reticence, no binding, no
Economy, the inordinate and tranquil prodigality
Of the creator.

Hugo

Chapter 14: "It Is the Key to Our Hearts"

1. E. Folger, "The Dream Come True."
2. The estate was not as simple as the *New York Times* suggested. In 1930, the law required that upon the death of a safety-deposit box owner, an appraisal of its contents
   must be made within one year. That inventory and appraisal of approximately 470
   of the most treasured and valuable books in the Folger collection were conducted
   by Edward Lazear of the Broad Street Bank where Henry kept a safety deposit box.
   Giles Dawson unpublished typescript. Inside the bank, under the watchful eye of
   the widow dressed in black, Lazear unpacked bundle after bundle of books. At that
   moment, no one alive but Emily knew the extent of their purchases. No one but
   she would know what, if anything, was missing. Now, for the first time, an outside
   appraiser would get an inkling of what had been squirreled away.

   The estate, whose value was composed foremost of the library building, the collection, and Standard Oil stock, was appraised and valued. "The account shows the
   net value of the estate at Mr. Folger's death on June 11, 1930 was $13,719,635."
   While Henry had hoped to bring the cost of the building in at a cost of less than
   $1 million, the building alone, according to the article, came in at around $1.75
   million.

   He bequeathed $10 million worth of Standard Oil stock to the trustees of Am-
   herst. As a result of the market crash in August 1929, the value of the Standard Oil
   stock had fallen and the monies were not sufficient to accomplish everything—
   the library, upkeep, continued acquisitions, fellowships, etc. Emily contributed
   substantial amounts from her own inheritance from Henry, and continued to
   make such donations for the rest of her life, as well as in her own bequests. If the
   fund dipped below $10 million, he stipulated, the library trustees were permitted
   to use only the income of the fund for expenses. If the estate grew and the fund
   was worth in excess of $10 million, it was permissible to use the money for acqui-
   sitions and development.

   Henry Folger's estate was valued as of June 1931. The estate was made up
   entirely of shares of oil stocks—from Standard of California, Indiana, New York,
   New Jersey, plus Prairie Oil and Gas; the total valuation was $2,999,852—a
   far cry from the $6.8 million it had been worth before the stock market crash
   on October 29, 1929. (Note that the valuation is mentioned on September 22,
   1931. "Almost half of the estate of the late Henry C. Folger, formerly president
   and chairman of the board of Standard Oil Company of New York . . . is represented by the investments in the Folger Shakespeare Library in Washington.
   This is shown by the intermediate account of Mrs. Emily C. J. Folger, widow
   and executrix, which was filed yesterday in the Surrogate's court at Mineola, L.I.
   [New York]."

   The valuation as of June 1931, conducted for the estate; attached was a list of
   securities, as well as their values as of June 1931.

720 shares	Prairie Oil & Gas Co	at 9	6,480
116 shares	Standard Oil Co Calif	at 36⅜	4,219.50
5,490 shares	Standard Oil Co Ind	at 25¼	138,622.50
36,494 shares	Standard Oil Co NJ	at 37	1,350,278

62,322 shares	Standard Oil Co NY	at 16	997,152
10,400 shares	Standard Oil Co Ind	at 25¼	262,000
6,500 shares	Standard Oil Co NJ	at 37	240,500
			2,999,852
Cash			148
Total			3,000,000

Folger Shakespeare Library, Folger archive, box 58.

Attached was a list of securities, as well as their values as of August 30, 1929, prior to the stock market crash; securities prices from the *New York Times*. Assuming the quantities were the same, the total valuation is given below.

720 shares	Prairie Oil & Gas Co	at 9	58⅜
116 shares	Standard Oil Co Calif	at 36⅜	76½
5,490 shares	Standard Oil Co Ind	at 25¼	57⅝
36,494 shares	Standard Oil Co NJ	at 37	71¾
62,322 shares	Standard Oil Co NY	at 16	44⅛
10,400 shares	Standard Oil Co Ind	at 25¼	57⅝
6,500 shares	Standard Oil Co NJ	at 37	71¾

August 30, 1929 $6,827,274

The market crash had cost Henry and Emily Folger half of their liquid assets.

3. Letter from William Slade to Emily Folger, Folger archive, box 58.
4. Rosenbach, *Henry Folger as a Collector*, 105.
5. Ibid.
6. 82 First Folios, about 50 Second Folios, at least 23 Third Folios, about 38 Fourth Folios, nearly 200 Shakespeare folios in all.
7. "Dear Shepherd now that I find thy saw of might,/Whoever loved that loved not at first sight." *As You Like It* (III, iv).
8. Sadly, the portrait is almost certainly not of Shakespeare. During the painting's 1979 restoration, details uncovered suggest the subject of the painting is Sir Hugh Hamersley, who was later Lord Mayor of London.
9. Joseph Quincy Adams, address at dedication of Folger Shakespeare Library, typed transcript, Folger archive, box 58.
10. E. Folger, "The Dream Come True."
11. In Henry Folger's own words: "It was well under way when two notable collections were added en bloc; The Halliwell-Phillipps Collection of Shakespeare Rarities was one of England's most famous assemblages of literary nuggets, 50 years ago. Its catalogue was as fascinating as a novel, for the clever collector told how each item earned its place with the other gems, and how he had tracked down his quarry, with patience and skill. This is a great Collection by itself, and adds much dignity to the library where it is now placed.

"Almost as notable is the charming Shakespeare Library from Warwick Castle, where it filled a room of size in that historic structure. It is especially distinguished for its Manuscripts, most notable of which is the play worked up in 1610 by Sir

Edward Deering, combining the two parts of *Henry IV*, the only surviving manuscript of any Shakespeare play prepared during his lifetime. Sir Edward may have worked with Shakespeare's own manuscript, or with that of the playhouse.

"But these are by no means the only Collections added to the Folger Library; Dr. John Gott, Bishop of Truro, had a shelf of 16 beautiful Quartos, purchased together after a quest most romantic. The story is too long—but far from too tedious, to be told here.

"The Lord Howe's marvelous group of 27 Quartos was secured on the very eve of the date set for their sale by auction. This was the culmination of negotiations extending back more than two years.

"Maurice Jonas added a fine lot of Shakepeariana, including many Quartos and Poems.

"Mention must also be made of the Collection of Samuel Timmins, the Shakespeare enthusiast, of Birmingham; of J. P. Colleri, the tireless student-editor; of Prof. Dowden, of Dublin University; of Dr. Ingleby, who set the student world at work seeking the books paying tribute to Shakespeare, or drawing inspiration from him. Mrs. Rose, the birthplace historian, a flame of passionate enthusiasm for the Bard, willed to the Library her Shakespeare treasures, not the least of which are her own manuscripts, lectures and notes.

"The list might be extended almost indefinitely.

"But we cannot overlook that glorious actor, David Garrick. He rescued the Shakespeare plays from their detractors, who were remodeling—in fact rewriting—Shakespeare. He went back to the text of the folios and quartos: We cannot be too grateful to him. So we are pleased to find here a long line of his Shakespeare Prompt Books, filled with his manuscript corrections; a large quantity of literary writing, and some 300 autograph letters. A busy man was Garrick; a great actor; a true friend.

"That recalls the splendid collection of Prompt Books made by Samuel Phelps, the English player, and a similar line prepared by our own sterling actor, Robert Mantell. We mention also the Shakespeare costumes of Sothern & Marlowe, and end this list with half a million Shakespeare playbills."

12. Emily Jordan Folger letter to William Slade. It is the last letter from Emily in the library's files. Folger archive, box 58.

13. Telegram to Joseph Quincy Adams from Edward J. Dimmock, the Folgers' nephew and executor of Henry Folger's will, Folger archive, box 58.

Epilogue

1. Georgianna Ziegler, "Duty and Enjoyment: The Folgers as Shakespeare Collectors in the Gilded Age" in *Shakespeare in American Life* (Washington, DC: Folger Shakespeare Library, 2007), 101.

Index

ANDREA MAYS, like Henry Folger, has been possessed by a life-long obsession with Shakespeare and his times. As a former student of Frank McCourt (who chronicled those days in his memoir, *Teacher Man*), Andrea spent much of her Manhattan girlhood holed up in the New York Public Library listening to vinyl LP recordings of performances by the Royal Shakespeare Company. When she was twelve years old, she costarred in the NBC network television show *Talking With a Giant*. For years, beginning in middle school, she carried around in her rucksack tattered paperback copies of the Folger Library editions of Shakespeare's plays and haunted the old Bouwerie Lane Theatre. A graduate of Stuyvesant High School, she was not only a protégé of McCourt but also of his own mentor, the legendary New York City public school teacher R'Lene Dahlberg.

Andrea has degrees in economics from the State University of New York at Binghamton and from UCLA, and teaches economics at California State University at Long Beach. She was a presidential appointee to the U.S. International Trade Commission in Washington D.C., where she served as economist to the chairman. She divides her time between California and Washington, where her Gilded Age townhouse—the residence of Daniel Chester French while he sculpted the Lincoln Memorial—stands in the shadow of the Folger Shakespeare Library. She hopes to own her own copy of the First Folio someday. This is her first book.

Follow her on Twitter @AndreaEMays.